Homos

exualities

A Study of Diversity
Among Men And Women

Alan P. Bell / Martin S. Weinberg

Simon and Schuster
New York

Designed by Irving Perkins
Manufactured in the United States of America
1   2   3   4   5   6   7   8   9   10

Published in association with Mitchell Beazley Publishers Ltd.

Library of Congress Cataloging in Publication Data

Bell, Alan P., 1932–
    Homosexualities.

    Report of a study made by the Institute for Sex Research.
    Bibliography: p.
    Includes index.
    1. Homosexuality—United States. I. Weinberg,
Martin S., joint author. II. Indiana. University.
Institute for Sex Research. III. Title.
HQ76.2.U5B45   301.41'57'0973   78-7398

                                    ISBN 0-671-24212-1

Contents

Preface

This book represents the fulfillment not only of years of work but of hope and a plan conceived by Dr. Alfred Kinsey some three decades ago. As a third volume following the famous "Male" and "Female" reports, he had intended to publish a study of homosexuality. To this end, he collected a very large number of case histories of predominately homosexual individuals, but he died before these data could be analyzed and published.

After his death, the Institute he founded became involved in other projects, and it was not until the late 1960s that its attention again focused on homosexuality. This took place because Dr. Stanley Yolles, then Director of the National Institute of Mental Health, recognized that homosexuality is a phenomenon affecting the emotional lives of literally millions of people and that no federal institution had had the courage to address the problem. He therefore established the National Institute of

Mental Health Task Force on Homosexuality, which held its first meeting in July 1967. Immediately it became evident that more research was needed. By this time, sex research had progressed beyond the pioneering stage, and it was necessary to consider homosexuality not only in terms of ages, techniques, frequencies, and partners, but also—and more importantly—in terms of how it interrelated with the social and psychological fundamentals of life shared by all human beings regardless of sexual orientation.

Therefore, the Institute for Sex Research embarked upon a new series of projects concerning homosexuality which involved, at one time or another, all of the research staff. This eventuated in a number of journal articles and book chapters, an annotated bibliography by Alan Bell and Martin Weinberg, and two books by Martin Weinberg and Colin Williams. While not all of these publications were, so to speak, ancestral to the present volume, they were an important part of the Institute's research on homosexuality. The direct predecessor of the present volume was a survey, mainly designed by Alan Bell and myself, of a homosexual community in Chicago. This project, funded by NIMH,* served as a pilot study for a far more extensive survey of homosexuality in the San Francisco area, the survey which constitutes the basis for this and a subsequent volume.

I am pleased to have been with Alan Bell the co-planner of the San Francisco study and to have been able to help launch the fieldwork. My only regret is that bureaucratic and other chores which inevitably accrete on administrators prevented me from taking a more active role in the fieldwork and precluded my involvement in the analyses and writing. My regret is sharpened by the realization that this is an important book, probably destined to be the definitive work on its subject for many years. It represents an enormous expenditure of time and effort, since the sample was large (second only to that of Kinsey) and the interviews extensive; consequently, the amount of data to be analyzed was correspondingly vast. It is not surprising that this long-awaited volume monopolized Dr. Bell's research time for seven years.

In summary, for more than a decade the Institute for Sex Research has devoted the major portion of its research to the subject of homosexuality, a subject of vital importance to the millions of homosexuals—and to the far greater number of heterosexuals who may gain an understanding and acceptance of them which I hope this book will foster. While written with a broader scope and with sophisticated statistical techniques unknown during Alfred Kinsey's lifetime, this volume not only makes important scientific contributions, but also maintains the combi-

* MH 12535, *Patterns of Adjustment in Deviant Populations.*

nation of objectivity and empathy which characterized his writings. He would have esteemed it as the volume for which he had hoped and planned.

Paul H. Gebhard, Director
Institute for Sex Research
Indiana University
Bloomington, Indiana

Background and Acknowledgments

It should be noted at the outset that the present work could not have been accomplished without the contribution which Alfred C. Kinsey originally made to our understanding of human sexuality. His painstaking work, begun in the 1930s and continuing into the 1950s despite the opposition of many powerful figures and institutions, involved the first wholehearted attempt to ascertain the sexual behaviors of American men and women. For almost two decades he and his small group of colleagues obtained sexual histories from thousands of people living in both ordinary and unusual circumstances all over the United States. Their reports, published in two widely read volumes, contained a vast amount of information about the sexual practices of American adults, much of which either shocked those who were unfamiliar with them or reassured those who had considered their own sexual experiences unique and therefore aberrant.

Not the least important discovery made by Kinsey and his associates was that large numbers of men and women had engaged in homosexual activity during adolescence and throughout adulthood, sometimes sporadically but often to the exclusion of any other form of sexual contact. And despite the uproar with which this information was received in many quarters, never again could the public remain under the illusion that homosexual interests and activity were simply adolescent phenomena or characteristic of only an insignificant number of adults. As a result of Kinsey's pioneering efforts, at least the fact of homosexuality, its incidence as well as the forms in which it was expressed, was finally "out of the closet." In addition, Kinsey's refusal to equate homosexuality with psychopathology, and his insistence that repressive laws concerning homosexual conduct be expunged, laid the groundwork for America's slow reappraisal of its attitudes toward and treatment of its homosexual citizens.

Prior to his untimely death, brought about in part by the numerous antagonisms generated by his work, Kinsey had planned to expand greatly the number of persons whom he and his colleagues would interview so as to obtain an even more comprehensive assessment of sexual behavior than that presented in the so-called "Kinsey Reports." It was also his intention to interview, in a separate study, large numbers of predominantly homosexual individuals in order to ascertain their sexual, social, and psychological circumstances more precisely. While we do not know exactly what form his own inquiry would have taken, in a very real sense the present work represents our attempt to fulfill Kinsey's plans for the work of the Institute for Sex Research.

Thanks in large part to the reputation for professional integrity which Kinsey and the Institute came to enjoy, we were invited by the National Institute of Mental Health (NIMH) to submit a proposal for a comprehensive study of the development and adult management of homosexuality. In the fall of 1967 our proposal, based upon many of the recommendations put forth by the NIMH Task Force on Homosexuality,[1] was reviewed and ultimately modified during site visitations and after extensive consultation with NIMH officials. We are especially indebted to Jack Wiener, Assistant Chief of NIMH's Center for Studies of Mental Health and Social Problems, who took a special interest in the project and has remained involved over what turned out to be a relatively long period of time. In addition to NIMH, we are grateful to Indiana University, which has been generous in its allocation of space and in its provision of personnel. Without the use of its computer facilities and of a programmer employed on a full-time basis, the vast amount of data we compiled could never have been analyzed.

During the initial stages of our work we consulted with a variety of

---

[1] The members of this group, as well as the names of others who served in various capacities on this research project, are listed on pages 491–494.

experts in the area of homosexuality who often held quite different points of view. Our correspondence and personal meetings with these individuals were of great help to us in constructing a viable interview schedule. While the final instrument, devised over many meetings of various Institute personnel, did not entirely please or represent the views of any one person associated with it, the interview schedule in its final form was the result of endless discussions and sometimes painful compromise on the part of many highly committed people. Preliminary interviews conducted by Institute personnel in Bloomington and Indianapolis were especially useful in helping us to establish the format of what amounts to the most extensive interview schedule ever used in research of this kind.

Needless to say, our work would never have got off the ground without the cooperation of various homophile organizations in the Bay Area and of educational institutions in the same locale from which were drawn our recruiters, interviewers, and ethnographers. These many individuals worked long hours in sometimes difficult circumstances in an effort to secure valid data from the wide assortment of people represented in our several samples. Many hours were devoted to their training. Every effort was made by our field directors and their staff to insure that we would get reliable information. The small field office, perched high over the city of San Francisco, was open day and night and over weekends, the center of constant activity on the part of numerous people who suffered both major and minor personal inconveniences on a daily basis over a period of a year. We wish to thank them again for their attention to detail and for their incredible investment of energy on our behalf.

Our special gratitude, of course, goes to the many people who consented to be interviewed. In addition to the hours they had to spend answering questions was the risk entailed for many of our respondents. Some made themselves known to us and consented to be interviewed even though they could not be absolutely convinced that we meant them no harm, that our work would not perpetuate long-held cultural myths about them, or that their anonymity would be preserved. The courage of these people and their patience with us deserve special mention even as we thank them again for their help.

The data gathered in the Bay Area were returned to the Institute in a fairly primitive state. Large numbers of people employed by the Institute in Bloomington had to go over the interview schedules with a fine-tooth comb. Coders spent months attending to the open-ended material. The closed-ended material had to be transferred to computer cards and ultimately to tapes. Two of the field directors, Kim Johnson and Helen Matthews, returned to Bloomington for the next stage of our work, which included endless discussions over the steps that had to be taken before we could analyze the data. Susanna Barrows, a graduate student at Indiana University, took charge of the coding procedures and suffered the monumentally difficult task of making sure that our open-ended data were coded reliably. Our project coordinators sometimes found themselves faced with too many equally demanding tasks, including that of organizing into a cohesive working unit large numbers of assistants, many of whom were not initially prepared for the attention to detail which their work required. Their work was often exasperating, and without their devotion to what they deemed an important research project, we would never have managed to complete our work.

Although we sometimes run the risk of overestimating the contributions of those most recently associated with an enterprise and of forgetting the enormous assistance of others in preceding years, we believe that special gratitude is due our most recent project coordinator and our editorial assistant. Barbara Gray acted as liaison to our programmer, hired and trained many different assistants, and took charge of the whereabouts of all our data. She participated in many of the decisions associated with this volume, suggested ways in which the data could best be presented, and her imprimatur given to our findings makes us rest assured that the information we report is correct. Linda DuPlantis, was especially helpful in her editing of the manuscript. Her talent in this area is impressive, as is her knack of telling the "story" in a creative way. She selected the open-ended material which has been used to illustrate various features of our respondents' lives and, together with Barbara Gray, was in charge of the volume's tabular format. Over a long period of time and on a daily basis, these two women did so much in our behalf that they deserve as much gratitude as anyone ever associated with our enterprise. It is our profound regret that the sudden and tragic death of Barbara Gray has precluded her ever realizing the depth of our appreciation for her contribution.

Finally, we wish to thank Lois Downey, our programmer, and Mickey Stentz, our statistical consultant, for their contributions to the present work. Lois Downey, working odd hours, usually late at night, always managed to get the necessary output to us on time. No job was ever too taxing for her, no procedures beyond the scope of her expertise. Mickey Stentz, a master statistician, was extremely helpful to us in our analysis of an enormous amount of data. Intrigued by the many, sometimes esoteric, ways in which statistics can be used in circumstances such as ours and responsible for the Statistical Package for the Social Sciences program at Indiana University, he sometimes had to settle for relatively simple statistical procedures so that our study could be understood by lay readers. We thank him for his work and especially for the manner in which it was always performed.

Our chief hope at this point is that we have not failed to mention or to name in our Contributors list anyone who contributed in any way to the work reflected in the present volume. In addition, it is our hope that we have produced a work which confirms others' faith in us and justifies all that they have done in our behalf.

A.P.B.
M.S.W.

Bloomington, Indiana

Part I
Introduction

Rationale

The present investigation was undertaken with several purposes in mind. First, we attempted to identify various sexual dimensions of homosexual experience and then to indicate the whereabouts of our homosexual respondents on each of these dimensions. Of course, as with heterosexuality, homosexuality encompasses far more than the direction of one's sexual preferences. It includes, for example, how interested a person is in sexual matters, the frequency with which sexual contact is pursued, and the number of sexual partners one may have during a given period of time. Dimensions of homosexuality which are not exactly comparable to or even extant in heterosexual experience include such additional matters as how much one regrets being homosexual and how overt one is (i.e., how many and which people know about one's homosexuality).

Most heterosexuals, unfamiliar with homosexual adults, tend to believe that homosexuals—regardless of their sex, race, age, or socioeconomic status—are alike in how they manage their homosexuality. These folk notions, or stereotypes, are reviewed in the present volume and examined for the extent to which our data support them. In addition, we compare our data with those of other investigators. Wherever the incidence of a given characteristic among homosexual men and women has been reported in the literature (e.g., their standings on the homosexual-heterosexual continuum, how many are involved in a quasi marriage with a same-sex partner), it has been compared with the incidence of that characteristic among our own homosexual samples. In addition, we also determine the extent to which our white homosexual male respondents are similar to other white homosexual men who were previously interviewed in Chicago by the Institute during the summer of 1967 (a study directed by Paul H. Gebhard, Director of the Institute). This pilot study utilized an interview schedule which, although it was less comprehensive, contained many questions identical to those used in the present study. Such comparisons allow the reader to determine how similar our respondents are to homosexuals investigated elsewhere and also to get some idea of what homosexual adults, at least those willing to be interviewed in studies of this kind, typically report about various features of their homosexuality.

It should be pointed out that reaching any consensus about the exact number of homosexual men or women exhibiting this or that characteristic is not an aim of the present study. The nonrepresentative nature of other investigators' samples as well as of our own precludes any generalization about the incidence of a particular phenomenon even to persons living in the locale where the interviews were conducted, much less to homosexuals in general. Nowhere has a random sample of American homosexual men and women ever been obtained, and given the variety of circumstances which discourage homosexuals from participating in research studies, it is unlikely that any investigator will ever be in a position to say that this or that is true of a given percentage of all homosexuals. We cannot stress too much that ours is not a representative sample. While we would have wished for a representative sample of homosexual adults and would have been pleased to be in a position to estimate the prevalence of a given characteristic among American homosexuals, the fact that this is neither possible nor, indeed, our interest has certain advantages. It means that we need not be as concerned with the fact that our interviews were restricted to a single location or that they were conducted as long ago as 1970. Rather, what we want to demonstrate is the relationship between homosexuals' sexual life-styles and their social and psychological adjustment, a relationship probably not affected very much by the nonrepresentative nature of our samples. For example, while we are not in a position to say that the average American homosexual man or woman has had a given number of sexual partners, we are able to differentiate homosexual individuals on the basis of a typology and to consider the relationship between the nature of their sexual partnerships and other aspects of their lives. Thus, even though homosexual (or heterosexual) persons may report larger or smaller numbers of partners in 1980 than in 1970, the relationship between such reports and respondents' psychological or social characteristics may remain substantially the same. We contend that where and when our respondents were interviewed might affect their reports to some degree, but the *relationship* between one set of variables and another is less apt to be affected by such circumstances. To take another example, it may be that the success of the gay activist movement has resulted in more positive attitudes toward homosexuality and that our respondents' attitudes, assessed in 1970, tend to be more negative than those of persons who have "come out" almost a decade later. For the purpose of the present investigation, the possibility of this disparity is almost beside the point. Homosexuals continue to differ in their acceptance of their own and others' homosexuality, and differences in this regard might still be related to differences in, for example, gender or educational level. It would be quite another matter if we were to find that *all* homosexuals today felt positively about homosexuality. In that case our investigation of how homosexuals' differential perceptions of homosexuality, evident in 1970, are related to other aspects of their lives would simply be irrelevant at the present time.

After comparing black and white and male and female homosexuals with respect to a variety of dimensions of homosexual experience, and considering any effects of age, education, and occupational level, we proceed to construct a typology of sexual experience among our male and female homosexuals. It is our conviction that if we are to learn more about homosexual men and women, various "types" or "kinds" of homosexual individuals must be identified and retained in the analysis (Bell, 1974, 1975b). We regret the fact that it was not possible similarly to delineate the heterosexual respondents. Ideally, "homosexualities" (i.e., the numerous ways in which one can be homosexual) should be exactly juxtaposed with "heterosexualities" in investigations of this kind so that the panoply of human sexuality can be observed and its relationships to other aspects of human functioning determined more precisely. Although the present study falls short of this ideal, it surpasses other investigations which either fail to make important distinctions among their homosexual respondents or else only consider a particular type of homosexual and are unable to show the ways in which he or she may differ from another kind of homosexual person. Our hope is that, at the very least, it will become increasingly clear to the reader that there is no such thing as *the* homosexual (or *the* heterosexual, for that matter) and that statements of any kind which are made about human beings on the basis of their sexual orientation must always be highly qualified.

It will become obvious to the reader that this perspective has determined the way in which we examine our respondents' social and psychological adjustment. For example, after showing the diversity of responses and comparing the white and the black homosexual males on a given item, we then determine whether the male homosexual subgroups or "sexual types" differ on that measure. This examination is followed by comparisons of the homosexual and the heterosexual men with respect to the item of interest and then by comparison of each type of homosexual male with the entire heterosexual male sample. The same sequence is followed among the female samples. In those instances where only the homosexual respondents were asked a particular question, comparisons are, of course, limited to the homosexual respondents, black versus white and the various subgroups. In addition, particularly large and interesting differences between homosexual men and women are noted.

The sequence of analysis just described represents a marked departure from others' investigations. Until now the unspoken assumption underlying most studies of homosexuality has been that homosexually oriented persons are very much alike. Most investigators have simply lumped together their homosexual respondents on the basis of their sexual preference and have then proceeded to compare them with a heterosexual control group in terms of various characteristics. Intergroup differences have usually meant disparities between homosexuals on the one hand and heterosexuals on the other. Our own interests are clearly quite different. A primary focus of this investigation is upon diversity—the ways in which homosexual persons differ from each other. Only after intergroup comparisons involving *homosexual* respondents have been made do we go on to compare the homosexual respondents with their heterosexual counterparts, with a consideration of whether homosexual-heterosexual differences depend upon the type of homosexual who is being compared. This procedure often shows that comparison of an undifferentiated homosexual sample with heterosexual men or women is not as productive as one in which the homosexual subgroups are delineated. In many instances, total sample differences were found to be produced by a particular type of homosexual, and sometimes it was the case that where total sample comparisons revealed no differences between homosexuals and heterosexuals, differences emerged in comparing the heterosexuals with the homosexual subgroups.

After having distinguished our homosexual respondents with respect to various aspects of their social and psychological adjustment, we present general "portraits" of the various types of homosexual adults. These not only provide evidence of the interrelationships of the sexual, social, and psychological features of their lives but also make it abundantly clear that homosexuality encompasses far more than people's sexual proclivities. Too often homosexuals have been viewed simply with reference to their sexual interests and activity. Usually the social context and psychological correlates of homosexual experience are largely ignored, making for a highly constricted image of the persons involved. The present study goes far in demonstrating the need for relatively comprehensive pictures of homosexual adults. Only then will come the much-needed realization that sexual orientation is not merely a matter of the direction of persons' sexual preference. Both homosexuality and heterosexuality generate numerous life-styles, and future research may indicate that these are far more important indications of people's whereabouts than is sexual orientation per se.

It should be noted that the present report is only one of a series of three books which have resulted from what we call our "San Francisco Study." Our first project, antedating our empirical research, involved a detailed survey of all the literature pertaining to homosexuality appearing in the English language between 1940 and 1968, which led to the publication of *Homosexuality: An Annotated Bibliography* (Weinberg & Bell, 1972). A second project, our most ambitious, based upon other data provided by the respondents in the present study, involves an attempt to ascertain the kinds of developmental experiences which are apt to lead to homosexuality or heterosexuality in men and women. This part of our investigation, in which a variety of theoretical perspectives will be explored, is to be reported in a subsequent volume. The latter book will bring to a conclusion the extensive attention which the Institute for Sex Research has given to the topic of homosexuality.[1]

Time limitations have made it impossible for us to analyze all of the data at our disposal, and we welcome other scholars' use of the large amount of data which remains unexplored. It is hoped that our ten-year investment of time and energy toward a greater understanding of homosexuality will prompt other much-needed and more focused investigations in this area and that it will also provide rich dividends to society as a whole. As long as homosexual men and women, as well as other groups of people who are simply seen as "different" from the majority of American citizens, continue to be viewed through stereotypical thinking, our society will pay the price inevitably exacted by fear and ignorance. We hope that our present work will help to diminish the forces of interpersonal alienation and enable people to become increasingly reconciled to themselves as well as to others.

[1] Other Institute publications dealing with homosexuality have included *Homosexuals and the Military: A Study of Less Than Honorable Discharge* (Williams & Weinberg, 1971) and *Male Homosexuals: Their Problems and Adaptations* (Weinberg & Williams, 1974, 1975a). A forthcoming volume (Klassen et al.) that uses a national probability sample will describe American adults' attitudes toward a number of sexual behaviors, including homosexuality.

Methods of Investigation

In planning the present study, one of our first decisions had to do with the locale from which our respondents would be drawn. Next we considered how we might obtain a diverse sample of homosexual respondents and a reasonably appropriate heterosexual comparison group. At the same time, we deliberated the content of our interview schedule, concerned that it be of sufficient depth and scope to tap important aspects of our respondents' lives—sexual, social, and psychological—and developed interviewing procedures. We also discussed at length what statistical methods might best be used to analyze the data we would collect. Finally, we gave a good deal of thought to ethnographic descriptions of our respondents' cultural milieu, for which we selected those settings and institutions that might influence and illustrate the conduct of our homosexual respondents at the time of the interview.

The sections of this chapter discuss each of these matters in detail. *Readers who are interested in only a few of these subjects may wish to skip the remaining sections and proceed directly to our findings, begin-ning in Part II, page 49.*

Study Site

We determined that the urban setting in which the present study was to take place should meet the following criteria: local homophile organi-zations and certain key individuals (homosexual and otherwise) must support the idea of the study; such organizations and individuals must be willing to help in the planning and execution of the study; there must be a large number of different sources from which potential respondents could be drawn; the community life-style must enhance the possibility of a successful conclusion of the study; and qualified individuals must be available to work as recruiters and interviewers and in other important capacities. After considering a number of possible cities, including New York, Los Angeles, New Orleans, San Francisco, and Boston, we de-cided that the San Francisco Bay Area would probably go further in meeting these criteria than any of the others.

The study site consists of six counties: Alameda, Contra Costa, Marin, San Francisco, San Mateo, and Santa Clara. The region com-prises some 3788 square miles and contains a population of more than four million. Within the six counties are more than seventy communities of varying size, ranging from San Francisco with a population of 750,000 and Oakland and San Jose with some 400,000 each, through Pacifica, a city of 35,000, down to Hercules with a population of 310. Since the Second World War the population of the Bay Area has more than dou-bled. Much of this population growth has been due to people migrating from other areas of the United States, attracted by the Bay Area's ex-panding economy, pleasant climate, and agreeable living conditions.

The city of San Francisco, if not the entire Bay Area, has been termed a "good scene" for homosexuals. In the mid-1950s, local homophile or-ganizations and other citizens' groups began to call public attention to homosexuals' social difficulties; since then there has been less and less official repression of homosexuals and an increasing sensitivity to their civil rights.

For example, the entrapment of homosexuals by police is rare in San Francisco. In the words of one informant:

The police leave us very much alone. I can make a complaint, and the police won't try to incriminate me because of my homosexuality. The police let gay people live their own lives in this city.

There was a time when

the "boys" [police] were out on their Hondas in the park, tearing all over Land's End, busting homosexuals left and right. . . .

but more recently the relations between the police and the homosexual minority have become reasonably amicable. For example, police are generally prompt and sympathetic in dealing with complaints of harassment. Scores of gay bars and restaurants operate openly and peacefully throughout the city. Unlike the situation in other cities, if a gay bar goes out of business, it is for reasons other than harassment by the police or the underworld. Pornographic bookstores, some with a large homosexual clientele, are left undisturbed. Gay baths, an important sexual setting for many homosexuals, are also allowed to conduct business without much interference. The absence of strong negative sanctions regarding homosexuality and the area's healthy economy make San Francisco attractive to homosexuals who migrate from rural or even other urban areas. As one informant put it:

You have a situation in San Francisco that's unique. You've got 7 by 7.9 miles. If you take the contiguous area, it's a 56-square-mile city. You have a huge, compact, cosmopolitan population. Within twenty minutes you can get anyplace that you want in this city. You can get any type of bar, any type of a pickup. So a young kid, or an older kid, is going to come here and he's going to say, "My God! Look, there's no harassment. There's everything I want. It's here within a short radius. I don't have to have a car. I can get a decent job at a transient level. I'm not really strapped down here. If I don't have enough money to buy a house, I can get into a gay rooming house or gay apartments. You've got it all right here!"

To a newcomer, the presence of other homosexuals is more apparent here than elsewhere, not only because of the numerous gay bars and restaurants but also because a variety of homophile organizations sponsor frequent activities that generate a unique sense of community. In such a setting one finds many opportunities for social contact, for camaraderie rather than the furtiveness which has characterized the homosexual "enclaves" of such cities as Chicago and Los Angeles. The fact that San Francisco's sexual permissiveness may be a precursor of what may soon obtain elsewhere in the country was an important factor in our selection of San Francisco as a study site.

Sampling Procedures

Recruiting Homosexual Respondents

Throughout the entire time that the project was in the field, a considerable amount of time and energy was devoted to obtaining a large number of potential respondents among the many homosexual adults living in the Bay Area. Various means were used to inform people about the study and about the need to conduct interviews with as many different persons as possible. We explained that all too often studies of human sexuality, and of homosexuality in particular, involved persons whose lives were hardly typical of many more people who, because of disinterest or concerns about their anonymity, were not included. We pointed out that if the myths which surround homosexuality were to be replaced by facts, information would have to be obtained from many more people than in previous studies. Those "in the closet" had to be convinced that their anonymity would be protected. Homosexuals who had lived successful lives had to be convinced that they had an obligation to their less fortunate colleagues. Those who had already been interviewed by others had to be convinced of the special importance of the present study. Some, who through hard experience had come to distrust the motivation of students in this area or who doubted that any good would come from their participation, had to be convinced of the investigators' objectivity and social concern. Although the Institute's past record was reassuring to many who would otherwise not have volunteered, the recruitment required extraordinary effort on the part of all concerned.

After the field office was set up in San Francisco, special recruitment cards were distributed in various locales. The three-by-five card had spaces for a person's first name or pseudonym, telephone number, age, education, sex, and race, and bore a notation of the recruiting source. A return envelope, addressed to the field office, was attached. Some of the cards were distributed to friends by people who had expressed interest in the study. Others who had heard of the study in local news reports telephoned the field office, volunteering to be interviewed; for them, the field office would fill in the card. These people occasionally would, in turn, refer others to the study.

The bulk of the recruitment, however, was undertaken by individuals hired specifically for this purpose. Most of the recruiting was conducted over a five-month period (June to October 1969). Many of the recruiters were homosexuals who were convinced of the value of the study. Most of them already had considerable knowledge of the various locales in which the recruiting was to take place.

Recruitment Sources

Almost five thousand men and women were recruited as potential homosexual respondents from the following sources: public advertising, bars, personal contacts, gay baths, organizations, mailing lists, and public places.

Public Advertising. Following a news conference announcing the study, feature articles appeared in three of the major newspapers which prompted numerous calls from people volunteering to be interviewed. Copies of a news release were also mailed to every radio and television station and newspaper in the Bay Area. In addition, the field director and staff were interviewed on radio and television, by newspapers, and by homophile organization publications, reiterating the need for potential respondents to volunteer.

Paid advertisements were placed in local newspapers over an eight-month period. Most of the people who volunteered in response to our advertising were those who had seen it in the "underground" newspapers (which after a short period of time carried our ads without charge). Advertising posters and matchbooks were left at various business establishments that had a considerable homosexual clientele. Boxes of recruitment cards were placed near each of the posters.

As a result of our public advertising, 914 white males, 132 white females, 35 black males, and 13 black females volunteered for interviews. Of this total, 150 were interviewed from this recruitment source. In addition, our advertising efforts informed large numbers of persons about the study, some of whom, we suspect, volunteered more readily in other recruitment settings. A number of people remarked that they had talked about the study with their friends long before a recruiter had asked them to be interviewed.

Bars. Recruiting was done in a total of eighty-two gay bars in the Bay Area, about three-quarters of them in San Francisco proper. Working from a list compiled from various gay publications and knowledgeable informants, recruiters regularly visited every gay bar that we knew of.

Recruiters were assigned to bars on the basis of their location, their clientele, and the extent to which they were already familiar to the recruiters. Male recruiters were never assigned to lesbian bars, where even female recruiters sometimes met with considerable resistance. Some of our female recruiters, however, worked quite effectively in male bars.

From the bars we recruited 994 white males, 205 white females, 110 black males, and 32 black females, a total of 1341 potential respondents of whom 227 were eventually interviewed.

Personal Contacts. As mentioned above, some persons who telephoned the field office volunteering to be interviewed had been told about the study by a friend. Others had been recruited at parties held in private homes or by members of the staff or by recruiters who had known them previously.

Staff members and recruiters made every effort to attend private parties, some of which were held for the express purpose of recruiting potential respondents. The party setting seemed much more conducive to recruiting than the public bars, for example, where people tended to be more on their guard with each other as well as with the recruiters.

Many individuals who called to sign up offered to hand out mailbacks to their friends. Because blacks (especially lesbians) and older homosexuals proved to be more difficult to find, toward the end of the recruitment period telephone calls were made to all the blacks and to the older whites who had been interviewed, asking them to try to get their friends to sign up. Some persons were even put to work on a volunteer basis and paid a small amount for every person they recruited.

Several homosexual friendship cliques provided another personal source, especially among females. Some who were not clique members but were acquainted with the members were also recruited in this way.

On the basis of personal contacts, 617 white males, 271 white females, 107 black males, and 61 black females were recruited. Of this number, 241 were interviewed.

Gay Baths. Recruiting was done in eight different gay baths. In the beginning, many recruiters at the baths hesitated to approach people directly, preferring instead to leave posters and cards in the lobby. Later, recruiters who were familiar with the baths met the clientele face to face, either in the lobby or in the steam room and hallways. One difficulty they encountered was that many potential respondents did not want to talk to them after learning why they were there. This was especially so in the steam and "orgy" rooms, where verbal communication of any kind is held to a minimum.

From the baths, 249 white males and 5 black males were recruited, of whom 91 were eventually interviewed.

Organizations. Twenty-three homophile organizations in the Bay Area whose memberships totaled about two thousand were advised of our need for respondents. With few exceptions, their leaders were extremely cooperative. The study was publicized in their newsletters and other publications and at their meetings, discussion groups, dances, picnics, and parties. Institute staff members attended many of these functions, and sometimes members of the organization helped them recruit others. Members of motorcycle clubs were less accessible, since many did not have formal meetings or newsletters. In one instance, though, a bike club member offered to recruit others on a weekend run, where he distributed hundreds of cards.

As a result of these activities, 222 white males were recruited, of whom 54 were interviewed. Because of the smaller number of females involved, the numbers of women recruited from organizations were combined with those recruited from mailing lists for a single recruitment source (see Mailing Lists, below).

It should be pointed out that not every member of a homophile organization welcomed the study or volunteered to be interviewed. In fact, some very active members of the gay community claimed that the time and energy they had invested in other research projects had done little to enhance the quality of life in the community. Some, indeed, had felt that previous researchers they had assisted were prejudiced against them. In certain gay liberation circles, some condemned the study as "exploitative" and "Establishment." However, these were not the usual reactions of homophile organizations or of their leadership, whose interest and support were important to the successful completion of our work.

Mailing Lists. During the initial phase of our fieldwork, officials of various homophile organizations and gay businesses gave permission for us to send out letters, mailback cards, and return envelopes to people on their mailing lists. We also used a colleague's mailing list of homophile organization members who had earlier said they would serve as research subjects. This resulted in mailings to almost six thousand people on the mailing lists of two bars, one private club, one bookstore, seven organizations, and that of our research colleague.

The mailback cards of 200 white males, 67 white females, 4 black males, and 4 black females were received from this source. Of these, 94 were eventually interviewed. As noted above, these figures include those women recruited from organizations as well.

Private Bars. Efforts were made to recruit persons in three "private bars" whose patrons paid for a membership card, sometimes yearly dues, and a regular admission fee. Although these establishments opened their doors early in the evening, they were most active after midnight, when their clientele would drift in from other bars to continue their drinking or to dance or, after 2:00 A.M. when the sale of liquor was prohibited, to drink coffee and converse. The recruiters operated in much the same way as in the regular bars, and with good results. Two hundred five white males and 20 black males were recruited from this source; of these, eventually 57 were interviewed.

Public Places. Probably the most difficult (and dangerous) recruiting took place in those public places where homosexual activity occurs or where sexual partners are sought. These included men's rooms (or "tea-rooms") in travel terminals, parking garages, hotels and restaurants, office buildings, parks, and theaters; theater lobbies and balconies; parks and beaches; and streets and public squares.

Originally, recruiters stationed themselves in a convenient spot at a given locale and simply handed a copy of the news release describing the study and a mailback card to anyone who would accept them. But almost no cards handed out in this way were returned, and many people were offended by the implication that they were looking for sexual contact, so these procedures were revised. In tearooms, for example, recruiters tried to identify individuals who appeared as if they were trying to make a sexual contact. Anyone who seemed to be lingering at a urinal or who repeatedly left and returned to the room was approached by the recruiter. The recruiter also attempted to engage the person in conversation and, if possible, sign him up on the spot. At the parks and beaches, the recruiters would either use the same technique or sometimes sit and wait for people to come to them. On the streets recruiters waited in obvious places or walked up and down, "cruising" the males who passed by. After a contact was made, the recruiter attempted to engage the person in conversation and sign him up.

Recruiting in public places was done primarily during the most active cruising hours. For example, theaters were visited most often on weekend evenings. Certain tearooms were only active on weekdays during business hours. Recruiting was done in the parks and on the beaches most often during the weekend daylight hours. The streets were most active on weekends, particularly after the bars had closed.

Although our recruiters made contact with several thousand males in public places, only 137 white males and 24 black males were recruited from this source. And of these numbers, over 30 percent could not be found afterward to set up interviews; they had either given a false address or moved away. We were finally able to interview 61 men who had been recruited in public places.

Recruitment Pool

In an attempt to obtain as much diversity as possible, we spent a great deal of time and expense in accumulating as many potential respondents as we could. Individuals who offered to be interviewed were placed in a "recruitment pool" and assigned to various categories, or cells, on the basis of their recruitment source, age, educational level, sex, and race (Table 2.1). In the effort to minimize sample error, we hoped to recruit many more prospective respondents than we would interview from each cell and then to select our respondents on a random basis, but this general procedure was not always possible. Homosexual men of a particular age or educational background are less apt to cruise in a particular locale and were thus more difficult to recruit from a given source, and homosexual women are simply not to be found in certain male cruising lo-cales. The homosexual men came from a wider variety of sources than the women did, and the white lesbians were more evenly distributed among the various recruitment sources than were their black counter-parts.

Among the homosexual men actually interviewed, the blacks were much more likely than the whites to have been recruited through per-sonal contacts (Table 2.2). While only between 9 percent and 20 percent of the white homosexual males were recruited from any given source, the black homosexual males display less diversity. Most of them were recruited from only three sources—personal contacts, gay bars, and public advertising. Similar differences between the white and the black sample sources are to be found among the lesbians, where almost two-thirds of the blacks but only about a third of the whites were recruited on the basis of personal contacts. The largest numbers of the lesbians were recruited from that source, followed by gay bars and public adver-tising. Much smaller numbers of them were recruited from homophile organizations or mailing lists.

Sizes of Our Samples

At the onset of the study we had hoped to interview approximately twice as many white males as females, together with enough blacks to provide a basis for racial comparisons. Several reasons prompted the differences in the sizes of our anticipated samples. First, because of their greater number and visibility, the problems and adaptations of ho-mosexual men were of greater interest to the sponsor of our study (the National Institute of Mental Health) than were those of lesbians. Sec-ond, since our Chicago pilot study had only to do with homosexual men and since others' research in this area has been chiefly confined to men, it seemed important for us to have a large enough sample of homosexual men to be able to compare our data with those of other studies. Finally, we supposed that it would be an easier task for us to find more male than female respondents because homosexual men tend to be more openly engaged in the gay world than are their female counterparts. This last consideration also affected our thinking about the sizes of our black samples: we expected to find fewer black than white homosexual adults and were prepared to be satisfied with relatively small black samples.

We did not want any recruitment source to yield a disproportionate amount of respondents. Thus we planned to draw from each source the relative number of respondents one would expect through that source. For example, although many homosexual men frequent gay bars, we did not want most of our respondents to have been recruited from there, but we did want more from bars than from public parks. Thus, approximately twice as many of our white homosexual male respondents were drawn from gay bars as from public places.

After about three months of recruiting we decided to begin our interviews. Over a twelve-month period, people to be interviewed were periodically selected on a random basis from the cells in the recruitment pool, while we continued to try to recruit more potential respondents, especially for those cells without many people in them. Among the white homosexual men, except for one cell (over forty-five years old, some college education, recruited in a gay bath), we had more potential respondents than were chosen for interviews. This was also true for the white homosexual women, except for three cells from which all those recruited ended up being interviewed. Among the blacks such stratifying procedures were generally not possible. Because of the difficulty we had in recruiting them, in many instances we were forced to interview all the blacks in a particular cell (Table 2.1).

Homosexual Respondents[2]: Demographic Characteristics (Table 2.2)

Following is the distribution of our homosexual respondents with regard to various demographic characteristics.

Age. We had hoped that each homosexual sample would contain approximately the same proportion of persons in each of four age categories: twenty-five years old or younger, twenty-six to thirty-five, thirty-six to forty-five, and forty-six or older. While we did achieve such distributions among the white respondents, they were simply not possible among the blacks. We had such difficulty in recruiting black homosexual men over twenty-five that they tend to be younger than either their female or their white male counterparts. Except for the black homosexual males, whose average age was twenty-seven, the homosexual respondents tended to be in their early to mid-thirties. The white homosexual males, whose average age was thirty-seven, were older than their counterparts interviewed in our pilot study, whose mean age was thirty-one.

---

[2] In reality, the ratio of homosexuality to heterosexuality in individuals' sexual behavior and feelings varies infinitely, but for statistical purposes it was obviously necessary for us arbitrarily to distinguish between "homosexual" and "heterosexual" respondents. Respondents were therefore assigned to one or the other group based on their self-ratings on the seven-point Kinsey Scale, which ranges from "exclusively heterosexual" (a score of 0) to "exclusively homosexual" (a score of 6); this scale is described more fully on page 53–4. If a respondent's score with respect to feelings, added to his or her score with respect to behaviors, amounted to 4 or more, he or she was assigned to the "homosexual" group. This meant, for example, that someone whose sexual behaviors, were exclusively heterosexual but whose sexual feelings were more homosexual than heterosexual would be considered a "homosexual" respondent. Such discrepancy was quite rare among the "homosexual" group, however; nearly 90 percent of our "homosexual" respondents (except for the black lesbians' 77%) scored 10 or more—i.e., predominantly or exclusively homosexual in both feelings and behaviors.

Education. Another variable on which we wanted relatively equal distributions was education, with equal proportions of each sample in three categories: high-school graduation or less, some college, and a college degree or more. However, on the basis of those recruited during the first three months, we were forced to revise our anticipated distributions. We found that although the white men versus women, and the black men versus women, did not differ in their educational level, the white respondents tended to have more formal education than the blacks. All of the groups, however, had respondents with some college education. The white homosexual males were similar to the pilot study males in their educational level.

Occupation. The occupational levels of our respondents, highly correlated with the amount of education they had received, were not determined before our interviews took place. Not surprisingly, among the men, the blacks tended to be employed at lower occupational levels than were their white counterparts. This was not the case among the homosexual women. All of the groups, however, had an average rank of level two (semiprofessional or small business) or three (skilled occupations), as did the pilot study men (Roe, 1956).

It should be noted that very few of the homosexual respondents were involved in stereotypically "gay" occupations. For example, less than 10 percent of the homosexual men worked as window dressers or decorators, hairdressers, nurses, designers, or dancers, and a similar proportion had "masculine" occupations such as the skilled crafts, engineering, and other technical work. Approximately one-tenth of the homosexual women worked in "masculine" occupations. It is also interesting to note the proportion of the homosexual respondents who had occupations that carry with them a certain amount of public trust, such as lawyers, teachers, counselors, or doctors. (When looking at Table 2.2, one should keep in mind that some of the occupations listed may now be more freely available to blacks or women than they were in 1970, when our study was conducted.)

Because of group differences in age, education, and occupational level, it was necessary for us to control for these variables in our analysis.

Residential Patterns. Most of the homosexual male respondents were not natives of the Bay Area. In fact, about a quarter of them had lived there less than 10 percent of their lives. Not many of them lived in "homosexual" neighborhoods: half thought that few or none of their neighbors were homosexual, and the largest numbers knew only a few of their neighbors by name. About one-half of the white homosexual males (WHMs) and almost two-thirds of the black homosexual males (BHMs) were living with one or more male roommates at the time of the interview. Somewhat smaller numbers were living by themselves. This is about the same number as those in the Chicago pilot sample.

As with the men, about one-quarter of the lesbians had lived less than 10 percent of their lives in the Bay Area, while somewhat less than a fifth had always lived there; but, compared with their male counterparts, the homosexual women tended to have spent a greater proportion of their lives in the Bay Area. More than two-thirds of the white homosexual females (WHFs) and most of the black homosexual females (BHFs) thought that only a few or none of their neighbors were homosexual, and the majority of each sample said they knew few or none of their neighbors by name. At the time of the interview, about half of the homosexual women were living with one or more female roommates, with about a quarter living by themselves.[3]

Religious Affiliation. About a quarter of the WHMs and more than a third of the BHMs listed themselves as Protestants. Thirteen percent of the WHMs and somewhat more of the BHMs were Roman Catholics. Only 2 percent of the WHMs, and none of the BHMs, were Jewish. Almost a quarter of the WHMs and fewer of the BHMs gave some other religious preference, while about one-third of the homosexual men said they were agnostics or atheists. The number claiming no religious affiliation is about the same as that found among the pilot study males.

Among the lesbians, about one-fifth of the WHFs and over a third of the BHFs belonged to a Protestant denomination. A smaller number said they were Roman Catholic, while hardly any of them were Jewish. Less than one-fifth of them listed some other religious preference, and almost half of the WHFs and a third of the BHFs reported that they were agnostics or atheists.

The Selection of Heterosexual Respondents

Considerable attention was given to how we might obtain the heterosexual comparison groups. We considered at great length the possibility of recruiting them from comparable sources. For example, we might have appealed to heterosexual adults through public advertising, mailing lists, singles bars, and various organizations. This idea was rejected, however, when we realized that very few sources are really comparable for homosexual and heterosexual adults. For example, a singles bar or even a neighborhood bar does not serve the same kind of function for heterosexual adults as the gay bar does for the homosexual community. In the same vein, a veterans' organization would not be expected to

---

[3] Ethnographic descriptions of our homosexual respondents' residential patterns can be found in Appendix A, pages 233–263.

provide representatives as typical of the study population as would a homophile organization. Thus, we finally decided to obtain our heterosexual samples from San Francisco's general population, using probability sampling with quotas. This procedure, developed by the National Opinion Research Center, uses random probability sampling to select census tracts and city blocks within the chosen tracts. Quota sampling is then used in each block. Each interviewer was instructed to begin at a selected point on a block and go clockwise around the block. Stopping at each dwelling, the interviewer would determine whether it contained a person satisfying the necessary requirements. (In our study, heterosexual respondents were chosen so as to match the homosexual respondents in terms of race, sex, age, and education.) The interviewer continued around the block until he or she had found such a person. Controls were imposed on the interviewer to insure that no dwelling units with potential respondents were skipped. (For further details, see Sudman, 1967.)

Unlike the comparison groups used in Saghir and Robins's study (1973), the heterosexuals whom we interviewed were not limited to unmarried individuals. The reason for this, again, has to do with comparability. While demographic characteristics such as age and education are comparable among homosexuals and heterosexuals, their marital status is not. For example, a middle-aged heterosexual man who is unmarried is clearly atypical of heterosexual males in general, while one would expect to find middle-aged homosexual males to be unmarried. In addition, many homosexual adults are involved in quasi marriages in which they and their partner live together, share expenses, and enjoy the same satisfactions as many married heterosexuals. Thus, we made no attempt to limit our heterosexual respondents to single men and women.

Heterosexual Respondents[4]: Demographic Characteristics

Age, Education, Occupation. As indicated above, heterosexual respondents were selected so as to be comparable to their homosexual respondents in age and education. Table 2.2 shows the distribution of

[4] As pointed out in footnote 2, in order to be able to make statistical comparisons we were forced to assign respondents to either the "homosexual" or the "heterosexual" group, even though these two elements of sexuality may actually occur in widely varying combinations among different individuals. A respondent was considered "heterosexual" if the sum of his or her sexual feelings and sexual behaviors scores (see page 53ff) was 3 or less. This meant, for example, that someone whose sexual feelings were exclusively heterosexual but whose behaviors were equally heterosexual and homosexual would be assigned to the "heterosexual" group. As it happened, however, the vast majority of the "heterosexual" respondents (three-quarters of the males and 90% of the females) had a total score of zero—i.e., they rated themselves exclusively heterosexual in both feelings and behaviors.

the four heterosexual samples with respect to these variables, and Table 2.3 compares them with the homosexual respondents. As can be seen from Table 2.3, the heterosexual groups did not differ from their homosexual counterparts in educational or occupational level, and they did not differ significantly in age except that the black heterosexual females tended to be somewhat younger than the black homosexual females. This disparity is due to the difficulties we had in finding black heterosexual females willing to be interviewed, forcing us to settle for a relatively small number of them as well as for a group significantly younger than their homosexual counterparts.

While the heterosexuals closely resembled their homosexual counterparts in occupational level, they differed from them in the kinds of work they did. The heterosexual men, white (WHTMs) and black (BHTMs), were less likely to be employed as office, personnel, or financial workers and more likely to work as engineers, factory foremen, contractors, and the like, than were the homosexual men. The BHTMs were also more likely than the BHMs to be employed in public or civil service occupations.

Among the female respondents, the white heterosexual women (WHTFs) were more likely than the WHFs to work in technological occupations such as chemists or geologists, factory technicians, or machine operators. The black heterosexual females (BHTFs) more often worked as teachers, librarians, or journalists than the BHFs did.

Residential Patterns. Both the WHTMs and the BHTMs tended to be less mobile than their homosexual counterparts; more had lived all their lives in the Bay Area, and fewer had spent less than 10 percent of their lives there. The heterosexual men did not think as many of their neighbors were homosexual as the homosexual men did, but the four male samples did not differ in knowing only a few of their neighbors by name. Another unsurprising difference between the heterosexual and the homosexual men is that at the time of our interview, fewer of the former were living alone or with male roommates. Most were living with their wives and a very small number with a female roommate.

The heterosexual women, like their male counterparts, tended to have lived longer in the Bay Area than the lesbians had. Compared with the homosexual women, they were less likely to think any of their neighbors were homosexual and more likely to know them by name. At the time of the interview, most were living with their husbands or with female roommates; fewer of the heterosexual than of the homosexual women were living alone.

Religious Affiliation. The heterosexual men hardly differed at all from their homosexual counterparts in their religious affiliation. About a quarter of the WHTMs and twice as many BHTMs listed themselves as Protestant, not quite a fifth as Catholic, and hardly any as Jewish. Two-fifths of the whites and a quarter of the blacks said they were atheists or agnostics. Differences in religious affiliation did appear between the heterosexual and homosexual female samples, however, with more of the heterosexual than of the homosexual women stating a religious affiliation of one kind or another, and a greater proportion of those who did so identifying themselves as Protestants.

Interview Schedule Development

As previously noted, in the summer of 1967 the Institute conducted a pilot study of male homosexuality (NIMH Grant No. MH 12535) in Chicago which involved interviews, each lasting about an hour and a half, with approximately 450 white homosexual males. Since the interview schedule used in that study covered many of the areas which the present investigation planned to include, and because of our interest in replicating as much of the present work as possible, each of the items in that schedule was examined for possible use in the present study.

The pilot interview schedule contained 165 general questions, some involving more than a single question, designed to explore the following areas: occupational history—the effect of one's homosexuality on one's career, whether homosexuals are employed compatibly with their training, the extent to which homosexual contacts enhance social mobility, and if so, in what occupations; social relationships—whether friendships are confined to other homosexuals, how homosexual and heterosexual friendships are managed, and how much they overlap; military service— the management of homosexuality in the service, differences between those honorably discharged and those discharged because of homosexuality; [5] family relationships and family background, in respondents' childhood and presently, including whether family members know of the respondents' homosexuality and if so, how this affects these relationships; involvement with the law—arrests and convictions and their context; the extent of the use of alcohol and other drugs; sexual relationships—the extent and nature of the respondents' homosexuality and heterosexuality, in the number of stable relationships with men or women, the number of sexual partners they had had, and attitudes toward sexual partners and lovers; attitudes toward sex in general and homosexuality in particular, including the degree of sexual inhibition;

---

[5] For a detailed exploration of this topic, see Williams and Weinberg, 1971.

incidence of being rolled or robbed or blackmailed; political activities and attitudes, including self-ratings on a liberal-conservative continuum; psychological adjustment, including current feeling states and psychosomatic symptomatology; contacts with therapists—their purpose and frequency and evaluation of their results.

In the item analysis we wanted to locate those items which had been of little use in the pilot study, which overlapped with other more useful items, or which were too extensive for the purposes of the present study. On this basis, we eliminated many of the items dealing with the subjects' work histories and friendship structures. Other items were lengthened or shortened or changed to an open-ended form. We ended up retaining in some fashion about two-thirds of the questions from the pilot study.

To these items we added a list of additional questions designed to provide for a more detailed investigation of the different ways in which people experience or express their homosexuality. These included questions about respondents' standings on the Kinsey Scale with regard to both sexual feelings and behaviors, the extent to which a wide variety of others knew about their homosexuality, their cruising activities, the sexual techniques they employed and those they liked best, how much sex appeal they thought they had, the number and nature of their sexual problems, and the level of their sexual interest and activity.

Questions about social adjustment, in addition to those from the pilot study, dealt with respondents' religious attitudes and, among the homosexual respondents, the nature of their social activities, and how their roommate relationships were handled. Many of the questions used in our pilot study to assess respondents' psychological adjustment were retained in the new interview schedule. Additional items, modified from the Minnesota Multiphasic Personality Inventory (Hathaway & McKinley, 1943), were used to measure our respondents' depression and paranoia. Rosenberg's (1965) measure of self-esteem was also included. Finally, respondents were questioned more extensively about their experiences of psychotherapy and their suicide attempts or ideation.

The new interview schedule, 175 pages in length, contained 528 questions, about one-third of which were derived from the pilot interview schedule. (Not all of the data generated by these questions have been reported in the present work. Some will appear in our subsequent volume and the rest in forthcoming journal articles.) Designed for use in a face-to-face interview, it normally took two to five hours to complete with the homosexual respondents and about half that time with the heterosexual men and women, since about one-third of the questions were asked only of the homosexual respondents.

Interviewing Procedures

All of the interviews were scheduled by telephone. If someone other than the prospective respondent answered our call, we simply asked when the particular person could be reached. Our callers never identified themselves, stated the reason for the call, or gave messages to anyone but the person named on the recruitment card. We also tried to find the new address or phone number of respondents who had moved away. We wrote letters to those who had not given a telephone number, asking them to call the field office.

The first element of the conversation with prospective respondents was to verify that the information on the recruitment card was correct. (If not, necessary corrections would be made and the person assigned to the appropriate cell, and an interview would not be scheduled just then.) Normally, arrangements would be made for an interview within the week at the respondent's convenience. The respondent would be assigned a field number, as a means of identification to the interviewer, and was asked to notify the field office if the interview appointment could not be kept. Although most persons preferred to be interviewed in their own homes (where we insisted utter privacy be provided), other interviewing locations in San Francisco, Palo Alto, and San Rafael were sometimes used. After an interview had been arranged, the field office would inform the person who was to conduct the interview. Normally an interviewer was assigned only to respondents of the same sex and race.

Interviewers

Needless to say, whom to entrust with the responsibility of interviewing was crucially important. Much time and effort had gone into the construction of the interview schedule. The community had been prepared for an extensive investigation of human sexuality. But the ultimate success of the study, the need for reliable and valid data, depended largely on the personalities and abilities of those who would be hired and trained as interviewers. Persons had to be found whose honesty could not be questioned; every aspect of their report had to be an exact reflection of what had actually occurred. They had to be personable, able to put others at ease, and sufficiently comfortable with themselves—especially sexually—that they would not be greatly disturbed by whatever the respondent might disclose. Socially, they had to be relatively unobtrusive, to present a neutral stimulus, so that nothing about their appearance or manner would unduly affect a respondent's answers. Regardless of their professional background, they had to be able to work under supervision, to be responsive to whatever suggestions the field directors made to them. At the same time they had to be able to work without constant reminders from their supervisors, to cope alone with situations that arose, and to seek help only when it was reasonable. They had to be flexible enough to tolerate whatever procedural changes might take place during the course of the project. Even if they were initially interested in interviewing because of the salary involved or simply out of curiosity about others' sexuality, they had basically to feel convinced that they were doing an essential job. Otherwise they would not be able to handle the difficulties (often, the boredom) which would sooner or later arise. They had to be perceptive individuals, able to recall whatever the respondent had said at any time during the interview, in order to catch and resolve discrepancies. Above all, they had to be able to conduct themselves as professionals at all times. Under no circumstances were they to discuss any aspects of an interview with anyone but the field office staff, since a bit of unusual information about a person might identify an otherwise unnamed respondent to someone else. In short, the interviewer had to be the kind of person who could be entrusted with information that was no one else's business (not even his or her own, once the interview was over) and who could behave in ways that justified the respondents' trust in the Institute.

Most of the interviewers were graduate students in local universities. All lived in the Bay Area within commuting distance of the field office. They attended a series of meetings in which they were familiarized with the interview schedule and the procedures in the interviewing manual. We stressed that they must read the questions exactly as they appeared in the schedule. The interviewers were also carefully trained in making additional probes when a response to an open-ended question needed elaboration or clarification. Since respondents' answers had to be recorded verbatim, a term or phrase that prompted probing was to be underlined and the interviewer's probe written in parentheses if it was directive (such as "but how did this make you feel?") or indicated by an X if it was neutral (such as "what do you mean by ————?"). By this means we would have a more accurate picture of what actually went on in the interview. In addition, after the respondent had satisfactorily answered an open-ended question, he or she would be asked once if there was anything more to add, and if not, the interviewer would go on to the next question. Immediately after the interview, the interviewer reviewed the schedule, clarified unusual abbreviations, corrected any recording errors, and circled the appropriate codes in areas not covered in the interview (for example, a person who had never married was not asked questions pertaining to marriage).

Each completed interview schedule was checked by the office staff for inconsistencies and the adequacy of probes and answers. Checkers' comments were discussed with the interviewer, giving particular attention to the interviewer's understanding of various questions, his or her handwriting and editing (if the handwriting was unclear, the interviewer would have to type up the response in question), how well he or she controlled the interview situation, any personal concerns arising during the interview, the degree of emotional involvement he or she felt with the respondent, and his or her general attitudes toward the project. Sometimes the interviewer had to get back in touch with the respondent to clarify an inadequate or missing answer.

Postinterview Contacts

The field staff made additional contact with at least half of the white men and women and almost all of the black men and women after their interviews. One reason for this was to check the competence of new interviewers; we were especially interested in whether the respondent felt that a good rapport had been established. Other reasons included arranging for family members to be interviewed if the respondent had agreed to this, or asking whether his or her friends might be willing to be interviewed. For example, in order to obtain additional older respondents, we attempted to call back all of our black respondents, white female respondents over forty, and white males in their fifties and sixties. Finally, in the few instances when a respondent had been paid for the interview, he or she was telephoned to ask if the payment had been made.

One important result of our having postinterview contact with so many of the respondents is that we have every reason to believe that those persons purportedly interviewed were, in fact, interviewed. Whenever an interviewing agency employs outside interviewers, there is always the possibility that such persons will forge an interview. It is therefore noteworthy that every one of the homosexual respondents whom we reached reported that he or she had, indeed, been interviewed. Our situation did make it unlikely that an interviewer would falsify the schedule. All of the interviews were arranged by the office staff and not by the interviewers themselves; the interviewer was paid for travel time and for the average time an interview would take even if the respondent did not show up; and, of course, the interviewer was well aware that the office would be getting back in touch with most respondents for one reason or another.

Ethnographic Procedures

In order to give readers a more vivid picture of our homosexual respondents' cultural milieu, we undertook an ethnographic survey that included on-the-spot descriptions of gay residential areas, bars and baths, clubs and restaurants, parties, other cruising areas, cruising activities, employment opportunities and businesses, and friendship groups. This ethnographic account of the social context from which our survey data were drawn, to be found in Appendix A of this book, illustrates the extent to which the San Francisco community maintains and reinforces various styles of homosexual life and behavior.

Reliability and Validity

All of our data are based on what respondents reported to be true of themselves in a face-to-face interview. The reliability of data gathered in this way can be affected by the respondent's reaction to a particular interviewer, by difficulties in remembering past experiences accurately, by fatigue or mood, by inadvertent or deliberate exaggeration, by misunderstanding a given question, and a host of other factors. In order to assure that our data were reasonably reliable, we used the test-retest method. Thus, we had a different interviewer reinterview a number of respondents six months after their first interview and compared their responses in both interviews. For most of our questions, we found high correlations between the two sets of responses—i.e., the retested respondents tended to answer in the same way both times. Where the correlation was low, we decided that the particular item did not yield reliable data and excluded it from our analysis.

In addition, in order to make sure that our data were valid—i.e., that our questions measured what we intended them to—we used several tests of convergent validity. By this means, a respondent would be questioned about the same general subject—e.g., his or her sexual activity—at various points in the interview that were widely separated in time (an hour or more), using a different wording and response category set at each point. When the answers to these sets of questions were consistent and made sense taken together, e.g., if the number of sexual partners a person reported having seemed to fit with how often he or she reported having had sex, we could feel some assurance that the related data were valid. The tests of convergent validity worked well enough to permit us to infer that the other data were reasonably valid as well.

Statistical Procedures

Several statistical techniques were used to process the large amount of data generated in this study. While many of these techniques may be less than intelligible to the average reader, they were used because of their power to summarize and organize an enormous amount of information. Some of these involve tests of statistical significance. Use of these tests is often based on the assumption of random sampling from a larger population of interest and is generally used by researchers to make inferences about that larger population. We do not claim to have drawn representative samples of all homosexual and heterosexual adults in the San Francisco Bay Area, and we do not believe that it is appropriate to make inferences to these larger populations or beyond them. However, we do report the probability levels these tests provide; for our purposes, these statistics only provide an occasional benchmark or index to the magnitude of a difference that exists in a sample of a particular size.

Other techniques used in the present study include cross-tabulation, correlation, factor analysis, cluster analysis, multiple linear regression analysis, chi-square analysis, multivariate analysis of variance, and multiple discriminant function analysis. A brief discussion of each of these techniques follows.

Cross-tabulations were performed on virtually all sexual, sociological, and psychological variables against the sex, race, and sexual orientation of the respondent.[6]

Correlation matrices were computed for the homosexual respondents on the major demographic variables (age, education, and occupational level) and all sexual experience variables. These matrices were used in a preliminary exploration of the dimensions of homosexual experience for males and for females. Orthogonal factor analysis was then used in an attempt to summarize these patterns for males and for females, and the resulting factors were contrasted. Factor analysis is a procedure by which relationships among a group of variables may be accounted for by a smaller number of variables called "factors."

[6] In order to classify respondents into "relatively low," "moderate," and "relatively high" categories, we divided the percentage distribution for the entire sample (white, black, male, female, homosexual, and [if applicable] heterosexual) into thirds and then distributed the group percentages accordingly.

Cluster analysis was used to explore the homosexual male and female samples separately for the existence of empirically distinct subgroups or types. The particular algorithm that we used is a hierarchical agglomerative one which clusters in a stepwise fashion individuals who are similar to each other. Plotting techniques were used as an adjunct to the cluster analysis to examine multivariate profiles of the cluster analysis–defined groups. Means and standard deviations were computed, where appropriate, for the various homosexual types: Close-Coupled, Open-Coupled, Functional, Dysfunctional, and Asexual.

Multiple linear regression analysis was used to examine each of the variables in the sexual, sociological, and psychological categories for males and then for females. The regression model varied depending on whether the particular variable was available for all the respondents or just for the homosexual samples. This technique allowed us to examine systematically the relationship of each of these variables to the race of the homosexual respondents and to sexual orientation. The regression model also allowed us to test systematically the usefulness of our homosexual typology in comparing the homosexual respondents among themselves and with their heterosexual counterparts. (If there were no differences among the homosexual types, they were considered one group for statistical purposes, and only the homosexual sample as a whole was compared with the heterosexual sample.)

Chi-square analysis was used to estimate the significance of differences in responses to discrete variables (i.e., those for which answers cannot be ranged along a "low-high" continuum). One computes the difference between how people's answers to a certain question varied and how much they would have varied if the answers were given randomly.

In general, for analytical reasons, blacks and whites were kept separate and were compared on every item to see whether the size of differences between them was significant. Throughout the book, we describe significant black-white differences with phrases such as "as opposed to," "compared with," or "but," as in "Most of the white males, as opposed to one-third of the blacks . . ." Where such a difference is not significant, we use "and," e.g., "Few of the whites and none of the blacks . . ."

Differences between the homosexual men and women were not a major analytic focus. Thus, they were not compared directly on each item (except as noted in the next paragraph). Nonetheless, the reader can be assured that the particularly large and interesting male-female differences that we do note were tested for statistical significance and had a significance level of at least .05.

With respect to our concluding overview chapter, analysis of variance was used in comparisons involving each type of homosexual men, each type of homosexual women, and "similar" types of homosexual men and women. The analysis of variance was followed by multiple discriminant function analysis. Although two groups may be very different on one variable, this difference may be spurious, i.e., actually due to the effect of other variables. This technique calculates standardized discriminant function coefficients for each of the comparison variables. These coefficients are similar to standardized multiple regression coefficients (beta weights); they reflect the relative importance of each variable in explaining group differences. We used this powerful statistical technique to summarize very complex within- and between-sex typology differences.

Part II

Dimensions
of
Sexual
Experience

In most research pertaining to homosexuality, investigators have not been concerned with the ways in which homosexual men and women may differ in the management or expression of their sexual interests and impulses. Instead, they have usually been focused on how homosexuals differ from heterosexuals in regard to certain variables, with neither group delineated as to how its members differ from one another in the dimensions of their sexual lives. It has been generally assumed that the chief distinguishing variable in sexual experience is one's sexual object choice—whether it is a person of the same or of the opposite sex—and that all one needs to know is whether a given individual is "homosexual" or "heterosexual" so that he or she can be assigned to a particular comparison group. The fact that homosexuals differ from each other in ways which make general conclusions about them problematic has led some clinicians and investigators to attempt more precise systems of classification (e.g., see Bell, 1975a). Up until now, probably the most usual kind of difference seen among homosexuals has had to do with the extent to which they display cross-gender characteristics. Among both homosexual men and women it has been suggested that there are two types: those who are "passive" and those who are "active" (Armstrong, 1955). Among lesbians, contrasts have been made between the "feminine type" and the "masculine type" (Ellis, 1964), among those who are "butch," "femme," or "neutral" (Giannell, 1966), and, among those in prison samples, between the "fish," "femme," or "mommy"—who takes on a feminine role—and the "butch," "stud broad," "stud," or "daddy"—who assumes a masculine role (Ward & Kassebaum, 1964; Sawyer, 1965; Giallombardo, 1966). Similar distinctions have been made between homosexual men, usually based upon the role they prefer in sexual contacts. The homosexual man who ordinarily acts as the inserter has been termed "active," while the man who prefers the role of "insertee" has been termed "passive" (McCreary, 1950; Erickson, 1961; Knight, 1965; Nash & Hayes, 1965; Oliver & Mosher, 1968). Among prison samples, "wolves," "jockers," or "voluntary aggressors"—those who are aggressively masculine—have been contrasted with "fags," "fairies," "effeminates," or "queens," and "punks" or "involuntary recruits"—who are thought to forfeit their masculinity (Lindner, 1951; Sykes, 1958; Kirkham, 1966; Sagarin, 1976). Gilbert (1954) devised four categories of homosexual men which, again, refer to their gender identifications: the "pure" homosexual who displays feminine characteristics such as dependency and passivity, the "heterosexual" who is more masculine than feminine but uncertain about his sexual identity, the "latent" type who cannot accept his feminine characteristics, and the "male partner" whose high sex drive renders him indifferent to the sex of the person with whom he happens to make sexual contact. Classifications of this kind have led one clinician (Becker, 1967) to propose that homosexuals be distinguished on the basis of where they stand on a masculine-feminine continuum with respect to their anatomy, physiology, personality, and overt behavior.

Another way in which homosexuals have been distinguished is in the degree of their heterosexual experience or potential. "Bisexuals" have been contrasted with "exclusives" (Neustatter, 1954) and the latter in turn with the "occasionally homosexual" (Caprio, 1955). A similar typology of homosexual women has been suggested by Landis et al. (1940), who distinguished among those whose homosexuality was "temporary," "consistent," or "sporadic." In one study, lesbians who were "exclusively homosexual" were compared with those categorized as "predominantly homosexual" (Kenyon, 1968b). Another study compared the psychological adjustment of homosexual men who had some heterosexual experience with that of those who had none (Dean, 1967b). A somewhat related system of classification appeared in a third investigation which distinguished those who had been homosexual since early childhood from those whose homosexuality came about after adolescence (Herman & Wortis, 1947).

Other attempts to delineate homosexuals more precisely have included categories reflecting the extent to which they are overt versus covert (Braaten & Darling, 1965; Myrick, 1974b), the nature of their partner preferences (Freund et al., 1974), the kind of relationship they seek (Rancourt & Limoges, 1967), whether or not they are currently involved in a "marital" relationship (Dickey, 1961), their preferences for anal intercourse as opposed to fellatio (DeLuca, 1966), how comfortable they are with their homosexuality (Nacht et al., 1956), the unconscious motivations prompting their homosexual sexual pursuits (Ovesey, 1964), and the degree to which their personalities are marked by pathology (Scott, 1957; Roth & Ball, 1964).

It should be noted that the various ways in which homosexuals have been distinguished from each other have usually not been used to determine the extent to which one "kind" of homosexual differs from another in other features of their lives. Those investigations which have actually proceeded with such comparisons have generally involved only one dimension of homosexuality in which homosexual respondents were shown to differ. An important exception is the work of Weinberg and Williams (1974, 1975a). These investigators delineated their homosexual male respondents from three different societies on the basis of the level of their sexual activity, whether they had ever been involved in an exclusive relationship, the degree of their effeminacy, their commitment and attitudes toward homosexuality, their sexual repertoires, their standings on the homosexual-heterosexual continuum, and the extent to which their homosexuality was known about by others. Their statistical analyses attempted to determine the degree to which these various dimensions of homosexuality were related to each other and the relationships between respondents' place on a given dimension and their social and psychological adjustment.

The present study includes an even greater array of the various features of homosexuality in which homosexuals are apt to differ. These include respondents' standing on the homosexual-heterosexual continuum as reflected by their self-ratings on the so-called Kinsey Scale; the extent to which they had revealed their homosexuality to others; the frequency of their sexual activity; their cruising patterns—how often they went out specifically in search of a sexual partner, whether they made the first approach to a prospective partner or waited for the other person to do so, where sexual contact was most apt to take place, the amount of time they usually spent with a pickup, the kinds and amount of worrying they did when they were out cruising; their sexual partnerships—how many partners they had had, what physical characteristics they preferred in their partners, how much they became nonsexually involved with their partners, the types of partners with whom they became sexually involved; how much sex appeal they thought they had to others of the same sex; the sexual techniques they most often employed and liked best; the level of their sexual interest; the nature and extent of their sexual problems; and how much, if at all, they regretted being homosexual. While these dimensions of sexual experience are not exhaustive, they are certainly more comprehensive than anything of the kind which has heretofore appeared in the literature. And while these variables deal only with the more explicitly sexual aspects of the respondents' homosexuality, other equally important ways in which homosexuals differ, socially and psychologically, are considered in succeeding sections of the book.

The purpose of the present section is to present our homosexual respondents' standings and their diversity on the above-mentioned dimensions of sexual experience; compare our distributions with those from other samples; examine the degree to which men and women and blacks and whites differ on each dimension; and, finally, devise a typology which is used in our succeeding analyses as the basis for comprehensive comparisons of the sexual, psychological, and social aspects of our respondents' lives.

The Homosexual-Heterosexual Continuum

Homosexuality-heterosexuality is not necessarily an either-or proposition. Rather, people can be distinguished on the basis of the degree to which their sexual responsiveness and behaviors are limited to persons of a particular sex (male or female). These facts should come as no surprise to anyone familiar with the literature. Kinsey and his associates (1948, 1953), using a seven-point scale to measure whether, and if so to what degree, their respondents were "homosexual" or "heterosexual" in their sexual behaviors, determined that nearly half of American males fell somewhere between "exclusively heterosexual" (a score of 0 on the scale) and "exclusively homosexual" (or 6). Women were likewise found to differ in their standings on this scale, although fewer were exclusively "homosexual." Only after an individual's standing on the homosexual-heterosexual continuum has been established can he or she be classified as "homosexual" or "heterosexual," with the clear understanding that such a classification refers merely to the balance between the person's sexual responsiveness to others of the same and of the opposite sex.

Some studies have found differences among homosexuals in how exclusively "homosexual" they are. For example, Bieber et al. (1962) found that psychiatrists described their homosexual patients as differing in terms of whether they ever had erotic heterosexual dreams. Saghir and Robins (1973) were able to distinguish their homosexual male and female respondents on the basis of their experience of heterosexual sexual arousal or contact. Two other studies found differences among lesbians in this regard (Gundlach, 1967; Schäfer, 1976). In an investigation of male homosexuals, Weinberg and Williams (1974, 1975a) found that respondents scoring 6 or 5 on the Kinsey Scale (exclusively or predominantly homosexual) could be distinguished from those who scored in a more bisexual direction (i.e., 4, 3, or 2) in their sexual, psychological, and social adjustment.

In the present study we asked respondents to classify themselves ("as you see yourself right now") on the Kinsey Scale, first as to their sexual behaviors and then as to their sexual feelings. We expected that separate ratings on these two dimensions would permit a more precise assessment of the nature of such ratings.[1] Besides the Kinsey Scale ratings, we considered whether our homosexual respondents had had any sexual contact with persons of the opposite sex during the past year, the incidence of orgasm in that context, whether their erotic dreams and masturbatory fantasies involved a heterosexual element, and whether they had ever been sexually aroused by a member of the opposite sex. In addition, respondents with both homosexual and heterosexual experience were asked to compare the two.

Findings: Men

Kinsey Ratings: Behaviors (Table 3.4)

About three-quarters of the white homosexual men (WHMs) and a somewhat smaller percentage of the black homosexual men (BHMs) considered themselves exclusively homosexual (or 6 on the Kinsey Scale) in their current sexual behavior. Moreover, most of those who did not give themselves an "exclusive" rating described themselves as

[1] Although respondents' ratings on each dimension have been considered separately, they have also been combined in a summary measure on which scores range from 0 (exclusively heterosexual in behaviors and in feelings) to 12 (exclusively homosexual on both dimensions). This summary measure is used in later chapters when respondents' standings on the homosexual-heterosexual continuum are discussed.

"mainly homosexual" (5). Thus, only a small minority of the homosexual male respondents could be considered "bisexual" (4—mainly homosexual with a substantial degree of heterosexuality; 3—as much heterosexual as homosexual; or 2—mainly heterosexual with a substantial degree of homosexuality) in terms of their sexual activity.

These self-estimates were generally related to what respondents reported about sexual contact with females (Table 3.7). While almost two-thirds of the WHMs and somewhat larger numbers of the BHMs said that they had had heterosexual coitus at least once in their lives (Table 3.4), smaller numbers (WHMs: 14%, BHMs: 22%) had engaged in it during the year prior to the interview. Fewer than half had ever engaged in oral-genital or manual-genital contact with a woman.

The incidence of heterosexual coitus among the white homosexual males in our sample is the same as that found in our pilot sample, about the same as that in Bieber et al.'s sample, and only slightly higher than that reported by Weinberg and Williams. Compared with our data, lower incidences of ever having had coitus are reported by Schofield (1965; 34%) and by Saghir and Robins (48%). In the latter sample, however, 10 percent were currently engaging in intercourse. Eighteen percent of our pilot study males had engaged in coitus during the current year, while 11 percent of the Weinberg and Williams males had engaged in coitus within six months of the time they filled out the questionnaire. Thus, although the above samples may differ with respect to the number who ever engaged in coital activity, the active incidences of such activity are nearly the same.

Of those who had ever had sex with women, approximately half of the whites, in comparison with five-eighths of the blacks, had always reached orgasm during such sexual contact. Despite these reports, however, about one-fifth of the respondents who had had sex with both males and females volunteered that they felt more competent in their sexual relationships with males. By far the largest numbers mentioned feeling more at ease or less fearful, nervous, or inhibited with males than with females:

I feel more relaxed, more earthy, more comfortable with males. There's always a fear with women, a fear that I am not my own.

It is more exciting with men.

There was always more of an emotional rapport with a male partner.

My homosexual experiences have been far and away more satisfactory, enjoyable, interesting, and fulfilling. My heterosexual experiences were primarily a sexual release for me. I felt indifferent about my female partner.

Kinsey Ratings: Feelings (Table 3.5)

The male respondents were less apt to consider themselves exclusively homosexual in their sexual feelings. Forty-two percent of the WHMs and more than half of the BHMs gave themselves a rating of 5 or less (i.e., not exclusively homosexual) on the scale; in fact, 6 percent of the WHMs and 8 percent of the BHMs believed that they were at least as heterosexual as homosexual in their sexual feelings. Clearly, the respondents' sexual feelings, which they can control less than their sexual behaviors (and on which they may not have the opportunity, time, or motivation to act), are less apt to fall at the extreme (exclusively homosexual) end of the continuum.

The relationships of these self-ratings to other measures of heterosexuality (Table 3.8) suggest that masturbatory fantasies, sex dreams, or heterosexual arousal may have made these men aware of a heterosexual responsiveness. One-third of the WHMs and almost half of the BHMs reported that at least some of their dreams involved sexual episodes with females. Somewhat smaller numbers occasionally imagined having sex with females while they were masturbating (Table 3.5). Respondents who did not rate themselves as exclusively homosexual in their sexual feelings also tended to recall one or more instances of having been sexually aroused by a female (Table 3.8). Seventy-two percent of the WHMs and even more of the BHMs said that they had been sexually aroused by a female at least once in their lives (Table 3.5).

With respect to other measures of heterosexuality in homosexual male samples, Bieber et al. found a higher incidence of heterosexual sex dreams (47%) than we did, but the incidence of heterosexual sexual fantasies and/or dreams reported by Saghir and Robins (36%) is about the same as our own. Nineteen percent of those in Saghir and Robins's sample had actually had nocturnal emissions with their heterosexual sex dreams. (These usually occurred in adolescence.) With regard to heterosexual sexual arousal, almost exactly the same percentage (73%) of the Saghir and Robins homosexual male sample as of ours reported having been heterosexually stimulated (in this case, to the point that they had an erection). These figures are higher than the number in Bieber et al.'s sample (49%) who ever experienced heterosexual sexual arousal and much higher than the percentage of homosexual males (8%) in Schofield's sample who ever felt a strong sexual attraction for a female.

Kinsey Ratings: Behaviors and Feelings (Table 3.6)

A majority of the WHMs and somewhat fewer BHMs considered themselves exclusively homosexual in both their sexual behavior *and* feelings. In both groups there was a slight tendency for the older respondents to rate themselves exclusively homosexual (Table 3.1). Respondents' ratings were not related to education or occupational level.

Our respondents' standings on the homosexual-heterosexual continuum are not unlike those found in the samples of other investigators. The same percentage of the white homosexual males in our Chicago sample (51%) and of those in the Weinberg and Williams United States sample (51%) gave this rating of themselves. In three other homosexual male samples, larger percentages have been described as exclusively homosexual. About three-quarters of those in Bieber et al.'s clinical sample were described as exclusively homosexual at the onset of therapy. Three-quarters of those in another sample (Manosevitz, 1972) were exclusively homosexual in their behaviors, and almost as many of those in Schofield's nonpatient, noninstitutionalized sample were considered exclusively homosexual. The greater number of exclusively homosexual males in these three samples may be due to an exclusive attention to sexual *behaviors*. Our data indicate that when respondents' sexual *feelings* are taken into account, smaller numbers can be considered to be exclusively homosexual.

About two-thirds of our male respondents rated themselves exactly the same way on each of these two dimensions of the continuum. Among those whose self-ratings were discrepant, more than three-quarters considered themselves more heterosexual in their feelings than in their behaviors. Thus, it would appear that few of them were engaged in heterosexuality to an extent that it interfered with their homosexual needs and interests. A more typical picture is that of a man whose sexual activity is homosexual, perhaps exclusively so, although he may feel a potential for sexual responsiveness to women.

Summary

These data clearly indicate that although the majority of our respondents fell at the homosexual end of the homosexual-heterosexual continuum, they differed from one another in the extent to which their sexual behaviors and feelings were chiefly or exclusively homosexual. Especially with respect to their sexual feelings, many could not be considered exclusively homosexual.

Findings: Women

Kinsey Ratings: Behaviors (Table 3.4)

Somewhat more than two-thirds of the white homosexual females (WHFs) and about three-fifths of the black homosexual females (BHFs) regarded themselves as exclusively homosexual in terms of their current sexual behaviors. Although the next largest number of them rated themselves 5 on the Kinsey Scale (i.e., mainly homosexual with a small degree of heterosexuality), 8 percent of the WHFs as compared to 17 percent of the BHFs rated themselves at least as heterosexual as homosexual with respect to their sexual behaviors. Thus, the WHFs scored in a more exclusively homosexual direction than did the BHFs.

These self-ratings tended to be related to the extent to which the female respondents had ever engaged in heterosexual sex (Table 3.9), although these relationships were not as clear as those among the males. And while most of the lesbians had experienced heterosexual coitus at least once in their lives, relatively small numbers had engaged in it during the year just prior to the interview (Table 3.4). The incidence of heterosexual coitus and the number of those currently involved in coital activity in our white homosexual female sample tended to be only slightly larger than what has been reported by other investigators. Seventy-nine percent of the women in Saghir and Robins's sample, 75 percent of the Gundlach and Riess (1968) sample, 73 percent of those in Schäfer's sample, and 62 percent of the women in *The Ladder* sample (1959) had ever experienced coitus. Nine percent of the female respondents in Saghir and Robins's sample were still having heterosexual intercourse when the study was conducted.

Finally, among those reporting any kind of sexual contact with a male, one-third of both the white and the black respondents said that they had never reached orgasm in this context. A majority had not reached orgasm during sex with men either most or all of the time. Of those who had both homosexual and heterosexual experiences, however, relatively few mentioned feeling less competent in their sexual contacts with males than with females. The largest number spoke in terms of having felt more joy and satisfaction and less fear in their sexual relationships with women:

My heterosexual experiences have been boring, very boring, whereas I have always felt very much alive in my relationships with women. They have always brought me much more emotional fulfillment.

My homosexual experiences are much more profound, more satisfying, and more sexually exciting.

I can share more of myself with a woman. I like the way a woman makes me feel.

With the exception of my husband, I've always enjoyed homosexual love more than heterosexual love. Heterosexual love seems more violent to me, sometimes frightening, and more selfish on the guy's part.

Kinsey Ratings: Feelings (Table 3.5)

Half of the WHFs and five-eighths of the BHFs rated their sexual feelings exclusively homosexual; another quarter of the women in each race gave themselves a "bisexual" feelings rating (i.e., a score of 4 or less). Among both groups, self-ratings with respect to their sexual feelings were related to the reports they gave about their sex dreams, masturbatory fantasies, and sexual arousal (Table 3.10). Fifty-five percent of the WHFs and 41 percent of the BHFs said that they had had sex dreams involving sexual activity with males, and approximately one-quarter of the lesbians had imagined having sex with males during masturbation (Table 3.5). Additional evidence of heterosexuality in the female respondents can be found in the number who reported ever having been sexually aroused by a male. More than three-quarters reported such arousal at some time in their lives. About the same number of the female respondents in Saghir and Robins's sample (70%) recalled ever having experienced heterosexual sexual arousal. However, larger numbers of our female respondents recalled a heterosexual content in erotic dreams than of those in the Saghir and Robins sample (33%) who had ever had heterosexual fantasies and/or a heterosexual content in their dreams.

Kinsey Ratings: Behaviors and Feelings (Table 3.6)

Sixty-two percent of the WHFs and 70 percent of the BHFs rated themselves the same on the two dimensions of their homosexual-heterosexual whereabouts. A minority of the WHFs and barely a majority of the BHFs rated themselves exclusively homosexual in both their sexual behaviors *and* feelings. Fairly large numbers, more of the lesbians than of their male counterparts, had at least one rating which fell toward the heterosexual end of the continuum. Three-fourths of the WHFs considered themselves more homosexual in their behaviors than in their feelings. Among the BHFs, however, about two-thirds thought that they were more homosexual in their feelings than in their behaviors. Although the respondents' ratings were not related to age or occupational level, the black lesbians with less education tended to score in a more exclusive direction than their better educated counterparts (Table 3.2).

The number of our white respondents who could be considered exclusively homosexual in both their feelings and their behaviors is about the same as the percentage (47%) in Kaye et al.'s sample (1967) who were described as exclusively homosexual at the onset of therapy. These percentages are slightly larger than the number (37%) of exclusively homosexual females in Kenyon's sample but smaller than the number (62%) in Schäfer's sample who were reported to be exclusively homosexual.

Summary

The white homosexual females were apt to rate themselves as more homosexual in their sexual behaviors than were the black lesbians. In addition, most of the white lesbians whose ratings differed as to behaviors and feelings believed that they were more homosexual in their sexual behaviors than in their feelings. This was not true, however, of the blacks, who tended to believe that they were more homosexual in their feelings than in their behaviors.

Overview

Respondents' ratings of themselves on the homosexual-heterosexual continuum were in agreement with their sexual histories. Those who rated themselves as exclusively homosexual were less apt ever to have engaged in sexual activity with persons of the opposite sex or ever to have been sexually aroused in a heterosexual context than were those respondents who scored in more of a heterosexual direction. As one moves from point to point along the seven-point Kinsey Scale (from 6 to 0), increasingly larger percentages reported more heterosexual experiences. At the very least, it would appear that respondents' self-ratings were valid reflections of their sexual whereabouts.

In addition, our data show evidence of more heterosexuality in the behaviors and feelings of the homosexual women than in their male counterparts. The further finding that the lesbians' ratings of themselves on the Kinsey Scale were less apt to agree with their actual sexual histories than were those of the males suggests that the women were less likely to behave sexually in accordance with their true interests. While they may have engaged in sexual activity with males, many might have done so with little satisfaction or sexual release. It is possible that the lesbians' greater heterosexuality simply reflects a history of accommodation to males in a sexual context or of conformity to societal expectations.

The extent to which our respondents' whereabouts on the homosexual-heterosexual continuum are similar to those in other samples is quite striking. None of these studies, including our own, pretends to have a representative sample of either homosexual males or females. None is chiefly interested in establishing the incidence of any particular characteristic among its homosexual subjects. However, on the basis of these several investigations it would not be unreasonable to suppose that a fairly strong heterosexual element is to be found in about one-third of those homosexual men most likely to participate in surveys of this kind. Even larger numbers of comparable homosexual women are apt to exhibit a "partial bisexual style" (Schäfer). Many homosexuals of both sexes have a history of sexual contact with persons of the opposite sex and, although they may not presently engage in such contact, sometimes are aware of their continuing potential for heterosexual sexual response. There are others, however, who have never been aroused sexually by a person of the opposite sex even though they may have engaged in some form of heterosexual contact. Clearly, among homosexual adults there is a diversity of experience on the homosexual-heterosexual continuum reflected in their sexual feelings, behaviors, dreams, and fantasies.

Overtness

Until fairly recently it had been generally supposed that almost all homosexuals went to great lengths to keep their homosexuality a secret. The homosexual person was seen as one who "dared not speak" (Hyde, 1970) of his or her sexual preferences to family members, friends, or colleagues, and who, even in gathering places for other homosexuals, preferred to remain anonymous. Such people were presumed to suffer the stress of extreme compartmentalization, forced to cope with two different worlds by assuming two quite different identities (Hatterer, 1970). No gay liberation movement had yet begun to challenge heterosexuals' stereotypes of homosexual individuals, assault the behemoth of social discrimination, or urge homosexuals to "come out of the closets and into the streets." Another reason that the image of the secretive homosexual prevailed was that it was based primarily on reports from homosexuals (usually male) seeking treatment for their sexual propensities. Most of these persons loathed their homosexuality and were anxious to keep it a secret from everyone but their therapists. Thus, it comes as no surprise that more than 90 percent of the homosexual male patients in one investigation were worried about the exposure of their homosexuality (Bieber et al., 1962).

More recently there has arisen a quite different image of homosexual candor. Many churches have reexamined their traditional attitudes toward homosexuality, a growing number of states have decriminalized homosexual activities, well-known and highly regarded persons have publicly acknowledged their homosexuality, and the mass media have discussed these events dispassionately. Hence, it is now frequently assumed that almost all homosexuals are frank about their sexual orientation or at least are becoming so.

Although it is reasonable to believe that many fewer homosexuals than formerly are still "in the closet," the fact remains that they continue to differ in the extent to which they disclose their homosexuality to others and/or to which others know about it. One recent study found that about half of the male and female respondents thought their parents knew about their homosexuality (Saghir & Robins, 1973). In addition, the degree to which homosexual men are "covert" or "overt" about their sexual preference has been found to be related to their socioeconomic status (Leznoff & Westley, 1956), their intellectual and social interests (Braaten & Darling, 1965), and their personal and social adjustment (Horowitz, 1964; Braaten & Darling, 1965; Myrick, 1974a; Weinberg & Williams, 1974, 1975a).

In the present study our repondents were asked whether their mothers, fathers, brothers, sisters, and relatives either knew about or suspected their homosexuality. They were also asked whether their employers knew or suspected them to be homosexual and how many of their heterosexual friends, fellow workers, and neighbors knew or suspected this.[1]

Findings: Men (Table 4)

Familial Overtness

Both the white and the black homosexual males were more likely to say that their mothers knew about their homosexuality than that their fathers did. In fact, the fathers were thought to be somewhat less likely to know about it than were the respondents' brothers and sisters.

---

[1] A summary measure, based upon the extent to which they thought those outside their families knew about or suspected their homosexuality, is used to indicate respondents' "overtness" in later chapters.

About two-fifths of the white homosexual males (WHMs) and fully half of the black homosexual males (BHMs) thought that their mothers definitely knew about their homosexuality; almost the same number of WHMs and fewer of the BHMs said that their mothers neither knew nor suspected it. Among those with siblings, one-third of the male respondents said that all of their brothers and sisters knew about their homosexuality. About half believed that none of their siblings knew about it. A third of the WHMs and somewhat more of the BHMs said that their fathers definitely knew them to be homosexual; slightly more than half of the WHMs and somewhat fewer BHMs believed that their fathers neither knew nor suspected this.

Not surprisingly, even smaller numbers of the respondents' other relatives allegedly knew about their homosexuality. Among those who had cousins, almost two-thirds of the WHMs as opposed to half of the BHMs said that none of their cousins knew they were homosexual. Similar percentages and racial differences appeared for other adult relatives.

Extrafamilial Overtness

Outside the family, about one-quarter of the respondents said that their employers and most of their fellow workers definitely knew they were homosexual. More than half believed that their employers and most fellow workers did not know or suspect this. About one-fifth of the respondents said that none of their heterosexual friends knew about their homosexuality, while approximately a third of them said that most of their heterosexual friends knew. Their neighbors were less likely to know.

Among both groups the less educated respondents were more likely to report that others outside their families knew about or suspected their homosexuality than were their better educated counterparts. Among the blacks, the younger respondents tended to be more overt than the older ones, while among the whites the respondents from lower occupational levels tended to be more overt (Tables 3.2, 3.1, 3.3). In addition, the degree to which respondents' homosexuality was known about by their family members tended to be related to the degree of their nonfamilial overtness.

The proportion of men in our Chicago pilot sample reporting that their mothers and that their fathers neither knew nor suspected that they were homosexual is very similar to the comparable proportions among our WHMs. Somewhat fewer of our white homosexual males than of those in Weinberg and Williams's United States sample (50%) thought that their mothers did not know or suspect that they were homosexual, but nearly as many of our WHMs as of the Weinberg and Williams males said their fathers did not know, and like our WHMs, about half thought that their brothers and sisters did not know. In Saghir and Robins's sample, 31 percent of the white males thought that their "families" did not know they were homosexual; in our sample, comparable figures are somewhat higher, ranging from 38 percent (for mothers) to 53 percent (for fathers). In Bieber et al.'s clinical sample, however, many more of the male homosexual psychiatric patients than of our WHMs said that their mothers or fathers did not know they were homosexual. Regarding extrafamilial overtness, the Weinberg and Williams males were similar to our WHMs, with 73 percent saying that their employers and most or all of their fellow workers did not know they were homosexual, and about one-fifth that none of their heterosexual friends knew.

Summary

Respondents' mothers were reported to be somewhat more likely than other family members to know that their sons were homosexual. In turn, their brothers and sisters were more likely to know about this than were their fathers. Almost half of the respondents, however, said that their siblings did not know they were homosexual; nearly as many said their fathers did not know; and somewhat lower numbers thought their mothers did not know about it. With regard to other relatives, the black men were more likely than the white men to report that their cousins and other adult relatives knew they were homosexual.

About a quarter of the respondents said that their employers knew about their homosexuality. About one-fourth also said that most of their fellow workers knew, while slightly more thought that none of their colleagues knew. About a third of the respondents said that most of their heterosexual friends knew they were homosexual and about a fifth that none of them knew it. Less than a fifth of the respondents reported that most of their neighbors knew of their homosexuality, with nearly half saying their neighbors definitely did not know. Except for the somewhat greater tendency of the blacks to believe that their employers and fellow workers neither knew nor suspected that they were homosexual, the two races showed almost no difference in their reports of extrafamilial overtness.

These data indicate that, compared with the whites, the black males' families were somewhat more likely to know about their homosexuality, while their employers and colleagues were somewhat less so. The proportion of the respondents' friends and neighbors who knew about it, however, is roughly the same for both races.

Findings: Women *(Table 4)*

Familial Overtness

As in the case of the men, the mothers of the female respondents were alleged to know about their homosexuality more often than were their fathers. Almost half of the white homosexual females (WHFs) and a majority of the black homosexual females (BHFs) thought that their mothers definitely knew about their homosexuality. Slightly more than one-quarter of them said that their mothers neither knew nor suspected that they were homosexual. With respect to their fathers, about two-fifths of each group said that their fathers definitely knew, while almost half thought that their fathers did not know of or suspect their homosexuality. Relatively large numbers of the female respondents thought that their brothers and sisters were aware of their homosexuality: about one-half reported that most or all of their siblings knew.

Outside the immediate family, almost four-fifths of the WHFs and about half of the BHFs said that none of their cousins definitely knew about their homosexuality, and slightly smaller numbers said that none of their other adult relatives knew about it.

Extrafamilial Overtness

Among those female respondents who were employed, less than one-fifth of them said that their employers definitely knew about their homosexuality, while about two-thirds said that their employers neither knew nor suspected. Smaller numbers reported that none of their fellow workers definitely knew about it. However, few of the female respondents said that none of their heterosexual friends knew they were homosexual, and more than one-third reported that most of these friends knew. Much smaller numbers reported this about their neighbors.

Among the white respondents, those with less education tended to report more instances of people outside the family knowing about their homosexuality. Among the blacks, those at lower occupational levels tended to be more overt (Tables 3.2, 3.3). In neither sample was age related to degree of overtness. In general, as for the males, female respondents' extents of familial and nonfamilial overtness were related.

About the same number of those in Schäfer's sample as of our white respondents said that their mothers (35%) and that their fathers (51%) definitely did not know about their homosexuality. The number of our white female respondents reporting that both their mothers and their fathers did not know about their homosexuality is also similar to the number (29%) of Saghir and Robins's female respondents who said their "parents" did not know about it. Outside the family, 21 percent of Schäfer's respondents, a proportion similar to that found among our WHFs, thought that none of their colleagues at work knew or suspected they were homosexual.

Summary

Among immediate family members, our female respondents were more likely to believe that their mothers and siblings knew about their homosexuality than that their fathers did. Nearly half of the white women, and fully half of the black women, reported this to be true of their mothers and of their brothers and sisters, while somewhat fewer of the respondents' fathers were reported to know definitely about it. Similarly, somewhat more of the fathers than of the mothers were described as definitely not knowing. The two races did not differ significantly on these measures. Most of the white females' cousins and other relatives allegedly did not know they were homosexual, while just under half of the black females reported this.

About two-thirds of the respondents said their employers did not know they were homosexual. Sizable minorities of both races said their fellow workers did not know. The white and the black females were quite similar in their responses to these questions.

Overview

A number of conclusions can be reached on the basis of these assorted data. First, homosexuals typically studied by survey researchers clearly differ in terms of how much their homosexuality is known about by others. Despite the expectation that homosexual men and women who volunteer for studies of this kind would be relatively overt, we found that the majority were relatively covert.

Second, while there is a relationship between members of a respondent's family and those outside the family knowing about his or her homosexuality, one cannot easily predict how generally candid such a respondent would be about it on the basis of reports from a single context. For example, some respondents who are still "in the closet" as regards their parents may work for a gay employer who actually hired them on the basis of their acknowledged homosexuality. The reverse, of course, is more apt to be true, with members of the family knowing about a person's homosexuality while other members of society do not. It should also be pointed out that the extent to which one's friends and neighbors, employer and work associates know about one's homosexuality is probably a better measure of "overtness" than is whether one's parents know about it. Parents may frequently become aware of a son's or daughter's homosexuality by deducing it from their own observations or through reports of third parties such as school authorities or police—not as the result of a freely given disclosure.[2] Such knowledge therefore may not always reflect what is usually meant by "overtness."

Third, it might be thought that women are more apt than men to stay involved with their families[3] and that female homosexuality is less stigmatized than male homosexuality.[4] Thus, a lesbian's family could be more likely to know about her homosexuality than would a homosexual man's family. Nonetheless, we found no significant difference between the homosexual men and the lesbians in our sample in this regard.

Fourth, some homosexual men and women may painstakingly conceal their homosexuality from their heterosexual friends, but in many cases such friends allegedly know about it.

Fifth, our female respondents were less likely than the men to say their employers or colleagues knew they were homosexual. This may reflect a tendency for women more than men to keep separate their working and their emotional lives. Or they may simply find greater ease in publicly avoiding the issue than men do, since the heterosexual majority is generally more suspicious of homosexuality in men than in women.

Finally, our data for white homosexual men and white lesbians confirm Leznoff and Westley's and Weinberg and Williams's findings that relatively overt homosexual men and women are apt to be of lower status than their covert counterparts. More educated and more well-employed homosexuals may feel they would have more to lose if their homosexuality were known. Interestingly, only among our black homosexual males did we find a tendency for the younger respondents to be more overt than the older ones. The lack of such a relationship among the other three samples may reflect the fact that at the time of our interviews, young adults less frequently made public acknowledgment of their homosexuality than they do now. It may also indicate, however, that regardless of gay activists' challenge to young people to "come out of the closet," many continue to hesitate disclosing their sexual whereabouts to parents or friends for whom they think such a revelation would be extremely stressful.

[2] For example, see Saghir and Robins (1973), pp. 170, 309.

[3] In the present study, this common notion was not supported. About half of the respondents of either sex reported that they saw their parents once a month or less often.

[4] Another Institute study (Klassen et al., forthcoming) found that respondents tended to be highly disapproving of adult homosexuality regardless of whether the homosexuals involved were male or female.

Level of Sexual Activity

The old stereotype of homosexuals as constantly engaged in all sorts of sexual activity, except during occasional breaks to eat or sleep, was first challenged by Kinsey and his associates (1948). These investigators reported that males whose behaviors were predominantly "homosexual" actually had less frequent sexual contacts than the "heterosexuals" did. More than a decade later, Westwood (1960) confirmed these findings.

Such studies encouraged the rise of another stereotype, more cognitively based: that homosexuals were relatively inactive sexually. This notion in turn has been called into question by more recent studies which found fairly high sexual frequencies among both male (Weinberg & Williams, 1974, 1975a; Saghir & Robins, 1973) and female homosexuals (Saghir & Robins, 1973).

We are not concerned here with a comparison of homosexuals' and heterosexuals' levels of sexual activity. Instead, we want to explore diversity among homosexual men and women. Accordingly, this chapter examines the number of times our respondents reported having had sex with partners of the same sex during the year just prior to the interview. The nature of these contacts will be considered in a succeeding chapter.

Findings: Men *(Table 5)*

We asked our male respondents how often during the past year they had had sex with others of the same sex. The largest numbers of the white homosexual males (WHMs) replied that this had occurred two to three times a week. Almost half of them reported an average frequency of at least twice a week. About one-quarter gave an average of once a week, and one-third said three times a month or less. (The latter group included fifteen who reported no homosexual contacts at all during the year.)

The black homosexual males (BHMs) reported significantly higher frequencies. Two-thirds of them reported having had homosexual sex at least twice a week; less than one-fifth reported an incidence of once a week; and the same number less than once a week. No BHMs had been sexually inactive during the past year. Respondents' levels of sexual activity were related to age, with the younger white respondents but the older blacks reporting higher frequencies (Table 3.1).

Our WHMs' levels of sexual contact are very similar to those of the men in our Chicago pilot sample. About two-thirds of each group had had sex with other men at least once a week. These figures are somewhat higher than the 50 percent reported by Weinberg and Williams but considerably lower than Saghir and Robins's finding that, depending on their male respondents' age (with those aged thirty to thirty-nine being the most active), at least 70 percent had four or more homosexual contacts per week. Among earlier studies, only 6 percent of Kinsey's samples and 11 percent of Westwood's averaged more than three such contacts.

Summary

Nearly half of the white homosexual males, and two-thirds of the black homosexual males, reported having had sex with other men at least twice a week during the year just prior to the interview. For each group, the most common incidence was two or three times a week. Fewer respondents of both races reported lower frequencies of homosexual contact, and a small number of the whites, but none of the blacks, reported none at all during the year.

Findings: Women *(Table 5)*

In response to the same question as that asked of the males, 20 percent of the white homosexual females (WHFs) said that they had had sex with other women about once a week. About a third reported a frequency of two or more times a week. Thus, nearly half of the WHFs had had homosexual sex less than once a week. The majority of the black homosexual females (BHFs) averaged two or more homosexual contacts per week. Nine percent reported an average of once a week, while the rest had had sex with other women less than once a week during the past year.

The reported level of sexual activity was higher among our younger female respondents (Table 3.1). When age was controlled in the regression, the differences between BHFs' and WHFs' activity levels seen in the percentages were reduced to a nonsignificant level. While occupational level was not related to level of sexual activity in either group, among the black lesbians the less educated tended to be more sexually active than their better educated counterparts (Table 3.2).

Our white female respondents reported lower frequencies of sexual activity than did those in Saghir and Robins's sample. For the latter group, the average reported incidence was between two and three times a week, a figure given by 80 percent of the females. Our finding that about half of the WHFs had had homosexual sex less than once a week does imply higher levels of activity than among Kinsey's sample, however, where the comparable proportion was three-fourths.

Summary

The black homosexual females tended to report more frequent homosexual sex than the white homosexual females did. The most common frequency for the whites was once per week, while that for the blacks was twice or more. Slightly more white than black lesbians had had sex with other women less than once a week, although for both races this proportion amounted to nearly half. The difference between our black and white females, however, is accounted for by the younger age of the blacks and becomes nonsignificant when age is controlled in the regression.

Overview

Our data lead us to conclude that homosexual men and women cannot be sexually stereotyped as either hyperactive or inactive. Rather, the amount of sexual activity they reported varied among individuals, with black males reporting more than white males, men reporting more than women, and (with the exception of the black males) younger people of either sex being more sexually active than their older counterparts.

The fact that homosexual men tended to be more sexually active than lesbians deserves special notice. It may be that males in general tend to be more sexually active than females and that, all else being equal, there will be more sexual activity in relationships involving only males. Perhaps this is due to an innate biological difference. In addition, it seems to accord with Gagnon and Simon's (1970) contention that the nature of females' socialization leads them—whether they be homosexual or heterosexual—to deemphasize the sexual features of their relationships. Since lesbian relationships do not involve a male, whose self-esteem may often be based on the frequency of his sexual contacts, it may be that they are characterized by a much less pronounced emphasis on explicitly sexual contact.

Cruising

A chief stereotypical notion of the homosexual person (especially the male) is that he or she is constantly on the lookout for sex, no matter where, no matter when. It is generally supposed that "cruising" (purposive search for a sexual partner) occupies a great deal of the homosexual individual's time and attention, with little regard given to the circumstances in which sex is solicited or even consummated. To be homosexual, it is thought, is to be "on the make"—at one's place of work, in a gay bar, or out on the street—and to be especially attracted to those locales where danger in cruising heightens the eroticism of the search.

Of particular interest to investigators of this aspect of homosexuality has been the gay bar. Numerous studies have dealt with how bars meet homosexuals' social and sexual needs (Hooker, 1965b; Cavan, 1966; Achilles, 1967; Dean, 1967a; Weinberg & Williams, 1974, 1975a). These explorations have led to the conclusion that the gay bar far outshadows any other cruising locale as a free market for sexual exchange.

Much less attention has been given to other places where cruising may occur. Descriptions of cruising in public rest rooms (Humphreys, 1970), gay baths (Weinberg & Williams, 1975b), parks (Rechy, 1967, 1977; Humphreys, 1971), beaches and streets (Rechy, 1963, 1977), movie theaters (Rechy, 1967), and highway rest stops (Troiden, 1974; Corzine & Cole, 1977) have, however, recently appeared. One reason for investigators' relative lack of interest in more precisely describing and specifying their subjects' cruising locales is that the settings in which sexual contacts are sought have been thought not nearly as important as the essential features which such contacts are believed to share, i.e., an opportunity for sexual exchange without obligation or commitment to one's partner (Hatterer, 1970). In other words, where one cruises is thought to be far less important than the absolute amount of cruising one does.

Protesting the popular notion that cruising occupies to an extravagant degree the free time of most homosexual individuals, Churchill (1967) argues that "for every 'homosexual' observed on the prowl . . . there must be any number of others sitting alone in their rooms" (p. 55) and that, in fact, many more people "never frequent the bars or cruise the parks and public lavatories, and . . . look upon this scene as a part of the demimonde" (p. 186). While this assertion may not be entirely correct, what little scientific evidence there is does suggest that cruising is not universal and that its nature and frequency depend upon one's demographic characteristics. For example, it has been found that although lesbians occasionally visit gay bars (and not necessarily in order to cruise), many more of their male counterparts are apt to do so (*Ladder*, 1959, 1960). Saghir and Robins (1973) found that, unlike homosexual men, lesbians almost never cruised in public places. They were much more apt to find a sexual partner among friends, at work, or at informal social gatherings. Only after the age of thirty were lesbians likely to be found cruising in a gay bar. The same investigators reported that even homosexual men's cruising habits were age-related. They found, for example, that while adolescent males often cruise in public places, bars become an important place to cruise after age nineteen, and older men are likely to turn to baths and certain public locales as well. Unfortunately, these investigators discuss cruising as inevitable for the homosexual man, affected only by his age, and prompted by his "basic selfishness," his "higher sex drive," and his "fascination with illegal activity." Except for their investigation of the incidence of those who limited their sexual exchanges to public places and of the relationship of a person's age to his willingness to sometimes engage in public sex, no attempt was made to explore the diversity of this phenomenon or to relate it to other features of the respondents' lives.

The present investigation examines a number of different aspects of cruising. These include the incidence and frequency with which our respondents cruised during the year prior to our interview in each of several specific locations (i.e., the streets, bars, public rest rooms, baths, etc.; for ethnographic descriptions of our respondents' cruising locales, see Appendix A, pages 233–263). Respondents were also asked about their cruising style (i.e., who made the first approach—they or the prospective partner), where they and their partner were most likely to go for sex, and how much time they usually spent with each other. Finally, respondents were asked how much they worried about various features of cruising and about sex consummated under these circumstances. The list included the prospect of being refused, difficulty conversing with the partner, the adequacy of their sexual performance, unwelcome sexual preferences on the part of the partner, being rolled or robbed by their partner, and having their homosexuality exposed, either out of the partner's carelessness or animosity or through police arrest.

Findings: Men (Table 6)

Incidence of Cruising

Nearly all of the white homosexual males (WHMs) and of their black counterparts (BHMs) said that during the last year they had "cruised" other males (i.e., had gone out specifically to look for a sexual partner). Among both the white and the black males, bars were by far the most popular cruising locale. Two-thirds of the WHMs and three-quarters of the BHMs had sought sexual partners in bars or nightclubs at least once during the past year. About half of both races had cruised on the streets, in baths, or at private parties, and less than a third at public parks and beaches. The lowest incidence of cruising, among both groups, was in "tearooms" (public rest rooms) and movie theaters.

Frequency of Cruising

The incidence of cruising in a given locale does not necessarily coincide with how frequently our respondents actually cruised there. One-fourth of the homosexual males who cruised in the past year had done so on the average of once a month or less; about the same number had cruised on the average of a few times a month. About two-fifths of both races had cruised at least once or twice a week over the year. Among the whites, the frequency of cruising they did was related to their age, with the younger men tending to cruise more (Table 3.1). Among the blacks, those employed at higher occupational levels tended to cruise more often than those of lower status (Table 3.3).

In terms of the frequency of cruising in particular places, of those who had ever cruised in a bar or nightclub during the past year, most had done so once or more a week, with a third of the respondents doing more than one-third of all their cruising in that locale. Of those who had cruised on the streets, 39 percent of the WHMs and more than half of the BHMs had done so on the average of once a week or more. Fourteen percent of the WHMs and about one-fifth of the BHMs cruised chiefly on the streets (i.e., they did one-third or more of their cruising there); the younger, less educated, and lower status white respondents were more likely to cruise in the streets (Tables 3.1, 3.2, 3.3). Of those who had gone to a bath to cruise, few had done so as often as once a week. The largest number had cruised at the baths once a month or less. Fourteen percent of the WHMs and 6 percent of the BHMs had cruised chiefly in baths; the older respondents and the better educated blacks tended to cruise more in that locale (Tables 3.1, 3.2). Of those who cruised at private parties, only a small minority did so as frequently as once a week, and only a few cruised chiefly in that setting. The older blacks were more likely to cruise at parties (Table 3.1).

The respondents tended to cruise infrequently in public parks or at the beach. Most of those who had cruised in a park had done so no more often than once a month, and hardly any of them cruised chiefly in parks. And most of those who had cruised on public beaches had done so on the average of a dozen times a year or less, with only 3 percent of the WHMs and none of the blacks cruising chiefly at the beach. Those blacks who cruised on beaches at all tended to be of higher occupational status (Table 3.3), while it was the younger whites who were more apt to do so (Table 3.1).

Of the relatively few who had done any cruising in tearooms during the past year, about one-half had done this once a month or less, and few cruised chiefly in this locale. And finally, of the still smaller number of respondents who had cruised in movie theaters, the majority had done so once a month or less. Only one of the respondents cruised chiefly in this setting.

Cruising Style

Almost half of the respondents said that during the course of their cruising it was usually their prospective partner and not they who made the first approach. Only about a quarter of the WHMs and somewhat fewer blacks were likely to approach first. (The remaining respondents said that they used both of these cruising styles.) Those who waited for the other person to make the approach gave a variety of reasons for this:

I'm just too shy to approach somebody myself. Besides that, I'd kind of like to know if they're interested in me.

I have difficulty talking—I just can't open my mouth when I'm cruising.

I don't have the self-confidence to cruise someone and then get rejected.

I feel safer, more secure if I am approached. I wouldn't want to stick my neck out and possibly get hurt. The other guy might not be gay.

The respondents who tended to make the first approach explained this in several ways:

It doesn't do any good to stand and wait. You have to grab the bull by the horns.

I never take the man that wants me. I want to be the hunter. Also, I don't trust them when they want me. When they want me, I feel used.

I like to dominate a sexual act. Contacts are made easier if you approach.

Because they won't come to me. I'm not good-looking enough, and I'm too old.

If you don't ask for it, you won't get it.

Where Sex Takes Place

Almost half of our respondents said that after a pickup had been made, they and their partner were most likely to go to the respondent's home for sexual activity. Smaller numbers reported that they were most likely to go to the partner's residence. About a fifth of the whites as compared to 12 percent of the blacks named some other location.

Time Spent with Partner

After they had gone someplace for sexual activity, the largest numbers of our respondents spent all night with their partners. About one-third of the WHMs and one-quarter of the BHMs spent an hour or more with their partners but not the entire night. A relatively small number said that they spent no more than an hour with their partner. Among both races it was the younger respondents who tended to spend the greatest amount of time with their sexual partners, and, among the blacks, the less educated respondents tended to spend more time with their partners (Tables 3.1, 3.2).

Cruising Worries

As to the extent to which our homosexual males worried while cruising, more than half reported that they worried considerably (i.e., "often" or "sometimes") about being refused by a prospective partner. Less than half of the WHMs, as compared to half as many BHMs, worried often or sometimes about being able to converse with their partners. Approximately a third of both races were concerned about catching venereal disease, over a quarter about responding to their partner's sexual requests, and fewer about being caught by the police, their sexual adequacy, being rolled or robbed, or having their homosexuality publicly exposed. The younger black respondents tended to worry more about carrying on a conversation with their partner, while the older and the better educated whites worried more about arrest, and the better educated whites about public exposure (Tables 3.1, 3.2).

It should be noted that while about the same numbers of whites and blacks worried much about their partner's possibly turning them down, about twice as many of the whites as of the blacks were much concerned about their ability to converse with their partner and about their ability to perform sexually. The blacks were also less likely to do much worrying about being publicly exposed.

Summary

The majority of the respondents had "cruised" other men in various locales at least a few times per month during the year just prior to the interview. Most of their cruising was done in bars, in baths, and on the street. Much less was done at private parties, in parks, at beaches, in public rest rooms, or in movie theaters. Only a very few tended to prefer a specific locale. The blacks were more apt to have cruised in the streets and in the bars than were their white counterparts, but the two groups did not differ in the total amount of cruising they did.

About half of the respondents, black and white, waited for a prospective partner to approach them first, and they were most likely to conduct their sexual activity in the privacy of their homes, usually spending the whole night with their partners. The older respondents tended to spend less time with their partners than did the younger ones.

The chief worry the men had while cruising was that their prospective partner might refuse them. Although they sometimes worried about being caught by the police or having their homosexuality publicly exposed, less than a quarter worried very much about these possibilities. Among the whites, these two particular concerns were more evident among the better educated respondents. Finally, the blacks tended to worry less than the whites about various aspects of cruising.

Findings: Women *(Table 6)*

Less than 20 percent of the homosexual females, black and white, had ever cruised during the past year, and the little cruising they did was almost entirely limited to bars and to private parties. The few who did any cruising were more likely than their male counterparts to make the first approach to a prospective partner and were apt to spend a much greater length of time with her.

Because such a small number of the lesbians had done any cruising, no attempt was made to analyze these data further.

Overview

The present investigation confirms Saghir and Robins's report that public cruising is infrequent among lesbians and that, among homosexual men who cruise in public places, most conduct their sexual activity in the privacy of their homes.

The significantly lower incidence of cruising among women is in keeping with other impressions of differences between homosexual men and women: that homosexual women are relatively uninterested in impersonal sexual encounters and are more apt to be involved in a continuing relationship that places a premium on mutual fidelity. To the extent that much of homosexual men's sexual activity involves cruising, they are apt to experience their homosexuality in a far different way than lesbians do.

While the present data do not confirm Churchill's impression that most homosexual men are not likely to engage in cruising, they also do not support the notion that such persons are apt to do little else but search for sexual partners. Almost 40 percent of our male respondents either did no cruising at all or did it no more than once a month.

The data also indicate that except for cruising on the streets, most of the homosexual males sought sexual partners in such relatively safe settings as the gay bar or bath, and few did much of their cruising in public rest rooms, movie theaters, or parks, where the danger of being arrested or physically assaulted is much greater. Perhaps this is why relatively few of them worried about the police or about being exposed or about being rolled and robbed. They were much more concerned about various aspects relating to their prospective partner.

Dimensions of Sexual Experience / **79**

Our finding that the gay bar is likely to be the most popular cruising locale supports others' impressions of the importance of this particular institution to the homosexual community. While the bar may serve a variety of other purposes, it clearly provides the homosexual with an opportunity to pursue his or her sexual interests.

While our next chapter, dealing with partnerships, speaks more to the matter of commitment and intimacy on the part of homosexual partners, it is apparently incorrect to assume that within the context of cruising, little more than sexual contact takes place between pickups. For some, their contact apparently allows just enough time for a nod to social preliminaries, their ejaculations, and some form of closure, but most of our respondents spent at least several hours with their partners. Indeed, nearly half of the white male respondents and a clear majority of the blacks customarily spent all night or even longer with such partners. Contacts with cruising pickups, then, must often involve friendly, non-sexual kinds of interaction. Since "one-night stands" are not unusual among our respondents, it is unfortunate that we did not ascertain anything more about their place in the lives of our male respondents.

Sexual Partnerships

One of the most predominant images of the homosexual man is that he is highly "promiscuous," unable to integrate his emotional and sexual needs, incapable of maintaining a long-standing sexual partnership, and doomed to an eternally hopeless quest for the ideal relationship. His proclivity for "impersonal, expedient, and fleeting encounters" (Humphreys, 1971) is frequently juxtaposed with the lesbian's supposed interest in a permanent "marriage" to another woman and her much greater preoccupation with sexual fidelity. These contrasting images make it appear that homosexual men are chiefly concerned with sexual release through genital contacts with other men and that homosexual women will often forfeit sexual contact in favor of warmth and closeness with their partners. Such stereotypes are not surprising. They conform to popular impressions of how men and women in general differ in their sociosexual expectations. Men, regardless of sexual orientation, are pictured as bent upon orgasmic release, and women as engaging in sexual activity so long as it involves affection and assurance of a deep commitment.

The contention that homosexual men are apt to have relatively large numbers of sexual partners is supported by several investigations. In one study, two-thirds of the homosexual male respondents were described as having been engaged in "promiscuous sexual patterns" (Braaten & Darling, 1965). Similarly, homosexual men have been found to have had significantly more partners than heterosexual men (Schofield, 1965; Saghir & Robins, 1973). Saghir and Robins also concluded that lesbians tend to be much less "promiscuous" than their male counterparts. These reports suggest that little credence can be given to the supposition that homosexual men's "promiscuity" has been overestimated (Liddicoat, 1956; Dean, 1967a).

In addition to the extent to which they may be "promiscuous," considerable attention has been given to the nature of homosexual individuals' sexual partnerships. Saghir and Robins (1973) reported that the great majority of the homosexual men and women in their sample had experienced several kinds of relationships: "casual-transient" (i.e., "one-night stands" or a series of contacts with another person lasting less than four months), "liaisons" (between four months and a year), and at least one "affair" (a longer-lasting involvement). In other samples of homosexual men, most were found to have been involved at some time or other in relatively monogamous relationships (Weinberg & Williams, 1974, 1975a; Harry, 1976). In a study of lesbians, the majority were found to be currently involved in a "love" relationship or "affair" with another woman (Ladder, 1959). These findings coincide with those of Oberstone and Sukoneck (1975), who reported that 80 percent of both the lesbians and the heterosexual women in their sample were currently involved in a love relationship.

Of particular interest to several investigators has been the durability of those relatively long-standing relationships in which the homosexual partners make, at least initially, important emotional investments. The usual impression is that lesbians are more likely to establish a permanent relationship with a partner than are their male counterparts (Hyde, 1970). It has been contended, however, that neither group is able to achieve anything more than a fleeting alliance with a homosexual partner (Caprio, 1956; Allen, 1961a; Bieber, 1969). In one investigation it was found that, of those who had ever been involved in a homosexual "affair," the men were, on the average, involved in such a relationship for about four years and the women a little more than six years (Liddicoat, 1961). In another investigation it was reported that, among those lesbians currently involved in an "affair," the average relationship had lasted between four and five years (Ladder, 1959). Greenberg (1973a) reported that the majority of the homosexual men in his sample had never maintained a relationship with a partner for as long as a year, and none had been involved in such a relationship any longer than ten years. In still another study it was found that the median duration of the homosexual men's "marital" relationships was somewhat less than ten years (Dean, 1967a). Finally, Saghir and Robins (1973) found that most of the affairs among both their male and their female homosexual respondents ended within three years. Interestingly, although a greater number of the lesbians in the latter study had ever been involved in an "affair," the affairs of the homosexual men tended to be somewhat more durable. These particular investigators also found that the homosexual men were more tolerant of a partner's infidelity, that lesbians' relationships were more likely to break up because one partner was unfaithful or wanted to renounce her homosexuality, and that homosexual men reacted less intensely to the termination of an affair.

There has been a good deal of conjecture as to the reasons for the instability which seems to characterize so many homosexual partnerships. Hoffman (1968) believes that society's antihomosexual attitudes arouse disabling anxieties in homosexual individuals which make it difficult for them to sustain lasting emotional commitments. Others suggest that homosexual "marriages" tend to be temporary because, unlike heterosexual marital relationships, they are not legally sanctioned (Cory & LeRoy, 1963; Harry, 1976). It has also been pointed out that the partners in a homosexual "marriage" are more apt to be culturally diverse than in heterosexual partnerships, and that differences in age, social class, ethnicity, etc. can create unresolvable tensions (Harry, 1976). Other reasons advanced for the instability of homosexual partnerships include the large marketplace for sociosexual contacts in the gay world (Allen, 1961a) and the likelihood that homosexual couples will meet many sexually available persons in their social milieu (Harry, 1976), conditions which may militate against fidelity to one's partner.

Clinicians have tended to stress the dynamics of homosexual relationships as contributing to partner disillusionment. Psychoanalytic thinkers, focusing on the transferential aspects of homosexual partnerships, have construed lesbian relationships as an attempt to recapitulate the mother-daughter or sister-sister dyad (Bergler, 1948; Rancourt & Limoges, 1967). Homosexual men have sometimes been seen as attempting to overcome feelings of unmanliness by seeking masculine qualities in their lovers (Bieber et al., 1962; Hatterer, 1970). Such dynamics, involving unrealistic goals and reflecting unfinished oedipal issues, are thought inevitably to sabotage homosexual partnerships.

With regard to homosexual men and women who live with their current sexual partner, some attention has been given to the extent to which homosexual roommate relationships are analogous to heterosexual marriages. The consensus is that such living arrangements often do not include sexual contact between the roommates and that even less often do they involve sex-role distinctions. It has been reported that most homosexual male roommates are members of the same friendship clique but are not necessarily lovers (Sonenschein, 1968), and that they are most apt to be close friends who share living arrangements primarily for economic reasons (Cotton, 1972). Among those whose relationship is more like a heterosexual marriage, it is thought that sex-role distinctions tend to be blurred (Hooker, 1967; Nuehring et al., 1974). In fact, it is believed that this lack of clear-cut male-female roles is what makes lesbian relationships so appealing to those involved (Martin & Lyon, 1970). Studies of lesbian couples, however, do not entirely support the notion that sex-role distinctions tend not to be made. One investigation of lesbian couples (Stephenson, 1971) found that most of them shared household duties and decisions equally and that the partners made about the same amount of money, but a similar study (Jensen, 1974) reported that roles like those of husband and wife were frequently adopted. The "masculine" partner, for example, tended to be older than her "wife," to earn a larger income, and to be more interested in conventionally masculine occupations. In a third study of black and white lesbian couples (Bass-Hass, 1968), it was reported that the blacks were more likely to dichotomize roles than the whites, and that fewer of them shared expenses.

In the present study respondents are compared on a wide range of partnership variables. The number of sexual partners they had had, both during the current year and throughout their lives, has been ascertained. Other variables include the types of partners they were apt to seek, the physical characteristics they prized in a partner, and the extent to which their contacts included more than genital involvement. Considerable attention has been given to respondents' affairs. The first "relatively steady relationship" is examined with respect to the partners' ages, its duration, whether they lived together, whether respondents were in love with their partner, the partners' relative social positions, what each got out of the relationship, how it differed from any later affairs, its impact on the respondent, the reasons for its termination, and the respondent's reactions to the breakup. Respondents' current affairs are examined in a similar fashion. Finally, we have ascertained the importance to our respondents of maintaining a living arrangement with one's sexual partner, looking at roommate relationships as to whether they involve sexual contact, and how the partners manage their domestic responsibilities.

Findings: Men (Table 7)

Sexual Partners

Almost one-half of the white homosexual males (WHMs) and one-third of the black homosexual males (BHMs) said that they had had at least five hundred different sexual partners during the course of their homosexual careers.[1] Another third of the WHMs and a quarter of the BHMs reported having had between one hundred and five hundred partners. Saghir and Robins reported that three-quarters of their male respondents had had more than thirty sexual partners over the course of their lives; over 90 percent of our white male respondents reported having twenty-five or more partners.

While almost all of the WHMs said that none or only a minority of their partners were black, about two-thirds of the blacks reported that more than half of their partners had been white. With respect to other partner characteristics, most of the whites and significantly fewer of the blacks said that more than half of their partners had been strangers prior to the day of their sexual contact. About a quarter of the respondents reported having felt some affection for more than half of their partners.

Most of the WHMs, as opposed to about a third of the BHMs, said that more than half of their partners were persons with whom they had sex only once. In the same vein, about two-thirds of the WHMs, compared with almost half of the BHMs, said that following their sexual contact, they had not seen most of their partners socially. At the same time, most respondents said that most of their partners had been people with whom they would have associated socially. Most of the partners had given respondents their addresses or telephone numbers, and had disclosed a fair amount about themselves. About a third of the respondents had told more than half of their partners a fair amount about themselves.

While a majority of the BHMs said that most of their partners had been older than they, only about half that number of the WHMs had had so many older partners. About a third of the male respondents said that more than half of their partners had been younger than they. One-quarter of the WHMs and 14 percent of the BHMs said that any of their sexual partners had been sixteen years old or younger (when the respondents were at least twenty-one years old).

---

[1] We are aware, of course, that these figures may reflect exaggeration on the part of some respondents.

Finally, three-quarters of the WHMs but almost two-thirds of the BHMs had never received money from any of their partners, and most had never paid any of their partners for sex. Among both groups, the older men were more likely than their younger counterparts to have paid for sex with their partners (Table 3.1).

With respect to the number of male sexual partners they had had during the current year, more than a quarter of the respondents said that they had had more than fifty partners. Another quarter had had between twenty and fifty sexual partners. About one-fifth of them had had fewer than six partners during the current year. Among the whites, the older men tended to have fewer partners than did the younger ones (Table 3.1).

When asked what physical characteristics they liked in a sexual partner, about one-quarter of the respondents mentioned one or more stereotypically "masculine" characteristics (such as a lot of body hair, muscular frame, large genitalia, etc.). Almost none of them mentioned a preference for some stereotypically "feminine" physical characteristic. More of the respondents showed some kind of special interest in the size or appearance of their partner's genitalia than in what his buttocks looked like. A relatively large number had a special interest in the partner's face, hair, or eyes.

Affairs

Virtually all of the male respondents had been involved in at least one affair (defined as a "relatively steady relationship" with another man) during the course of their lives. Less than a quarter of them had had only one affair, while about a third had had four or more relatively steady relationships with another male since they reached age seventeen.

All of the males in Saghir and Robins's sample had formed a special relationship with another man at least once in their lives. The majority of them, like the majority of those in our sample, had had between three and five such relationships. Somewhat fewer of the nonpatient and nonincarcerated homosexual males in Schofield's sample had had at least one affair with another man.

First Affair. One-third of the WHMs were between the ages of twenty and twenty-three when they began their first affair with another man. A few more were twenty-four or older and a few less, under the age of twenty. Among the black respondents, the greatest number—43 percent—were nineteen or younger at the start of their first affair, another forty percent were twenty to twenty-three years old, and about one-sixth twenty-four or more. On the average, the WHMs were twenty-three and the BHMs twenty-one when their first affair began. (When demographic characteristics were controlled, however, there was no significant difference between the races in their age at the beginning of their first affair.) No more than a quarter of the respondents reported that their first partner in an affair had been younger than they. Sixty percent of the WHMs and about three-quarters of the BHMs had been younger than their first partner. In the majority of instances they and their partners had been within five years of age, had lived with each other, and had been in love. More than half of the whites and two-fifths of the blacks had had the same social position as their partner.

In the largest number of instances, the first affair lasted between one and three years. For some, the relationship lasted four or more years, while smaller numbers said their first affair lasted three months or less.

The largest number of the respondents said that they, and not their partners, had initiated the breakup of their first affair, and that it had been due either to factors beyond their control or to dissatisfaction with the partner's behavior:

I moved to Berkeley to go to school, so we had to break up.

He was recalled into the service.

I felt I was being used, and rather unscrupulously, by someone who was emotionally dishonest.

He became very jealous and antagonistic and bitchy and threw a violent tantrum one night. He thought I was cheating. His second tantrum was so violent, I moved out for my own safety.

Others said that the relationship itself was too weak to last long and/or that they or their partner got romantically involved with someone else:

We were too dissimilar. Different interests, different personalities. We just drifted apart.

Because there wasn't anything to it. I was young and new to the life and had a lot to learn. It was a mutual breakup.

I believe I was too possessive. I made unreasonable demands. Eventually, he met someone else he was interested in and I wouldn't permit that, so I moved out.

Almost half of the respondents said they were extremely upset and unhappy when their first affair came to an end, but a fairly large number were sad but also relieved that it was over.

Asked what they thought they got out of their first affair, almost two-thirds of the WHMs and nearly half of the BHMs mentioned the warmth and love and understanding they had received; others described ways in which they themselves had become better persons:

A feeling of being wanted. Companionship. Security. We had things in common. And the other people in the gay community respected us for having a relationship going.

I got a feeling of being loved and having my love accepted. It was a great feeling—companionship and mutual dependence.

It made me capable of loving others. I used to withdraw and be afraid of people, but now my main orientation is toward people.

Some mentioned that they had become more mature and realistic and had gained insight into themselves:

Maturity—that really sums it up. I learned what the gay world was all about. And I learned what you have to do to maintain a relationship.

I learned a good deal about the homosexual scheme of things, also about giving a little of myself. He was good, wise, tolerant, and I was a young shit at the time. He helped to mature me.

I learned the kind of love I'm capable of—I can be self-sacrificing and very strong. I'm steady and affectionate, even if I'm not so much to look at.

With respect to what they believed their partner got out of their first affair, more than a quarter of those who spoke of positive changes in the partner believed that, like themselves, he became more mature. A somewhat smaller number said that he had become a better person as a result of their relationship. Still others spoke of the partner's new aspirations for himself and an improvement in his general life-style:

He broke from a possessive mother and got out into the world.

He got some education—he hadn't completed high school. I guess I helped him to become worldly and sophisticated.

Again, however, the largest number of our respondents (more than half of them) mentioned the warmth and love their partner had received from them. A smaller but sizable number of respondents said that their partner had received sexual satisfactions from the relationship:

I turned him on, and that's what he wanted.

Good sex, companionship, and someone to nurse him through his drunk spells. The whole relationship really took place in the bedroom. It was basically sexual.

In comparing their first affair with their subsequent relationships, about half of the respondents said that in their first affair they had had a lot to learn or that the relationship had been comparatively superficial:

I was so young. I didn't know about life or what it meant to have a lover. I couldn't make any commitments.

I was much younger, more unstable and awkward. I threw myself more freely and passionately into it without understanding the problems of maintaining it. I was surprised when it was over.

It was a new beginning and very exciting. It was mostly infatuation, though, and not as deep as my other relationships. It wasn't as emotionally satisfying, it wasn't based on as many common interests.

A few mentioned having become afraid to get involved again:

I became a little more cautious about choosing a partner after this. The question of trust became an issue. I was more careful not to get caught in a non-trusting relationship.

I discovered I was too willing to give of myself before I'd analyzed the situation fully. In the future I'll be more careful before committing myself.

Current Affair. At the time of the interview, about half of the male respondents were currently involved in an affair with another man. Of these, less than a quarter were still involved in their first affair.[2] The number currently involved in an affair is the same as those in our Chicago pilot sample and in Schofield's sample, and about the same as the number in *The Ladder.*

In almost half of the WHMs' current relationships and in almost two-thirds of the BHMs', discrepancies in age between themselves and their partners amounted to no more than five years. Most of the respondents who were currently involved in an affair reported that they and their partner were living together and that they were in love with their partner. About two-thirds of the currently involved WHMs and two-fifths of

[2] In considering the nature of our respondents' current affairs, we have excluded those still involved in their first affair in order to be able to examine differences between the respondents' current and past involvements.

their black counterparts had the same social status as their partner. Somewhat less than half of the currently involved BHMs said that their partner had a higher social position; this was true for 14 percent of the WHMs. Of those involved in a current affair, about three-quarters of the WHMs and almost half of the BHMs had been involved for at least a year at the time of the interview.

When asked what they were getting out of their current affair, about a third of the respondents who mentioned positive changes in themselves spoke in terms of becoming a better or more complete person. Much larger numbers, however, spoke of the warmth and love and understanding they were getting from their partners. About a quarter of them referred to the peace and happiness they were experiencing in their relationship. Others made mention of the quality of the sexual relationship they were having with their partner.

With regard to what they thought their partner was getting out of the relationship, about a quarter of those mentioning positive changes in the partner thought he had achieved greater self-actualization. The majority mentioned the warmth and love the partner was receiving. Only a very small number said that their partner was getting something materialistic out of the relationship:

He'll be a full partner when I open up my antique business. Everything I have is *ours*—the car, the house. And I trust him completely.

He was poor and sees me as a financial asset.

So far, he's got two and a half months' free entertainment in San Francisco.

In answer to the question of how they thought their current affair was different from others they had had, a few spoke in terms of being more mature and capable of handling a relationship of this kind. Somewhat more of the respondents were more emotionally involved with their current partners than they had been in their previous relationships or said that the relationship itself was more complete and satisfying:

I'm in love with the guy. I'd say that's very different.

No comparison at all. The others were just flings. This is the first time I've felt I'm accomplishing something important.

This is the island we dream about, security, the last road for me—where I plan to end my days. It's lasted, that's how it's different, and we like each other beyond the sex. We have complete trust. It's a friendship as well as a romance.

We don't worry about outsiders. Neither of us are ashamed—we don't really care what the world thinks anymore.

Finally, it should be noted that although a majority of the male respondents reported a current affair with another man (for some, the first), approximately half of those reporting a current affair were not "coupled"—i.e., they were not living with their partner. In other words, 29 percent of all the homosexual men were currently "coupled." [3] It is also interesting to note that only a third of the homosexual men said that having a permanent living arrangement with a male sexual partner was very important to them at the beginning of their homosexual careers. At the time of the interview, however, two-thirds considered such an arrangement at least somewhat important.

Among the "coupled" respondents, slightly less than half of the WHMs and a little more than a quarter of the BHMs kept their incomes separate. The others combined them entirely or at least in part. Among the "coupled" males, more of the whites than of the blacks said they earned more than their roommate, but this racial difference proved to be due to differences in age and occupational level. In response to questioning about the effect of income disparity upon the relationship, more than two-thirds of the respondents involved in this situation said that it had no particular effect.

With respect to the way in which various household responsibilities were carried out, almost two-thirds of the "coupled" respondents said that they and their partner shared equally in the housework. Nearly half said that they and their partner did household shopping together. Smaller numbers said that they and their partner both did about the same amount of home repairs, household bookkeeping, or cooking. Very few reported that either they or their partner did all of the tasks usually undertaken by a traditional wife in a heterosexual marriage. Almost a quarter of the "coupled" WHMs, compared with fewer than a tenth of the BHMs, said that they usually did the tasks associated with a traditional husband in a heterosexual marriage, and less than 10 percent reported that their partners had entirely assumed a "masculine" role in the household.

[3] Of all those living with a male roommate, about two-thirds reported that they and their roommate were having sex with each other. Among those who said that they were not having sex with their roommate, about half said that this had not always been so. Of these, more than two-thirds reported that at first there had been sexual contact between them but that it had stopped, usually at some time after they had begun living together. Only ten WHMs and four BHMs said that they and their roommate had been sexually involved only before and not after they had started living together. Among those reporting sexual contact with their roommate, the majority said that they and/or their partner were having sex with others as well.

Summary

The homosexual male respondents were apt to report a large number (i.e., hundreds) of sexual partners over the course of their lives. While the whites tended to limit their sexual contacts to others of their race, the blacks, by contrast, were apt to have had mostly white partners. Among both groups, partners tended to be strangers, but our respondents reported spending a fair amount of time with them and described such encounters as often involving some exchange of personal information, implying that more than just sex was shared. A majority had never had sex with prostitutes or minors. A chief interest which many of our respondents had in a prospective sexual partner was the degree to which he conformed to a stereotypically "masculine" image.

Almost all of the respondents had had at least one affair with another man (i.e., a "relatively steady relationship"). The first affair was apt to have begun when the respondent was in his early twenties. Their first-affair partner tended to be somewhat older than they and of much the same social position. In most instances, the partners lived together, and most of the respondents felt they were in love. The first affair usually lasted between one and three years, coming to an end either due to factors beyond their control or else upon the respondent's becoming dissatisfied with various aspects of the relationship. Many were extremely unhappy over the termination of their first affair. Large numbers believed that they did a lot of growing up through their first involvement of this kind and appreciated the love and acceptance which the relationship provided them. They were apt to believe that their partner got much the same thing out of the affair and, in many instances, that it had helped the partner to fulfill himself. The first affair tended to be viewed as an important and necessary preparation for subsequent involvements, though some became more hesitant about becoming involved again.

Just over half of the respondents were currently involved in an affair at the time of the interview. In comparison with their first affair, the respondents' current involvement was somewhat more likely to have involved living together and being in love with their partner. Among the whites the respondents were also more likely to have the same social position as their partner; the blacks were most likely, on the other hand, to say that their partner had a higher social position, but this was explained by differences in age and occupational level.

At the time of the interview, most respondents had been involved in their current affair for no more than three years. Many of them spoke of how they had become better persons as a result of the relationship. They believed this also to be true of their partners. There was a tendency for them to think that their current affair involved a more complete relationship for both themselves and their partners than any of their previous involvements. About a quarter of all the male respondents were currently in a homosexual "couple," meaning that they and their partner lived together and were having sex with each other. Among such couples, there was generally little evidence of a "masculine/feminine" sex-role dichotomy in the performance of household tasks.

Findings: Women *(Table 7)*

Sexual Partners

The majority of the homosexual female respondents, whether white (WHFs) or black (BHFs), had had fewer than ten female sexual partners throughout the course of their homosexual careers. About a quarter had had fewer than five, nearly one-third between five and nine, and an additional third had had between ten and fifty partners. Much larger numbers of our white lesbians than of those in Kenyon's sample (11%) had had ten or more sexual partners during the course of their homosexual careers.

About three-quarters of the WHFs said that all of their partners had been of the same race as they, while less than a quarter of the BHFs reported that their sexual partners had been limited to blacks. Most of the respondents said that none of their partners had been strangers, that more than half of their partners had told them a fair amount about themselves, and that most of them had been willing to give the respondents their addresses or phone numbers. Four-fifths of the WHFs, compared with almost two-thirds of the BHFs, reported that the majority of their homosexual partners had been persons whom they cared about and for whom they had some affection. Close to half of the female respondents said that none of their partners were onetime sexual contacts. Less than one-fifth reported that most of their partners were women they never saw again socially after the time of their first sexual contact; very few WHFs and no BHFs believed that most of their partners were people with whom they would not have associated except for sex. The relatively high level of nonsexual involvement which the female respondents tended to have with their partners is reflected further in that three-fourths of the WHFs, as compared with half of the BHFs, reported having told the majority of their partners a fair amount about themselves. Virtually all of the respondents said that they had never paid a sexual partner to have sex with them. An equally large number reported never having been paid by a sexual partner for having sex with her. Finally, about a third of the WHFs and somewhat more of the BHFs said that more than half of their partners had been older than they. About three-quarters of the female respondents said that a minority of their partners had been younger than they. Almost none of them said that any of their partners had been sixteen years of age or younger (when the respondents were twenty-one or older).

During the year prior to the interview, the majority of our female respondents had had either one or two sexual partners. Only very small numbers of the females of either race reported more than ten partners, while about a quarter of the WHFs and a third of the BHFs had had sex with three to ten different women in the past year. Among both groups, the younger women tended to report a larger number of partners (Table 3.1).

In response to the question of what kinds of physical characteristics they most desired in a sexual partner, those who mentioned any at all most frequently expressed a special interest in their partner's body type or frame. Somewhat smaller numbers mentioned their partner's face, hair, or eyes. Even fewer had a special interest in the size or appearance of their partner's breasts. Finally, more mentioned a fondness for one or more stereotypically "feminine" physical characteristics in their partner than for "masculine" characteristics. It should be noted, however, that only a few of the respondents spoke at all of such gender-related characteristics.

Affairs

Practically all of the female respondents had had at least one affair (or "relatively steady relationship") with another woman since age seventeen. The majority reported between one and three such relationships.

First Affair. The respondents were, on the average, twenty-two years old when they began their first affair with another woman, and in the majority of such instances they were younger than their partner. It should be noted, however, that of those who had ever had an affair, a majority of the WHFs and more than a third of the BHFs had been no more than two years younger or older than their partners in their first affair. Almost all of them had been in love with their partner, and, among the whites, were likely to have lived with her. Two-thirds of the WHFs and about a third of the BHFs reported that they and their partner had had similar social positions. Another third of the BHFs reported that their partner's social position was higher, and slightly fewer than a third that their partner's social position was lower.

Almost half of the first affairs lasted between one and three years. For more than a quarter of the respondents, their first affair had lasted four or more years. Almost half reported that it was their partner who had initiated the breakup, but nearly as many said it was they who had done so. The breakup of their first affair was most often due to one or both partners' involvement with another person—female or male:

I met somebody else who was more compatible and more interesting and more gratifying all around.

She came back after summer vacation and said it was over and she felt guilty and that it was wrong and she had started sleeping with a boy.

I met my present partner and fell in love with her.

A somewhat smaller number mentioned various dissatisfactions with the relationship itself:

I couldn't take being used anymore. I felt like a meal ticket.

She discovered she wasn't homosexual after all—and I got sick of paying her bills while she went out with men on the side. I decided the relationship was a little masochistic so I threw her out.

Her insane jealousy. She made a terrific scene in front of my insurance sales-man. I told her I wouldn't tolerate that from anyone. I was embarrassed. He knew what was going on. I never saw him or her ever again.

About half of the respondents were extremely upset and unhappy when their first affair came to an end, but about a third of the WHFs and a quarter of the BHFs were unhappy but also relieved that it was over.

With respect to the positive changes which occurred in themselves as a result of their first relatively steady relationship, about a third of the female respondents spoke of gaining self-insight or greater maturity:

I grew up a great deal, learned a lot—emotionally, psychologically, intellec-tually.

I got a hell of a lot, but I can't put it in words. I learned how to love and care about someone. I started to mature a teensy-weensy bit.

I got a deeper understanding of the meaning of love, of myself and what I was capable of, an understanding of another person's capacity for feeling.

Other results which were mentioned had to do with all the good feelings that came from the relationship:

There was a great deal of respect, a very close feeling—consideration, enjoy-ment. Usually there were other roommates, but the two of us shared a bed. We both knew and said we loved each other. We took care of each other. We're still very close.

In terms of what they thought their partner got out of the first affair, some of the whites who commented about positive changes in their partner spoke of the partner's new aspirations for herself, her clearer goals and broader horizons:

I felt she needed more of a domineering force and I think I kind of steered her in a little better direction than she had been heading as far as improving herself and her own appearance and so on.

I gave her a new lease on life, "a sense of renewed youth," she described it. She also said many times that she had felt for six or seven years like she was dead and now she'd come back to life.

About a fifth of the blacks who commented about positive changes in their partner said that she became a better and more fulfilled individual:

She learned what it is to love somebody besides yourself and seriously mean it for once. She's gotten a lot. She learned how to smile for a change.

Since she's been with me she's felt more acceptance and satisfaction. She feels more settled—not always paranoid, not so tense.

The majority who commented about other things their partner got out of the relationship spoke of warmth, affection, and other positive feelings:

Security, understanding, companionship, satisfaction, and happiness.

She got a lifelong love and friendship; a gentleness that we could share together.

In response to the question of how their first affair differed from their subsequent relationships, the largest number commented that there was a lot they had to learn at that time or that the relationship was more superficial:

It was the first. It was like two kids in a playground trying out the swings for the first time.

It was more experimental and less sincere. It didn't really last as long and was not very sexual really—we had very little sexual contact, and we didn't know what to do, really.

I was much less committed in this relationship. I was much less sure of my own feelings. I was selfish. Also I think we were groping more then.

Interestingly, almost 15 percent of the respondents referred to having more emotional involvement with their first affair partner than with any later partner:

I was in love with her. It was more romantic, more like a marriage than some of the others. It was more like the romantic notions of marriage.

It was a very deep thing. My feelings lasted longer.

When asked about the way in which they had become a different person as a result of their first involvement (or "affair") with another woman, almost a fifth of the respondents said they had become more committed or reconciled to their homosexuality:

I became an aware homosexual.

She brought me out. After her, I became exclusively homosexual.

I was confirmed in my homosexual leanings. I felt more self-assured as a result of this—that people would like me.

Current Affair. Almost three-fourths of the female respondents, and significantly more of the older white lesbians (Table 3.1), were currently involved in a relatively stable relationship with another woman. Of these, somewhat less than a quarter were currently involved in their first affair.[4] The proportion of our white female respondents who were committed to an alliance with another woman at the time of our study is exactly the same as the proportion reported by *The Ladder*'s investigators and only slightly less than the proportion reported by Oberstone and Sukoneck or by Armon (1958, 1960).

On the average, the WHFs were thirty-two years old and the BHFs thirty years old at the start of their current affair. While close to half were older than their partner, almost as many were younger. In two-thirds of the WHFs' partnerships and in about half of the BHFs', the discrepancy in age between themselves and their partners was five years or less. Most of those currently involved were living with their partners, were in love with them, and shared the same social position. The largest number of the respondents' current affairs (more than a third of them)

---

[4] As with their male counterparts, data from respondents still involved in their first affair have not been used in our consideration of respondents' descriptions of their current affair.

had been going on for one to three years. For a little more than one-tenth of the respondents, the current affair was of more than five years' duration. The duration of our respondents' current affairs is the same as that reported by *The Ladder* investigators and longer than the two-year duration reported by Armon or the three years reported by Saghir and Robins, but shorter than the six-year average in Liddicoat's sample.

Some of those respondents who commented about positive changes in themselves as a result of their current involvement said that they had become more complete persons or had higher aspirations for themselves:

She's shown me how to be loyal, and how to relax and live with my hang-ups. She's given me a sense of responsibility about my duties and a great deal more confidence in myself.

I'm opening up to a lot of things that I never thought existed before. She's teaching me how to communicate and that there is beauty in ugliness and that there is more than just my little square in the world.

Some of the blacks commented that they had gained insight into themselves:

Even more of a deeper understanding of myself, and a sense of accepting your responsibility—and I mean, it is a responsibility being gay.

I'm learning to look at myself in a proper perspective—being honest with myself. She is the sort of person who shocks you into taking an honest look at things.

In addition, just as they had done regarding their first affair, the majority of all the lesbians spoke of the warmth, love, and understanding they were receiving, or positive feelings about the relationship generally:

I'm sexually satisfied. I feel loved and needed, and most of all I feel creative. I can relax because I feel secure.

Stability, kindness, a generous spirit. Tender loving care, no pressure. Someone who is totally fair—no petty ego problems. She's someone who *gives*.

There was a tendency for the respondents who mentioned positive changes in their partner to mention the same kind of changes as they saw in themselves: becoming a better person, acquiring insight into herself, and higher aspirations for herself. About one-fifth of them said their partner was becoming more mature:

She's a lot more steady than she used to be. She's settled down. She's gained maturity; we both have.

She's gotten independence; responsibility, especially with money. She's grown up a lot and learned how to deal with the world.

Comparing their current affair with previous ones, two-thirds of the respondents said that it was a more complete relationship:

It's a deeper and richer relationship—emotionally, intellectually, and physically.

I feel we are more tuned in to each other, more compatible with each other. Our interests and our backgrounds are similar. Most people take us as twins, twin sisters. Most of my family feel very fond of her—she is completely accepted. We're not seeking anyone else, we're not frequenting the bars.

A smaller number mentioned a more positive emotional involvement with their current partner, and others thought that they were more mature and better able to handle the relationship.

Of those who were currently involved in a relatively steady relationship (or affair) with another woman, the majority were in what we have termed a homosexual "couple"; i.e., they were living with their partner and involved in sexual activity with her. Thus, nearly half of all the lesbians were "coupled" at the time of the interview.

Over half of the WHFs and a third of the BHFs said that when they first considered themselves to be homosexual, having a permanent living arrangement with a female sexual partner was very important to them. Such an arrangement was, at the outset, more important to the lesbians than to their male counterparts. At the time of the interview, somewhat more of the homosexual women were likely to consider it important. Less than one-fifth thought that this kind of arrangement was of no particular importance.[5]

Among the "coupled" homosexual women, the majority reported that they combined their incomes and that they earned more than their partner. Of those reporting any income disparity, two-thirds said that it had no particular effect on the relationship. With regard to ways in which household responsibilities were handled, a majority of the "coupleds"

---

[5] By far the greatest number of those living with another woman were having sex with her. The incidence of ongoing sexual contact between roommates was considerably higher among the lesbians than among the homosexual men. An even greater difference between the homosexual men and women appears in terms of the monogamy they reported. About three-quarters of the WHFs and more than half of the BHFs reported that they and their roommate were having sex with each other exclusively.

said that they and their partner took equal responsibility for the house-work and for shopping. At the same time, a majority reported that either they or their partner were more likely to do repairs around the house, keep the books, or do the cooking. However, like their male counter-parts, few of the "coupled" shared all household responsibilities equally with their partner. Less than a tenth of them said that either they or their partner took over all the traditional wife's tasks in the household, while somewhat greater numbers managed all of the traditional husband's chores (i.e., they did the repairs and presided over the financial affairs of the household).

Summary

Most of the female respondents had had fewer than ten female sexual partners during the course of their adult lives, with almost all of these partners being persons whom they knew beforehand, who exchanged nonsexual intimacies with them, and with whom they had sex more than once. Most of the respondents had been monogamous, or nearly so, dur-ing the current year; only a very few had had more than five sexual partners during this period.

Almost all of the lesbians had had at least one affair with another woman since the age of seventeen. The respondents were, on the aver-age, twenty-two years old at the beginning of their first affair; they tended to be somewhat younger than their first partner and to be in love with her; and the two were likely to have lived together. Among those whose first affair had come to an end, its termination was due chiefly to one of the partners' involvement with another person or to other dissat-isfactions about the relationship itself. Many of the respondents were very upset and unhappy when the first affair ended. They acknowledged the fact that their first relationship of this kind had given them insight into themselves, had made them more mature, and had provided them with feelings of peace and happiness. They believed that their first part-ner was also likely to have ended up with greater maturity and to have attained a higher measure of self-fulfillment. In contrasting their first af-fair with any of their subsequent involvements, many mentioned the fact that at the time of their first affair they had had a lot to learn and that the relationship was more superficial than subsequent ones, although a num-ber thought that it was more romantic. Some said that as a result of their first affair they had become more committed to their homosexuality.

Almost all of the respondents were involved in an affair at the time of the interview. This relationship, generally begun in their early thirties, tended to involve partners who lived together, shared similar social posi-tions, and were in love (at least on the part of the respondent). The current affairs tended to be described in much the same way as the first affairs. Such differences as were mentioned often included the notion that the present involvement was a more complete relationship than previous ones, that respondents (except for a few) were more emotionally involved with their current partner, and that they were more able to handle such a relationship than they had been earlier. Nearly half of the lesbians and their current partners were "coupled"—that is, the two were living together and were sexually involved. As with their male counterparts, few of the "coupled" respondents described a domestic situation in which one partner took on only "wifely" tasks and the other the "husbandly" ones.

Overview

Several conclusions can be drawn on the basis of our own and others' data. Perhaps the most important involve differences between homosexual men and women with respect to this particular dimension of sexual experience. Clearly, homosexual men tend to have many more partners than do homosexual women and are more apt to engage in sexual activity with persons who are virtual strangers to them. This phenomenon, evident in other aspects of their homosexual activity, has already been attributed to the greater tendency of males in general to separate sex from affection, to estimate their personal worth on the basis of how much sex they have, and to view fidelity as an undesirable restriction upon their freedom and independence. Frequently, what is ego-syntonic for the female is ego-alien for the male, and nowhere is this better illustrated than in the way they conduct their sexual lives. Another important reason for homosexual men's large number of sexual partners could be the fact that society provides them with little or no opportunity to meet on anything more than a sexual basis. Driven underground, segregated in what have been termed "sexual marketplaces," threatened but perhaps also stimulated by the danger of their enterprise, homosexual men would be expected to have an enormous number of fleeting sexual encounters. Sex with persons other than strangers can, in fact, be a liability, the occasion for blackmail and unwanted public exposure. In other words, sex without commitment or much involvement may reflect an even greater commitment to the reality of their circumstances, given the "homoerotophobic" society (Churchill, 1967) in which they live.

Social attitudes may also account for the greater number of homosexual women involved in quasi marriages: fewer questions are raised when two women live together in the same household. It is interesting to note, however, that while our male respondents were less likely to live with their love partner, they did not differ from their female counterparts in terms of how many affairs they ever had, nor did they differ on the basis of how long they had been involved in their current affair. The latter similarity may be mere coincidence, since how recently an affair began tells us nothing about how long it will last. Nevertheless, while the lesbian's first affair may last longer than that of the homosexual male, it may be a mistake to assume that his subsequent involvements are rarer or less enduring than hers.

The chief differences between the male and female groups with respect to their affairs include the greater sexual fidelity on the part of lesbian partners, the greater likelihood that they break up when one of them becomes at all involved with someone else, and less of a diversity in age or social position among female than among male couples. Another interesting difference between the two groups is the relative importance of the female's first affair in helping her to accept her homosexuality. In some cases, apparently, the homosexual woman's first significant and extended involvement with another woman becomes the occasion for a much deeper awareness of her sexuality and offers an enduring model of how homosexuality is most comfortably expressed. Such circumstances are quite different from those of her male counterpart, who is apt to have engaged in numerous sexual activities with other males at a relatively early age and whose model of homosexuality consists chiefly of men "on the make," of sex without commitment, of the excitement of sexual pursuit. Their respective introductions to homosexuality may influence many of the differences we find between homosexual men and women.

Finally, our data tend to belie the notion that homosexual affairs are apt to be inferior imitations of heterosexuals' premarital or marital involvements. The fact that homosexual liaisons, unlike those of their heterosexual counterparts, are not encouraged or legally sanctioned by society probably accounts for their relative instability. But the stability of a relationship may not be the only or even the chief criterion for judging its quality. Our data indicate that a relatively steady relationship with a love partner is a very meaningful event in the life of a homosexual man or woman. From our respondents' descriptions, these affairs are apt to involve an emotional exchange and commitment similar to the kinds that heterosexuals experience, and most of the homosexual respondents thought that they and their partners had benefited personally from their involvement and were at least somewhat unhappy when it was over. The fact that they generally went on to a subsequent affair with another partner seems to suggest a parallel with heterosexuals' remarriage after divorce rather than any particular emotional immaturity or maladjustment. In any case, most of our homosexual respondents spoke of these special relationships in positive terms and clearly were not content to limit their sexual contacts to impersonal sex.

Sex Appeal

It has been assumed that the homosexual subculture exists mostly in terms of sexual successes and disappointments. But no study, to our knowledge, has ever explored the relationship between homosexuals' estimates of their sex appeal and other aspects of their lives. Supposedly they would base such estimates upon how successful they have been in arousing others' sexual interest, how attractive their friends say they are, and, perhaps, how positive their self-concept is.

In addition, how people rate their sex appeal may be related to how old they are. This might be especially true for homosexuals, since it is widely supposed (by both homosexuals and heterosexuals) that older homosexuals are especially unlikely to be as sexually appealing as younger ones. It would certainly depend upon how much a person believes that he or she conforms to the cultural ideal of sexual attractiveness. This could include whether one's physical attributes (such as breast or genital size, height, weight, or facial appearance) are of the kind highly valued in the sexual marketplace.

Regardless of what may influence homosexuals' estimates of their sex appeal, such estimates would be expected to reflect and to influence many other aspects of their lives. Our respondents accordingly were asked to rate their sex appeal to members of the same sex on a five-point scale, ranging from "definitely below average" to "definitely above average."

Findings: Men *(Table 8)*

A majority of the homosexual men, white (WHMs) and black (BHMs), rated their sex appeal to other males as "a bit" to "definitely" above average. Less than a fifth of them considered their sex appeal "definitely" above average. Younger males were more likely than older respondents to rate their sex appeal favorably (Table 3.1). In addition, black males of lower socioeconomic status and less education tended to give themselves higher ratings than did those of higher status; these relationships did not appear among the WHMs (Tables 3.3, 3.2).

The only other sample with which we can compare our respondents' sex appeal self-ratings is that of the Chicago pilot study's homosexual men. More of them (28%) than of our WHMs rated their sex appeal to other men as below average.

Summary

The majority of the male respondents thought their sex appeal to other men was at least somewhat above average. The younger respondents of both races were more likely to consider themselves sexually appealing to other men, as were the blacks of lower educational and occupational levels.

Findings: Women *(Table 8)*

Half of the white homosexual females (WHFs) and close to two-thirds of the black homosexual females (BHFs) rated their sex appeal to members of the same sex as above average to some degree, with one-quarter of the BHFs and nearly a fifth of the WHFs rating themselves "definitely" above average. Only around one-tenth of them rated their sex appeal to other women as below average. The lesbians' estimates of their sex appeal were not related for either race to their age, occupational, or educational levels.

Summary

Half of the white homosexual females and almost two-thirds of the black lesbians considered their homosexual sex appeal to be above average. Relatively few respondents of either race rated themselves low on this measure.

Overview

Despite differences in how sexually appealing they believed they were, most of our homosexual respondents tended to rate themselves as at least average. Younger men tended to rate their sex appeal higher than the older men did, although no such relationship was found among the women; this suggests that the homosexual male subculture may value youthfulness more than the lesbian subculture does. The fact that respondents of high education and social status did not tend to rate their sex appeal any higher than did their lower status counterparts suggests that these ratings did not reflect a general sense of social prestige or that it is of no particular advantage in the sexual marketplace. In fact, among the black men lower status and education were associated with high ratings on sex appeal. The reason for this is not clear, but it could be that certain homosexual males find such persons especially appealing and that the blacks' self-ratings reflect this phenomenon.

Sexual Techniques

One variable on which most people have recognized differences among homosexuals is what sexual techniques they most often employ, or prefer to employ, in their sexual contacts. In fact, this recognition has led some people, especially therapists, to conclude that homosexual men and women generally adhere to a particular technique or sex role in their sexual activities. This conclusion also assumes that an individual's propensity for taking either an "active" or "passive" role is related to his or her gender identification, personality configuration, and the kind of nonsexual, social role he or she adopts with a partner. Whether homosexuals should be dichotomized according to sex role has been questioned in that adherence to a particular role or technique seems highly unusual, that the techniques employed can depend largely upon people's age and the nature of the sexual partnership. It has been observed, for example, that sexual partners involved in a long-standing relationship are apt to employ a diversity of techniques and to engage in whatever reversals of role are prompted by their momentary emotional exchange

(Hooker, 1965a). This impression has led many to believe that what homosexuals do sexually is of no particular importance, since the manner of their sexual exchanges is so diverse and relatively unpredictable.

Such an impression is furthered by research which indicates that homosexual men and women are apt to have experienced a panoply of sexual techniques by the time they reach middle age. Several studies attest to the diversity of techniques and sexual roles engaged in by homosexual men (Greenberg, 1973a; Saghir & Robins, 1973; Weinberg & Williams, 1974, 1975a) and women (Saghir & Robins, 1973). Most such studies report no marked role preference in homosexual men, although in Bieber et al.'s clinical sample (1962), a majority did prefer to be either the inserter or the insertee.

The present study addresses itself in several ways to homosexuals' use of various sexual techniques. One measure is concerned with whether our respondents employed any of a variety of techniques during the year prior to the interview. Another indicates how frequently persons engaged in a particular technique, and a third, which techniques were the respondents' favorites. Finally, the respondents have been distinguished as to the extent of their sexual repertoire.

Findings: Men *(Table 9)*

Incidence of Techniques Employed

The male respondents were asked to indicate whether, during the past twelve months, they had ever engaged in seven different homosexual sexual techniques: reaching orgasm by rubbing their body against the body of a partner, masturbating a partner, being masturbated by a partner, performing fellatio, receiving fellatio, performing anal intercourse, and receiving anal intercourse. Almost all of the white homosexual males (WHMs) and of their black counterparts (BHMs) had engaged in five or more of these techniques during the past year. About one-quarter of the WHMs and somewhat more of the BHMs had experienced all seven of these particular forms of sexual contact. The extent of our respondents' sexual repertoires was related to age, with the younger males, both black and white, tending to have engaged in a greater variety of sexual techniques than had the older males (Table 3.1).

In decreasing order of incidence (i.e., whether they had ever engaged in a particular sexual technique during that year), the white men were most likely to have fellated their partner or to have been fellated by him. Next most prevalent was being masturbated by their partner, followed by masturbating their partner, performing anal intercourse, having anal intercourse performed on them, and reaching orgasm through body-rubbing. The order for the black males was quite similar, except that they were somewhat less likely to have performed fellatio.

Frequency of Techniques Employed

The order of frequency with which the male respondents actually engaged in a particular form of sexual contact did not always correspond with its incidence. Among both the white and the black males, fellatio was the sexual technique in which they had most frequently engaged. About half of them had performed fellatio at least once a week. About the same numbers of the WHMs and somewhat more of the BHMs had received fellatio once a week or more. Among the white males, the older men tended to spend a greater proportion of their sexual activity performing (or, less often, receiving) fellatio, but the younger men were more likely to have engaged frequently in any of the seven activities listed (Table 3.1).

Among the white respondents, the next most frequent sexual technique was hand-genital contact. About one-quarter had masturbated their partners or had been masturbated by them at least once a week. Somewhat smaller numbers had performed anal intercourse or had received it weekly or more often, and only a few had reached orgasm through body-rubbing at least once a week; this technique was more common among the lower status men (Table 3.3).

The order of the frequency with which the black homosexual respondents had engaged in a particular sexual technique is somewhat different. After fellatio, they were significantly more likely than the whites to list performing anal intercourse as their most frequent activity (of those engaged in at least once a week). Other techniques, in decreasing order of frequency, were performing or receiving masturbation, receiving anal intercourse, and body-rubbing (significantly more than the whites). The less educated black males were especially likely to report having been masturbated by their partner (Table 3.2), and the higher status respondents to have performed anal intercourse (Table 3.3).

Favorite Sexual Technique

With respect to favorite sexual techniques, the largest numbers of the WHMs said they liked receiving fellatio (27%) or performing anal intercourse (26%) best. Almost one-half of the black respondents said that performing anal intercourse was their special preference, and approximately a fifth most preferred receiving fellatio.

Summary

Almost all of the homosexual men had used a considerable variety of sexual techniques during the year prior to the interview. And almost none of them had exclusively engaged in one particular form of sexual contact. Fellatio was the sexual technique most frequently employed by members of both races. While some form of hand-genital contact was the technique next most frequently employed by the white men, the blacks were next most likely to have engaged in performing anal intercourse. About half of the white men most preferred either having fellatio performed on them or performing anal intercourse on their partners, while more of the blacks preferred performing anal intercourse.

Findings: Women *(Table 9)*

Incidence of Techniques Employed

The forms of sexual contact about which the female respondents were questioned included: reaching orgasm through body-rubbing, masturbating their partner, being masturbated, performing cunnilingus, and receiving cunnilingus. More than three-quarters of either the white female respondents (WHFs) or their black counterparts (BHFs) had employed three or more of these techniques during the year prior to the interview. More than one-quarter of the WHFs, as opposed to a majority of the BHFs, had used all five of them. Among the white respondents, the younger women were apt to have had a more extensive repertoire than the older ones (Table 3.1).

The female respondents were most apt to have experienced being masturbated by their partner or masturbating her. In decreasing order of incidence, the whites were less apt to have performed cunnilingus or to have received it. This order was reversed for the blacks, who (after masturbation) were next most likely to have received cunnilingus, followed by performing it. Both groups were least likely to have reached orgasm through body-rubbing.

Frequency of Techniques Employed

Masturbation (of or by their partner) was not only the form of sexual contact which the female respondents were most apt to have experienced. It was also the technique which they most frequently employed.

Forty percent of the WHFs had masturbated their partners or had been masturbated by their partners once a week or more during the twelve-month period. The frequency with which manual-genital contact between partners was a sexual outlet for the white respondents is related to their age, with younger females more apt to have employed this technique relatively often (Table 3.1). Similarly, almost half of the BHFs had masturbated their partners, and half of them had been masturbated by their partners, at least once a week. Cunnilingus was the sexual technique next most frequently engaged in by the respondents. About one-quarter of the WHFs and nearly half of the BHFs had performed cunnilingus, and significantly more blacks had received it, once a week or more; the younger white lesbians tended to engage in cunnilingus more often than the older ones (Table 3.1). About one-fifth of the WHFs and two-fifths of the BHFs had reached orgasm at least weekly through body-rubbing. Among both the black and the white groups, the younger and the less educated females were more apt to have engaged relatively often in body-rubbing with their partners (Tables 3.1, 3.2), as were the lower status white lesbians (Table 3.3).

Favorite Sexual Technique

The sexual technique most preferred by the female respondents was cunnilingus, with about half ranking this first. Among the whites, the next most preferred techniques were being masturbated by their partners or engaging in mutual masturbation, while the BHFs were likely to mention body-rubbing with their partners.

Summary

Most of the female respondents had engaged in a number of different forms of sexual contact with their partners, with the blacks tending to have a more extensive sexual repertoire than their white counterparts. The lesbians most frequently engaged in some form of masturbation with their partners. The next most frequent technique was cunnilingus. The largest number of them said that they most preferred cunnilingus. The white lesbians were next most likely to say they liked some form of masturbation best and the black women to mention body-rubbing.

Overview

While our data are not exactly comparable to those of other studies, our findings are consonant with others' reports that homosexual men and women are apt to engage in many different forms of sexual contact with their partners and that a very strict adherence to a particular sexual role is quite uncommon.

Comparing our various samples, we find only one demographic characteristic—age—to be related to the extent of sexual repertoire among any of our respondents. The fact that during the last year the younger whites (male and female) and the younger black males were apt to have employed a wider variety of sexual techniques than their older counterparts could be due to several things. It is not unreasonable to suppose that younger homosexuals are often involved in sexual experimentation, and that, in general, they may be less inhibited than their older colleagues. In turn, the older ones may have engaged in just as many different forms of sexual contact at some time in their lives but through the years may have settled on only two or three techniques, either by preference or in order to please a partner. It should be noted that although performing fellatio was the sexual technique in which the white male respondents most frequently engaged, the older men were especially apt to have used this technique. This may be due to older homosexual males' greater difficulty in finding a partner willing to reciprocate their attentions.

The fact that homosexual men and women are apt to engage in a number of different forms of sexual contact does not mean that they have no favorite. When asked to state their preferred sexual technique, virtually all of our respondents did so. Men and women of both races specified receiving oral-genital sex. The males also mentioned performing anal intercourse, and the black females, body-rubbing. This is hardly surprising, since, in general, all of these activities are organized around the respondent's rather than the partner's orgasm; it suggests, furthermore, that speculation about sexual "roles" (e.g., active/passive) may simply be missing the point.

Level of Sexual Interest

Differences between levels of sexual interest on the part of homosexual men and women have not heretofore been acknowledged, much less explored, by any investigators. A common stereotypical notion of homosexual men is that they are constantly preoccupied with sexual matters—that they eroticize their relationships with other men, spend their time daydreaming about sex when they are not actually engaging in it, and consider sex much more important than heterosexual men do. On the other hand, many people suppose that lesbians are asexual, that their activities are usually limited to nongenital displays of affection; but there are also those who believe that homosexual women, like their male counterparts, are hypersexual, with a sexual interest and aggressiveness far exceeding that of heterosexual women.

The stereotype of the hypersexual homosexual for whom sex is "figure" and all else is "ground" is not difficult to understand. First, the heterosexual majority tends to define homosexuals basically in terms of their sexual preference. Knowing little about other aspects of homosexuals' lives, many people assume that the label "homosexual" reflects or even summarizes the homosexual's place and purpose in the world. Second, nonmarital sex is more "visible," e.g., cruising in public places. Third, sexual preoccupations or an "undue" emphasis upon sexual matters tend to be alien to the values of the heterosexual majority. Attributing these characteristics to homosexual men and women makes it possible for heterosexuals to disavow their own levels of sexual interest and to express revulsion and disdain for those they perceive as different from themselves. Thus they can believe that while heterosexuals are (and others should be) chiefly concerned with the quality of the relationships they have with their partners, homosexuals are far more interested in sex for its own sake. Finally, the heterosexual majority can account for the willingness of homosexuals to risk a host of negative social consequences by seeing them as helplessly dominated by their sexual impulses and preferences. Only sex-ridden individuals, they conclude, would pay such a high price for their sexual proclivities.

The supposition of the present study is, of course, that homosexual men and women, like their heterosexual counterparts, differ among themselves in the levels of their sexual interest. Two questions were asked: "How often during the day do you think about sexual things?" and "Is sex a very important part of your life, fairly important, not very important, or an unimportant part?" Answers to the first question may denote the extent to which respondents were preoccupied with sex, trying to cope with a sexual difficulty, or less active sexually than they would have liked to be. Answers to the second may reflect the standing of sexuality in respondents' hierarchy of values. At the very least they reflect the prominence of sex in our respondents' thinking.[1]

Findings: Men (Table 10)

With regard to the first question, about one-third of the white homosexual males (WHMs) and almost the same number of black homosexual males (BHMs) said that they thought "quite a bit" about sex during the course of a day. The largest numbers in each sample did "some" thinking about sexual matters, and less than a quarter of them said they thought hardly at all about sex. With regard to the importance of sex in their lives, about half of the male respondents said that it was a "fairly" important part of their lives. The amount of sexual interest the men dis-

---

[1] A summary measure that combines responses to both of these questions is used in later chapters in discussions of respondents' level of sexual interest.

played was not notably affected by their race, age, education, or occupational level.

The men in our Chicago pilot study tended to report lower levels of sexual interest than did our white homosexual male respondents. Thirty-six percent of the Chicago men, twice as many as in our WHM sample, did not think very much or at all about sex during the day. Similarly, only 27 percent of the pilot study respondents, but 40 percent of our WHMs, considered sex a "very important" part of their lives. (These differences may reflect the nature of the samples' respective milieus. Perhaps San Francisco has a more sex-charged atmosphere than Chicago, and the Bay Area sample may include individuals who moved there in anticipation of such an atmosphere.)

Summary

More than two-thirds of the male respondents said that sex was a "fairly" or a "very" important part of their lives. Regarding how often they said that they thought about sex during the course of the day, the most common response—given by nearly half of either the blacks or the whites—was that they did "some" such thinking, with smaller numbers saying they did "quite a bit." Less than a quarter of the black males, and less than a fifth of the whites, said that they seldom thought about sexual matters.

Findings: Women *(Table 10)*

More than a third of the white homosexual females (WHFs) and a quarter of the black homosexual females (BHFs) said that they did not think very much, if at all, about sex during the course of a day, and only about one-quarter of them thought "quite a bit" about sexual things during their waking hours. The largest numbers in each of the female samples said that they did "some" thinking about sex. The female respondents tended to score higher on the extent to which they thought sex was an important part of their lives. About three-quarters of them believed that sex was either a "fairly" or a "very" important part of their lives. Among the white homosexual females, but not the blacks, younger respondents and those with relatively lower-ranking jobs tended to score higher in sexual interest than did their older or higher status counterparts (Tables 3.1, 3.3).

Summary

In terms of level of sexual interest, approximately one-quarter of the women in each race said they thought "quite a bit" about sex, about one-quarter said they hardly ever thought about it, and close to half said they sometimes did so. Approximately three-quarters of the women said that sex was at least a "fairly" important part of their lives.

Overview

Besides demonstrating the diversity of sexual interest among our respondents, these data fail to support the idea that homosexual men and women are sex-ridden people who think constantly of sexual matters or consider sex the most important part of their lives. It would appear that for most homosexuals, sex is not a particularly predominant concern. Regardless of their race or gender, the largest numbers of those in our samples did only "some" thinking about sex and said that sex was only a "fairly" important aspect of their lives. It is little wonder that so many homosexual men and women reject the label "homosexual," in that it exaggerates the sexual component of their lives, and prefer such terms as "gay," "lesbian," or "homophile." These terms connote much more an entire life-style, a way of being in the world which only incidentally involves sexual activity with persons of the same sex. And, of course, they spend much more of their time at work or with friends or on household chores than in explicitly sexual contexts.

Finally, our data tend to confirm the impression that homosexual men are more interested in sex than lesbians are. This notion was borne out among the whites. It is not supported by the black data, however, where the women's levels of sexual interest did not differ significantly from their male counterparts'.

Sexual Problems

The heterosexual majority has so generally regarded homosexuality per se as a sexual problem that almost no consideration has been given to whether homosexuals may differ in how many problems they have in their sexual functioning. This omission may stem from the notion that homosexuality is chiefly the way certain persons cope with a failure to perform heterosexually, retreating to a less threatening mode of sexual functioning that inevitably results in "successful," albeit immature and incomplete, sexual contacts. More certainly it proceeds from clinicians' disinclination to assess or ameliorate homosexuals' sexual problems for fear that such efforts may reinforce behaviors which they consider unfortunate, if not pathological.

The first perspective, that homosexuality is an easier achievement than heterosexuality and therefore usually mechanically, if not emotionally, fulfilling, received consideration in the work of Kinsey and his associates (1953). They found that a significantly larger proportion of predominantly homosexual women were almost always orgasmic in their homosexual sex relations than were a comparable group of heterosexual women in coital activity with their husbands. Concluding that homosexual sexual encounters may be more "effective" (more likely to result in orgasm) than heterosexual contacts, these investigators reasoned that same-sex partners are more likely to understand and to respond to each other's needs because they are so similar to their own.

Regarding how clinicians deal with homosexuals' sexual problems, there is a paucity of literature. Bieber and his associates (1962) reported that approximately one-half of the homosexual male patients in their sample entered treatment for a "sex problem" but did not specify whether their sexual orientation in itself constituted the "problem." One isolated finding, however, is specified: the "bisexual" men in this study were less apt to report potency difficulty in their homosexual sexual relations than were the exclusively homosexual men.

In the present study respondents are compared with regard to the extent to which they reported problems in their sexual lives. Such problems include orgasmic difficulties in themselves or their partners, ejaculatory control and erectile problems (among males), insufficient frequency, difficulties finding a suitable partner, their own or their partners' failure to respond to whatever sexual requests were made of them, concerns about their ability to perform sexually, difficulties in maintaining affection for their sexual partners, and whether they had ever contracted a venereal disease from homosexual contact.

Findings: Men *(Table 11)*

Incidence of Sexual Difficulties

Asked whether they had ever experienced various sexual difficulties, the male respondents of both races were most likely to say that at some time they had had difficulty getting a partner to respond to their sexual requests. In addition, about three-quarters of the white homosexual males (WHMs), compared with approximately two-thirds of the black homosexual males (BHMs), said they had had trouble finding a suitable sexual partner. About two-thirds of both races also mentioned at least occasional difficulty in responding to their partner's sexual requests or finding sexual contacts frequently enough. A majority of the WHMs and significantly fewer BHMs had had trouble with getting or maintaining an erection, lack of orgasm in their partner, being unable to maintain affection for their partner, "coming" too fast, or feelings of sexual inadequacy. Not quite half of both races, at one time or another, had had difficulty achieving orgasm.

Severity of Sexual Difficulties

The extent to which respondents reporting any of these experiences considered them to be very much of a problem in their sexual lives did not necessarily correspond to how likely they were to report ever having had a given experience. For example, although the majority of both races said that they had sometimes had trouble finding a suitable partner, and even though this experience was most often mentioned as a problem, less than a fifth said it was very problematic for them. There was a tendency for the younger and the lower status black respondents to think that finding a partner was especially problematic (Tables 3.1, 3.3). Similarly, although a lack of sexual frequency was next most often mentioned as a problem, only 11 percent of the WHMs and fewer blacks said it was very much of a problem for them. For all the other difficulties listed, very small numbers of either race—less than 10 percent, and in most cases less than 5 percent—said that the given difficulty was very much of a problem. However, among the whites the younger males were more likely to report that maintaining affection for their partner was a problem. The older WHMs, on the other hand, were more apt to have erectile problems (Table 3.1).

Incidence of Venereal Disease

About two-thirds of the males in each race had at some time contracted a venereal disease as a result of homosexual sex, but of these, most had had it only once or twice.

Summary

The black and the white homosexual males differed somewhat in terms of whether they had experienced various sexual difficulties, but in either race the respondents were most likely to mention difficulties in finding a suitable sexual partner or their partner's not responding to their sexual requests. Smaller numbers cited not getting enough sex or having difficulties responding to their partner's sexual requests. The other experiences were reported less often. The two difficulties most often described as constituting much of a problem were finding a partner and infrequent sexual contact. At the same time, very few of the homosexual males indicated that any of these experiences were very much of a problem. Finally, approximately two-thirds of the homosexual males had had a venereal disease at one time or another.

Findings: Women *(Table 11)*

Incidence of Sexual Difficulties

The homosexual women, whether white (WHFs) or black (BHFs), tended to have experienced fewer sexual difficulties than their male counterparts did. They most often mentioned not having sex often enough, followed by difficulties in getting a partner to respond to their sexual requests, finding a suitable partner, or, at one time or another, attaining orgasm. Among other difficulties they might have encountered, somewhat over 40 percent of the lesbians of either race had sometimes had trouble meeting their partner's sexual requests. Approximately one-third to two-fifths noted occasional difficulty in maintaining affection for their partner, a lack of orgasm in the partner, or concerns about their own sexual adequacy.

Severity of Sexual Difficulties

While a lack of sexual frequency was the experience most often reported by both races, it was not the one considered the most problematic. As with the males, the female respondents generally did not report that any of the specified experiences were very much of a problem for them. Difficulty finding a suitable partner was very much a problem for the greatest numbers. Next most often mentioned was insufficient sexual frequency. Fewer had had problems with a lack of orgasm, concerns over being sexually adequate, whether sexual requests were met, or maintaining affection for their sexual partner; these difficulties were described as very much of a problem only by small numbers, less than 10 percent of either race. The younger BHFs, however, did tend to mention more often having difficulty responding to their partner's sexual requests (Table 3.1).

Incidence of Venereal Disease

None of the WHFs, and only one of the BHFs, had ever caught venereal disease from homosexual sexual contact.

Summary

The sexual difficulty that the homosexual women were most likely ever to have had was feeling that sexual contact was too infrequent. In

Dimensions of Sexual Experience / **119**

terms of whether their sex difficulties constituted problems for them, the few lesbians who did have such problems most often cited trouble finding a suitable partner. Only one of them had ever contracted a venereal disease from homosexual activity.

Overview

In general, our data show less incidence or severity of sexual difficulties among lesbians than among their male counterparts. These differences between the male and female respondents, much more marked among the whites than the blacks, were especially pronounced with respect to the incidence of difficulties in finding a suitable sexual partner, maintaining affection for their partner, and meeting one another's sexual requests. The lower incidence of these problems among our female respondents confirms the general impression that lesbians, as compared with homosexual men, are less apt to be engaged in the pursuit of many different partners or kinds of sexual acts and more apt to be involved with a partner for whom they have deep affection.

Finally, although some 20 to 80 percent of our respondents reported having experienced some difficulty in one or another aspect of their sexual circumstances, in almost every instance the largest number said that the particular "problem" concerned them very little. In all instances one-fifth to less than 10 percent of our respondents considered a particular matter to be of some or much concern to them. These data tend to convey the impression that only a lack of frequency and difficulties in finding a suitable sexual partner may be at all problematic for a fairly large number of homosexual men and women. In other respects, our respondents appeared to function with minimal difficulty.

Acceptance of Homosexuality

Given the homoerotophobic features of our society, it is understandable that some writers have stressed the ways in which homosexual men and women assimilate the heterosexual majority's negative views of homosexuality, thus becoming alienated from their deepest sexual needs and interests. It is taken for granted that homosexual people, lacking others' endorsement of their private identities (Simon & Gagnon, 1967), raised in a society whose sexual values oppose the usual homosexual life-style (Cory, 1952), and discriminated against in important areas of their lives (Cory, 1951), are bound to have extremely ambivalent feelings about their own and others' homosexuality. One example of this presupposition is the tendency for many therapists to view a homosexual client's homosexuality as the central problem and to assume that the client would gladly relinquish it if possible.

It is certainly true that homosexuals share with other minority groups a "legacy of subordination" (Bertelson, 1970)—a tradition of expecting prejudice and harsh treatment as they go about their daily lives—and this is an important concern for social justice. Nevertheless, the fact remains that homosexuals' feelings about being homosexual depend in large part upon their age, sex, social circumstances, and psychological makeup. For a variety of reasons, some loathe their homosexuality while others are satisfied and content with it. Numerous investigations of homosexuals' attitudes toward their homosexuality have demonstrated that it is a psychological and social burden for some but an energizing influence for others.

Weinberg and Williams (1974, 1975a) found that homosexual men could, indeed, be distinguished on the basis of their commitment to homosexuality (i.e., their inclination or disinclination to give up their sexual orientation if they could). Saghir and Robins (1973) reported that lesbians felt less guilty and fearful about their sexual practices than did homosexual men and that such negative reactions were more evident in younger subjects of both sexes. In addition, they found that while large numbers of their homosexual respondents fully accepted their homosexuality, others were either in "deep conflict" about or only "partially accepting" of their sexual orientation. Even Bieber et al. (1962) found that although most of the homosexual male psychiatric patients in their sample wanted to be "cured" of their homosexuality, fully one-third of them had no such desire at all.

Studies such as these prompt our interest in determining the extent to which our own homosexual respondents differ in their acceptance of their homosexuality. Measures employed include the amount of regret the respondents had over their homosexuality, whether they ever considered discontinuing their homosexual activity, whether they wished they had been given a magic pill at birth which would have guaranteed their becoming heterosexual, and whether they would take such a pill today if one were offered to them. Respondents were also asked how much it was a problem for them to be engaging in activities they had been raised to believe were immoral, the extent to which they agreed with those who view homosexuality as an emotional disorder, and, finally, how upset they would be if a child of their own were to become homosexual. In addition to these items, the respondents were asked whether they had ever made an actual attempt to discontinue their homosexuality.

Findings: Men (Table 12)

Regret of Homosexuality

Almost half of the white homosexual males (WHMs) and somewhat over half of the black homosexual males (BHMs) said that they had no regret whatsoever about being homosexual. This is about the same number as those in our Chicago pilot sample. About a quarter of the WHMs and a somewhat smaller number of the BHMs reported some or a great deal of regret over their homosexuality.

Among those who regretted the fact that they were homosexual, many mentioned having to live in a rejecting society, not being able to have children, or feeling lonely:

My regret is not being a homosexual but being a homosexual in this society. My problem is dealing with society and how I can function as a complete human being. For example, I'd like to be a teacher right now. I really would. But I won't go where I have to live a lie and where homosexuals are not accepted or welcome.

I don't like fingers pointed at us all the time. I don't like being a freak. Otherwise I wouldn't care.

It's lonely. Marriage and children are guarantees against loneliness. Although I've made up for this, in part, by being a teacher, I still regret not having had my own children.

Smaller numbers spoke in terms of the way their homosexuality tended to restrict their options (such as jobs or friendships):

Had I been born heterosexual, many things would have been much easier and more pleasant for me—"in the mainstream." But a lot of the things, like certain jobs, I've had to reject.

I think it has severely hampered my main energy drive in professional activities. I'm a lot less ambitious than I would be if I were less anxious about my sex life.

Attempts to Discontinue Homosexuality

On another measure of the degree to which our respondents accepted their homosexuality, most of them said they had never seriously considered discontinuing it. Somewhat more (40%) of the pilot study respondents had, compared to only about one-quarter of our respondents. Of those of our respondents who did, about one-third of the WHMs, compared with more than half of the BHMs, had made no serious attempt to stop their homosexual activity or to reduce their homosexual proclivities. Of those who had made such an attempt, most tried it no more than twice. These attempts often involved an effort to withdraw from the gay world:

I just stopped going to bars. I didn't allow myself to get in a situation where I might engage in homosexual activities.

I just stopped going to the usual places and seeing people I knew. I wanted to avoid temptation.

I stepped out of gay society. I left my roommate twice. I just moved out and stayed out. I tried the religion bit but that didn't work. I thought I could pray it out of me.

Some began to date women and engage in heterosexual sex or sought professional help. Other attempts included the resolution not to engage in homosexual sexual fantasies nor to act on their sexual impulses:

My only sexual activity was masturbation, and there I didn't allow myself to fantasize about men.

I tried to completely forget men. I tried to stop thinking about them or looking at them, but I don't think it had any effect at all on my behavior or attitudes.

Only fifteen WHMs and none of the BHMs got married with the thought that this would enable them to stop their homosexuality.

Negative Feelings About Homosexuality

On other measures of respondents' attitudes toward homosexuality, we find varying degrees of negativity. Twenty-eight percent of the WHMs and almost half of the BHMs reported some guilt over their homosexual sexual activities, compared with 55 percent of those in Saghir and Robins's sample. About one-quarter of both the WHMs and the BHMs agreed that homosexuality is an emotional disorder. Approximately the same number said they would be somewhat or very upset if a child of theirs were to become homosexual. A similar number wished that they had been given a magic pill at birth which would have guaranteed their becoming completely heterosexual. Smaller numbers (WHMs: 14%; BHMs: 13%) said that they would take such a pill today. Much larger numbers of the psychiatric patients in Bieber et al.'s sample (66%) wished that they could become heterosexual. Compared with those in our WHM sample who would have wanted a magic pill today, only a few more in the pilot sample (24%) or in Weinberg and Williams's sample (28%) said that they would give up their homosexuality if it were at all possible.

Summary

It would appear that the vast majority of our male respondents accepted their homosexuality. Only about a quarter of them regretted it or had seriously considered stopping their homosexual activity. The same numbers tended to think of homosexuality as an emotional disorder, thought they might be upset if their own child turned out to be homosexual, and wished that they had been given a magic pill for heterosexuality when they were born. The degree to which they accepted their homosexuality did not appear to be related to race. Slightly more blacks than whites had thought about giving up their homosexual activity, but more whites than blacks had actually tried to do so, and the two races did not differ significantly on the other measures.

Findings: Women *(Table 12)*

Regret of Homosexuality

Almost two-thirds of the white homosexual females (WHFs) and an even larger percentage of the black homosexual females (BHFs) said that they had no regret at all about being homosexual. Approximately one-fifth of the female respondents reported "very little" regret, and even smaller numbers had some or a great deal of regret over their homosexuality.

Of those who had any regret at all, the most frequent reason they gave for their feelings had to do with having to live in a society that was disinclined to accept them:

Most of the world doesn't really like gay people, and I feel a little separated from straight people. Like, I can't be completely open about being gay at work.

It's because of society's attitudes. I think there are happier ways of life, although I'm not sure that heterosexuals are all that happy.

It's not a natural way of life. It requires too many repressions and involves too many repercussions, conscious energy that you consume guarding against discovery.

The next most frequent reasons they gave had to do with feeling restricted by their homosexual status in terms of such things as friendship, housing, and job opportunities, and not being able to have children:

The person I love and live with might someday want a child, and I could never give it to her, nor could she to me. This is often important to women.

Anyone who is different has problems, especially when you're younger. It's inhibiting. And that inhibits relationships. You can't be upfront, and that's limiting—you have to give up your gains.

Well, your mobility is reduced. Like wanting to change jobs or move to another town or area—small-towners don't have a generous spirit, they'd never tolerate us. And if it were known in my work that I was homosexual, they'd fire me, and I'd have to lie to another employer.

Attempts to Discontinue Homosexuality

About one-third of the respondents had seriously considered discontinuing their homosexual activity, and of these, the majority had made at least one serious attempt to stop their homosexuality. Those who had ever made such an attempt were likely to have dated or even married men or tried becoming less involved in the gay world:

I just stopped going out and associating with other homosexuals. But you get tired of staying home, so you start going out again.

I threw out all my slacks. I never sat next to a woman in public places. I started going to heterosexual social affairs and saw less of my gay male friends. I thought, it's easier and less hassle to meet men—I enjoy their company. I thought I could do the straight thing. I tried for two years.

I went out with men and tried to feel that it was O.K. to have sex with them, but I didn't like it.

The psychiatrist and I figured I was basically bisexual and that it was easier to be heterosexual in our society. So I found a boyfriend, and we went together for a year and a half. He was not very sexually satisfying, but I liked him a lot and thought that in time everything would work out nicely and we'd have a happy marriage. Then one day an old girlfriend came to visit. We went to bed together, and I remembered what sex was all about, and that was the end of my trying to be heterosexual.

I married him because I thought maybe I'd get over being homosexual, but it didn't work. I just couldn't have any sex with him. I tried it but I just couldn't force myself. He was nice about it, but I figured it wasn't fair to him.

Negative Feelings About Homosexuality

Additional measures of the lesbians' attitudes toward homosexuality indicate that relatively few of them thought of it in negative terms. About one-fifth of the WHFs and a third of the BHFs felt some degree of guilt over their sexual activities with other women. More of the lesbians in Saghir and Robins's sample (37%) reported feeling some guilt about their homosexual practices. Less than a quarter of the WHFs or BHFs thought homosexuality was an emotional disorder. About a third of the WHFs and a quarter of the BHFs thought that they might be upset if a child of theirs became homosexual. Only a few of the respondents wished that they had been given a magic pill at birth which would have guaranteed their becoming heterosexual, and, like their male counterparts, even fewer said that they would take such a pill today if it were available. Much smaller numbers of our WHFs (5%) and of those in Schäfer's sample (3%) than of those in Kaye et al.'s clinical sample (37%) wanted to be "cured" of their homosexuality.

Summary

A minority of our homosexual female respondents appeared to have difficulty accepting their homosexuality. Majorities of both the white and the black women said they did not at all regret being homosexual, had never seriously considered discontinuing their homosexuality, did not think of it as an emotional disorder, would not mind if a child of theirs became homosexual, and would not want a magic pill causing heterosexuality to have been given them either at birth or currently. The two races did not differ much in their acceptance of their homosexuality, but one measure on which the blacks appeared to be less accepting involved their greater tendency to feel guilty over engaging in sexual activities which they had been raised to believe were wrong or immoral.

Overview

More women than men in our samples, although a minority in each case, had seriously considered stopping their homosexuality, and among those who considered this, more women than men had made actual attempts to do so. Nevertheless, since at the time of the interview more men than women regretted their homosexuality or wished for a pill to "cure" it, it seems reasonable to conclude that homosexual men are more likely than lesbians to have difficulties in accepting their homosexuality. It may be that homosexuality is more frequently construed by males as a failure to achieve a "masculine" sexual adjustment, while lesbians, many of whom have experienced considerable sexual contact with males, more often experience their homosexuality as a freely chosen rejection of heterosexual relationships.

Another obvious and understandable finding is that clinical samples of homosexual men and women are much more apt to include persons who regret their homosexuality. Unfortunately it is these conflicted people's determination to become heterosexual which has been most evident in the literature and which has prompted clinicians to believe that homosexuality is inevitably problematic for those involved. Our data show that many homosexual men and women appear to come to terms with their homosexuality.

A Typology of Sexual Experience

As one would expect, the various dimensions of homosexual experience are related in varying degrees to each other (Tables 13.1, 13.2). Not only do their interrelationships, or lack thereof, help us to obtain a more complete picture of how homosexual men and women function; they also provide evidence of the validity (and internal consistency) of the measures used in the present investigation. It should be noted that our respondents were asked about these items at various points in the interview, not all at once. For example, they were questioned about their sexual problems about an hour before they were asked how much they regretted being homosexual. Thus, the fact that measures such as these are related as they are, always in a predictable direction and usually for both the male and the female respondents, lends credence to our research enterprise. And where two particular measures are related to each other among the women but not the men, or vice versa, they cast additional light on whatever differences there might be between male and female experiences of homosexuality.

The correlation matrices in Tables 13.1 and 13.2 show the interrelationships among the measures discussed in preceding chapters. Notice first the way in which involvement in a quasi marriage (i.e., being "coupled") or in an affair, amount of regret over being homosexual, number of worries while cruising, and number of sexual problems are related to each other. Those who were "coupled" or involved in an affair tended to have fewer sexual problems than their uninvolved counterparts. The extent to which one regretted being homosexual tended to be related to how many sexual problems one had; in turn, the extent of problems was related to the extent of cruising worries. Looking next at other measures, "involved" men and women tended to report relatively high levels of sexual activity. For the women, being involved in an affair or "coupled" was also related to being more exclusively homosexual in both behaviors and feelings and to having more extensive sexual repertoires. Predictably, the "coupled" men tended to report a smaller number of sexual partners than did the other men, and both the men and the women who cruised the most tended to report the most worries in connection with their cruising. Among both men and women, those reporting the greatest number of sexual problems tended to be less sexually active than the others.[1]

Tables 13.1 and 13.2 also show relationships among some of the other measures. As one would expect, respondents with high levels of sexual interest tended to report a greater number of sexual partners, higher levels of sexual activity, and more cruising. The "high interest" females also tended to have more extensive sexual repertoires than the "low interest" women. Those who thought they had more homosexual sex appeal tended to have more extensive repertoires and more sexual activity. Respondents reporting relatively large numbers of sexual partners understandably also tended to cruise more and to be more sexually active than those reporting fewer partners. Among both groups, the more they cruised, the more partners they reported having, and, among the men, higher frequencies of cruising were related to higher levels of sexual activity and to more extensive repertoires. Male and female respondents with extensive sexual repertoires tended to be more active sexually and to report larger numbers of partners than those who had used less of a variety of sexual techniques.

Finally, except for the tendency for the more "exclusively homosexual" women to be "coupled" or else involved in an affair and thus to report fewer sexual partners but higher levels of sexual activity, respondents' ratings of themselves on the homosexual-heterosexual continuum

[1] Since two of the sexual problems included are trouble finding a sexual partner and lack of sexual frequency, this relationship may appear to have a tautological element; however, the correlation remains significant (p <.001) when these two problems are excluded from the summary measure "amount of sexual problems."

were not highly related to the other measures; and the degree to which others outside the family knew about respondents' homosexuality was not especially related to the other variables.

Factor analysis was employed to group these interrelationships. Table 13.3 presents loadings of each item on four factors which emerged from among our various measures concerning the homosexual men. The loadings confirm the foregoing impressions from the correlation matrix. The number of sexual problems they reported having loaded heavily on the first factor, the amount of worrying they did while cruising on the second; the number of partners they had, their level of sexual activity, how much cruising they did, and the extent of their sexual repertoires had strong loadings on the third factor, while being "coupled" and being involved in an affair had high loadings on the fourth factor. This clustering of items initially suggested to us that the homosexual men might be distinguished at least on the basis of how much their sexuality was problematic for them, how sexually active they were, and whether they were involved in a relatively permanent sexual relationship.

Similar factors appeared for the lesbians (Table 13.4). The amount of cruising they did and how much they experienced cruising worries loaded strongly on the first factor, the number of sexual problems they had on the second. Being "coupled" or involved in an affair had a strong loading on the third factor, while the fourth factor was made up primarily of the extent of their sexual repertoires, the level of their sexual activity, and the number of sexual partners they had. Thus, as with the males, it appeared that we could assign the female respondents to groups on the basis of the extent to which their sexuality was problematic for them, whether they were "coupled" or involved in an affair, and how sexually active or involved they were.

With these data we created a typology that would allow us to compare different "types" of homosexuals with each other and with the heterosexual sample in terms of the sociological and psychological aspects of their lives. We were especially concerned about demonstrating the importance of using such a typology in studies that compare homosexuals with heterosexuals. Thus, we hoped that differences among homosexuals would emerge more clearly when the types were employed in the analysis and that the various types would compare in different ways with the heterosexuals. We did find this to be so.

In this chapter we create the typology on the basis of sexual parameters. Part III then presents our social adjustment findings, and Part IV our psychological adjustment findings, with relationships to our typology when they occur.

The first step in our construction of a typology of homosexual experience involved a cluster analysis of our male respondents on the basis of their standard scores on the major measures of sexual experience. Comparisons of the different group profiles that emerged suggested the existence of five major groups of homosexual males. Not all of the sexual variables were critical in distinguishing these five groups. The highly discriminating variables, already suggested by the factor analysis, included whether the respondents were "coupled" (i.e., involved in a quasi marriage), how much they regretted being homosexual, the number of sexual problems they had, how many sexual partners they reported having over the past year, the amount of cruising they did, and the level of their sexual activity. Using profiles of the different groups as models, specific criteria were set for respondents' standard scores on these measures (Table 13.5). Using these procedures, which are spelled out in greater detail in Appendix B, 485 white and black homosexual respondents (or 71% of the homosexual male sample) were assigned to five "pure" types: (I) Close-Coupled; (II) Open-Coupled; (III) Functional; (IV) Dysfunctional; and (V) Asexual.[2] The exact criteria we used in determining assignment to these types are shown in Table 13.5.

I. Close-Coupled

The sixty-seven homosexual men assigned to this group had to be in a quasi marriage with a male partner (i.e., they were living with him as a sexual partner). Their standard scores on number of sexual problems, number of sexual partners, and amount of cruising also had to be *low*. Thus, the Close-Coupleds had fewer sexual problems and fewer partners, and did less cruising, than the typical male respondent. With respect to the noncriterion measures, the Close-Coupleds also tended to have fewer cruising worries (among those who cruised), fewer difficulties in finding a suitable partner and in maintaining affection for him, and less regret about their homosexuality, and to be more sexually active than the typical respondent. The group members did not differ from the rest of the respondents in terms of their demographic characteristics.

[2] The only demographic characteristic on which those who could be assigned to a subgroup differed from the 201 unassigned males is that of age. The assigned males were somewhat older than their unassigned counterparts but did not differ with respect to race or occupational or educational level.

II. Open-Coupled

The 120 individuals assigned to this group had to be involved in a "marital" relationship with another man, and their standard scores had to be *high* on one or more of the following variables: number of sexual partners, number of sexual problems, and amount of cruising. Thus, even though they were "coupled," these respondents' scores indicated that they could not be classified as "fulfilled romantics" whose special relationship with another male had reduced their sexual problems or their interest in having a variety of sexual contacts. In addition to their scores on these criterion variables, the Open-Coupleds tended to be more exclusively homosexual, to do more worrying in connection with their cruising, to report somewhat higher levels of sexual activity, to have engaged in a wider variety of sexual techniques, and to have more regret about their homosexuality. Their partner's failure to respond to their sexual requests was the most prevalent sexual problem for this type. Finally, there was nothing notable about the Open-Coupleds' demographic characteristics.

III. Functional

One hundred and two individuals were assigned to this group. They had to be "single" (i.e., not "coupled," although they might have been involved in an affair), and with regard to other criteria, their standard scores were required to be *high* on number of sexual partners and level of sexual activity, and *low* on regret over their homosexuality and number of sexual problems. Thus, compared with the total sample, the Functionals had more sexual partners and higher levels of sexual activity, much less regret over their homosexuality, and fewer sexual problems. In terms of noncriterion variables, they did more cruising than the typical respondent, yet they were less apt to worry about their homosexuality being exposed through this activity. They also tended to be more overt, to have a higher level of sexual interest and somewhat more extensive sexual repertoires, and to rate their sex appeal higher. They were less likely than the average homosexual respondent to experience sexual problems regarding feeling that they did not have enough sex, that they were sexually inadequate, or that their homosexual activity was immoral. All of these differences clearly justify the use of the term "functional" in describing members of this particular group. Compared with the rest of the respondents, the Functionals tended to be younger, and the black respondents were overrepresented in their membership. There were no other distinguishing demographic characteristics.

IV. Dysfunctional

Eighty-six individuals were assigned to this group on the basis of the pattern of their standard scores. By definition none of them were "coupled," and while they had to score *high* with respect to the number of partners or the level of their sexual activity, their standard scores also had to be *high* on number of sexual problems and regret over their homosexuality. Thus, the Dysfunctionals tended to have much more regret about being homosexual and many more sexual problems but also more sexual activity with a greater number of partners than the typical respondent. In terms of noncriterion variables, the Dysfunctionals' sexual problems had to do chiefly with concerns that they were not sexually adequate and difficulties in reaching orgasm, finding a suitable sexual partner, and maintaining affection for their partner. Although the Dysfunctionals tended to have more formal education than the typical male respondent, they did not differ from the other respondents in terms of their other demographic characteristics.

V. Asexual

One hundred and ten male respondents were considered relatively "asexual" on the basis of certain standard scores. None could be "coupled," and, compared with the typical respondent, they had to score *low* in level of sexual activity, number of partners, and amount of cruising. In addition, the Asexuals were found to have more sexual problems (their chief complaints pertained to difficulties in finding a partner and to infrequent sexual activity), much lower levels of sexual interest, less extensive sexual repertoires, and more regret over their homosexuality, and to be less exclusively homosexual and more covert than other respondents. They were also less apt to be involved in an affair or to think that they were sexually appealing to other men. Members of this group tended to be older than the other male respondents, and blacks were underrepresented in its membership.

Women

The same methods used in the assignment of the male respondents to a particular group were used in connection with the homosexual women. Although we had no particular interest in creating comparable or even the same number of male and female groups, they happen to be identical in number, are called by the same names, and are directly comparable in most respects. The degree to which they are not exactly comparable represents our interest in classifying as many of the female respondents as possible and in doing justice to whatever is distinctive about their experience of homosexuality.

Two hundred eleven of the lesbians (or three-quarters of the entire homosexual female sample) were assigned to five groups on the basis of their standard scores on the different dimensions of sexual experience (Table 13.6): whether they were "coupled," regret over their homosexuality, number of sexual problems, amount of cruising, and how much sex appeal they thought they had for other females. Like their male counterparts, the females have been classified as (I) Close-Coupled, (II) Open-Coupled, (III) Functional, (IV) Dysfunctional, and (V) Asexual.[3] The exact criteria we used in determining assignment to these types are shown in Table 13.6.

I. Close-Coupled

The eighty-one individuals assigned to this group were all, by definition, "coupled" with another woman, and, compared with the other respondents, their standard scores had to be *low* on number of sexual problems, amount of cruising, and number of partners. Thus, the Close-Coupled homosexual women tended to have few sexual problems (they were particularly unlikely to mention finding a suitable sexual partner, not reaching orgasm, and concerns about one's sexual adequacy). They had fewer partners and did less cruising (and were found to have fewer cruising worries) than the typical female respondent. Persons in this group were also found to have less regret over their homosexuality, to be more sexually active, to have lower levels of sexual interest, to engage in a wider variety of sexual techniques, and to be more exclusively homosexual in their sexual behaviors and feelings than the typical respondent. Finally, the Close-Coupleds did not differ at all from the average female respondent with respect to their demographic characteristics.

II. Open-Coupled

Fifty-one persons, all of them by definition "coupled," were assigned to this particular group. In addition, their standard scores had to be *high* on one or more of the following: number of sexual problems, number of partners, and amount of cruising. In comparison with all of the other female respondents, the Open-Coupleds actually had only somewhat more sexual problems, did a little more cruising, and had a somewhat

[3] The women who could be classified in some way did not differ from those not assigned to a particular subgroup with respect to race, age, education, or occupational level.

greater number of sexual partners. In addition, they were found to be more sexually active, more overt, more exclusively homosexual, to do more worrying in connection with cruising (particularly with regard to exposure), and to have somewhat more regret over their homosexuality and more extensive sexual repertoires than the typical female respondent. They were also more likely to experience difficulty responding to their partner's sexual requests. In terms of their demographic characteristics, the Open-Coupleds tended to be younger than the rest of the females.

III. Functional

Thirty individuals were assigned to this group. By definition none were "coupled," and their standard score on regret over being homosexual had to be *low*. In addition, their standard scores had to be *high* on level of sexual activity and sex appeal, and *low* on number of sexual problems. Thus, the Functional lesbians, compared with all the other members of the sample, had less regret about their homosexuality and fewer sexual problems, were more sexually active, and rated themselves higher on sex appeal. In addition, they were found to cruise more and to have higher levels of sexual interest, more extensive sexual repertoires, and more sexual partners than the typical female respondent. They were also less likely to experience difficulty responding to their partner's sexual requests or to be concerned with their sexual adequacy. There is nothing notable about the demographic characteristics of this particular group.

IV. Dysfunctional

Only sixteen women could be termed "dysfunctional" on the basis of our criteria. By definition none of these persons were "coupled." Their self-ratings on sex appeal had to be *low* but with a *high* frequency of sexual activity. In addition, their standard scores on regret over their homosexuality and their scores on number of sexual problems had to be *high*. Given these criteria, the Dysfunctionals, compared with all of the other lesbians, had much more regret and many more sexual problems and were less likely to believe that they had much sex appeal for other women. With regard to noncriterion variables, they were found to be less exclusively homosexual, to have more sexual partners, to have somewhat higher levels of sexual interest and somewhat more extensive sexual repertoires, and to worry a little more in connection with their cruising activity. They were more likely to experience difficulty reaching orgasm and responding to their partner's sexual requests. Like the Open-Coupleds, and even to a greater degree, the Dysfunctionals tended to be younger than the typical respondent.

V. Asexual

The thirty-three homosexual women assigned to this group were by definition not "coupled." Their standard scores on number of sexual partners, amount of cruising, and level of sexual activity had to be *low*. The female Asexuals were thus less active sexually than the rest of the respondents, had fewer partners, and did less cruising. In addition, they were found to be less often involved in an affair as well as to have more sexual problems (they had special difficulties finding suitable sexual partners and concerns that they were not sexually adequate) and much less extensive sexual repertoires, to be more likely to believe they had little sex appeal to other women, and to be more apt to rate themselves in a bisexual direction on the homosexual-heterosexual continuum. The Asexuals also tended to be older than the sample as a whole.

Overview

It should be noted that we make no claim that the preceding typology exhausts the ways in which homosexual adults can be meaningfully classified or even that our own respondents could only be classified in these particular ways. For example, had we chosen to emphasize respondents' standings on the homosexual-heterosexual continuum, we might have ended up with quite different classifications. Our only claim is that after examining our particular respondents' whereabouts on the many different dimensions of sexual experience, we were able to come up with what appeared to be a sensible and potentially useful typology. There was no question but that our respondents could be distinguished on the basis of their involvement in a quasi marriage (i.e., whether or not they were "coupled") and of their management of that kind of relationship, of the degree to which their homosexuality was problematic, and of the extent to which they were disengaged from the explicitly sexual aspects of gay life. Hopefully our efforts will inspire other investigators to develop typologies of homosexual experience which are at once more comprehensive and discriminating.

Although it is not our intention to establish our typology as definitive in any sense or to draw conclusions from it with regard to homosexual men and women not interviewed in this particular study, several of its aspects do deserve additional comment. For example, it is interesting to note that almost one-quarter of the homosexual men could be considered relatively "asexual." That is, large numbers of them, and perhaps of homosexual men in general, defied the stereotypical notion that all homosexual males are inevitably caught up and chiefly interested in the explicitly sexual aspects of their lives. The fact that more than one-third of the males were either Close-Coupled or Functional and that only one-fifth could be classified as Dysfunctional is also worth noting. It would appear that relatively large numbers of homosexual men manage their homosexuality with little difficulty, while a homosexual way of life is problematic for only a distinct minority. It should also be noted, however, that there were many more Open-Coupleds than Close-Coupleds among the male respondents. This suggests that a monogamous quasi marriage between homosexual men is probably difficult to achieve, and that most such relationships involve the pursuit of sexual contacts with persons other than one's partner.

Among the homosexual women, in contrast to their male counterparts, there were more Close-Coupleds than Open-Coupleds. Indeed, the former group contained more members than any other. These findings confirm our earlier impressions of how homosexual men and women differ in their experience of homosexuality. More women than men are apt to be involved in a quasi marriage marked by a relatively high degree of sexual fidelity. In fact, since so few of the female respondents could be classified as Functional (i.e., not "coupled" but with a good adjustment), it would appear that the most viable option for most lesbians may be that of a fulfilling and relatively monogamous "marital" relationship with another woman. Those not involved in such a relationship may be apt to experience their homosexuality as more problematic on one count or another.[4] This has not been the case for homosexual men.

Finally, it should be noted that the various types of homosexual adults tended to differ from the overall sample on dimensions of sexual experience not used as selection criteria and in other ways that seem to provide for tests of convergent validity—e.g., the Asexual males and females had less extensive sexual repertoires than the rest of the respondents; the male Functionals, highly involved in the sexual aspects of the gay world, were younger than the average respondent; and the Asexuals were older. Differences such as these are encouraging to the extent that they can be understood as additional evidence of the validity of our measurements and selection procedures.

[4] With the advent of the feminist movement, however, this may change.

Part III
Social
Adjustment

The preoccupation clinicians and researchers have had with the sexual aspects of homosexual individuals' lives has often resulted in a disregard of their social circumstances. The truncated picture of homosexuality which emerges for the most part from the literature makes it appear as if a homosexual orientation has to do entirely with genital activity involving persons of the same sex and maintained by an aversion to sexual involvements with those of the opposite sex. Homosexuals' chief gratifications are thought to involve orgasmic release and/or the escape from sexual situations which they view as potentially destructive. Thus, the maintenance of homosexual interests and activity among men or women has been "explained" primarily by the nature of their sexual and intrapsychic motivations.

Only within the last decade has very much attention been given to those social aspects of homosexuals' lives which may profoundly affect and reflect their experience of homosexuality. This attention, given for the most part by sociologists and by some anthropologists, has resulted in the construction of homosexuality as a way of life or "life-style" as much as it is an indication of a sexual affinity for persons of the same sex. According to this view, whatever the reason for the original development of homosexuality in an individual, it is ultimately expressed in a social context the nature of which must be understood if much more is to be learned about the lives of homosexual men and women. We shall extend this view to include an examination of the numerous life-styles found among homosexuals, and how they spend their waking lives going to work, dealing with friends, deciding how to spend their leisure time, etc.

In addition to whatever rewarding activities may be pursued in a social context, homosexual men and women, probably to a degree not found among heterosexuals, must concern themselves with certain malevolent features of their society. They must learn to manage their homosexuality in a way that minimizes the likelihood of their being victimized by a homoerotophobic society which seeks them out for special punishment. Homosexual men, in particular, run the risk of police entrapment and arrest, of blackmail, and of dismissal from their jobs if their sexual orientation is made known to their employers. The special social stress which many homosexual individuals are subject to is obviously another important feature of homosexuals' lives which must be taken into account if their lives are to be more thoroughly understood.

What follows represents an attempt to discover the various social "life-styles" of our homosexual respondents. These include the nature of their work situation and the effect of homosexuality on their careers; their religiousness and the effect of being homosexual on their religious feelings; the nature and extent of their political involvements and how their homosexuality has affected them; their experience with marriage; the number of friends they have, the extent to which their friendships are restricted to persons of the same sex and sexual orientation, and differences in their attitudes toward men and women; the amount of time they spend alone and at home, and the kinds of activities they pursue in their leisure time; and the degree to which they have encountered such social difficulties as arrest, extortion, blackmail, and dismissal from their place of employment.

Work

To the extent that some people equate homosexuality with emotional instability, they may assume that homosexual men and women are likely to have unstable work records. In addition, they may think of homosexuals as less tied down than heterosexuals and thus more likely to leave a job they do not especially like. (Conversely, it could be posited that the lesbian would be less mobile because, unlike her heterosexual counterpart, she cannot rely upon a husband's income and must make do in a work situation which a heterosexual woman might not tolerate.) The notion that homosexuals are likely to move from job to job is supported further by the impression that they are likely to be fired if their homosexuality becomes known. In this view, homosexuals are seen as always "on the run," never secure in their employment and even resigning if they feel that otherwise they will soon be fired. Such a view, of course, emphasizes the risk of being homosexual in a society like ours and includes the expectation that homosexuals are likely to be in a particularly disadvantageous position with respect to their work and their employability.

With regard to how stable homosexual men's and women's work histories are likely to be, the evidence is not at all clear-cut. One investigator found that the employment records of homosexual men were no less stable than those of their heterosexual counterparts (Liddicoat, 1956). In another study, however, homosexual men were found to have held more full-time jobs, and to have been fired more often, than were the heterosexual men with whom they were compared (Saghir & Robins, 1973). Interestingly, relatively few of those who had been fired reported that it had something to do with their homosexuality. These investigators also found greater job instability among lesbians than among heterosexual women, a finding shared by Kenyon (1968a). These data, however, do not agree with those of Simon and Gagnon (1967), who reported that lesbians are more seriously committed to work than other women are and tend to have relatively stable work histories.

As to the effect of being homosexual on other aspects of one's working life, it has been reported by Freedman (1967) that lesbians are apt to be *more* satisfied with their work than are heterosexual women. In another study, about two-thirds of the homosexual men reported that their homosexuality had little to do with their occupational choice and that it was not a disruptive influence on their work performance (Westwood, 1960). In a study of lesbians, many stated that their employers knew about their homosexuality and considered it an advantage in the belief that homosexual women, compared with heterosexuals, would be more dependent on their income and better able to adapt to such unusual working conditions as split shifts and travel (Bass-Hass, 1968). Seventy percent of the homosexual men in Weinberg and Williams's study (1974, 1975a) reported few or no job problems arising from others' knowing or suspecting that they were homosexual. Wolff (1971), however, reported that significantly more of the lesbians than of the heterosexual controls in her sample had difficulties relating to their colleagues, a function of many lesbians' need to keep their homosexuality a secret.

In the present study we determined the number of job changes our homosexual and heterosexual respondents had made in the past five years. We also ascertained their satisfaction or dissatisfaction with various aspects of their present jobs. Finally, the homosexual respondents were asked how they thought their homosexuality had affected their careers.[1]

---

[1] Ethnographic descriptions of our homosexual respondents' working situations can be found in Appendix A, pages 245–247.

Findings: Men

Job Stability

Almost half of the white homosexual males (WHMs), compared with about a quarter of the black homosexual males (BHMs), had not changed employment at all in the last five years. Less than a third of the WHMs and almost half of the BHMs had had one or two job changes during that period (Table 14.1). The homosexual subgroups did not differ significantly on these measures of work adjustment. In addition, the homosexual and the heterosexual men did not differ with regard to how many job changes they had made during the past five years.

Job Satisfaction

The majority of the homosexual men were, on the whole, reasonably satisfied with various aspects of their job situation, i.e., the kind of work they did, their co-workers, their employers, opportunities for advancement, and the amount of money they were making (Table 14.2). The members of the various homosexual subgroups did not differ in how satisfying their jobs were to them; however, the homosexual men as a whole were more satisfied with their jobs than were the heterosexual men.

Effect of Homosexuality on Career

More than three-fifths of the homosexual male respondents believed that their homosexuality had had no particular effect upon their careers (Table 14.3). However, about a quarter of the WHMs thought that it had had a harmful effect, while 11 percent believed that it had actually been helpful to them in some way. It is interesting to note that the BHMs more often said their homosexuality had been helpful rather than harmful and were significantly less likely than the whites to say it had been harmful. In terms of our homosexual typology, the Dysfunctionals were more likely to report that their homosexuality had had some negative effect upon their careers, while the Close-Coupleds were least apt to think so.

Some said they had lost or almost lost their jobs because of their homosexuality (Table 14.4):

The other people used to abuse me because of it. Finally I got tired of pussyfooting around and complained about it; and they told me I was through.

On my last job, I was told I'd be rehired after the layoffs, and then when I got a blackmail call at work they told me I was terminated.

My arrest record caused my California teacher's license to be rescinded. I'm not allowed to teach in public schools in California because of it.

I went to prison. Because of the stigma of the sex charge and the prison record, my whole background as a good worker was wiped out. I had a very good job but the company wouldn't tolerate my coming back.

I was working for the Coast Guard as a civilian. They found out I was gay and terminated me.

Others felt that their homosexuality had restricted their vocational options or impeded their advancement:

My whole goals are affected. I have to choose a kind of job where I won't be discriminated against.

Because I'm gay, others on the job discriminate against me. I remain second-best on the job though I'm obviously the best worker. I was given a lower position with less pay than another person on the same job.

In my firm, the employers are skeptical about giving people who are unmarried a good deal of responsibility, since anyone who's unmarried and over thirty-five is suspected of being homosexual, and they consider a homosexual emotionally unstable and unbalanced.

I shy away from people who homosexuality might make a difference to. So it limits the professions I might choose.

Others mentioned the fact that, as homosexuals, they had experienced fears and tension which interfered with their job performance:

I was a clergyman before I got this job. If I had been caught, it would have been disastrous. So I was constantly aware of having to hide my homosexuality.

I just feel paranoid. Because of my arrest record for homosexuality—I'm nervous and fearful of being found out.

It can't help but be harmful. There are times, always, when you have to be on your guard, even though I've never felt personally that anybody had any question about me. Like when straight guys would discuss their sex exploits, I had to keep quiet and felt uncomfortable.

Because of the way society looks at homosexuality, you have to hide it. It puts added pressure on you. It's hard to find the kind of job where you're not shackled by having to keep up a heterosexual image.

Some, however, thought that their homosexuality particularly qualified them for their work:

The floral company's acceptance and understanding of homosexuality—they prefer to hire gays because of their benevolent attitude.

There is a number of gays in this field [interior decorating], and it makes things easier in terms of the rest of society. They kind of expect it.

My homosexuality has assisted my creativity. I'm more aware of things and more sensitive to others' feelings and distresses.

The people I work with are homosexual. Women usually expect a hairdresser to be homosexual. They aren't threatened by it.

Still others, especially those in the black group, thought that their homosexuality and/or their contacts with other homosexuals had been helpful in their careers, regardless of their original qualifications:

I'm myself in my business and have a large homosexual clientele. It has freed me from having to do business in a conventional way.

Most people in display are queer. It's been easier at times to get ahead because I am homosexual.

I think it has helped me to advance on my present job because of the association with my supervisors and co-workers, who are also homosexual.

Summary

The homosexual men did not show evidence of greater job instability than did their heterosexual counterparts. The black homosexual males tended to report more job changes in the past five years than the white homosexual males, but the homosexual men in general did not differ from the heterosexuals in this regard. In terms of job satisfaction, the homosexual men actually tended to like their jobs better than the heterosexual men did theirs.

When asked whether and in what ways being homosexual had affected their careers, the majority of both the white and the black homosexual males said it had had no effect at all. The white men, however, were more likely than the blacks to describe a negative effect, such as having been fired or feeling their opportunities were restricted. The black respondents more often mentioned a positive effect, e.g., that other homosexuals in their place of work had helped them to advance in their careers.

Findings: Women

Job Stability

Two-thirds of the white homosexual females (WHFs) and three-quarters of their black counterparts (BHFs) had changed jobs no more than twice, if at all, during the last five years (Table 14.1). The homosexual women tended to report more job changes than did the heterosexual women. There were no differences among the homosexual subgroups in terms of job stability.

Job Satisfaction[2]

The black homosexual women tended to be less satisfied with their jobs than their white counterparts (Table 14.2). One-quarter of the WHFs, compared with two-fifths of the BHFs, reported relatively low job satisfaction. The homosexual subgroups did not differ significantly on this variable, nor did the homosexual and the heterosexual women in general.

Effect of Homosexuality on Career

More than three-quarters of the homosexual women said that their homosexuality had not had any particular effect upon their careers (Table 14.3). Of the WHFs who thought that their homosexuality had affected their careers in some way, twice as many thought that it had been harmful as that it had been helpful. Only a few of the BHFs believed that their careers had been either harmed or helped by their homosexuality.

[2] For a fuller description of this composite measure, see page 143.

Some of the women mentioned the fact that they had lost or almost lost their jobs when their homosexuality became known to their employer (Table 14.4):

I became involved with a patient who needed help. I thought I could give her comfort and understanding. But in the course of it, I revealed my homosexuality. She told my boss and they called for my resignation. I should have known better.

If they find out that you're homosexual, they fire you. That happened to me in New York.

Others talked about the fears and tensions their homosexuality caused and how their job performance was adversely affected:

I've had chronic, severe anxiety—to the point of being incapacitated on the job. It is still difficult. I can't work under tension or stress. It's the loneliness, the feelings of guilt, fear of rejection.

Still others felt that there was something about their being homosexual that made them especially qualified for the work they did:

It's given me a better understanding of people, especially the ones I work for. Having a problem myself, I am able to see others' problems more clearly.

Because I work with people, people who have experienced one or another form of societal rejection due to one form or another of deviant behavior. It's given me a certain sympathetic sense.

The Foundation wanted to hire a gay person to coordinate the task force. I would never have my present job if I were not a lesbian.

Summary

The homosexual women tended to report more job changes than did those in the heterosexual group. They did not differ, however, in terms of job satisfaction. More than three-quarters of the lesbians thought that their homosexuality had had no particular effect on their careers, either positive or negative.

The most striking feature of our data about homosexual male respondents' working lives seems to be that they refute the popular notions about homosexual men shifting from job to job as their sexual orientation becomes (or threatens to become) known, or being forced on account of it to stay in an unpleasant, perhaps poorly paid position. They reported work histories fully as stable as the heterosexual men's and described themselves as even more satisfied with their working situations and salaries. Many of them said that being homosexual had not particularly affected their careers, but some felt pressure in this regard or thought that their homosexuality had restricted their job opportunities. On the other hand, a small number reported that being homosexual was advantageous to them in getting a job or furthering their careers; this was especially true among the blacks. Thus, it appears that while some homosexual men pay vocational penalties for their sexual preference, a sizable number do not.

The picture is less clear with respect to the homosexual women. The lesbians in our samples changed jobs more often than did the heterosexual women, although they did not differ in how satisfied they were with their current jobs, and the great majority of them said that their homosexuality had had no special effect on their careers. We did not ask our female respondents to what extent their status as women had affected their careers, but it is possible that the lesbians, already sensitive to possible discrimination based on their sexual preference, might also have been more sensitive to discrimination based on their gender than the heterosexual women were. On the other hand, it could be that the homosexual women's greater number of job changes reflects more personal ambition on their part and a consequently greater effort to improve their working circumstances. Perhaps, given the rise of the feminist movement since our data were collected, we would find less of a difference between the lesbians and the heterosexual women if we interviewed them today. In any case, it appears that for the majority of our homosexual respondents, male and female, the fact that they happened to be homosexual had little to do with their experiences at work or the satisfaction they derived from them.

Religiousness

Numerous writers, reviewing traditional Judeo-Christian attitudes toward homosexuality, believe that organized religion is largely responsible both for the heterosexual majority's aversion to homosexuality and for feelings of alienation among large numbers of homosexuals (e.g., see Katz, 1967; McNeill, 1976). Most such theorists construe these views as the result of several factors: certain Biblical passages have been unjustifiably interpreted; Old Testament authors were preoccupied with procreative sexuality, anxious to maintain salient distinctions between Jews and pagans; and the influence of Stoic philosophy upon early Christian theology led to the renunciation of sexual passion per se and to regarding any kind of nonreproductive sexuality as irrational, therefore unacceptable.

These recent analyses, by theologians of many religious persuasions, have led some churches to question the merit and the social consequences of their traditional points of view. They have enabled gay activists to stimulate communication among homosexual men and women, lay people, and religious authorities. In a growing number of instances these efforts have led established churches formally to change their policies toward homosexuals. Such changes include condemning discrimination against homosexuals and calling for the decriminalization of homosexuality. Some churches have actively welcomed homosexual members and provided social support for gay liberation groups (cf. Humphreys, 1972, pp. 144–145) and, more recently, have admitted overt homosexuals to the ministry.

In some churches that have resisted changing their views of homosexuality, groups have been formed to sensitize the membership to the plight of the homosexual members in their midst and to help the latter feel more at ease with their own sexuality. Central to such groups' message is the conviction that the motivations and ethics involved in any sexual activity are far more morally important than the nature of the activity itself and that all human beings, regardless of sexual orientation, are responsible for what they intend in what they do. Proponents of this point of view argue that sexual contact involving mutual respect, genuine affection, and an enduring commitment cannot be viewed as morally reprehensible.

Beyond these important theological and political discussions, relatively little is known about the religious proclivities of homosexual men and women. The tendency for homosexual adults to reject organized religion has been noted by several investigators (Schofield, 1965; Kenyon, 1968a; Philipp, 1968; Saghir & Robins, 1973). Two other studies, however, did not find homosexual males to be particularly alienated from formal religion. McGuire (1966) found no differences in religious attitudes between the homosexual and the heterosexual groups in her sample, and Westwood (1960) even found an especial commitment to religion among many of the homosexual males he studied. Almost one-quarter of them attended church regularly, and another 20 percent maintained strong religious beliefs even though they did not go to church.

It appears that homosexual adults who are serious about their religion experience far more conflict over their homosexuality than do those who have renounced their religious background. Gigl (1970) found greater guilt among homosexual males who reported a religious affiliation, and Greenberg (1973b) found that conventionally religious homosexual males, especially those who were Roman Catholic, tended to be markedly low in self-esteem and to feel extremely alienated. Other correlates of homosexual males' religious devotion have been found to include a low commitment to homosexuality, a restricted sexual repertoire, a low degree of social involvement with other homosexuals, and much concern about remaining as covert as possible (Weinberg & Williams, 1974, 1975a).

In this chapter, we compare our respondents in terms of the degree to which they considered themselves conventionally religious and how often they attended church or religious functions. In addition, the homosexual respondents were asked how they felt their homosexuality had affected their religious involvement.

Findings: Men

Religiosity

One-half of the white homosexual males (WHMs)—twice the number of those in the pilot sample—said they were not at all religious in the conventional sense; one-quarter described themselves as "not too religious," and fewer than a quarter of them thought of themselves as either moderately or very religious (Table 15.1). Their black counterparts (BHMs) were much more likely to view themselves as conventionally religious. Less than a third of them said that they were not at all religious, and more than one-third of them viewed themselves as moderately or very religious. The homosexual subgroups did not differ significantly on this variable, and the homosexual men did not differ from the heterosexual respondents in how religious they considered themselves.

Church Attendance

While the majority of both races had not gone to church at all during the three months just prior to the interview, twice as many of the BHMs as WHMs reported that they had attended church at least a few times a month during that period (Table 15.2). The pilot study males reported somewhat higher frequencies of church attendance than did the WHMs. The Open-Coupleds attended church less often and the Asexuals more often than the other subgroups, and the homosexual men as a whole had attended church less frequently during the past three months than had the heterosexual men.

Effect of Homosexuality on Religious Feelings

About half of the homosexual males said that their homosexuality had not affected their religiousness in any way, but about a third of them reported that the fact that they were homosexual tended to weaken their religious feelings. Significantly more whites than blacks reported this effect (Table 15.3); fewer of the pilot study males said their religiosity had been weakened.

Summary

The black homosexual men defined themselves as conventionally religious much more often than their white counterparts did. They were also more likely than the whites to have attended church recently. The homosexual respondents had gone to church less often than the heterosexual men. With respect to the effect of homosexuality on their religiousness, the black and the white homosexual males were most apt to say that being homosexual had not affected their religious feelings at all, although more whites than blacks said it had tended to weaken these feelings.

Findings: Women

Religiosity

A majority of the white homosexual females (WHFs) but only about a quarter of the black lesbians (BHFs) reported that they were not at all religious in the conventional sense (Table 15.1). Similarly, less than a fifth of the WHFs, compared with more than a third of the BHFs, thought that they were either moderately or very religious. Compared with the homosexual women, many more of the heterosexuals considered themselves to be conventionally religious. There were no differences among the homosexual subgroups in this respect.

Church Attendance

The black and the white homosexual females differed much less with respect to how often they had attended church during the three months before the interview. Close to three-quarters of them had not gone to church at all. Only a fifth of the BHFs (and significantly fewer WHFs) had gone as often as a few times per month during that period (Table 15.2). Among the homosexual subgroups, the Functionals were the least frequent church attenders. Except for the Dysfunctionals, the homosexual women attended church much less frequently than those in the heterosexual group. More than twice as many of the heterosexual women attended church on a somewhat regular basis.

Effect of Homosexuality on Religious Feelings

About two-thirds of the homosexual women said that their homosexuality had neither weakened nor strengthened their religiousness (Table

15.3). However, about a quarter of the WHFs and exactly one-third of the BHFs reported that their homosexuality had tended to weaken whatever religious feelings they had had.

Summary

More of the black homosexual women than of the whites described themselves as religious in the conventional sense. The heterosexual women of either race, however, were much more likely than their homosexual counterparts to report this about themselves. The great majority of the lesbians, black and white, were not even infrequent churchgoers, while more of the heterosexual women said they attended church with some regularity. The homosexual women tended to believe that being homosexual had not affected their religious feelings in any way, although some said they were less religious because of it.

Overview

These data confirm to a limited extent others' findings and impressions that homosexual adults tend to be more alienated from formal religion than are heterosexuals. The men in our samples, regardless of sexual orientation, tended not to be conventionally religious. Religiosity and such matters as church attendance are not very characteristic of men in our culture. Nevertheless, while the majority of the homosexual men said that their lack of interest in religion had little to do with the fact that they were homosexual, they did go to church less often than the heterosexuals, and a fairly large minority reported that their homosexual status had weakened their religiousness to some degree.

Clearly, our homosexual female respondents were much less apt to participate in religious activity than were their heterosexual counterparts. It may be that conventional religiosity, an important feature of the traditional female role, is but another aspect of "femininity" that lesbians tend to reject. Among Christians, it is women and children who are most likely to be found occupied with religious matters. Women (and couples) without children are much less likely to carry out religious obligations of various kinds. Thus, lesbians, living apart from such a milieu, would be expected to show less religious conformity than heterosexual women. Homosexual women are not reminded that partners who "pray together, stay together." Instead, they may be sensitive to the patriarchal features of Judeo-Christian religion or to the fact that churches are only beginning to appoint women to responsible positions in their organizations. Like their male counterparts, homosexual women may be disinclined to be conventionally religious, either because of guilt over their homosexuality or of disagreement with theological treatises, or else because their special social circumstances do not encourage the usual forms of religious commitment.

Politics

Little is known about the political affiliations or activity of homosexual men and women. In the past, fears of exposure and victimization required them to keep silent and avoid drawing attention to themselves, so that they seldom tried to alleviate their oppression either through participation or protest. Only within the past decade or so have homosexual men and women begun to make their presence, and their difficulties, known. They have protested at political gatherings and tried to engender political awareness in their largely anonymous membership. Gay activists have publicly endorsed political candidates and exhorted their fellow gays to vote en bloc. At major political party conventions, the issue of homosexuals' civil rights has been raised. Most recently, avowed homosexuals have won election to public office.

As homosexual men and women become less reticent about disclosing their sexual orientation, their effect on politics is likely to grow. Political candidates may actively seek gay support, and major political party platforms may come to include homosexuals' rights and views as they now do those of other (sometimes smaller) disadvantaged groups. In the meantime, however, the extent and nature of homosexuals' political involvement remains unclear. Whether overt homosexuals tend to be politically radicalized, whether those "in the closet" are likely to be more conservative, how one's homosexual (or other minority) status is apt to affect one's political stance, are as yet basically unknown.

The scant empirical data obtained in this area hardly begin to answer such questions. One study has suggested that the highly secretive homosexual man, the so-called "closet queen," is apt to be a political conservative, in fact a "moral crusader" who publicly supports police efforts to intimidate those who engage in homosexual activity (Humphreys, 1970). In another study, homosexual men were found to be more authoritarian than heterosexual men, although their attitudes toward government policies did not significantly differ (McGuire, 1966). Among the men in Saghir and Robins's (1973) samples, most—homosexual or heterosexual—who claimed political affiliation were Democrats, and only a slightly larger number of heterosexuals than homosexuals described themselves as politically conservative. Both the homosexual men and women in this study were more likely to belong to a political party than were their heterosexual counterparts.

In the present study our respondents have been compared with respect to their political party affiliations, how they classified themselves on the politically conservative-liberal continuum, the extent of their political involvement, and, in the case of the homosexual respondents, how their homosexuality had affected them politically.

Findings: Men

Political Affiliation

Slightly less than half of the homosexual men said they were political Independents (Table 16.1). About half of the blacks (BHMs), compared with about a third of the whites (WHMs), thought of themselves as Democrats, while more of the WHMs than of their black counterparts were Republicans. The white heterosexual men (WHTMs) could not be distinguished from their homosexual counterparts on the basis of their political affiliation. Among the blacks, however, fewer of the heterosexual men (BHTMs) than BHMs claimed to be Independents.

The Liberal-Conservative Continuum

Most of the homosexual men considered themselves politically liberal or radical (Table 16.2). Compared with the heterosexual men, those in the homosexual group were significantly more liberal. The homosexual subgroups did not differ among one another on this measure.

Political Involvement

Our composite measure of political involvement included how often respondents said they kept up with political affairs through magazines, newspapers, or television; how often they voted in local elections; and how much they participated in such political activities as campaigns and rallies. Approximately 40 percent of both the WHMs and the BHMs scored moderate on this measure. The homosexual and the heterosexual men did not differ in this regard. The homosexual subgroups also could not be distinguished with respect to the extent of their political involvement (Table 16.3).

Effect of Homosexuality on Political Stance

When asked in what way their homosexuality had affected them politically, a majority of the WHMs and significantly more BHMs reported that their attitudes or involvement had not been affected at all (Table 16.4). About a third of the WHMs said that the fact that they were homosexual had made them more politically liberal (Table 16.5). None of the BHMs reported this about themselves; in fact, some of them thought that they had become *less* liberal. Only about one-fifth of the WHMs and an even smaller number of the BHMs specifically mentioned having less confidence in the present political system as a result of their homosexual status (Table 16.6). A few of the respondents said that their being homosexual had made them more politically active (Table 16.7).

Summary

In giving their political affiliations, both the heterosexual and the homosexual white male respondents were most likely to describe themselves as Independents and least likely to say that they were Republicans. Among the blacks, both the homosexual and the heterosexual men were most apt to identify themselves as Democrats, and more of the former group than the latter said they were Independents. Most of the homosexual men said that they were either liberal or radical in their politics, with the heterosexuals tending to be slightly more conservative. On a composite measure assessing the extent of their involvement in politics, the homosexual and the heterosexual men did not differ.

With respect to how being homosexual had affected them politically, the homosexual men of both races were most likely to say that it had not affected them at all in this way. Some of the white homosexual males said that because of their homosexuality they were more politically liberal than formerly, but a few of the blacks said it had made them less liberal. Small numbers thought that their homosexual status had led them to have less confidence in the present political system or to be more active in politics.

Findings: Women

Political Affiliation

About half of the homosexual women, black (BHFs) or white (WHFs), considered themselves Democrats (Table 16.1). Approximately one-third of them claimed to be political Independents; like their male counterparts, relatively few were Republicans. The WHFs, compared with the white heterosexual women (WHTFs), were less apt to be Republicans, while twice as many of the BHFs as of their heterosexual counterparts (BHTFs) were Independents.

The Liberal-Conservative Continuum

The majority of the homosexual women placed themselves at the liberal end of the liberal-conservative continuum (Table 16.2). The homosexual subgroups did not differ from one another on this variable. Compared with the homosexual women as a whole, the heterosexual women were significantly more conservative politically.

Political Involvement [1]

Neither the homosexual subgroups nor the homosexual and the heterosexual women as a whole differed on the composite measure used to assess the degree of their political involvement (Table 16.3). About one-third of all the female respondents indicated a moderate degree of political involvement.

Effect of Homosexuality on Political Stance

Most of the homosexual women said that their homosexuality had not affected them politically in any way (Table 16.4). A few of the WHFs said that their homosexual status had made them less liberal politically, but almost the same number of BHFs had become *more* liberal (Table

[1] For a fuller description of this composite measure, see page 157.

16.5). Only a small number mentioned the fact that their homosexuality had made them less confident in the present political system (Table 16.6) or that they had become more active politically as a result of their homosexuality (Table 16.7).

Summary

About half of the female respondents (white or black) were Democrats, and another third identified themselves as Independents. Compared with their heterosexual counterparts, the white homosexual females were less likely to say they were Republicans, and the black homosexual females were more likely to be Independents. The lesbians of both races were much more likely to describe themselves as politically liberal or radical than were the heterosexual women. In terms of their involvement in politics, however, the homosexual and the heterosexual women did not differ.

The homosexual women were not likely to believe that being homosexual had affected them politically. A few of the white lesbians thought that they were less liberal as a result, but about as many of the blacks thought they were more liberal. Hardly any thought they now had less confidence in the present political system, or had become more active in politics, because of their homosexuality.

Overview

These data indicate that political matters are of no more importance or interest to homosexual men and women than they are to their heterosexual counterparts. That so many of our homosexual respondents reported that being homosexual had hardly affected their political outlook or activity may simply reflect the fact that the gay activist movement had barely got off the ground at that time. On the other hand, these data may be but further evidence that American men and women, regardless of whether they describe themselves as liberal, or of the extent to which they are aware of oppressive features in their environment, are not inclined to seek political solutions. Recent voting statistics would seem to bear this out. The homosexual man or woman who lives in San Francisco may find his or her circumstances favorable enough that further amelioration takes low priority. In addition, our other data indicate that few of our homosexual respondents (especially the women) had ever suffered negative social consequences as a result of their homosexuality, and this may account for the political moderation we find among them.

Marriage

Several investigations have found that approximately 20 percent of homosexual men and even more lesbians have been married at least once (Curran & Parr, 1957; Parr, 1957; Saghir & Robins, 1973). The actual incidence of heterosexual marriage among homosexual men and women is, of course, impossible to determine because investigators' samples are probably not representative and presently married homosexuals are probably less likely to participate in such surveys. In this regard, Weinberg and Williams (1974, 1975a), for example, found that the homosexual men in their sample who were currently married tended to be the most covert, the most worried about having their homosexuality exposed, and less integrated into the gay world than their unmarried counterparts.

Although how many homosexual men and women ever marry may never be known, the literature shows that marriages between homosexuals and persons of the opposite sex, while not commonplace, are neither extremely unusual. Several studies have suggested a number of reasons for this phenomenon, including a desire to conceal one's true sexual orientation, to test one's heterosexual sexual responsiveness, and to deny one's homosexuality to oneself or, more actively, to vanquish homosexual impulses. Such a marriage, it has been thought, may also reflect accommodation to social pressures, flight from an intolerable parental relationship, disappointment with homosexual lovers together with a desire for a more stable and permanent relationship, and, of course, a genuine affection for one's spouse and/or the desire for children (Cory, 1951; Westwood, 1960; Dank, 1972; Ross, 1972).

Whatever the reasons, it has been found that marriages between homosexuals and heterosexuals (marriages between homosexual men and homosexual women are rarely reported) are apt to be unhappy and relatively short-lived. Some writers have pointed to the strain involved in having to conceal one's homosexuality from one's spouse (Cory, 1951; Allen, 1961b). Ross (1972) reported that such marriages are likely to be troubled with sexual problems such as aversion or indifference toward sex with one's spouse, inability to function sexually in a heterosexual context, and guilt or jealousy over homosexual involvements outside the marriage. Philipp (1968) suggested that most such marriages are apt to become increasingly platonic to such a degree that other, nonsexual, satisfactions in the relationship are insufficient to sustain it. Almost all such marriages have been found to end in separation or divorce, with the marriages of homosexual men tending to be of shorter duration than those of lesbians (Saghir & Robins, 1973). The spouse originally ignorant of the partner's homosexuality may learn about it and find it intolerable. The spouse who had some idea prior to the marriage that the partner was homosexual may finally conclude that he or she can neither change nor compete with these circumstances. The spouse who originally welcomed the partner's lack of sexual aggressiveness, perhaps because of his or her own sexual inhibitions, may come to want more sexual fulfillment than the partner can provide. Within three or four years, and not infrequently after the birth of one or more children, such "odd couples" (Ross, 1972) are apt to split up.

The data ascertained in the present study include the incidence of heterosexual marriage among our respondents and the number of times they were ever married. Since almost all of those ever married were married only once, further information is limited to their first marriage. This includes how old they were when they first married, how happy the marriage was, and how long it lasted. In addition, coital frequency during the first and the last year of the marriage, and the number of children in the marriage, were ascertained. The homosexual respondents were also asked about their fantasies during coitus, whether they told their spouse about their homosexuality prior to the marriage, and, if so, what they told their spouse they would do about it. Those with children aged twelve or older were asked whether the children knew about the respondent's homosexuality, how they had found out about it, how they reacted, and what effect this had on their relationship with the respondent.

Findings: Men

Incidence of Marriage

One-fifth of the white homosexual men (WHMs) and a slightly smaller number of their black counterparts (BHMs) had been married at some time (Table 17.1); the various homosexual subgroups did not differ in this regard. The number of WHMs ever married is about the same as that of the pilot study men and only slightly higher than the number of homosexual men in other samples who had ever been married (Saghir & Robins: 18%; Weinberg & Williams: 17%; *Ladder:* 15%; Manosevitz: 12%). Not surprisingly, many more of the heterosexual men had been married at least once in their lives. The vast majority of those in each sample who had ever been married had been married only once (Table 17.2), and the number of persons who were married more than once is so small that the analysis which follows pertains only to the respondents' first marriages.

Nature of the First Marriage

The homosexual men were, on the average, 24 years old when they were married the first time. Of the subgroups, the Close-Coupleds were the youngest and the Asexuals the oldest at the time of their first marriage. As a whole, the homosexual men did not differ from the heterosexual men in this regard, but both the Close- and the Open-Coupleds were significantly younger than the heterosexual men when they were first married (Table 17.3). The largest number of the homosexual men who had ever been married believed that their (first) marriage had been "moderately happy" (Table 17.4). There were no differences among the homosexual subgroups, but the homosexual men as a whole rated their first marriages as less happy than did the heterosexual men.

Sex During the First Marriage

Of those who had ever been married, about a third of the WHMs and half of the BHMs had intercourse or "sexual relations" two to four times per week during the first year of their marriage (Table 17.5). During the last year of their first marriage, almost half of the WHMs and about a fifth of the BHMs were having sexual relations less than once a month. About one-quarter of the homosexual men, however, had sex with their wives twice a week or more during the last year of their marriage (Table 17.6). There were no differences among the homosexual subgroups in terms of coital frequency during either the first or the last year of the first marriage. The heterosexual men, however, were more active coitally than were their homosexual counterparts during both the first and the last years of their marriage.

One-third of the WHMs and a fifth of the BHMs said that during sexual relations with their wives, they often fantasized sex with men (Table 17.7), while some 40 percent had done so on occasion. Another third, however, had never engaged in homosexual sexual fantasy during coitus. The homosexual subgroups did not differ significantly on this item. Less than a third of the homosexual men had told their wives about their homosexuality prior to the marriage (Table 17.8), but of those who did, most did not tell their spouse that they were going to do anything about it after they were married (Table 17.9).

Ending of the First Marriage

More than half of the homosexual males who had ever been married reported that their (first) marriage had lasted three years or longer (Table 17.10). The marriages of the heterosexual men were of longer duration than those of their homosexual counterparts as a whole; there were no differences among the homosexual subgroups in this regard. And although a majority of the white homosexual men said that homosexuality had had something to do with the disruption of their marriage, only about a quarter of the BHMs said that this was the case (Table 17.11). The Asexuals were the least likely of the homosexual subgroups to report this. Of those who reported that homosexuality had something to do with the ending of their marriage, almost half of the WHMs and both of the BHMs concerned said they had become involved with another man (Table 17.12):

I desired to live with another man instead of a woman. I left her because I wanted to live full-time with him, that's all.

I was having more and more homosexual activity, and she assumed that it was frequent. So I decided to go gay and left her for another guy I was having an affair with at the time.

About the ninth year of marriage I discovered that there were many other homosexuals and that a homosexual life was possible. I decided to go this route. I had this lover I had had for about two years.

A smaller number mentioned their lack of interest in sexual contact with their wives as a precipitating factor:

I finally told her, "That's it—no more sex," and she moved out. I just couldn't get over wanting sex with guys more than with her.

We weren't getting along. I wanted to go out [cruise]. My sex life with her wasn't satisfactory.

I wasn't an adequate sexual partner for her. At first it was a novelty for me and I went wild—then I realized it didn't fill the bill for me. I wasn't interested anymore, and she left.

An equally small number said that their wives had found out about their homosexuality and had reacted negatively:

I got discharged from the Air Force for it. She found out, and after that our marriage went downhill.

She caught me having sex with her youngest brother. She didn't want the kids to know, so she just left with them.

After I told her I was homosexual, we bickered and fought. After all kinds of accusations, it finally came to an end.

Children

Half of the WHMs who had ever been married and 71 percent of the BHMs had one or more children from their (first) marriage (Table 17.13). There were no differences among the homosexual subgroups in the number of children they reported having. The heterosexual men had more children than the homosexual men.

Eighteen WHMs had one or two children (either their own, adopted, or stepchildren) twelve years of age or older, who either suspected or definitely knew about their father's homosexuality (Table 17.14). The Open-Coupleds had the greatest number and the Asexuals the smallest number of children who were aware of their father's homosexuality. These children were about equally likely to have learned about this from their father, from their mother, or by figuring it out themselves (Table 17.15); the homosexual subgroups did not differ from one another in this regard. When asked how this had affected their relationship with them, these WHMs claimed that it had not affected it at all and that their children had been tolerant and understanding (Tables 17.16, 17.17):

My daughter is glad I'm having some sex. She's not upset about it at all.

When I told my son about it, it didn't appear to bother him. We are still quite close. It probably doesn't bother him because he's pretty much of a freethinker.

It hasn't affected our relationship one bit. I've been a very good father. I get along well with the two of them. We are really able to communicate.

Summary

About one-fifth of the homosexual male respondents, compared with most of the heterosexual males, had been married at some time in their lives. Most of the males of either sexual orientation had been married only once. The homosexual and the heterosexual men did not differ in how old they were at the time of their first marriage, most being in their mid-twenties, but the heterosexuals more often said their marriages were happy.

The heterosexual men also reported more frequent sexual activity with their wives during the first and last years of their first marriage than did the homosexual men, many of whom had at some time or other fantasized about a male during sex with their wives. The homosexual men tended not to have told their wives about their homosexuality before marriage nor to have promised to do anything about it.

The heterosexual men reported a longer-lasting first marriage than did their homosexual counterparts, although more than half of the latter said it had lasted more than three years. The white homosexual men were more likely than the blacks to say that their homosexuality was involved in the breakup of their first marriage. Those of both races who reported this tended to specify that they had become involved with another man, although some said they were uninterested in or inadequate at sex with their wives or that their wives could not tolerate the respondents' homosexuality.

The homosexual male respondents who had ever been married tended to report that they had had children in their first marriage. Only a few of the whites and none of the blacks reported having children aged twelve or older who suspected or knew of their homosexuality. Those who did have such children tended to say that the parent-child relationship was unaffected by this knowledge.

Incidence of Marriage

More than a third of the white homosexual females (WHFs) and significantly more (almost half) of their black counterparts (BHFs) had been married at least once (Table 17.1). The number of the white lesbians in our sample who had ever been married is only somewhat higher than the numbers reported by Gundlach and Riess (29%), *Ladder* (27%), and Saghir and Robins (25%), but a much larger number than that reported by Kenyon (18%). Of the homosexual subgroups, the Functionals were most likely to have been married. Although the homosexual women were less apt to have been married than were their heterosexual counterparts (WHTFs, BHTFs), they were more likely to have been married than were the homosexual men. Approximately three-quarters of the homosexual women who had ever been married had been married only once; the Functionals were most likely of the subgroups to have been married more than once (Table 17.2). Thus, as in the findings relating to marital experience among the men, the data which follow pertain only to their first (and sometimes current) marriages.

Nature of the First Marriage

The homosexual women who had ever been married were, on the average, twenty-one years old when they were married the first time. There were no differences among the homosexual subgroups in this regard (Table 17.3). The heterosexual women were somewhat older than the lesbians at the time of their first marriage. Among those ever married, the majority of the homosexual women, compared with significantly fewer heterosexuals, rated their marriage as "moderately" or "very" unhappy (Table 17.4).

Sex During the First Marriage

The homosexual women were much less active coitally during both the first and the last years of their marriage than were the heterosexual women (Tables 17.5, 17.6). For example, more than a third of the homosexual women, compared with 18 percent of the WHTFs and 8 percent of the BHTFs, had sexual intercourse less than twice a week during the first year of their marriage. Similarly, eight WHFs and one BHF did not engage in coitus at all during the first year of their marriage, and about a quarter of the lesbians but less than 10 percent of the heterosexual women were not coitally active at all during the last year of their marriage. About half of the homosexual women never or only rarely fantasized sexual relations with women during coitus with their husbands (Table 17.7).

Almost one-half of the WHFs and about a quarter of the BHFs did not consider themselves homosexual prior to their marriage (Table 17.8). Most of the BHFs and nearly half of the WHFs who thought they were homosexual at that time did not tell their husbands about it. Of those whose husbands knew about their homosexuality, most did not tell their spouses what, if anything, they were going to do about it once they were married. Five WHFs had told their husbands that they would no longer engage in homosexual activity, but four WHFs and two BHFs had said that they would continue as before (Table 17.9).

Ending of the First Marriage

About one-half of the WHFs who had ever been married reported that their first marriage had lasted less than three years, as did 30 percent of the black lesbians (Table 17.10). Not surprisingly, the marriages of the homosexual women were of shorter duration than those of their heterosexual counterparts. The majority of the WHFs and slightly fewer of the BHFs said that their homosexuality had been a precipitating factor in the breakup of their first marriage (Table 17.11). Of these, the largest number said that they had become involved with another woman (Table 17.12):

My first lover came back into my life. I had a very strong remembered attraction for her. For no one else would I have left him.

In the two weeks that I lived with him, I got very close to my next-door neighbor. So, I filed for divorce and so did she, and we've been together nine years now.

I wanted to live with this chick that I was having an affair with. My husband and I didn't have anything going.

A smaller number reported that they had become uninterested in sex with their husbands:

I didn't enjoy heterosexual sex. I wanted to find out about my own homosexuality.

I couldn't stand to go to bed with him anymore because it disgusted me.

I was not able to respond to him.

I felt like he wasn't doing nothing but pumping babies in me. I was not satisfied sexually.

Children

Of those who had ever been married, half of the WHFs, compared with significantly more of the BHFs, had one or more children from their first marriage (Table 17.13). There were no significant differences among the subgroups, but the homosexual women as a whole had fewer children than did the heterosexual women. Eighteen WHFs and fourteen BHFs had children (their own, adopted, or stepchildren) who were at least twelve years of age and suspected or definitely knew about their mother's homosexuality (Table 17.14). Most often, they had either surmised it on their own or else the respondents themselves had told them (Table 17.15). In most instances respondents said that these circumstances had had no particular effect upon their relationships with their children (Tables 17.16, 17.17):

It hasn't affected us. We've been fairly close.

Not at all. Being the younger generation and all, she kind of accepts it.

It didn't affect them. We have a real good relationship. They can dig it.

Summary

A fairly large minority of the homosexual female respondents reported having been married at least once, most of them only once. The heterosexual women were much more likely ever to have been married and also tended to report only one marriage. They were likely to be somewhat older than their homosexual counterparts at the time they were first married and to report greater marital happiness.

The homosexual women reported much lower levels of sexual activity with their husbands than did the heterosexual women. The lesbians rarely fantasized during marital sex that their partner was female, although a bare majority of the white homosexual females and three-quarters of the blacks had considered themselves homosexual prior to marriage. Those who did feel this way tended to report that they had not told their husbands about it; among those who did tell them, most had not said they would do anything about it.

The heterosexual women reported longer-lasting marriages than did the lesbians, a fair number of whom said they had been married less than

three years. The lesbians also tended to say that homosexuality was involved in the breakup of their first marriage, many citing an involvement
with another woman, with others reporting a lack of sexual interest in
their husbands.

Among those homosexual women who had ever been married, the
blacks were more likely than the whites to say they had had children in
their first marriage. Those respondents whose children aged twelve or
older knew about their mother's homosexuality tended to report that this
knowledge had not affected their relationships with their children.

Overview

Up until now the most that has been said about marriage on the part of
homosexual men and women is that it is more common than most people
suppose, that the incidence of marriage is higher among lesbians than
among their male counterparts, and that such marriages are usually
short-lived. Our data agree with others' findings of this kind. About one-
quarter of our homosexual respondents had been married at least once in
their lives. More than a third of the homosexual women had been married, compared with fewer than a fifth of their male counterparts. In
addition, most of the black homosexual respondents (male and female)
who had ever been married, and about half of their white counterparts,
had children.

Connected with the higher incidence of marriage among lesbians may
be the fact that, unlike men, women can participate in coitus with little
or no sexual arousal. Thus a woman who finds heterosexual sex uninter-
esting or distasteful may feign arousal or passively accommodate her
partner, whereas a man who feels this way is simply unable to participate. Since more lesbians than homosexual men had ever married, it
seems possible that this difference may have been involved. (Among our
homosexual respondents who had married, however, the women as well
as the men engaged in coitus less frequently than their heterosexual
counterparts during both their first and their last year of marriage.)

It may be that a large number of homosexual men who marry tend to
have a degree of sexual interest in women and that for some of them
marriage may be an important testing ground for their heterosexual potential. Their female counterparts, on the other hand, may be a far less
select group, marrying for no other reason than the fact that social factors encourage it and/or that they do not find a sexual relationship with a
man completely intolerable or impossible. Unlike their male counterparts, a number of our homosexual female respondents were not even

aware of their homosexuality prior to marriage. Only a few had engaged in sexual fantasies about women during sex with their husbands. Apparently, only after their involvement in a marital relationship, one frequently more distasteful to them than to their male counterparts, did a number of the female respondents develop a particular aversion to heterosexual relationships. The fact that, contrary to Saghir and Robins's findings, the lesbians' marriages tended not to last as long as those of the homosexual men coincides with our other data and supports the general impression that while homosexual women are more likely ever to have been married than are homosexual men, their marital experiences may also be much less satisfying.

Finally, it is noteworthy that while homosexual men and women who are parents probably do not go out of their way to inform their older children about their sexual orientation, those few of our respondents whose children did know tended to report that their older children's knowledge or suspicion about their homosexuality had no particular effect upon the relationship they had with them. It may be that children find it difficult to imagine parents, regardless of their sexual orientation, in any sexual context, and that the quality of parent-child relationships is determined early in life, when affectionate contact is the basis of the child's experience of the parent. In addition, these responses may reflect San Francisco's particularly liberal ethos.

Friendships

An important aspect of the social adjustment of homosexual men and women is the number and nature of their friendships. Both individual friendships and a circle of friends or clique can provide them with much-needed emotional support, models of alternative life-styles, new objects of identification, opportunities to meet new sexual partners, and, above all, with the sense that they are not alone in what might otherwise seem a hostile or indifferent world.

There are basically two opposing views of homosexuals' interpersonal contacts. The first emphasizes the negative aspects of their plight in both the gay and the straight worlds. This view sees them as alienated individuals, unhappy in a gay world characterized by sexual competition and mutual hostility, and rejected by the heterosexual majority. Accordingly, the homosexual person would have a very small number of friends, mostly of the same sex and sexual orientation. By contrast, the second view sees the homosexual as a "social butterfly," spending the better part of his or her life in a splendid array of social contacts and cultivating a wide circle of friends (Cotton, 1972). Such a view might presume that homosexuals' friendships are apt to be more heterogeneous than those of the typical heterosexual person and that they are much more likely to include sexual involvement. Lacking the emotional support provided by a family, homosexual men and women might also be thought to need a surrogate family to whom they can turn for meaningful contact in an increasingly depersonalized society and thus to treasure friendships more than heterosexuals would.

Little is actually known about the number and nature of homosexual people's friendships. One study, examining whether homosexual men and women have more or fewer friends than their heterosexual counterparts, reported that the white homosexual men interviewed had significantly more friends than did the heterosexual men; the white lesbians, however, had significantly fewer friends than either the homosexual men or the heterosexual women (Saghir & Robins, 1973). These investigators also found that although most of those in their homosexual samples reported that all their close friends were predominantly homosexual, one-quarter of the men and even more of the women had as many heterosexual as homosexual friends. Other studies have also indicated that homosexual men and women not uncommonly have heterosexual friends (Simon & Gagnon, 1967; Hedblom, 1972). Despite these findings, almost half of the homosexual men and about a quarter of the homosexual women in Saghir and Robins's (1973) sample felt that their homosexuality tended to restrict their social lives somewhat, particularly with regard to having heterosexual friends.

There is evidence that homosexual men can be distinguished on the basis of whether they tend to restrict their interpersonal involvements to other homosexuals. Weinberg and Williams (1974, 1975a) found that those men who were more involved with the straight world were less apt to anticipate rejection and discrimination from heterosexuals, less concerned about their homosexuality being exposed, and less bothered about being labeled homosexual. These investigators also found that respondents who were relatively uninvolved with other homosexual men tended to be less self-accepting, more depressed, more negative about their homosexuality, and more apt to seek psychiatric treatment.

Finally, given the long-held view that homosexual men and women feel indifferent, hostile, fearful, or contemptuous toward members of the opposite sex, it would be commonly supposed that their friendships would be limited to members of the same sex. While research in this area tends to support the notion that homosexual men and women are apt to have negative feelings about those of the opposite sex (Wheeler, 1949; Armon, 1958, 1960; Bass-Hass, 1968; Wolff, 1971), it appears that their predominant feeling is one of emotional (and, of course, sexual) indifference (Saghir & Robins, 1973). The degree to which such a feeling induces homosexual men and women to find friends only among their own sex has not, however, been empirically determined.

In the present study we asked our respondents how many good, close friends they had. Such friends were defined as "people [they] could talk to or go to for help about relatively intimate matters." They were then asked to estimate what proportion of their close and fairly good friends were men, and, of these, how many were predominantly or exclusively homosexual. The same questions were asked concerning their female friends.[1] In order to ascertain more fully the reasons for differences in the monosexuality of friendship patterns, we have also compared the respondents' open-ended statements about how their attitudes or feelings toward men and women differed.

Findings: Men

Number of Friends

Most of the white homosexual men (WHMs) had more than five good, close friends, while their black counterparts (BHMs) tended to report no more than four very close friendships (Table 18.1); this difference, however, was not statistically significant. The Chicago pilot study men tended to have somewhat fewer close friends. Only a very small number of the homosexual men in the present study were without the kinds of friends to whom they could talk or go to for help about relatively intimate matters. In fact, they reported having more close friends than did the heterosexuals. Only the Close-Coupleds and the Asexuals could not be distinguished from the heterosexual men on the basis of the total number of close friends they reported having. Among the homosexual subgroups, the Open-Coupleds tended to have the largest number of close friends.

Nature of Friends

About one-quarter of the homosexual men said that all of their friends were men (Table 18.2). An additional two-thirds said that most (but not all) of their friends were men. Among the homosexual subgroups, the Functionals had the highest and the Asexuals the lowest proportion of male friends. All of the homosexual male subgroups, compared with the

---

[1] Ethnographic descriptions of our respondents' friendship groups can be found in Appendix A, pages 247–249.

heterosexual men, tended to report much higher proportions of male friends.

Almost half of the homosexual respondents said that all of their men friends were homosexual (Table 18.3). The Open-Coupleds and the Functionals tended to have the largest number of male friends who were homosexual, while the Asexuals had the lowest proportion of homosexual male friends. Nevertheless, as would be expected, all five of the homosexual subgroups reported higher proportions of male homosexual friends than did the heterosexuals.

Differences in Attitudes Toward Men and Women

When asked to compare their attitudes toward men and women in general, the largest number of homosexual men commented on the fact that they could not look upon women as prospective sexual partners (Table 18.4):

I'm only physically attracted to males.

I can think of men sexually, but I can't think about a woman sexually. I think a man's body is attractive, period. I enjoy women's company but it's for friendship sake only, not for sexual reasons.

To me, men are obviously more attractive. Females are attractive to me too, but not sexually. They look nice and they *are* capable of sexual activity. But they're just attractive as people, not sexually.

The largest number of the heterosexual men said that they did not look upon other *men* in a sexual way:

The natural and normal thing for sex is a woman. Men have no attraction for me.

They're completely the opposite. With a man, I have no sexual attitudes. My feelings about women are that there's always the feminine mystique; there's always something that can stir your imagination.

To meet a woman—there's always a sexual thing underlying. With a man, not so. I don't feel you can have a complete relationship with a woman without having sex.

The homosexual men also said that men possess more desirable psychological characteristics than women do, and interestingly, almost the same number of heterosexual as homosexual men indicated a greater enjoyment of men's company:

I tend to think of women as being demanding and selfish, insincere. They play roles and act out parts a lot of the time. They pretend to be helpless. I think men are much more likely to speak out and say what they like and don't like. (H)

I'm more friendly to men. I can identify better with a man and his feelings. I simply relate better, more easily with men. (H)

I enjoy associating with men almost exclusively. Men are easier to talk to and get along with. (HT)

My friends are men; that's as it should be. I do things with men: cards, sports, and drinking. Those aren't things for women. (HT)

Summary

Both the black and the white homosexual men reported having more good, close friends than the heterosexual men did, and when the total number of friends was considered, the homosexual men had a much greater proportion of male friends and more homosexual friends. With regard to differences they perceived between men and women in general, the homosexual men were most likely to specify that women were not sexually attractive to them, and the heterosexual men to say that they were not sexually interested in other men. The homosexual men also said that males in general have better personalities, and all the male respondents, regardless of sexual orientation, tended to think that other men were more enjoyable to socialize with.

Findings: Women

Number of Friends

A majority of the white homosexual women (WHFs) reported that they had five or more good, close friends, while most of the black lesbians (BHFs) had no more than four close friends to whom they could talk or go to for help about relatively intimate matters; as with the males, however, this difference was not statistically significant (Table 18.1). The homosexual female sample as a whole reported having more such friends than did the heterosexual women. The greater number of close friendships found among the homosexual women is especially evident among the Functionals (who had more friends than any of the other subgroups), the Close-Coupleds, and the Open-Coupleds. The Dysfunctionals and the Asexuals did not differ from the heterosexuals in how many close friends they reported having.

Nature of Friends

Less than a quarter of the homosexual women said that all of their friends were women, although an additional two-thirds of the WHFs and almost that number of BHFs said that most but not all of their friends were of the same sex (Table 18.2). Compared with those of their heterosexual counterparts, the homosexual women's friends were more apt to be women. With respect to their female friendships, one-fourth of the WHFs and about a fifth of the BHFs said that all of their women friends were lesbians (Table 18.3). Among the homosexual subgroups, the Open-Coupleds had the largest percentage of women friends who were homosexual. All of the homosexual subgroups, however, reported a higher proportion of homosexual same-sex friends than did the heterosexual women.

Differences in Attitudes Toward Men and Women

With respect to their attitudes toward men and women in general, many of the homosexual women expressed the belief that women possess more desirable psychological characteristics than men do or that women's company is more enjoyable (Table 18.4):

Men can't get inside you, understand you. They're always proving their maleness, liking football, doing the put-on things, the male role-playing.

Men strike me as being basically more insecure, more self-centered. They aren't as sensitive about your feelings—more manipulative.

Women are more sensitive and gentle. They can give more love and understanding. Men seem more demanding and demand a subordinate role of a woman.

I feel more open and trusting with women than toward men. I feel like it's harder to get close to men; you have to go through more shit to get close to them.

I feel more comfortable with chicks. I tend to socialize more with them. Trouble is, when you get socially interested with guys, they want sex right away.

It is interesting to note that a not inconsiderable number of the heterosexual women spoke in terms of *men* possessing more desirable psychological characteristics or enjoying their company more:

I think men are more patient than women, and they're more stable emotionally on the whole.

I think of men as being strong and women as being silly, stupid, and sort of bitchy, generally.

I find it easier to be with men, more relaxing. I don't feel competitive with men as I do with women. I can admire them more.

I can communicate with men easier, generally. Men are more truthful and my statements with them are less guarded. My relationships with women are more put-on and pretentious.

Some of the lesbians spoke of their disinclination to relate to men in a sexual way:

Males don't turn me on. I find myself at a loss with them.

For me, men exist as people but they don't exist as sexual entities. I even have difficulty remembering their names, even the gay ones. They all seem to look alike. I think this is all largely on a sexual plane.

I'm not interested in the sexual part of males. The problem is that becoming friends with them usually leads up to sexual advances and how do you tell them you're homosexual? Sex isn't Number One with a woman; like, males are usually pretty sex-oriented.

I look at men as friends, and at women as potential sex partners.

A relatively small number of the heterosexual women said that an important difference in their experience of men versus women was the fact that they were not sexually attracted to women:

When I meet a man there's a sexual overtone to it. I act differently in the company of men than with women, I talk differently—it's that sexual awareness at work.

I don't think I'd enjoy having sex with women. With men it's just the opposite. When I'm with a man I want to be close to him. I enjoy being affectionate if I really like him.

I think I'm more apt to think about my reaction to men—I ask myself am I attracted or repelled, but when I meet women I'm less aware of them. I'm more aware of the opposite sex.

Summary

The homosexual women, white and black, tended to have more good, close friends than their heterosexual counterparts did. They also reported a greater proportion of female friends. As might be expected, the heterosexual women had fewer homosexual female friends than the lesbians did. When asked how they felt men and women differed, the female respondents were likely to mention superior psychological characteristics or greater enjoyment of the company of one sex or the other, with the lesbians being likely to prefer women and the heterosexuals to prefer men. Fewer of the women mentioned sexual object choice as the difference between their perceptions of males and of females.

Overview

Certain aspects of our respondents' friendship patterns are worth noting. First, it would appear that homosexual men and women are apt to have more close friends than heterosexuals do. Whether this is because they have a larger range of interpersonal contacts or because of their greater need for an "extended family," which can serve as an important support system in a hostile environment, remains a moot point. The fact that heterosexual men and women are more likely to be involved in family commitments of one kind or another may account for the smaller number of close friends they are likely to have.

Second, our data show that, for obvious reasons, homosexual people are apt to number both homosexuals and heterosexuals among their friends, whereas relatively few heterosexuals have one or more friends of the same sex who they know are homosexual. The fact that there are many more heterosexuals than homosexuals in the general population probably accounts for much of this particular disparity. On the other hand, heterosexuals are less apt to restrict their close friendships to persons of the same sex. The tendency for them not to do so and for homosexual men and women to be more fully engaged with only same-sex persons could be a function of the nature of their sexual attractions. It has been thought that close friendships often include an erotic component which brings life to the relationship and encourages continuing contact. Where that component is missing, for example in homosexual males' contacts with women, very close friendships may sometimes be inhibited.

Finally, the data support the notion that homosexual men and women are likely to have less favorable impressions of people of the opposite sex than do heterosexuals. It is interesting to note that whereas the homosexual women tended to ascribe more favorable characteristics to other women, the reverse was true of their heterosexual counterparts. The latter, as other literature would have predicted, tended to see more positive attributes in men, which would account, of course, for their attraction to men, for their seeking of fulfillment through ongoing relationships with men, and possibly for their accommodation to traditional roles.

Social Activities

In considering how homosexual men and women spend their leisure time, the place that comes most readily to mind is the so-called "gay bar." As the central social institution of the gay world (Hoffman, 1968), the gay bar has been described as a principal meeting place for friends (Cory, 1951), a place of refuge from heterosexual society (Cory & LeRoy, 1963), and a communications center where people can keep up with what is going on in the gay world (Hooker, 1967). While most people tend to emphasize the importance of the gay bar as a place to meet prospective sexual partners, much in the literature indicates that gay bars tend to serve more of a social than a sexual purpose.

The attention given to the place and purpose of the gay bar in the life of homosexual men and women has tended to obscure the many other kinds of social activities they may pursue. Social occasions often take the form of dinner and cocktail parties and the celebration of birthdays or "wedding" anniversaries (Hooker, 1967). Members of a particular clique may spend much of their time visiting each other's houses (Leznoff & Westley, 1956). This is thought to be especially true of middle- and upper-middle-class homosexuals, who tend to avoid public places (Cotton, 1972). In addition, Hedblom's (1972) findings suggest that the nature of homosexuals' social activities may be gender-related as well. Most of the lesbians in his sample reported that their social activities involved attending private parties and group outings which, unlike bar-hopping, were arranged so as to make their homosexuality relatively unapparent.

In the present study we have ascertained the number of evenings during an average week that our homosexual respondents spent at home and how much of their leisure time they spent alone. In addition, they were asked how frequently they went to the theater, concerts, movies, sports events, bars, and baths. We also questioned them about the amount of contact they had with their friends. This included how frequently they ate out at restaurants with friends, went to their friends' houses, and entertained friends at home.[1] Finally, because participation in homophile organizations can be an important social as well as political outlet for an increasing number of homosexual men and women, we asked our respondents whether they belonged to such organizations and, if so, how often they had been involved in organization activities.[2]

Findings: Men

Time Alone

More than half of the white homosexual men (WHMs) and about two-thirds of the blacks (BHMs) said that they spent less than half of their leisure time by themselves (Table 19.1). How much time they reported spending alone depended a great deal on the type of homosexual they happened to be. Not surprisingly, both the Close-Coupleds and the Open-Coupleds spent a relatively small proportion of their leisure time alone, while the Dysfunctionals and the Asexuals tended to spend more time alone.

Time at Home

The majority of the homosexual men said they spent four or five evenings a week at home (Table 19.2). Thus, most stayed at home more often during the week than they went out. Again, this depended on the

[1] Ethnographic descriptions of our respondents' leisure activities can be found in Appendix A, pages 249–263.
[2] Heterosexuals were not queried with regard to their social activities.

subgroup to which they belonged. The Close-Coupleds and the Open-Coupleds spent more evenings at home than either the Functionals or the Dysfunctionals.

Contact with Friends

Only two of the WHMs, and none of the BHMs, had had no contact whatsoever with friends during the past year; i.e., they had not gone to friends' houses, had friends visit them, or eaten out at a restaurant with friends. The Functionals, not surprisingly, tended to score higher on this composite measure (i.e., they had more contact with friends) than members of the other groups; the Asexuals, on the other hand, were the lowest scoring group (Table 19.3).

Entertainment and Sports

A fair amount of the male respondents' leisure-time activity included going to movies, live theater, and concerts (Tables 19.4, 19.5, 19.6). By far the most frequent form of entertainment was going to movies, which virtually all of them had done during the past year. The subgroups did not differ in terms of their attendance at movies or concerts. However, the Functionals had gone to the theater more often, and the Asexuals less often, than the other respondents.

Attending or participating in sports events was not particularly popular among the homosexual men. Most of the WHMs and almost half of the BHMs had not done this at all during the past year (Tables 19.7, 19.8).

Bar Attendance

Almost half of the WHMs, compared with nearly two-thirds of the BHMs, had gone out to bars at least once a week during the past year (Table 19.9). Less than a tenth of the WHMs and none of their black counterparts said they had not gone to a bar even once in the year. Thus, in general, our male respondents frequented bars on a fairly regular basis. Among those in our sample, the Close-Coupleds and the Asexuals went to bars less frequently than either the Functionals or the Dysfunctionals, presumably because they were less interested in the kinds of sexual pursuits that are typically conducted there.

Gay Baths

Gay baths are men's health clubs that provide a setting for impersonal homosexual sex (for a description of the baths, see Weinberg & Williams, 1975b). Our homosexual male respondents went to baths far less often than they did bars. While the whites had gone significantly more often than the blacks, more than a third of the WHMs and almost half of the BHMs had not gone to a gay bath during the past year. Another third of each sample had gone only a few times (Table 19.10). The Dysfunctionals and the Functionals were most apt to have gone to the baths, while, again, the Close-Coupleds and the Asexuals tended to spend less of their time there. The fact that a much larger percentage of the pilot study men (69%) had not gone to the baths is probably due to the smaller number of gay baths in Chicago.

Homophile Organizations

Not many of our male respondents had been very much involved in homophile organizations. About three-quarters of the WHMs and nine-tenths of the BHMs did not belong to such organizations (Table 19.11), and of those who did, most had been involved only once a month or less often (Table 19.12). The Functionals were the most likely of all the subgroups to belong to a homophile organization.

Summary

The majority of the homosexual men, black and white, said that they spent less than half of their leisure time alone and that most of this time was spent at home. They tended to spend a fair amount of their spare time getting together with friends. As regards other entertainments, they were most likely to report having gone to the movies and least likely to have attended or played in sports events.

Special institutions of the homosexual community also accounted for much of our respondents' leisure time away from home. They were particularly likely to have gone to gay bars, with the black homosexual males reporting more frequent visits to the bars than did the whites. On the other hand, the white men were more likely to have gone to gay baths, although far fewer respondents of either race reported having gone to the baths at all. Attendance at homophile organization events was quite rare among the homosexual males, and the majority said they were not even current members of such organizations.

Findings: Women

Time Alone

Almost three-quarters of the white lesbians (WHFs) and more than two-thirds of their black counterparts (BHFs) reported that they spent less than half of their leisure time alone (Table 19.1). The Asexuals were more apt to be alone relatively often, while the Close-Coupleds and the Open-Coupleds tended to spend little of their leisure time by themselves.

Time at Home

The majority of both homosexual female samples spent five or more evenings a week at home (Table 19.2). The Close-Coupleds, Open-Coupleds, and Asexuals were more likely to stay home during the week than were either the Functionals or the Dysfunctionals.

Contact with Friends[3]

The homosexual women tended to have a good bit of contact with their friends during their leisure hours (Table 19.3). The Functionals saw their friends most often and the Asexuals the least.

Entertainment and Sports

The homosexual women were not very involved in other forms of entertainment (Tables 19.4, 19.5, 19.6). They seldom went to concerts or the theater, and the majority went to movies no more than once a month. The BHFs attended concerts more often than the WHFs, but the subgroups could not be distinguished on the basis of how frequently they sought entertainment of these kinds.

Few of the female respondents went to or took part in sporting events, but more of them than of their male counterparts did so (Tables 19.7, 19.8).

Bar Attendance

More than one-third of the lesbian respondents never went to gay bars or went to them only on special occasions (Table 19.9). Another third, however, went to bars at least once a week.

Gay Baths

At the time of our study, there were no gay baths for women in the Bay Area.

[3] This composite measure is described more fully on page 182.

About three-fourths of the WHFs and nine-tenths of the BHFs were not current members of any homophile organizations (Table 19.11). Of those who were, about two-thirds of the WHFs and four-fifths of the BHFs had gone to organization meetings once a month or more. The Functionals attended such meetings more frequently than members of the other subgroups (Table 19.12).

Summary

Most of the lesbian respondents said that they spent less than half of their leisure time alone, and they tended to spend this time at home. A fair amount of their leisure activities involved seeing their friends, and they were less likely to attend outside entertainments such as movies, concerts, or the theater. Not very many reported going to or taking part in sports.

Few homosexual women were involved in gay institutions. Some went to gay bars, but relatively few claimed membership in a homophile organization or had gone to its meetings.

Overview

The nature of homosexuals' social activities and the extent to which they are socially involved clearly depend upon their gender and upon the type of homosexual they happen to be. Our data support others' impressions that lesbians are much less likely than homosexual men to be very much involved with others or in activities outside the home and that, since more of them tend to have an ongoing relationship with a lover and to set up housekeeping with such a partner, they are less apt to spend very much time alone. Thus, the lesbians were significantly more likely than the homosexual men to spend their leisure time at home and to go to movies, the theater, and concerts less often.

Our findings indicate that the "coupled" homosexual men or women spent less of their leisure time alone and more of their time at home. On the other hand, both the Functionals and the Dysfunctionals, male or female, tended to spend less time at home. Among both the male and the female respondents, the Functionals tended to have the most contact with friends and the Asexuals the least. Differences between these two groups in this regard coincide with our other impressions of them. The Functionals, interested in sexual pursuits and having little regret about their homosexuality, would be expected to cultivate a variety of support systems and to be enlivened by their many friendships. The Asexuals, on the other hand, little interested in sexual contact and relatively withdrawn from the gay world, would be expected not to display much interpersonal involvement.

Among the men, our typology is useful in considering how often homosexual men frequent gay bars and baths. Not surprisingly, the Close-Coupleds and the Asexuals spent less of their time in bars or baths than did the Functionals or the Dysfunctionals. These locales, often termed "sexual marketplaces," are obviously of greater importance to persons in the latter groups. In the area of social activities, then, the typology is useful in helping to specify the diversity of life-styles among our homosexual respondents.

Social Difficulties

In all but nineteen states[1] homosexual activity, even between consenting adults in private, is considered a criminal offense.[2] And even where homosexual activity between consenting adults is not legally proscribed, homosexual men in particular are subject to considerable police harassment. Police frequently hold the conventionally punitive attitude toward homosexuality and have been known to arrest people they suspect of homosexual sexual interests on such grounds as loitering, disorderly conduct, or solicitation. In any number of instances, they have spied upon homosexual persons in various cruising locales or in places where homosexual activity is apt to take place, and even police entrapment is not uncommon.

Abolishing laws against homosexuality may do little to ameliorate so-

[1] As of November 1977.
[2] For a relatively detailed overview of this topic, see "Homosexuality and the Law," pp. 454–499 in Martin S. Weinberg and Alan P. Bell, eds., *Homosexuality: An Annotated Bibliography* (New York: Harper & Row, 1972).

ciety's hostility toward homosexuals (Gagnon & Simon, 1968); but as long as these laws remain on the books, homosexuals will remain vulnerable to many kinds of social oppression. Besides the continual threat of arrest, they sometimes suffer extortion and blackmail by police, by persons posing as police, by hostile sexual partners, or by a disenchanted friend. Since such persons threaten to expose their victim's homosexuality if their demands are not met, more often than not the victims will not turn to the police for help when this happens, lest they themselves be arrested or their sexual orientation become known after all. Understandably, they fear publicity at least as much as whatever legal penalties might ensue. In a homoerotophobic society such as ours, many persons feel free to rob or assault homosexuals, knowing that their victims are not likely to press charges and even feeling that they are getting just what they deserve.

Given all of these circumstances, there are probably many people who suppose that homosexuality inevitably includes social disaster and who wonder why, in such perilous circumstances, people would persist in homosexual pursuits. Even the efforts of well-meaning gay activists, rightly pointing out the extent of these kinds of oppression, may contribute to the notion that a homosexual life-style is generally masochistic. At the same time, the great majority of the homosexual men in various study samples had never been arrested on account of their homosexuality (Westwood, 1960; Dean, 1967b; Kepner, 1971; Saghir & Robins, 1973), blackmailed (Curran & Parr, 1957; Westwood, 1960; Kepner, 1971; Saghir & Robins, 1973), robbed or assaulted (Westwood, 1960; Kepner, 1971; Saghir & Robins, 1973).

Whether a homosexual adult is ever victimized seems to depend on several factors. For example, the literature clearly demonstrates that lesbians are much less likely than homosexual men to encounter such difficulties. In one study it was found that the homosexual men who had been convicted for homosexual offenses were apt to have lower educational and socioeconomic levels than those who had never been convicted (Schofield, 1965). This study also reported that those who had been convicted of a homosexual offense were more likely to have been bisexual, to have had more sexual partners, and to have sought sexual partners in public places. Another study found that those who had paid or been paid for sex were more likely to have been arrested at some time (Saghir & Robins, 1973). Finally, two investigations found more victimization among those who had ever received psychiatric treatment (Kepner, 1971; Weinberg & Williams, 1974, 1975a).

In this chapter we consider the incidence and nature of respondents' arrests, whether they were ever booked or convicted, and if so, whether homosexuality was involved. We also examine respondents' experience of police extortion, blackmail, and being rolled or robbed.

Findings: Men

Arrests

About half of the white homosexual men (WHMs) and a third of the blacks (BHMs) had been arrested or picked up by the police, for other than traffic offenses, at least once (Table 20.1). Fewer of the Chicago pilot study men reported this, but they were asked only about actual arrest, not less formal pickups as well. Among the heterosexual men, less than a third of the whites but almost half of the blacks had been arrested or picked up. The Dysfunctionals were more likely ever to have had this experience than were any of the other homosexual subgroups, and they were the only subgroup to differ in this way from the heterosexuals.

In terms of how many times they had been arrested or picked up, the Functionals reported more arrests than the other subgroups. However, the homosexual men did not differ from the heterosexual men in this regard, either as a whole or among the various subgroups (Table 20.2).

Fewer than one-third of the WHMs and about one-tenth of the BHMs reported having been arrested in connection with their homosexuality (Table 20.3); this experience was most common among the Functionals. Our WHMs are similar to the pilot study and the Weinberg and Williams males in this respect, while somewhat more of the homosexual men in Saghir and Robin's sample had been arrested for such offenses.

Two-fifths of the WHMs and about a quarter of the BHMs had ever been booked by the police (Table 20.4). The Dysfunctionals were the most likely to have been booked and were the only subgroup to differ from the heterosexuals on this measure. Bookings related to their homosexuality were reported by 24 percent of the WHMs and 10 percent of the BHMs, most often by the Functionals (Table 20.5). With regard to convictions for any kind of offense (Table 20.6), the Dysfunctionals were more likely than the other homosexuals to report ever having been convicted, and the homosexual men as a whole reported it more often than the heterosexual men did. Convictions specifically related to their homosexuality were relatively uncommon among the homosexual men, but this had happened more often to the Functionals (Table 20.7).

Extortion

Less than a tenth of the homosexual respondents had ever had to make payoffs to police (or people impersonating police) who had threatened to arrest them on account of their homosexuality or to reveal it publicly (Table 20.8). Police extortion thus appears to be rare in the gay world, although more of the Dysfunctionals reported this experience than did members of the other groups.

Assault and Robbery

In contrast to their reports of police extortion, more than a third of the WHMs and about a fifth of the BHMs said they had been rolled or robbed at least once in connection with their homosexuality (Table 20.9). One-third of those in the pilot sample also reported this experience. Among the men in the present sample, the Dysfunctionals were most apt ever to have been rolled or robbed and the Close-Coupleds the least so.

Blackmail

About a seventh of the homosexual men said that at one time, someone (other than police) had threatened to expose their homosexuality in order to get something from them (Table 20.10). Interestingly, the Close-Coupleds had been "blackmailed" more often than any other group. Among the men who reported this experience, the largest number said that the blackmailer had wanted money or material goods from them (Table 20.11):

He wanted five dollars. It was somebody that knew me. When I was home from college he said he'd tell my mother. I told him to go right ahead.

My wife wanted unreasonably high alimony.

I was managing a clothing store and they wanted lots of clothes. I defied them and won out.

A colleague. He wanted money and for me to leave the city. He thought he could get my job if I was out of the picture.

A couple of times, people I picked up demanded money afterwards.

In some instances the blackmailer had made sexual demands:

He wanted me. He was homosexual also. I would have been blacklisted if he'd exposed me, but even though I refused him, he didn't do it.

They wanted me to blow them.

They wanted sex with me and they threatened to tell my father if I didn't come across.

Sometimes the person threatening to expose the respondent's homosexuality was a lover actually trying to keep him from breaking up their relationship:

I wanted out of the relationship and he threatened to expose me to my parents.

I was living with him and when I was going to leave, he threatened to expose me. Yes, I "escaped."

My ex-lover wanted me to go back to him.

Summary

Nearly half of the white homosexual men and about one-third of the blacks had been arrested or picked up by the police. Of the homosexual men ever arrested, however, the majority were charged with some offense that did not have to do with their homosexuality. Similarly, among the homosexual men who had ever been booked, these bookings were usually not related to their homosexuality, and relatively few had ever been convicted of an offense involving homosexuality. Nevertheless, the homosexual men as a whole were significantly more likely than the heterosexual men ever to have been arrested, booked, or convicted for any reason.

Other social difficulties a homosexual might encounter were less frequent among our respondents. A small number reported that they had had to pay police (or police impostors) to keep their sexual orientation secret or to avoid arrest, while slightly more had been blackmailed by other persons threatening to expose their homosexuality. The number of those who had ever been robbed or assaulted on account of their homosexuality was greater, however, constituting a sizable minority.

Findings: Women

Arrests

A quarter of the homosexual women, whether black (BHFs) or white (WHFs), had ever been arrested or picked up by the police for other than traffic offenses (Table 20.1). Although this is a much smaller number than the finding for their male counterparts, more of the lesbians than of the heterosexual women (WHTFs, BHTFs) had been arrested or picked up by law officials at least once in their lives. There were no differences among the various subgroups on this measure. Among those who had ever been arrested, the homosexual and the heterosexual women did not differ in how many times this had happened (Table 20.2). Unlike their male counterparts, virtually none of the homosexual women—nine WHFs and three BHFs—had ever been arrested or picked up for reasons having to do with their homosexuality (Table 20.3).

Less than a fifth of the homosexual women had ever been booked for any kind of offense (Table 20.4). No particular subgroup differed from any of the others, but as a whole the lesbians were more likely to have been booked than were the heterosexual women. Of the twelve in our sample who had ever been arrested in connection with their homosexuality, seven had been booked for this reason (Table 20.5). Fewer homosexual women than men had ever been convicted of any kind of offense (Table 20.6), but the homosexual women were more likely than the heterosexual women to have been convicted. Only two WHFs were ever convicted for a reason related to their homosexuality (Table 20.7).

Extortion

None of the homosexual women had ever experienced police extortion (Table 20.8).

Assault and Robbery

Assault and robbery were much more common among the homosexual men than among the lesbians. Only four WHFs and three BHFs had ever been rolled or robbed in connection with being homosexual (Table 20.9).

Blackmail

About one-quarter of the WHFs and a smaller number of the BHFs reported that anyone (other than police) had ever threatened to expose their homosexuality in order to get something from them. Thus, the incidence of blackmail among the homosexual women is about the same as that for their male counterparts (Table 20.10). The person and the motive of the blackmailer, however, tended to be different. Whereas the men were most apt to have been blackmailed by someone wanting money from them, the homosexual women were more likely to be threatened by a lover intent upon keeping their relationship from breaking up (Table 20.11):

She said she'd call my job and get me fired. She wanted me to stay with her, not leave her.

He wanted me to marry him. He threatened to expose me at school and at my job, but I don't think he will.

It was this married man I was seeing. When I wanted to end our affair, out of revenge he threatened to tell my parents and other men.

After our affair was over, she threatened to tell my relatives if I didn't stay with her.

Summary

One-fourth of the homosexual female respondents had ever been arrested or picked up by the police. This experience was more likely to have happened to the lesbians of either race than to the heterosexual women. These arrests, among the homosexual women, seldom had anything to do with homosexuality. Similarly, the female respondents of either sexual orientation were unlikely ever to have been booked or convicted, and among the lesbians who had experienced this, homosexuality was virtually never involved.

The homosexual women were less likely ever to have experienced robbery or assault in connection with their homosexuality, and none at all had ever undergone police extortion. The incidence of blackmail among them, however, was not uncommon, and the person threatening them was usually a disenchanted lover wanting to maintain the relationship rather than someone asking for money.

Overview

These data tend to confirm others' findings that experiencing a variety of social difficulties as a result of one's homosexuality is a feature of the lives of some homosexuals, particularly men. While the majority of the homosexual men and women in our samples had never been arrested, robbed, blackmailed, assaulted, or suffered police extortion on account of homosexuality, these things did happen to a fair number of them.

Although the homosexual men were more likely ever to have been arrested for any reason than the heterosexual men, few of them had been arrested on account of their homosexuality. The Functional men, however, were more likely than the others to have been arrested, booked, and convicted for homosexual offenses. This finding may reflect the fact that the Functionals cruise more, go to gay bars and baths more, and stay at home less, than members of the other groups; this greater involvement in the gay world may expose them to greater likelihood of arrest. Still, most of the Functionals had never experienced this. Clearly, the social difficulties they did experience did not lead to consequences dire enough to cause problems of well-being for them. The homosexual men who had experienced extortion, robbery, assault, or blackmail in connection with their sexual orientation were not as numerous as those who had had trouble with the police. The fact that most of our homosexual respondents had not had these difficulties is also noteworthy, however, in that it suggests that a homosexual life-style is not necessarily perilous.

The homosexual women experienced far fewer social difficulties than their male counterparts did, but they were more likely than the heterosexual women ever to have been arrested for any reason. Since those lesbians who had been arrested tended to report that it was for reasons other than homosexuality, it is possible to suppose that their greater incidence of arrest was influenced by their leading less conventional lives than the heterosexual women did.

In considering these data, it is important to remember that members of homosexual communities in less permissive cities than San Francisco might report a much higher incidence of social difficulties. Presumably, such difficulties will become less and less common as public policies and attitudes toward homosexuality continue to change, until they are experienced by only a few rather than by the sometimes sizable minorities in our present samples.

Part IV

Psychological Adjustment

From the beginning of our Judeo-Christian civilization, the heterosexual majority's antipathy toward homosexual behavior has been manifested and justified in countless ways. The Jews' preoccupation with survival as a people, expressed in their emphasis on procreative sexuality and their determination to distinguish themselves from the alien people surrounding them, led them to denounce homosexuality in the severest terms (McNeill, 1976). This denunciation continued to be fostered by the Christian Church, whose authorities were convinced that any engagement in homosexual acts would bring about divine retribution upon the whole society. Such acts, believed to be "against nature," were considered mortal sins whose only remedy was confession, penance, and sometimes the sentence of death. Thus, in most corners of Western civilization, homosexuality came to be labeled both sinful and criminal, an outrage to God and man, indicative of social decay. This view persisted for more than nineteen centuries until it was replaced, at least in some quarters, by medical authorities' equation of homosexuality with disease. This ostensibly more humane view contended that the punishment of homosexual behavior should be supplanted by medical treatment of those who engaged in it, that these people could be cured of their aberration and find their rightful place among the normal heterosexual majority. This relatively recent medical model, fostered in large part by Freud's view of psychosexual development, construed homosexuality in terms of "arrested development," unresolved oedipal conflicts, and irrational phobias. Homosexuality was thought to be ipso facto pathological and chiefly the result of abnormal familial circumstances. Until fairly recently it was this view of homosexuality which appeared most frequently in the literature. The latter is replete with case histories provided, for the most part, by psychoanalytic clinicians whose findings appeared to justify their theoretical point of view. This point of view includes the notion that homosexuality involves a "pathological elaboration of an unresolved masochistic attachment to the pre-Oedipal mother" (Bergler, 1958), a defense against castration anxiety (Bromberg, 1965), an immature ego characterized by fetishistic, narcissistic, and oral-sadistic elements (Bychowski, 1961), and inevitably an underlying psychopathology (Gershman, 1953; Caprio, 1955; Bozarth & Gross, 1962; Socarides, 1968). Clinical case histories have described homosexual individuals as, among other things, psychopaths, obsessive-compulsives, tyrannized by castration anxieties and father fixations, involved in dependency conflicts, filled with suicidal ideation, given to hysterical displays, and possessing marked transvestic tendencies. Nowhere has the stereotype of the homosexual as a pathetic caricature of a fully functioning human being been more clearly put forth than in a recent popular work which promised to enlighten the public on various aspects of sexuality (Reuben, 1969). The stereotype has suffered an extremely slow death. In fact, it was never very seriously challenged until the work of Kinsey and his colleagues (1948, 1953) indicated that millions of Americans had engaged in homosexual behavior. These investigators, pointing out the considerable incidence of such behavior even among infrahuman species, went on to conclude that it was simply a natural variation of sexual expression. Their findings, and particularly their conclusions, led to widespread controversy and eventually to a reconsideration of the nature of homosexuality. Growing numbers of people, including clinicians, came to disagree with the long-held view that homosexual persons were necessarily less well adjusted than were their heterosexual counterparts. The new view, ultimately upheld by the American Psychiatric Association in a vote of its membership, was put quite succinctly by a most distinguished psychoanalyst:

Surely the time has come for psychiatry to give up the archaic practice of classifying the millions of men and women who accept or prefer homosexual object choices as being, by virtue of that fact alone, mentally ill. The fact that their alternative life-style happens to be out of favor with current cultural conventions must not be a basis in itself for a diagnosis of pathology (Marmor, 1973).

Numerous investigations have failed to show any consistent or clearcut differences between homosexuals and heterosexuals in terms of their psychological adjustment. Among those studies which have found more pathology among homosexual than heterosexual samples, one investigator reported that his homosexual male subjects scored significantly higher on measures of neuroticism, hysteria, mania, depression, autism, and paranoia (Bruce, 1942). Doidge (1956), using a battery of ten psychological tests, found higher levels of anxiety among homosexual men. Kenyon (1968c) found lesbians to be more neurotic and more severely disturbed in their moods and feelings than were heterosexual women. Saghir and Robins (1973) found a somewhat higher incidence of affective disorders among those in their lesbian sample, while Weinberg and Williams (1974, 1975a) reported less happiness (but not less self-acceptance or more psychosomatic symptoms) among their homosexual male respondents than among men in the general population. Myrick (1974a) found homosexual men to have lower self-esteem and self-acceptance than those in his heterosexual control group, and Friedberg (1975) found homosexual male respondents to be more paranoid than their heterosexual counterparts.

Many other studies have been unable to distinguish homosexual and heterosexual individuals on the basis of their psychological adjustment. Chang and Block (1960) reported that the homosexual and heterosexual men in their sample did not differ significantly in the degree of their self-acceptance, while Freedman (1967), using an extensive battery of objective measures, found that homosexual and heterosexual women also did not differ in their self-acceptance. In another study it was found that the Szondi Test failed to discriminate homosexuals from heterosexuals (David & Rabinowitz, 1952), while another investigation, employing the Blacky Pictures Test, found no differences between the two groups (DeLuca, 1967). In Hooker's famous study (1957), experts were unable to distinguish homosexual and heterosexual men on the basis of their Rorschach protocols or their responses to the Thematic Apperception Test (TAT) cards or to the Make A Picture Story Test. These results led Hooker to conclude that homosexuality is a "deviation in sexual pattern which is still within the normal range psychologically." In a study of men in the military, the Rorschach and the TAT were again found to be useless in distinguishing homosexuals from heterosexuals (Wayne et al., 1947). In yet another study of homosexual and heterosexual men (Clark, 1975), sexual orientation was not found to be related to their scores on the Tennessee Self-Concept Scale (including measures of self-criticism, neurosis, personality integration, etc.). Saghir and Robins (1973) found no differences between the homosexual and the heterosexual men in their sample with regard to the extent of their depression, anxiety, or psychosomatic symptoms. Approximately three-quarters of each group were judged to be free of any manifest psychopathology. Finally, contrary to what most experts would have anticipated, Riess et al. (1974) found lesbians to be *more* self-accepting and less depressed than their heterosexual counterparts, while Wilson and Greene (1971) found a higher degree of neuroticism among the heterosexual women than among the lesbians they studied.

In the section which follows, our respondents have been compared on various measures of psychological adjustment. These include their current feeling states, their general state of health, self-acceptance, psychosomatic symptoms, the incidence of suicidal ideation and attempts, and the extent of their involvement in treatment for emotional disorders.

Findings: Men

General Health

Most of the men, regardless of race or sexual orientation and including those in the Chicago pilot study sample, reported that they were in good or excellent health (Table 21.1). Among the homosexual subgroups, the Asexuals scored significantly lower on our measure of general health, and while no differences emerged between the health reports of the homosexual and the heterosexual men as a whole, the Asexuals did tend to give poorer health reports than did the heterosexual men.

Psychosomatic Symptoms

On a composite measure consisting of the frequency with which, during the past three months, the respondents had been seriously bothered by headaches, dizziness, general aches and pains, muscle twitches, nervousness, and rapid heartbeat, the Functionals reported fewer symptoms than did the other homosexual subgroups (Table 21.2). While the heterosexual men reported fewer psychosomatic symptoms than the homosexual men, the Close-Coupleds and the Functionals did not differ from the heterosexual males (WHTMs, BHTMs) on this particular measure.

Happiness

The majority in each of the male groups (as well as of those in Weinberg and Williams's sample) said that they were feeling "pretty happy." The Close-Coupleds and Functionals were the happiest of the homosexual groups, while the Dysfunctionals and Asexuals were the least happy. In addition, although the Asexuals and the Dysfunctionals were less happy than the heterosexual men, the Close-Coupleds tended to report even more happiness than those in the heterosexual group (Table 21.3).

Except for the BHTMs, more than two-thirds of the male respondents (and 70% of the Chicago pilot study men) said that they were happier now than they were five years ago (Table 21.4). More of the BHMs than of the WHMs, however, said that they were less happy at the present time. Among the homosexual subgroups the Asexuals and Dysfunctionals scored lowest on this measure. The Close-Coupleds, who were the highest scoring group, were more likely than the heterosexual men to report being happier currently than they were five years ago.

Exuberance

This composite measure consists of how often during the past three months the respondents had felt "on top of the world," were "particularly excited or interested in something," "pleased about having accomplished something," and "proud because someone complimented [them] on something [they] had done." The homosexual men actually tended to score higher than the heterosexual men on this measure (Table 21.5). The Functionals were much more likely to report feelings of exuberance than were the heterosexuals, and more exuberance was also reported by both the Close and the Open-Coupleds. The Dysfunctionals and the Asexuals, who were less exuberant than the other homosexual groups, did not differ from the heterosexual men in terms of how much exuberance they reported.

Self-Acceptance

Our self-acceptance composite measure consists of the frequency with which a respondent took a positive attitude toward himself, wished that he could have more respect for himself, and thought of himself as no good at all. The homosexual men in general (unlike those in Weinberg and Williams's study) scored lower on this measure than did the heterosexuals (Table 21.6). At the same time, we find that it was the Dysfunctionals and the Asexuals, significantly lower in self-acceptance than the other homosexual respondents, who had much lower levels of self-acceptance than the heterosexual men. While the Open-Coupleds also tended to score lower on this measure, the Functionals and Close-Coupleds, the highest scoring of the homosexual subgroups, did not differ at all from the heterosexual men in their self-acceptance.

Loneliness

A little more than a third of the WHMs (versus 45% of the Chicago pilot study men), and significantly more of the BHMs, said that they sometimes or often felt lonely (Table 21.7). While the homosexual men were more apt to report feelings of loneliness than the heterosexual men did, the difference is chiefly confined to the Dysfunctionals and the Asexuals, who reported greater feelings of loneliness than either the other homosexuals or those in the heterosexual group. The Functionals also tended to be more lonely than the heterosexual men; they were, however, less lonely than the other homosexual men, as were the Close- and Open-Coupleds, who in fact did not differ from the heterosexual men on this measure.

Worry

About one-quarter of the homosexual men (and about the same number in the Chicago pilot sample) reported that they did a great deal of worrying (Table 21.8). Among the homosexual subgroups, the Functionals reported the least and the Dysfunctionals the greatest amount of worry. Except for the Functionals, who could not be distinguished from the heterosexual men on the basis of how much worrying they did, the homosexuals tended to worry more than those in the heterosexual sample. The Dysfunctionals did much more worrying than the heterosexual men, and the Asexuals and the Close- and Open-Coupleds also reported more worries than the heterosexual men.

Depression

This composite measure consists of the respondents' reports of how frequently they felt life was worthwhile, had difficulty starting to do things, felt their daily lives were full of things that kept them interested, could not take care of things because they could not get going, experienced hurt feelings, felt blue, and did not care about anything even though everything was going fine for them. The Close-Coupleds and Functionals were the least depressed and the Dysfunctionals and Asexuals the most depressed among the homosexual subgroups. The homosexual men were more likely to report feelings of depression than the heterosexual men (Table 21.9); it should be noted, however, that the Close-Coupleds and the Functionals did not differ from the heterosexual men in terms of their depression.

Tension

On a composite measure consisting of how often during the past month the respondents had felt bored, so restless that they could not sit still long, and vaguely uneasy about something without knowing why, the BHMs scored significantly higher than the WHMs (Table 21.10). Among the homosexual subgroups the Close-Coupleds were the least tense and the Dysfunctionals and Asexuals the most tense. The homosexual men were significantly more tense than their heterosexual counterparts. This is especially true of the Dysfunctionals and, to a lesser degree, of the Asexuals. The Open-Coupleds and even the Functionals also reported more feelings of tension than did the heterosexual men, but the latter are indistinguishable from the Close-Coupleds on this measure.

Paranoia

This composite measure consists of the frequency with which the respondents felt that strangers were looking at them critically, tended to be on their guard with people who were unexpectedly friendly, and wondered what hidden reason another person might have had for doing something nice for them. The Close-Coupleds and the Functionals were the least paranoid of the homosexual subgroups, while the Dysfunctionals and the Asexuals were the most so. Although the homosexual men as a whole were apt to report more feelings of distrust and suspicion than those in the heterosexual group, the difference between the two groups is not very large (Table 21.11). In fact, it is only the Dysfunctionals and the Asexuals who were more paranoid than the heterosexual men; the other groups' scores on this composite measure did not differ significantly from those of the heterosexual men.

Suicidal Feelings and Impulses

About three-eighths of the homosexual men had idly thought about but never seriously considered committing suicide (Table 21.12). Another 19 percent of the WHMs, as contrasted to 4 percent of the BHMs, had seriously considered it. These experiences were significantly less common among the heterosexual men.

Among those who had ever seriously considered suicide, many of the homosexual respondents did not directly relate their feelings of desperation to their being homosexual (Table 21.13). Some, however, said that they had reached this state as a result of difficulties with their lovers or because of their inability to establish a meaningful sociosexual relationship:

My lover was going to leave me.

A love affair. After the time I had accepted that I was gay, I was going with a person for over a year, and he fell in love with someone else.

I was generally depressed and tired of all the hang-ups in the gay world. There is just no structure in society to aid a homosexual relationship—it's so underground.

I felt I was being neglected by my lover. I didn't stop to think.

Much smaller numbers had seriously considered suicide because they could not accept their homosexuality:

It was because of my homosexuality. I was completely depressed that my homosexuality was leading me nowhere. My life seemed to be going around in a circle. I was still fighting against recognition of my homosexuality. I knew what I was but I didn't want to be.

I felt scared, lost, trapped. Suicide is a kind of a way out. I don't want to be a dirty old man living in an old hotel room—to go out and pay a kid $10 to lay on his back for a few minutes.

The feeling that homosexuality was a hopeless existence. I felt there was no future in it, that I was doomed to be alone. And from my Catholic background, I felt that homosexuality was very evil.

I was guilty and upset about being gay.

About 20 percent of the homosexual men (exactly the same number as those in the Chicago pilot study and about three times the number of those in Saghir and Robins's samples), compared with less than 4 percent of the heterosexual men, reported that they had actually attempted suicide on one or more occasions (Table 21.14). The incidence of suicidal ideation and gestures, not significantly higher or lower in any particular homosexual group, was markedly higher among the homosexual men than among those in the heterosexual group (Tables 21.12, 21.14). Among those men who had made such an attempt, the homosexual and the heterosexual respondents did not differ in terms of how old they were at the time of their first suicide attempt or gesture (Table 21.15). Most were in their late teens or early twenties.

Although the reasons they gave for their first suicide attempt corresponded to those they gave in connection with their having seriously considered it (Table 21.16), almost two-thirds of the WHMs (compared with 76% of the Chicago pilot study men) and nearly one-half of the BHMs who had ever attempted suicide said that their first attempt had something to do with the fact that they were homosexual (Table 21.17). This usually involved problems generated by unstable relationships with a valued partner or the difficulties they had in accepting the fact that they were homosexual (Table 21.18).

Most of the homosexual men who had ever attempted suicide reported that their first attempt had brought about important changes in their lives (Table 21.19). Many spoke of having gained a new perspective on things (Table 21.20):

A total personality change. Each time I became more selective of a love object. I became more tolerant of people and more understanding of their shortcomings. Before the attempt, I was concerned with financial success; now I am concerned with happiness.

I'm beginning to get out of my shell, seeing myself and my life as it really is. I don't feel uncomfortable now about being homosexual, I'd admit it to anyone. My old goals are back; I've come alive again. My feeling of fear is gone—that's most important.

I realized by my lover's reaction that he really loved me very deeply. I became more happy and more content, more secure, less ill at ease. Before, I was living hard and fast, hitting the bars. Afterwards, I realized that I didn't have to run, that I had someone that really loved me.

I saw that life was worth living. I saw that my family wouldn't be hurt by my being a homosexual.

Other results which they mentioned included others' greater compassion for them and an attempt to get help for themselves from a professional therapist.

Professional Help

Fifty-eight percent of the WHMs and significantly fewer (but almost half) of the BHMs had had contact with a professional person in connection with what they or others had construed as an emotional problem (Table 21.21). (These numbers are much like the 51% in the Chicago pilot sample and almost half of those in Manosevitz's sample, compared with about a third of Weinberg and Williams's respondents, who had been "in psychotherapy" at one time or another in their lives. This compares with about one-quarter of the males in Saghir and Robins's study.) Of all the homosexual subgroups, the Open-Coupleds were least apt to have sought help from a professional. Far smaller numbers of the heterosexual men reported having had this kind of professional contact than did the homosexual men (either as a whole or among the various subgroups). Among the homosexual men ever in therapy (or its equivalent), less than a quarter (versus 64% of those in Bieber et al.'s sample) had sought help in connection with their wanting to give up their homosexuality (Table 21.22).

Among those who had ever been in treatment for an emotional problem, the homosexual men tended to be younger than the heterosexual men at the time of their first professional contact (Table 21.23), although most (like those in the Chicago pilot study) were in their middle twenties when they sought help for the first time. They also differed in connection with their reasons for seeking help of this kind (Table 21.24). The heterosexual men went to a therapist because of various feelings of distress unrelated to their sexual orientation; among the homosexual men, however, difficulties with their homosexuality on one basis or another (but not necessarily wanting to give it up) were what usually prompted them to seek professional help. In addition, more of the homosexual men (a greater number than in the Chicago pilot sample) than of their heterosexual counterparts said that the reason they went in the first place was that they had been required to by others:

I got arrested for homosexuality, and my sentence was to get therapy.

My mother sent me, about my homosexuality.

Because I told my wife I was homosexual, and she wouldn't stay with me unless I went.

I was forced to go. I was in the Army and I'd been found in bed with another soldier.

With respect to their first professional contacts, the homosexual and the heterosexual men did not differ in the number of times they saw their counselor; most of those who had ever sought help went no more than a dozen times (Table 21.25). (Those in the Chicago pilot study sample tended to have seen the professional more frequently.) They also did not differ in terms of how helpful they thought the professional contact was to them (Table 21.26). Most respondents tended to think that these contacts were helpful to some extent, although the Functionals reported having got less help than did the other homosexual subgroups.

When asked to comment on the ways in which their contacts with professionals had been helpful to them, the largest number of the homosexual (and the heterosexual) male respondents spoke in terms of having gained insight into themselves (Table 21.27):

It helps you to understand yourself a little bit better and to sort of take your problems a little bit easier—being able to cope with them.

I've tried to bare more of my own feelings. I'm trying to open myself more to people. I've tried to discover myself, more what I *am,* not just "a professor" or "a homosexual."

It's simply helping me to be able to live with myself, to recognize myself.

He helped me to analyze myself. He helped me to see and solve my own problems.

Others commented about feelings of well-being:

The world is still a marvelous place, they made me realize that.

They taught me to cope with whatever causes my stomach to kick up, to face issues rather than avoid them. I used to have to go to the hospital about twice a year for stomach trouble and I don't anymore.

I learned to adjust to myself and have no guilt now. Relationships are more rewarding now that I accept my homosexuality, and I've been able to really cut down on worrying and cruising. I'm more accepting of the heterosexual part of my life too. I have more confidence in myself.

Relatively large numbers said that their contacts with professionals had not been helpful at all (Table 21.28):

They were generally pretty unhelpful. One psychiatrist assured my mother that nothing could really be done to help me. Another made me do all the work—he said very few words.

Well, he encouraged me to talk and I didn't have anything to say, so I just rambled. And I tried to get him to say something and he wouldn't.

I can't recall them having ever been helpful.

It wasn't at all helpful. Outside of just sitting down and talking with you, a person can't help you. A person has to realize his own problems and solve them himself.

The respondents' complaints about their professional contacts had to do most frequently with the way in which the counselor had related to them:

He didn't seem to understand my basic problem, which was homosexuality. He didn't seem that involved with my needs.

Detachment. The lack of personal involvement that you feel. They carry the detachment bit too far. I think they might accomplish a lot more and faster if they became a friend. I think a lot of people probably feel it's not accomplishing anything because the guy isn't interested at all in them.

The doctor told me homosexuality was bad.

I still resent paying $25 a week for him saying nothing.

The psychiatrist just couldn't communicate with me at all. I don't know, I always felt worse when I left his office. I got the feeling he only wanted my money.

Some reported that they had learned virtually nothing about themselves or their problems:

It seemed like I didn't find out anything I didn't already know about myself.

They didn't do anything. No help, no enlightenment, no perceptions given.

I still didn't know myself any better.

Others said that their feelings of distress had not been reduced as a result of their professional contact:

They have never helped me eradicate my guilt or change my life so I could function better in society.

He made me feel more guilty about my homosexuality. I had to worry about *not* being heterosexual as well as about *being* homosexual.

It made me depressed. He brought out the disadvantages of homosexuality and it made me unhappy and depressed. He just wanted to reform everybody.

Summary

The black homosexual males differed from the white homosexual males on several measures of psychological adjustment. They tended to be less likely to feel happier at the present time than five years ago, to feel more tension, and to feel lonely more frequently. On the other hand, the blacks tended to be less likely ever to have considered suicide or to have sought professional help for an emotional problem, and they worried less often. They did not differ from the whites in terms of their general health, their psychosomatic symptoms, their happiness at the present time, their level of exuberance, their self-acceptance, or how paranoid or depressed they were. Among those who had ever sought professional counseling, the black and the white homosexual males did not differ in terms of why they did so, how old they were at the time, how many times they went, or their reaction to the counseling they got.

The homosexual and the heterosexual men did not differ in their tendencies to report that they were in good physical health, were feeling pretty happy overall at the time of the interview, and were happier at that time than five years previously. On other measures of psychological adjustment, however, differences did emerge. The homosexual men tended to feel less self-accepting and more lonely, depressed, and tense than did the heterosexual men. They also tended to worry more and to display more paranoia and psychosomatic symptoms. On the other hand, the homosexual men tended to be more exuberant than their heterosexual counterparts. They were much more likely to have considered or attempted suicide, although, according to the respondents, this was not necessarily connected to their homosexuality. Far more of the homosexual than of the heterosexual men had ever sought professional help for an emotional problem, but among those who did, there was no difference in how long they went or what they felt they had got out of it. Not unexpectedly, their reasons for going differed, with the homosexual men more likely to mention difficulties with respect to their sexual orientation or to report that they had been coerced to seek counseling.

In the measures above, differences between the homosexual and the heterosexual men in general were sometimes due to only one or two of the homosexual subgroups differing from the heterosexuals. In such cases, the remaining subgroups tended to appear as well adjusted as the heterosexuals or, occasionally, even more so. At other times, only by comparing the heterosexuals with the various subgroups did any differences emerge. To give several examples, the Asexuals were the only group less healthy than the heterosexual sample. They had the largest number of psychosomatic symptoms, were less happy or self-accepting than the heterosexuals, and felt lonely more often. They worried more, were more depressed and tense, and showed more paranoia than the heterosexuals. By contrast, the Functionals did not differ from the heterosexuals in terms of psychosomatic symptoms, self-acceptance, amount of worrying, depression, or paranoia; and the Close-Coupleds were the only group that felt no more tense, and were even happier, than the heterosexual men.

Findings: Women

General Health

Like their male counterparts, most of the female respondents, no matter their race or sexual orientation, believed they were in good or excellent health (Table 21.1). The white homosexual females (WHFs), however, were more likely to report excellent health than were their black counterparts (BHFs). The homosexual and the heterosexual respondents did not differ with respect to how healthy they believed themselves to be, and no particular type of lesbian scored higher on this variable.

Psychosomatic Symptoms [1]

While the BHFs tended to report more psychosomatic symptoms than the WHFs did, subgroup comparisons revealed no differences with respect to scores on this composite measure (Table 21.2). The homosexual women as a whole also did not differ from the heterosexual respondents in how frequently they experienced psychosomatic symptoms.

Happiness

Again like their male counterparts, most of the women, homosexual or heterosexual, considered themselves "pretty happy," and relatively few said they were either "not too happy" or "very unhappy" (Table 21.3). The BHFs and the WHFs did not differ on this measure. The Close-Coupleds were the happiest of the lesbian groups. The homosexual women in general reported less happiness than the heterosexual women, but among homosexual types, only the Dysfunctionals were less happy than those in the heterosexual group.

At least two-thirds of all the female respondents said that they were happier now than they were five years ago (Table 21.4). Although there

---

[1] See page 198 for a description of the items which make up this composite measure.

were no differences between the homosexual women as a whole and the heterosexual women, the Close-Coupleds scored higher on this measure than any of the other subgroups and were more likely to report being happier at the present time (than they were five years before) than were those in the heterosexual group.

Exuberance[2]

In terms of homosexual subgroup comparisons, the Functionals were the most exuberant and the Dysfunctionals the least so. In addition, the Dysfunctionals were less exuberant and the Functionals more exuberant than the heterosexual women. The homosexual women as a whole, however, did not differ from the heterosexuals on this measure of their psychological adjustment (Table 21.5).

Self-Acceptance[3]

Among the homosexual subgroups, the Close-Coupleds scored highest and the Open-Coupleds lowest on self-acceptance. Although the homosexual women tended to report lower levels of self-acceptance than did their heterosexual counterparts (Table 21.6), it was actually only the Open-Coupleds and the Dysfunctionals who could be distinguished from the heterosexual women on this measure. Those in the other homosexual groups did not report significantly less self-acceptance than the heterosexual respondents.

Loneliness

Most of the female respondents reported that they had rarely or never felt lonely during the past month (Table 21.7). The BHFs, however, reported significantly more loneliness than the WHFs did. The Close-Coupleds were the least lonely and the Asexuals the most lonely of all the subgroups. The homosexual women as a whole were no more lonely than the heterosexuals, but the Asexuals were apt to be more lonely and the Close-Coupleds less lonely than the women in the heterosexual group.

Worry

About one-quarter of the female respondents reported that they worried "a great deal" (Table 21.8). The BHFs and the WHFs did not differ

---

[2] See page 199 for a description of this composite measure.
[3] See page 199 for a more complete description of this composite measure.

on this item, nor did the homosexual and the heterosexual respondents. In addition, no particular type of lesbian differed from the other types in terms of the amount of worrying they did.

Depression[4]

The female respondents hardly differed at all with respect to how depressed they felt at the time of the interview (Table 21.9). The Close-Coupleds and the Functionals were less depressed than the other subgroups. The homosexual women, regardless of race or subgroup, did not differ from the heterosexual women on this variable.

Tension[5]

The BHFs reported significantly more tension than the WHFs, and among the subgroups, the Close-Coupleds were significantly less tense than the rest of the lesbians. Although the homosexual and the heterosexual women in general did not differ on this measure, the Asexuals were apt to report being more tense than those in the heterosexual group (Table 21.10).

Paranoia[6]

The BHFs displayed significantly more paranoia than did their white counterparts (Table 21.11). While the Close-Coupleds scored significantly lower on this measure than members of the other homosexual subgroups, the homosexual women as a whole did not differ significantly from the heterosexual respondents in terms of how paranoid they felt. The Open-Coupleds and Asexuals, however, appeared more paranoid than the heterosexual women.

Suicidal Feelings and Impulses

Somewhat over a third of the lesbians had imagined but not seriously considered committing suicide (Table 21.12). Another 16 percent of the WHFs, as opposed to half as many BHFs, said they had seriously considered it at one time or another. Although the total sample comparisons revealed a higher incidence of suicidal ideation among the homosexual respondents, only the Asexuals (who reported more suicidal ideation than those in the other groups) differed significantly from the heterosexual women with regard to suicidal feelings.

[4] See page 200 for a description of the items which make up this measure.
[5] See page 201 for a fuller description of this composite measure.
[6] See page 201 for a detailed description of this measure.

Among those homosexual respondents who had seriously considered committing suicide, the greatest number gave as their reason unbearable feeling states not explicitly related to their homosexuality (Table 21.13). Some described a particularly stressful situation:

Everything seemed to be going wrong. I lost my job, I didn't have any money, I was doing very badly in school, I was rejected by a lover—just everything!

I was pregnant. At twenty-nine, I found out I was pregnant! I messed up on the rhythm system. I was going to shoot myself. I knew I didn't have the temperament to be a fit mother.

A neighbor gave me money to pay the rent and I spent or lost some of it. My mother said to go out and get it, but instead of prostitution, I drank iodine.

Others spoke solely in terms of the feelings they were experiencing:

I just couldn't see any point to it. Things weren't going to get any better and I was never going to be any different. I couldn't be the kind of person I wanted to be.

Nothing dramatic. Sometimes life seems a general bummer and I just think, "screw it."

I felt I couldn't go on. Life was too painful, too much of a struggle. I didn't know where I fit in, who I was, where I belonged—a pervasive loneliness.

Like their male counterparts, a good number of the lesbians had thought about committing suicide when a relationship with a lover had come to an end:

I felt that I would never find anyone to marry—to settle down with seriously. I had a marriage with a girl for about three years. Then she went straight. Now I wish I could fall in love again.

I was afraid of losing my lover.

Unrequited love. I wanted to "show" my lover—and I was depressed.

One-quarter of the WHFs (about the same as the number in Schäfer's sample but three times the number of those in Saghir and Robins's sample) and one-sixth of the BHFs had actually attempted suicide (Table 21.14). The homosexual and the heterosexual women did not differ with respect to how often they had attempted suicide. (In considering these findings, one should keep in mind that San Francisco has one of the highest suicide rates in the country.) Among those who had ever attempted suicide, the heterosexual and the homosexual women did not differ in terms of how old they were at the time of their first attempt (Table 21.15). Unlike their male counterparts, most of these homosexual women (more than half of the WHFs and almost three-quarters of the BHFs) reported that their first attempt had nothing to do with the fact that they were homosexual (Tables 21.16, 21.17). Among those who said that their first attempt did have something to do with their homosexuality, most mentioned the difficulties they had in dealing with the breakup of a significant relationship with another woman or adjusting to their homosexuality (Table 21.18).

Like the homosexual men, most of the female respondents who had ever attempted suicide said that the attempt had brought about important changes in their lives (Tables 21.19, 21.20):

I won't try it again. It's stupid. The body wasn't causing the problem; why punish it?

I really didn't want to withdraw from life, die, or be dead. I saw that there was a lot ahead of me, a lot I wanted to be involved in. I realized that it wasn't the end of the world and maybe I started maturing a little bit then. I decided to just do my own thing, to hell with society, if they didn't like it they could lump it.

A complete personality change. I felt like a new person, a rebirth, so grateful for not being dead and to be alive and do things. Since then I've been fortunate to be able to help a few others.

Besides their getting a new perspective on life, a small number began getting professional help as a result of their unsuccessful suicide attempt:

I took a much more positive outlook and sought professional help.

I came to value being alive. I got a sense of needing to do something more worthwhile with my life. I also felt there must be better ways of handling my emotional responses. That's when I began seeing a psychiatrist.

I started seeing a therapist. I got more self-confident.

Professional Help

About two-thirds of the WHFs and slightly over half of the BHFs reported having been involved with one or more professional counselors in connection with an emotional problem (Table 21.21). (Only 37% of the lesbians in Saghir and Robins's sample had ever been "in psychotherapy.") While the homosexual women were more apt to have been "in therapy" than were their heterosexual counterparts, it was actually the Dysfunctionals, Asexuals, and Open-Coupleds who differed from the heterosexual women in this regard; the Close-Coupleds (the subgroup least likely to have sought professional help) and the Functionals did not have a significantly higher incidence of professional contact. Of those homosexual respondents reporting professional contact, less than one-fifth said that they had gone to a professional at least once in order to give up their homosexuality (Table 21.22). (The number of homosexual women in our sample who sought professional help for this purpose is considerably smaller than the 30% of Kaye et al.'s sample who entered therapy in order to be "cured" of their homosexuality.) Among the homosexual subgroups, the Asexuals were most likely to have sought help for this purpose.

The homosexual women who had ever seen a professional for some form of therapy were somewhat younger at the time of their first professional contact than were their heterosexual counterparts (Table 21.23). Like the men, the homosexual women were more likely to have been involved with a professional because they had been required to do so or in connection with feelings of distress directly related to their sexual orientation (Table 21.24).

Despite the above differences, the homosexual and the heterosexual respondents who had seen a counselor did not differ in terms of how frequently they saw their first professional (Table 21.25). Most reported no more than sixteen visits. Among the homosexual subgroups, the Asexuals saw their first counselor the smallest number of times, while the Dysfunctionals went more often than the others. The Dysfunctionals also tended to have seen their first professional more frequently than did the heterosexual women. The homosexual and the heterosexual women did not differ in terms of how helpful they thought their first professional contact had been to them (Table 21.26).[7]

Like the men who had ever sought professional help, the homosexual women who regarded their contacts with professionals as helpful spoke in terms of the insight into themselves that they had gained (Table 21.27):

He taught me to see myself as I am, to set my goals realistically. He taught me to analyze myself and to release my emotions—particularly angry ones—instead of letting them build up. He let me see myself freed of my mother, acting like a responsible adult, accepting my sexual partner. He gave me many tools for living my own life.

[7] Not enough women had had contact with more than one professional for us to analyze responses to subsequent counselors meaningfully.

It helped me see myself more clearly. I wondered what I was all about, but not anymore. I do what I want and what feels comfortable, with myself in general and as a homosexual.

Others mentioned that they became more self-accepting:

I've come to accept the possibility of my homosexuality and to accept myself more as a person—to get more in contact with my emotions. I'd repressed them and couldn't get them out. I'm continuing to learn self-acceptance and how to express myself.

In helping me to accept myself. In general, I grew up with a feeling of unworthiness. I felt I was a failure and a disappointment to everyone. He helped me recognize certain factors that were operating in my relationship to other people. But the main thing was learning to know myself better and accept myself as I was.

Still others appreciated the opportunity for getting in touch with others and sharing their feelings with another human being:

I think these things clarify in your own mind what's eating you. A third ear develops when you're talking with another person which helps to see yourself objectively.

It was helpful to have someone to act as a reflector for my problems and confusions. I could look more objectively.

It allowed me to ventilate my feelings. When you actually say what you feel, it sounds different. It allowed me to express some hostility.

As with their male counterparts, the chief complaint which the female respondents had about their contacts with professionals had to do with the professional's manner and way of relating to them (Table 21.28):

He was cold toward me, not interested in me, didn't understand my problems. I really disliked him.

My therapist made a pass at me to see if I was really homosexual. Instead of feeling good, I left with some hostile feelings about men that he had previously erased.

I felt they didn't understand me. It was too personal to him—like I was confronting him. I felt all the time I went to them that they were more interested in my history than what was happening to me at the present time.

Summary

Compared with the white homosexual females, the black lesbians tended to report poorer health and more psychosomatic symptoms, to feel lonely more often, and to display more tension and paranoia. However, the whites were more likely than the blacks ever to have considered committing suicide. The black and the white homosexual females did not differ with respect to how happy they felt either at the present time or five years ago, how exuberant, self-accepting, or depressed they felt, or how much they worried. They also did not differ in the number of or reasons for the suicide attempts they reported or in their experiences with psychotherapy.

Unlike the case with the male samples, the homosexual females did not differ from the heterosexual females in many measures of psychological adjustment. All the female respondents tended to score similarly in terms of their general health, the extent of their psychosomatic symptoms, how happy they were compared with five years ago, their exuberance, how often they felt lonely, how much they worried, how depressed, paranoid, or tense they tended to be, how often they had attempted suicide (among those who ever did), or how old they were at the time. The homosexual women did tend to report less current happiness, less self-esteem, more suicidal ideation, and more contact with professional counselors, than did the heterosexual women.

Some of these differences, however, were due to the scores of only one or two of the homosexual subgroups. On the other hand, in some cases where the homosexuals and heterosexuals as a whole did not differ, one or more of the subgroups did differ from the heterosexual sample. For example, the Close-Coupled lesbians were more likely than the heterosexual women to say they were happier at present than five years ago; they were also less lonely than the heterosexuals. The Dysfunctionals, by contrast, were the only subgroup less happy and less exuberant than the heterosexuals. They were also less self-accepting.

Overview

These data confirm our conviction that studies which compare homosexual men and women with their heterosexual counterparts in terms of their adult psychological adjustment are more informative when homosexual types are delineated. If we had not done this ourselves, we would have been forced to conclude that homosexual adults in general tend to be less well adjusted psychologically than heterosexual men and women. In fact, however, among both the males and the females, it is primarily the Dysfunctionals and the Asexuals who appeared to be less well off psychologically than those in the heterosexual groups.

Among the men, the Close-Coupleds could not be distinguished from the heterosexuals on various measures of psychological adjustment and actually scored higher on the two happiness measures. The Functionals, as well, hardly differed at all from the heterosexual men in terms of their psychological adjustment. Among the women, the need for delineating the homosexual adults on the basis of "type" is similarly striking. Like their male counterparts, the Close-Coupleds and the Functionals looked much like the heterosexuals psychologically. In fact, the Close-Coupled lesbians reported less loneliness than the heterosexual women, while the Functionals appeared to be more exuberant.

It would appear that homosexual adults who have come to terms with their homosexuality, who do not regret their sexual orientation, and who can function effectively sexually and socially, are no more distressed psychologically than are heterosexual men and women. Clearly, the therapist who continues to believe that it is by fiat his or her job to change a homosexual client's sexual orientation is ignorant of the true issues involved. What is required, at least initially, is a consideration of why a particular person's homosexuality is problematic and to examine the ways in which his or her life-style can be made more satisfying. Of particular importance, perhaps, might be the individual's failure to establish an ongoing relationship with a same-sex partner. Our data indicate that such a failure may be even more consequential and problematic for most homosexual adults than whatever difficulties they might have in accepting their homosexuality. Suicidal ideation and suicide attempts are apt to occur at the time of the breakdown or dissolution of a significant "couple" relationship. Such extreme reactions on the part of those involved need not lead us to conclude that homosexual adults have some special deficit in their personalities. Rather, homosexual partnerships may involve more mutual interdependence than is found among heterosexual couples and, for that reason alone, their disruption may be more debilitating for those involved. What is required is counselors sensitive to the special difficulties and challenges homosexuals face in their attempt to maintain viable partnerships. Such professionals should be prepared to work as frequently with homosexual couples as with individuals, either in an effort to reopen lines of communication and to modify the partners' expectations or to make their eventual parting an occasion for personal growth instead of alienation.

Part V

A Concluding Overview

We are pleased at the extent to which the aims of our investigation of homosexual men and women have been realized. The tables in Appendix C show clearly that homosexual adults are a remarkably diverse group. Seldom do we find the vast majority of a given sample responding to a particular question in exactly the same way. Whether they were reporting about an aspect of their sexual lives, their social adjustment, or their emotional feelings, our respondents tended to say widely different things. This, of course, accounts for the many useful response distributions to be found in connection with almost every item. Needless to say, if we had not obtained samples from so many different sources, or if our respondents had been very similar demographically or only men or only women, the diversity of homosexual experience would not have been so evident. Again and again our data have demonstrated the need for specifying the race, sex, age, and sometimes educational or occupational level of homosexual adults before drawing any particular conclusions about them.

In addition, we were able to delineate our respondents beyond what their demographic characteristics would suggest. Initially based on differences in how they experienced and expressed their homosexuality, our typology proved to be more comprehensive. The types demonstrate important relationships between homosexual adults' sexually related behaviors and feelings and their social and psychological adjustment. These relationships, evident in the more comprehensive typologies described below, make it clear that the sexual, social, and psychological spheres of human life are inevitably related to each other, that experiences in one sphere frequently coincide with and influence what occurs in another. An important lesson to be learned from our data is that homosexual men and women are best understood when they are seen as whole human beings, not just in terms of what they do sexually, despite the connection between sex and other aspects of their lives.

Another lesson our data provide is that future research in this area should attend increasingly to differences among homosexual adults. Researchers must be made keenly aware of the necessity to develop more precise typologies than the one in the present study, and for heterosexuals as well. These should refer not only to the sexual features of people's lives but also to the variety of contexts in which sexual feelings and impulses are expressed and to their social and psychological correlates.

Our data show that using a typology of homosexual experience helps to clarify whatever differences there might be between homosexual and heterosexual adults. In many instances a much greater amount of the variance was accounted for when the heterosexual group was compared with various types of homosexuals than when the comparisons involved simply the two undifferentiated groups. In some cases, if we had not distinguished one type of homosexual male or female from another and had not been able to compare each type with those in the heterosexual group, we would have concluded that homosexual men and women in general are quite different from their heterosexual counterparts, both socially and psychologically. In fact, however, the Close-Coupled homosexual men and women, similar perhaps to many of the married men and women in the heterosexual group, hardly differed at all from the heterosexual sample and in some cases actually appeared better adjusted; the same was true of the Functional homosexuals. Usually it was the Dysfunctional and Asexual homosexuals who differed from the heterosexual respondents, and often in much the same way that they differed from other homosexual respondents. There is no question but that the heterosexual population has its share of types equivalent to those found among homosexuals and that if we had been in a position to develop a corresponding heterosexual typology, we might have concluded that the chief difference between the two groups involves only the nature of their sexual preference.

Returning to the *raison d'être* of our study, it should be clear by now that we do not do justice to people's sexual orientation when we refer to it by a singular noun. There are "homosexualities" and there are "heterosexualities," each involving a variety of different interrelated dimensions. Before one can say very much about a person on the basis of his or her sexual orientation, one must make a comprehensive appraisal of the relationships among a host of features pertaining to the person's life and decide very little about him or her until a more complete and highly developed picture appears.

In what follows we present composite pictures of the types of homosexual men and women that emerged from our samples, involving their standings on the various measures of sexual experience and social and psychological adjustment. The descriptions are based on comparisons reported throughout this book and, in those instances where additional comparisons were made in order to determine differences between particular types (the Close-Coupleds versus the Functionals, the Dysfunctionals versus the Asexuals, etc.), on our multivariate analysis of variance. The statistical results of these additional analyses are to be found in Tables 22.1, 22.2, and 22.3. Each composite picture will include descriptions of some of the actual respondents assigned to the particular type. These descriptions are excerpts of "thumbnail sketches" prepared for each respondent by his or her interviewer, who, of course, did not know we would be "typing" the homosexual respondents.

Close-Coupleds

We resisted the temptation to call this group "happily married," although some of its members described themselves that way, because we did not want to imply that heterosexual relationships and marriage in particular are standards by which to judge people's adjustment. Instead, we use the word "close" in two senses. First, the partners in this kind of relationships are closely bound together. Second, the partnership is closed in that the Close-Coupleds tend to look to each other rather than to outsiders for sexual and interpersonal satisfactions.

The ways in which the Close-Coupleds differ from respondents in other homosexual groups bear out this description. They were the least likely to seek partners outside their special relationship, had the smallest amount of sexual problems, and were unlikely to regret being homosexual. They tended to spend more evenings at home and less leisure time by themselves, and the men in this group seldom went to such popular cruising spots as bars or baths. Although the Close-Coupleds did not have the highest level of sexual activity, they reported more than most respondents, and their sexual lives were evidently gratifying to them. They were likely to have engaged in a wide variety of sexual techniques and tended not to report the kinds of problems that might arise from a lack of communication between partners.

The Close-Coupleds' superior adjustment is demonstrated in other aspects of their lives. The men in this group had rarely experienced difficulties related to their sexual orientation such as being arrested, trouble at work, or assault and robbery. They were less tense or paranoid and more exuberant than the average respondent. The Close-Coupled lesbians were the least likely of all the groups ever to have been concerned enough about a personal problem to have sought professional help for it. Both the men and the women were more self-accepting and less depressed or lonely than any of the others, and they were the happiest of all.

Our interviewers described some of the Close-Coupled respondents as follows:

There was an obvious warmth and caring between him and his roommate. Altogether I felt that he had his life in better order than the vast majority of people I've met.

Although he and his roommate do not think of themselves as husband and wife, there seemed to be some consistent division of roles. For example, his roommate does most of the cooking and serving, while he does more about keeping their finances in order. They seem to have a very good relationship. Although they did not display physical affection in my presence, they clearly like each other.

She was very friendly, interested, talkative, and open. I felt like I was a friend whom she was inviting in to share part of her life. I liked her paintings, her roommate's photographs of the Bay Area, and the warm togetherness of their home. She and her roommate were obviously very much in love. Like most people who have a good, stable, five-year relationship, they seemed comfortable together, sort of part of one another, able to joke, obviously fulfilled in their relationship. They work together, have the same times off from work, do most of their leisure activities together. She is helping her roommate to learn to paint, while her roommate is teaching her about photography. They sent me home with a plateful of cookies, a good symbolic gesture of the kind of welcome and warmth I felt in their home.

The apartment which he shares with his lover is very clearly "their" home. A lot of love went into fixing it up. Interestingly, when I asked him questions about his own siblings, he called in his roommate to help him out with the answers!

The room was filled with *their* things—paintings her roommate had done, their books and records, etc. The relationship seemed quite stable and satisfying to them both.

She lives in a nice modern home with her girlfriend, who is in real estate. They really have a loving, happy thing going together. Although she's had previous relationships, she says she's really happy for the first time.

I got the feeling that both were warm and loving people and had their heads together as to what they were doing and wanted.

The salience of a viable "coupled" relationship among our homosexual respondents is evident in comparisons between the Close-Coupleds and the next group to be described, the Open-Coupleds. The latter are not as fully committed to their special partner, placing more reliance on a large circle of homosexual friends and less stress on the importance of their relationship with their partner. They are also less happy, self-accepting, and relaxed than the Close-Coupleds. These differences seem to suggest that the Open-Coupled relationship reflects a conflict between the ideal of fulfilled monogamy and dissatisfactions within the partnership.

Open-Coupleds

Like their Close-Coupled counterparts, the men and women in this group were living with a special sexual partner. They were not happy with their circumstances, however, and tended (despite spending a fair amount of time at home) to seek satisfactions with people outside their partnership. For example, the Open-Coupled men did more cruising than average, and the lesbians in this group cruised more than any of the other female respondents. Concomitantly, the Open-Coupleds worried about their cruising, especially about the possibility of being arrested or otherwise publicly exposed—perhaps because of their partner's ignorance of their cruising activities. In addition, the Open-Coupleds reported more sexual activity than the typical homosexual respondent and broader sexual repertoires, but the men tended to have trouble getting their partner to meet their sexual requests, and the women had the greatest worry about their partner wanting to do unwelcome sexual things or about being unable to carry on a conversation with her.

In most respects of their social and psychological adjustment, the Open-Coupleds could not be distinguished from the homosexual respondents as a whole. For example, they were not notable in how they spent their leisure time, how often they had experienced various social difficulties connected with homosexuality, or how many other people knew about their sexual orientation. Psychologically, they were about as happy, exuberant, depressed, tense, paranoid, or worrisome as the average homosexual respondent. However, the Open-Coupled lesbians were less self-accepting than any of the other groups.

He tries to give the appearance of happiness with his roommate but cruises continually, feels grave guilt about this, and says that it contributes to his domestic travail. He stopped me from introducing myself to his roommate, as if I were a pickup he wanted to keep secret.

At first he wanted his roommate to sit in on the interview but later acknowledged that he was glad I hadn't allowed this, since his roommate doesn't know he cruises.

He indicated that he has never had moral qualms about his homosexuality, but he is upset about his promiscuity.

As she talked, I discovered that her lover is very jealous and that she (the respondent) would like to date men and explore her own sexual orientation further, but that her lover was demanding a long-term commitment and she was not free to try out other relationships.

He is having a serious problem with his lover right now. The latter jumped off a third-floor porch on Christmas Day in an alcoholic stupor.

His partner is eleven years older than he and has begun slowing down sexually, which is a problem for them both. He has another friend with whom he's sexually compatible, but he doesn't want to end his present relationship. He appears troubled by this dilemma.

In discussing her current affair, she said that they had had sex twice and that she doesn't care to again and that she is not involved emotionally with her partner.

He was disappointed that he and his lover do not have sex anymore.

He said that he could not say whether he was in love with his roommate because he did not know what love really is.

It should be noted that the Open-Coupleds were the modal type among the males but relatively rare among the females, many more of whom were Close-Coupled. Whether lesbians find it easier than do homosexual males to achieve a stable and satisfying relationship with just one person, or whether they are more strongly motivated by romantic feelings than the men are, is not clear. However, our analysis of variance did show that the Open-Coupled males expressed more self-acceptance and less loneliness than the females did. This kind of relationship, then, is apparently more trying for the lesbian than for her male counterpart.

Compared with members of the other groups, the Open-Coupleds are intermediate in their adjustment. They went out more often and also spent more time alone than the Close-Coupleds did, and among the males, felt more lonely. On the other hand, the Open-Coupled males appear much better off than the Dysfunctional males do. The latter were less likely to have many homosexual friends or to value having a special partner, and the Open-Coupleds were significantly better adjusted psychologically, reporting more happiness and self-acceptance and less worry, paranoia, tension, or depression. Since the Open-Coupled lesbians did not differ from their Dysfunctional counterparts in these ways, it seems possible that managing a less than exclusive homosexual relationship is more difficult for women than for men.

Functionals

If Close- and Open-Coupled respondents are in some respects like married heterosexuals, the Functionals come closest to the notion of "swinging singles." These men and women seem to organize their lives around their sexual experiences. They reported more sexual activity with a greater number of partners than did any of the other groups, and the Functional lesbians had been married more times than the rest of the female respondents. The Functional men and women were least likely to regret being homosexual, cruised frequently, and generally displayed a great deal of involvement in the gay world. They were not particularly interested in finding a special partner to settle down with, engaged in a wide variety of sexual activities, considered their sex appeal very high, and had few if any sexual problems. They were particularly unlikely to complain about not getting enough sex or difficulties in their sexual performance. Of all the groups, they were the most interested in sex, the most exuberant, and the most involved with their many friends. In addition, the Functional men had the fewest psychosomatic symptoms. They were also the most likely ever to have been arrested, booked, or convicted for a "homosexual" offense; this may be related to their greater overtness, their high attendance at gay bars, and perhaps as well their relative lack of worry or suspicion of others—or even a certain degree of recklessness.

He lived in a very neat apartment. A music lover, he must have had close to a thousand blues and jazz records on the shelf. He also had three motorcycle trophies.

He seemed very self-assured, and it was enjoyable interviewing him.

He was a very energetic and open kid, looking much younger than twenty-seven. He seemed to be feeling very happy, likes his job in the Merchant Marine, and enjoys being back for just short stays. Although this militates against long-term relationships, he really enjoys his feelings of independence.

Just a warm, lovely lady.

She was friendly and completely comfortable during the interview. She had a very pleasant, lively personality.

A very calm, well-adjusted "man's man" type. His social skills were most evident.

He is a crusty but likable old Yankee from Maine, a warm, friendly person who lives in a renovated Victorian house full of gay roomers. He has plenty of money and seems beautifully adjusted.

He is a well-adjusted, confident, relaxed homosexual male: obvious but not flamboyant.

The Functionals' good adjustment seems to be a function of their particular personalities. They are energetic and self-reliant, cheerful and optimistic, and comfortable with their highly emphasized sexuality. One should not conclude, however, that Functionals are an ideal type as regards coping with a homosexual orientation. It is rather the Close-Coupled men and women who have made the best adjustment. For example, while the Functionals had few sexual problems and were not very depressed or unhappy, the Close-Coupleds surpass them in these respects. When the two groups are compared directly, we see that the Functionals understandably spend less time at home and see their friends more often, but the males are more tense, unhappy, and lonely than their Close-Coupled counterparts.

Dysfunctionals

The Dysfunctionals are the group in our sample which most closely accords with the stereotype of the tormented homosexual. They are troubled people whose lives offer them little gratification, and in fact they seem to have a great deal of difficulty managing their existence. Sexually, socially, and psychologically, wherever they could be distinguished from the homosexual respondents as a whole, the Dysfunctionals displayed poorer adjustment.

In terms of their sexual lives, the Dysfunctionals were the most regretful about their homosexuality. They reported more sexual problems than any other group, and they were especially prone to worry about their sexual adequacy, how they could maintain affection for their partner, and whether they or their partner would attain orgasm. Despite fairly frequent cruising (among the males) and a relatively high number of partners, they tended to complain about not having sex often enough and were most likely of all the groups to report that they and their partner could not agree on what kind of sexual activity should take place. In addition, the men had trouble finding a suitable partner and were the most likely ever to have experienced impotence and premature ejaculation. Not surprisingly, with all these difficulties, the Dysfunctionals tended to think they were sexually unappealing.

Other aspects of the Dysfunctionals' lives were similarly problematic for them. Among the men in this group, there were more reports of robbery, assault, extortion, or job difficulties due to their being homosexual; they were also more likely ever to have been arrested, booked, or convicted regardless of the reason. The Dysfunctional lesbians were the least exuberant and the most likely to have needed long-term professional help for an emotional problem, and their male counterparts were more lonely, worrisome, paranoid, depressed, tense, and unhappy than any of the other men.

He is a bookkeeper type, prim and a little stuffy, not a warm person. He lives alone with his ledgers.

He has a languid, apathetic manner.

He seems to have an adolescent religious hang-up. I see his admission to being a "chicken queen" as a way for him to relive or act out his lost youth. He drives to the Tenderloin "meat rack," picks up young hustlers, drives them to Redwood City, and then pays them for sex.

He tends to project his own inadequacies onto others. For example, he claims that others are shallow and not desirous of lasting relationships, and yet he's had more than a thousand partners in the past two years.

He lives in an ugly, bleak two-room apartment, where he seems to devote most of his time to watching TV. He has no close friends, and those he has he seldom sees. All relationships seem casual and unimportant to him.

He wanted very much to be an Episcopal priest, but his moral conflict over his homosexuality stood in his way. He seemed very depressed and low in self-esteem.

I felt a horrible sense of resignation about him, of surrender to a dead-end fate.

She seemed quiet, somewhat stiff, almost cold.

He says he enjoys drinking more than sex. He kept referring to his drinking when I asked a question about sex.

She seemed very well put together for someone with two psychotic breaks to her record.

Direct comparisons of the Dysfunctionals with other groups strengthen the impression of their general distress. The Dysfunctional men differ significantly from both the Functionals and the Open-Coupleds on virtually every measure of psychological adjustment. If we had numbered only Dysfunctionals among our respondents, we very likely would have had to conclude that homosexuals in general are conflict-ridden social misfits.

Asexuals

The most prominent characteristic of the Asexual men and women in our samples is their lack of involvement with others. They scored the lowest of all the groups in the level of their sexual activity, reported few partners, had narrow sexual repertoires, rated their sex appeal very low, and tended to have a fair number of sexual problems. In this regard, the Asexual males tended to mention trouble finding a partner and not having sex often enough, but they were also less interested in sex than the other men. The Asexuals were the least likely of all the groups to describe themselves as exclusively homosexual, and among the males, they were less overt about their homosexuality and had fewer same-sex homosexual friends. Both the men and the women in this group tended to spend their leisure time alone and to have infrequent contact with their friends. They described themselves as lonely and (among the men) unhappy; the Asexual lesbians were most apt to have sought professional help concerning their sexual orientation but also to have given up counseling quickly, and they had the highest incidence of suicidal thoughts (not necessarily related to their homosexuality).

This woman now lives alone, has had no sexual experience with a partner in the past year, and seems never to have had any deep commitments to anyone. I can't imagine her really responding with warmth to any person or any need.

Quite subdued and reticent, he lives alone in his apartment with five cats. There are five different cat food bowls on the floor in the kitchen. One for each cat.

When the interview came to an end, he asked me why he had difficulty relating to people and why people didn't like him, exclaiming, "I'm always clean, neat, polite, proper . . ." He seems very lonely to me.

He seemed like a totally ineffectual, frightened, withdrawn sort of person. He was desperately shy and seemed very afraid of me for the first part of the interview. The house was a fantastic state of rubble, full of boxes of junk, files, and furniture. He explained them by saying simply, "I collect things."

He has to be one of the saddest, most forlorn human beings I've ever met. He said to me, "Here I've made it financially and professionally. I could travel anywhere or do anything, but why bother? I'm more lonesome away than I am at home, and I'm desperately lonesome at home." He has a big dog named Chipper who is very important in his life.

She says no one has ever loved her. Indubitable!

She was a bit cool and businesslike. Her difficulties with interpersonal relations were hinted at when she said she tends to be suspicious of people who are "too nice." When the interview was over she was pleasant, but it felt superficial.

He lives alone in a run-down Nob Hill apartment. He's over fifty years old and engages only in solitary masturbation with male fantasies. This has been the case for over four years.

He was a very soft-spoken and shy person. I couldn't imagine this short, timid little guy driving a big bus around the city.

The Asexual life-style is a solitary one. Despite their complaints of loneliness, Asexuals are not very interested in establishing a relationship with a special partner or in any of the rewards the gay world might offer them. For example, in addition to their lack of involvement with friends, the Asexual men seldom went to gay bars and did less cruising than any of the other groups except the Close-Coupleds. When compared directly with the Dysfunctionals, the Asexuals differed from them chiefly in terms of their disengagement from others. Nevertheless, since the Asexuals of either sex did not differ from the sample as a whole in many respects of psychological adjustment or in the extent to which being homosexual had caused them difficulty, it seems reasonable to infer that these people's quiet, withdrawn lives are the inevitable product of an underlying apathy toward the panoply of human experience.

Epilogue

It would be unfortunate to conclude this study of homosexual men and women without making its meaning more explicit and urging serious attention by those for whom our findings have special import. Such persons include state legislators involved in debates over the decriminalization of homosexual conduct, community leaders addressing themselves to the matter of civil rights for gays, governmental and business executives charged with the responsibility of hiring and firing personnel, educators and lay people dealing with sex education, religious leaders who are reexamining their churches' sexual beliefs and values, counselors with homosexual clients, and, finally, homosexual men and women themselves.

Until now, almost without exception, people in general, as well as those above, have been outraged, fearful, or despairing toward homosexuality because of the stereotypes they hold. Not only have they believed that homosexuals are pretty much alike, but that this similarity necessarily involves irresponsible sexual conduct, a contribution to social decay, and, of course, psychological pain and maladjustment. Given such a stereotype, it is little wonder that the heterosexual majority has seen fit to discourage the acceptance of homosexuality by criminalizing homosexual behaviors and ferreting out people who engage in them, refusing to employ homosexuals, withholding from homosexual men and women the civil rights enjoyed by the majority and by a growing number of other minority groups, trying to cure homosexuals of their "aberration," and feeling grief or shame at the discovery that a loved one is "afflicted" by homosexual propensities. Reactions such as these to the millions of homosexual men and women in America and elsewhere are understandable in the light of common notions about what it means to be homosexual.

The present investigation, however, amply demonstrates that relatively few homosexual men and women conform to the hideous stereotype most people have of them. In addition, it is reasonable to suppose that objectionable sexual advances are far more apt to be made by a heterosexual (usually, by a man toward a woman) than a homosexual. In the same vein, seduction of an adolescent girl by a male teacher is probably more frequent than the seduction of young people by homosexual teachers, who are more apt to regard the class as a surrogate family than as a target for their sexual interests. And outside the classroom, the seduction of "innocents" far more likely involves an older male, often a relative, and a pre- or postpubescent female. Moreover, rape and sexual violence more frequently occur in a heterosexual than a homosexual context. Rape (outside of prisons) generally involves sexual attacks made by men upon women, while the relatively rare violence occurring in a homosexual context is usually the result of male youths "hunting queers" or a man's guilt and disgust over a sexual episode just concluded. Finally, with respect to homosexuals' sexual activity itself, as our study notes, it commonly begins with highly cautious pursuits in places not normally frequented by heterosexuals or in more public surroundings where heterosexuals are not aware of what is taking place. Most often it is consummated with the full consent of the persons involved and in the privacy of one of the partners' homes. Even this description, however, disregards the numerous instances in which homosexual contact occurs solely between persons whose commitment to each other includes sharing a household.

As for homosexuals' social and psychological adjustment, we have found that much depends upon the type of homosexual being considered. Many could very well serve as models of social comportment and psychological maturity. Most are indistinguishable from the heterosexual majority with respect to most of the nonsexual aspects of their lives, and whatever differences there are between homosexuals' and heterosexuals' social adjustment certainly do not reflect any malevolent influence on society on the part of the homosexuals concerned. Close-Coupleds and Open-Coupleds behave much like married heterosexuals. Functionals draw on a host of support systems and display joy and exuberance in their particular life-style. To be sure, Dysfunctionals and Asexuals have a difficult time of it, but there are certainly equivalent groups among heterosexuals. Clearly, a deviation from the sexual norms of our society does not inevitably entail a course of life with disastrous consequences. The homosexual who is afraid that he might end up a "dirty old man," desperately lonely, should be assured that such a plight is not inevitable and that, given our society's failure to meet the needs of aging people, heterosexuality hardly guarantees well-being in old age. Between the time of their "coming out" and whatever years remain, homosexual men and women must become increasingly aware of the array of options they have in their lives.

Perhaps the least ambiguous finding of our investigation is that homosexuality is not necessarily related to pathology. Thus, decisions about homosexual men and women, whether they have to do with employment or child custody or counseling, should never be made on the basis of sexual orientation alone. Moreover, it should be recognized that what has survival value in a heterosexual context may be destructive in a homosexual context, and vice versa. Life-enhancing mechanisms used by heterosexual men or women should not necessarily be used as the standard by which to judge the degree of homosexuals' adjustment. Even their personality characteristics must be appraised in the light of how functional they are in a setting that may be quite different from the dominant cultural milieu. It must also be remembered that even a particular type of homosexual is never entirely like others categorized in the same way, much less like those whose life-styles barely resemble his or her own. And while the present study has taken a step forward in its delineation of types of homosexuals, it too fails to capture the full diversity that must be understood if society is ever fully to respect, and ever to appreciate, the way in which individual homosexual men and women live their lives.

Appendix A / Ethnography of the Bay Area Homosexual Scene

The reports that follow were compiled by our team of ethnographers at the same time that the interviews were being conducted. Where the passage of time has outdated them, so that they no longer reflect the Bay Area environment, we apologize. Nevertheless, they still stand as a portrait of the social context in which our respondents gave their reports and lived their lives. (Note: the bars and restaurants mentioned have been given fictitious names.)

Residence Patterns

Although in many cases our homosexual respondents did not appear to be very different from the heterosexuals, some did display distinctive residential patterns. Homosexual men tended to eschew family neighborhoods and instead to buy old Victorian houses in areas of San Francisco where property values were low and housing cheap. These old buildings, though many had been converted into apartments, had high ceilings, large windows, spacious and well-proportioned rooms (evident even where recent partitions divided them), carved decorations, and sometimes the original, elaborate fixtures, all of which made them potentially lovely accommodations. Homosexual men's reputation for skillfully and imaginatively renovating such houses—an avocation that invariably enhanced neighborhood property values—was so well-known among realtors and banks that they seldom had trouble acquiring mortgages, although on occasion lenders would insist that only one of a couple be the borrower of record.

The neighborhoods where many homosexual men lived (the Upper Market, Lower Pacific Heights, and Polk Street areas, for instance) had the additional advantage of being close to the "action." Cruising areas, gay bars, and other subcultural institutions were close by. What was most striking to the observer, however, was the beauty of their meticulously restored houses. On many such streets the monotony of rows of architecturally identical houses would be sharply broken, as the following examples attest.

In one such neighborhood stood a row of two-story stucco houses. On the first floor of each house was a garage with a wooden door of ordinary size located a few feet to the right. To enter, one walked up a concrete staircase at the side to a doorway on the second-floor level. On this level there was also a large window facing the street, set precisely in the middle of the house. The window trim and eaves, if the rest of the house was white, were painted green or blue or red. If the house was painted putty color, the trim would be white. These color combinations were quite standard.

Standing out from these houses was one painted a soft, drab moss green with black trim around the windows. On the lower half of the windows were dark-stained, wooden louver blinds, and starkly white shades covered the upper portion. This house looked so different from its neighbors that one might assume its basic design differed as well. Directly across the street, on its highest point, were two three-story, older, wood-frame houses. One had been painted a deep mustard with black trim around the windows and on the carved eaves. There was a dull-black, wrought-iron banister encircling the front porch. The other house was dark olive with mahogany trim. Its front yard was fenced in by weathered-gray, carved wooden seats.

Around the corner opposite several dingy apartment buildings, two houses were undergoing extensive remodeling. One was being paneled on the outside with pale red unstained wood. On the second floor the old wood had been removed and replaced with these panels, and modern windows had been set into the walls. On the inside the owner had stripped away the old walls and floorboards. A third floor was as yet unfinished. Here, a modern house had been superimposed on a Victorian frame. The house next door had recently been covered with pre-aged wooden shingles and the trim painted black. Elaborate wrought-iron railings encircled the porch, the second-story balcony, and the upper part of the garden. At this time the third story was still pink and green; the remodeling, apparently, was proceeding as the owner could afford.

In another area, two homosexual men's houses stood out from the rest. One had been shingled during the past few years in a medium red-brown shade. The trim under the eaves and around the windows was shiny black. There were four hand-carved, dark brown doors with elaborate gold numbers, door knockers, and knobs, and white, shirred curtains in the large front window. Inside, the owner had remodeled extensively, enlarging the rooms, extending the breakfast nook to include the porch, and adding a new sun porch. The other house was painted bright yellow. The carved curlicue trim around the windows and under the eaves was painted with glossy white enamel. The small false balconies at the bases of the windows were glossy black.

In addition, landlords tended to regard homosexual men as favorable tenants because they paid rent on time, took great care of the property, and in general behaved in unobtrusive and discreet ways so as not to draw attention to themselves. At the time of our study, people were much more likely to be distrustful of blacks or hippies.

The housing circumstances of lesbians in San Francisco were markedly different. Landlords were disinclined to rent to them—or to women generally—for reasons opposite those above. They believed that homosexual women were careless about rent payments, poor at housekeeping, contentious about repairs, and disturbingly noisy tenants. Consequently, lesbians were more likely to choose to live in outlying suburbs. Those who could afford it were likely to purchase modest homes of bland appearance and, their reputations as tenants notwithstanding, to live quiet, conventional lives like their heterosexual neighbors. The fact that suburban living required lesbians to commute, in contrast to the men who preferred living near "the scene," probably worked to their advantage: pleading extensive driving distance, they could avoid social gatherings with work associates and thus perhaps conceal their homosexual life-style. Those lesbians who did live in San Francisco proper were subject to the kinds of suspicion from landlords (or mortgagors) mentioned above and often had to settle for unpleasant accommodations. Since 1970, however, legislative attention to women's equal rights in borrowing and renting may have ameliorated these difficulties.

Cruising

Most of our homosexual male respondents and some of the lesbians went out cruising—looking for a sexual partner. Cruising took place in a variety of settings which were known in the homosexual community as places where partners might be found with relative ease and safety. Chief among these settings was the gay bar.

Gay Bars

At the time of our interview there were several dozen bars catering mostly or exclusively to homosexuals in the Bay Area. (Gay bars and restaurants, their varying ambiance and clientele, are discussed more fully in the Social Activities section, below.) While the gay bar functions as an important gathering place in which to socialize with one's friends, it is also—like heterosexual singles bars—a comparatively safe place to pursue and find sexual partners. Even though patrons well understood this, the approaches which were made were remarkably cautious. Bar cruising did not necessarily begin in the bar itself. Men might come to a gay bar with people they had picked up in the streets, parks, or other public places. Or one man might see another enter a bar and, following him inside, begin to cruise him. An ethnographer reported:

Outside The Pit I sat in my car and watched the cruising scene on this busy Tenderloin corner. A man about forty stood on the corner for half an hour or so until another man the same age came along. They looked each other over for a while, the newcomer looking as if he were waiting for a taxi or something. Eventually he walked down the street a few yards and stood in front of the door to The Pit. The first man began to walk toward the bar also and eventually went in after him. Later, I went into the bar and observed them standing and having a beer. About ten minutes after that, they left together.

An informant-hustler whom I watched work Market Street a couple nights told me about a transaction I observed tonight. One man cruised him and he wasn't interested; another came along a little drunk and tried to get into the action. From where I was standing it appeared that it was a three-way sex proposition, but the informant said that the men did not know each other. He said the two of them exchanged introductory words and one invited the other to have a drink and dance at the Meeting Place.

Inside the gay bar, cruising could take many forms. The initiator might buy his prospective partner a drink or engage him in small talk. In the dancing bars he might ask him to dance. If the cruiser was successful, at some point during the evening the two would leave the premises for sexual activity, often in one or the other's home. Not infrequently an approach, at the point that it became direct, would be met with a "No, thank you," "Maybe some other time," or "I'm waiting for someone else," and the prevailing courtesy generally meant that the cruiser would desist.

The moment I entered the bar I noticed men casually, sometimes surreptitiously, sometimes directly, looking at each other. The bar had a lighted entrance designed to allow maximum viewing by people sitting at the bar. From the moment a man enters the bar he is checked out.

I sat at the end of the bar and watched two men sitting six stools apart. Each would look at the other periodically, casting short and quick glances. This process went on for nearly an hour. Eventually one of the men got up to leave, walked to the door, and stopped to look at some posters on the wall there. The other man got up and followed the other and stood beside him. They talked briefly with each other. The one man went back to the bar and picked up his jacket and both left together.

I noticed a handsome older man leaning against the end of the bar looking at the dance floor at a young blond man who was very popular with the customers because of his age and attractiveness. The young man was dancing with many others, yet the older man made no approach. Over an hour passed before the younger man noticed that the older man was paying him attention, and then there were many people in between them. Finally, the young man nonchalantly walked over to the bar and stood next to the older man, who asked him to dance. They danced one dance and then left the bar together.

In the Purple Zebra I noticed one young man kept going into the rest room. Eventually I went in after him and noticed him exposing an erection to another at the urinal. Soon both men left, and as I looked out the front door I noticed that, as frequently happens, one was waiting in his car for the other to get his own car and follow him to their rendezvous.

At the Clock, where customers stand four deep in front of the bar, the standard cruising procedure is to stand against a wall next to the person you are interested in. You sort of sidle up backwards to the wall, excusing yourself to the person you want to cruise. You are then in a good position to get acquainted (there is nothing else to do but leave) and the bumping and excusing allows for a good opener, e.g., "Gee, it's crowded here tonight."

Just before closing time everyone in the place appears as if he is looking for a lost contact lens which is somehow floating at eye level in the room. Seven people asked me if I needed a ride.

At the Circus customers will go and sit near the door at closing time to get looked over and to look over others who are leaving at that time. There are lots of smiles and pats on the head and some "Hey, let's go for coffee." All this after many hours of being together and drinking without an overture to conversation.

A cruise in the Tiger may take the form of asking the waiter (who is popular with everyone) to perform introductions. He says he gets a lot of tips this way.

Standing outside of The Hangout on a Tenderloin street, I could see dozens of gay men cruising, hopping from one bar to another—it was nearly closing time. Three cruised me while I was standing there, each with the same approach, "Wanna catch a last-minute drink?" It was like my first trip to New York, where it seemed that at least a million people were running toward me as I got off the bus. I realized that two eyes, a drinking hand, and an imbibing mouth are the only functional anatomical parts necessary to be in that bar near closing. The bar is really structured so that people don't need to communicate verbally.

Cruising the bars and the streets outside them are also a number of male hustlers. They are particularly apparent near closing time, when those who have not yet found a partner may be more willing to hire them. Most bars, wary of trouble with the police, discourage hustlers from coming inside (and for the same reason close fifteen or twenty minutes before the statutory time) except during bad weather. In a few, however, hustlers are an integral part of the scene. Along the wall opposite the bar there are usually a few hustlers, many of whom spend most of the day there. One said many of his customers come directly to this bar to find a hustler, rather than using the street. Other hustlers drop by from time to time for a drink. Tonight I saw quite a few hustlers come into the bar for a drink, I guess to talk about what they were going to do sexually and where. I spoke to one and he stated that he often suggests that he and his "score" come to the bar for a drink; he felt it loosened up the "score" and he might pay more money for the services. Several of the customers who knew the hustlers said hello and talked briefly with them, sometimes jabbing them or patting them on the back. The wall was apparently reserved primarily for the hustlers, for few others stood by it or leaned against it.

I met an ex-Marine tonight in the Circus. He was hard as nails, almost a stereotype of the tough Marine. He said he came to the bar just about every night. Some months before, he had hustled the streets, but found more reliable and better-paying customers here in the bar. He would sit in the middle of the bar and talk to whoever would buy a drink and feel them out for sexual interest. He was very aggressive and would at times demand a drink from someone. He said he didn't like this routine particularly, but it turned some men on.

Gay Baths

Another important feature of gay life is the gay baths (or "tubs").[1] They are not a central part of social life as the bars are, and unlike the bars they have not even a remote counterpart in the straight world. The baths, despite the services they provide (steam rooms, whirlpool baths, and in some, masseurs, manicurists, entertainment, etc.), exist principally to facilitate impersonal sexual encounters among homosexual men.

The baths have been an institution in San Francisco gay life for at least thirty years. Some began as "legitimate" health clubs catering to the general public. But by the time of our interviews, they were widely understood as exclusively homosexual places. This meant that the baths had to be careful to operate so as not to jeopardize their licenses. One method was to discourage or prohibit heterosexual patrons who might be offended by sexual activities in the baths. It was assumed, for instance, that anyone who called for an appointment was straight and was therefore told that schedules were filled. Some receptionists and stewards would candidly say that the bath catered to homosexuals. The covert acceptance of gay baths by the local authorities was probably an indication of their "live and let live" philosophy.

The major function of the gay bath is to provide an inexpensive place where homosexual men can engage in frequent, anonymous sexual activity without fear of social or legal reprisal. The larger baths could accommodate at least two hundred people, who usually stayed up to twelve hours. The cost was low, much cheaper than a motel room, and a patron might have nearly a dozen sexual encounters while he was there.

An important feature of the baths is the anonymity and privacy they afford their customers. Each person, on arriving, would put his clothes in a locker and wrap a towel around his waist. An ethnographer commented:

Visiting a downtown gay bath was in many ways like revisiting a high-school gym—everyone wearing the same towel, in the same color, on the same part of the body. There was no status consciousness in the social-stratification sense; the towel or loincloth created a sort of equal-status social group.

Dim, colored lights throughout the baths made it difficult to ascertain people's ages or physical merits:

[1] For a sociological description of gay baths, see Weinberg and Williams (1975b).

There was an almost surrealistic use of lighting—multicolored, indirect, dim, and changing. People often appeared to be moving to and fro in slow motion, as though they were dancing to the background music of a highly charged sexual atmosphere. In the (well-lit) shower room it was astonishing to see that a man who a few minutes earlier had appeared to be twenty-five was in fact forty or fifty years old. With visual cues kept to a minimum, I would guess that touch, hearing, and smell become most important.

Each of the baths had a large number of private rooms. Most were equipped with a dimly lit sitting area, a single cot, a small table with an ashtray, and a clothing rack (for clothes removed from lockers once a room became available).

There were always more patrons in the baths than there were individual rooms; on busy evenings or weekends, a majority of the clientele would not have rooms. They cruised the showers, steam rooms, and lounges, also glancing into private rooms where the occupant had invitingly left the door open.

The shower rooms, steam rooms, and the large "orgy" room were also frequently used for sex. The orgy room was understood to exist specifically for that purpose:

About seventy people were walking and creeping around the "maze" on the second floor of the bath. Some were having sex (usually mutual masturbation) standing up at various parts of the maze. In one corner was the orgy room. In the room was a large circular couch on which, for a few brief moments, were some eleven men, mostly drunk, playfully jumping on each other. Soon, three couples joined in a sex act while singing some popular song. It appeared that the sexual activity stopped short of orgasm since there was no sign of semen on the floor or couch. The atmosphere was that of a carnival or Fellini film.

This popular Tenderloin bath has a TV room which is essentially an orgy room after 8:00 P.M. On the third floor, up a short flight of stairs, it is a very dimly lit room with benches around the walls. Two couples were kissing, standing in the middle of the room with several men standing around watching. On the benches several people were fondling each other. All at once everyone in the room moved over to the west wall. A young black man was performing fellatio on a very young blond man. Soon almost everyone in the room was rubbing against the other in what was much like some tribal initiation ceremony. After the young white man ejaculated, he and the black youth embraced. The atmosphere in the room at that point was more brotherly than sexual.

And in the steam room:

As I sat down on a slatted bench, a middle-aged man slid under me, trying to perform anal intercourse. I told him I wanted to relax; he said, "Maybe later." The room was terribly hot and humid. It was difficult to see anything. The unbearable climate was made more bearable by the joking of two inebriated men who could not maintain their erections. One said to the other, "I guess it has been parboiled."

Not every area of the bathhouse was used for sexual activity. Those who stayed for several hours might make use of food vending machines, reading material, sunlamps, and a TV room where conversation took place. Especially in the baths frequented by younger persons, marijuana was often used. On Friday and Saturday nights the baths were packed, especially just after the bars closed for the night. At other times men would stop by the baths on their way to work or during their lunch hour or while waiting to return home by train or bus. At one bath a group of workingmen would congregate early in the morning once or twice a week for sex, followed by breakfast. One informant regularly slept at the baths two nights a week rather than commuting twenty miles every day.

There were a variety of reasons for going to the baths. Older or less attractive men found it easier to get a partner in the baths where the lighting did not make a person's age so apparent and other people who had not yet found a partner for the night were apt to be less choosy. Anyone who wanted to keep his identity a secret liked the semiprivate nature of the baths. A few "tub freaks" had sex only at the baths, and some hustlers liked to bring their scores there, but for most patrons, baths were simply an alternative cruising locale where partners were readily and anonymously available.

Public Places

Although bars and baths were important cruising locales, homosexual men cruised in other areas too. More public locales, such as certain streets or neighborhoods, men's rest rooms in various public facilities, and public parks, were popular with some gay men. While bars and baths were recognized cruising areas, public cruising required much more discretion, and a system of subtle cues helped cruisers identify each other.

Many street cruisers were hustlers, usually attractive young men who might work only part-time at what seemed relatively easy money. Some only received fellatio and therefore rejected a homosexual label; others were "in the life" for whatever the market would bear. A male hustler might earn ten to twenty dollars a trick, spending only a few minutes with a score. Male homosexual hustlers cruised during the noon hour, late afternoon, and at bar-closing time, and those who were particularly attractive (e.g., those with a "student" youthful image—indeed, many were college students or servicemen) might charge extra for a night's company.

Other street cruisers were simply looking for quick, impersonal sex. In the Tenderloin area, heterosexuals as well as homosexuals might be cruised by effeminate or "drag queen" men; here the object was not profit but anonymous pleasure. By far the most common kind of street cruiser, however, was one seeking a partner to spend the night or all weekend. An ethnographer reported:

Two sections of Polk Street—between California and Washington streets and between Chestnut and Union streets—have become widely known as a cruising area for large numbers of San Francisco homosexual men. It is an area where many homosexual men and women live; much of the cruising is quite open and casual. In the early evening, just before and after dinnertime, and on weekends at brunchtime or early afternoons and evenings, as many as two hundred people may cruise on Polk Street. Dressed in conventional business suits or slacks and sweaters or in mod clothes, these people (most of them white and between twenty-five and forty-five years old) will stroll casually up a few blocks of the street, cross over, and then return on the other side. The cruiser may stop in at one of the many coffee shops or soda fountains on the street, or strike up conversations with friends, neighbors, or shopkeepers. During weekdays potential sexual partners may meet each other over dinner in one of the area's restaurants. People also cruised around bus stops and phone booths.

The Great Highway is a one-mile stretch of road fronting the beach area at the end of Golden Gate Park. Dividing the beach area from the highway is a long seawall which runs the entire length of the area. From dawn to dusk, when the days are mild, homosexuals can be found cruising in the area, leaning, sitting, or walking on the wall. Sometimes people cruise in cars. Persons cruising each other on the highway may go to the adjacent parks for sex or accompany each other home for various lengths of time or just share each other's company on or around the beach area. There are several rest rooms in the vicinity which are sometimes used for sex. On warm days, homosexuals in pairs or in groups may gather on the beach. A nude beach in the Land's End area has recently been established, and homosexuals have begun to share this location with other, usually young, people from the metropolitan area.

The cruising sequence usually began with a person positioning himself on a street or public area. When he spotted a potential sexual partner, the cruiser moved within range by driving, walking, or lingering near the person he was cruising. Sometimes this involved looking into the same store window or up at the same marquee or standing together at the same newsstand. Next he made some kind of contact (or waited for the prospective partner to do so). This might involve a smile, a stare, or a lingering eye contact, or it might be verbal: "Do you happen to have the time?" "That's a nice shirt in the window," or more personally, "That's a nice shirt you have on." If the other responded agreeably, the cruiser then suggested getting together in private: "Do you want to come to my place?" "Let's make love," or even, "What do you say we get some coffee?" Soon thereafter, the two would come to an agreement about what to do and where and would stroll (or drive) off together.

Tearooms

Public rest rooms, or "tearooms," are sometimes used for cruising. They are an easily accessible source of potential sexual partners and permit immediate, somewhat private, sexual activity, as well as being places where members of the same sex share close yet anonymous physical proximity.

However, tearoom cruising is quite dangerous. Unlike other locales such as bars and baths, where most patrons are homosexual and at least expect that cruising may occur, tearooms are used by the general public, and one runs the risk of cruising a heterosexual who might be outraged enough to report or assault him. In addition, tearoom cruising is comparatively disreputable in the gay community. Despite the risks and the lack of aesthetic appeal, though, it does provide for quick consummation and preserves anonymity.

Certain public rest rooms, often near homosexual neighborhoods, were known by the gay community as cruising sites. They might be outdoors in parks, in travel terminals, theaters, or restaurants, or in office or university buildings. To qualify as a tearoom, a public rest room had to be not too publicly visible (so no one would notice if a person kept going in and out or stayed a long time), easy to get away from in case of trouble, and, often, seldom used except by other homosexuals. It should have structural features—lockable stalls and/or outer doors, for example—that would permit sex to take place privately and without interruption. A third person who could act as lookout was very useful in those tearooms that fell short of this criterion.

A person who was approaching a known tearoom, especially if he seemed to linger outside it, was assumed to be cruising. Thus, tearoom cruising was much less elaborate in style than street cruising, and contact between partners might be made without going inside at all:

At the X Terminal I stationed myself at a bench outside of the john and periodically would follow individuals into the john. I found myself and several other people engaged in a circular walking pattern from the lobby to the rest room to the urinal and back out to the lobby. On four different occasions, people said to me without a word from me to them that they were busy or didn't have time now! One person said while I was standing next to him at the urinal, "I have a meeting tonight, but maybe we could get together tomorrow night." Another said that people were not cruising there just now because the janitor who acted as a lookout was fired, and people were now afraid that they might get caught.

In some tearooms, certain stalls were reserved for sex. They might be more private, farther away from the door, or more fully partitioned. The wall between two such stalls might have a "glory hole" in it through which a man would insert his penis for fellatio by his next-stall neighbor. The modern public men's room is usually designed, or has been refurbished, to include metal or other easily maintained materials. When rest rooms were made of wood, the glory hole was easier to make, but we observed them in marble, plastic, metal, and opaque glass partitions. Some must have taken weeks to create. In other rest rooms, sex took place more openly:

Upon entering the men's room of the X Theater, I saw five middle-aged men standing in the doorway of the stall to the toilet. One man had his pants dropped, while another man was performing fellatio on him, and another was performing anal intercourse from behind. Two men were leaning against the wall and masturbating. I was told I would have to stand in line.

Regardless of whether sex took place in the tearoom or elsewhere, cruising methods tended to be simple and concise:

In a welfare office rest room, I noticed two men standing by the washbasins. One was washing his hands, the other combing his hair. The one who was combing his hair kept reaching down and grabbing his genitals through his clothing. The other man washed his hands again and glanced at him in the mirror. I left the rest room and waited outside. They did not come out and I went back in and noticed that one of the stalls was occupied.

While I was at the urinal in a Golden Gate Park men's room, a white man in his thirties came in and stood beside me. He kept looking over and smiling at me. I noticed he was not urinating. He kept looking at the general area of my genitals. Once when he did so he said, "Nice!" He turned partially to face me and I noticed he had an erection and he played with himself for a while. I told him I wasn't interested and he said, "That's a shame."

Cruising also took place at parties and other social gatherings. These are described later in the Social Activities section.

Work

Most of our respondents were indistinguishable from the heterosexual groups in terms of the kind of work they did. Some, however, owned or were employed by businesses which catered especially to homosexuals. The following sections describe employment opportunities in the Bay Area and several gay businesses that were operating at the time of our interviews.

Employment Opportunities

The Bay Area is a major manufacturing center, a rich agricultural area, and the largest foreign trade port on the West Coast. San Francisco is also a commercial and retail center with many insurance companies and financial exchanges. When our study was conducted, most people who worked there were white-collar; factories were more common in other parts of the six-county area. Space Age and heavier industries, as well as dairy, food-processing, and agricultural enterprises, provided Bay Area residents with a variety of employment opportunities.

At the time of our interviews, Bay Area residents enjoyed greater purchasing power than most other Americans, although the level of wages in the area had not quite kept pace with rapidly rising sales and profit figures. This discrepancy affected employment practices, as most of our informants (employment agents and the like) suggested, in that prospective employers preferred the kind of applicant who would not be likely to leave his or her job on account of an apparently low salary. An ideal applicant, they agreed, would be young—preferably well under thirty, in keeping with the general youthfulness of San Francisco's population—and encumbered by familial and financial responsibilities (mortgage, car payments, etc.). Such a person would have to keep on in his or her present job until another opportunity came up and could not afford to take off several months for job-hunting.

These criteria notwithstanding, our informants said that there was little discrimination against homosexuals in employment. They mentioned advising long-haired male clients to cut their hair and noticeably effeminate ones to tone down their "campy" mannerisms before a job interview. But they also pointed out that only those who had difficulty finding jobs on their own would be apt to seek the services of an employment agency. A person with few marketable skills and/or gaps in his or her work history (due perhaps to periods of incarceration, being on welfare, or being "kept" by a partner) might be rejected as a job applicant solely on such a basis, regardless of sexual orientation. Some area corporations, such as insurance companies, reputedly preferred married male applicants for positions that would provide advancement, but with the emphasis on equal employment opportunity and affirmative action that has arisen since our 1970 survey, this may no longer be entirely true. In any case, most of our homosexual respondents did report that they were employed full-time at jobs they found reasonably satisfying (or else were students).

Gay Businesses

Many of the homosexual men and women in the Bay Area owned, operated, or were employed by gay businesses (in addition to gay bars and baths) whose clientele was predominantly homosexual. Such establishments were unlike those of heterosexuals, which catered to the business of a particular neighborhood. Rather, they advertised in homophile publications and other subcultural media in the effort to attract the trade of homosexuals throughout the area.

We spoke with the owners of several such establishments, the first a pet shop. Its owners, who operated in two locations as partners, believed that homosexuals made especially good customers since their pets served as substitutes for the children they could not have. This meant that, first, homosexuals' pets had a special standing in the household, and second, that they could afford to spend more money on their pets than people with children; thus they would take better care of their animals. The pet store owners were homosexual but not active in either the homosexual subculture or in the local merchants' association, which they considered aging and unimaginative.

The owners of a men's clothing store complained that despite their four-year-long efforts to cultivate a homosexual clientele, too many potential customers were still shopping at discount stores. They also felt discriminated against by other, conservative merchants, and mentioned that even their customers had been harassed as "hippies" or "faggots." They expected, however, that the latter difficulties would subside as police patrols became more frequent in the area.

Finally, the owner of a hairstyling shop for men reported that most of her business came from homosexuals, whom she described as being much more interested in their personal appearance than straight men. They were also more faithful customers and more appreciative of the services provided. She and her four male employees maintained contacts with the homosexual clientele by visiting the bars and by supporting the activities of various homophile organizations. In addition to a regular homophile-newsletter advertisement, the shop was advertised in the programs for gay benefits and performances and on posters displayed in many of the gay bars.

In addition to the three described above, Bay Area gay businesses included stationers, florists, liquor stores, employment agencies, printing firms, import-export houses, furniture and upholstery outlets, and pornography distributors. About half of all the owners we interviewed acknowledged their own homosexuality, but all stressed that the "gay" emphasis in their business—their choice of advertising media, for example—had to do with the clientele they sought rather than their own sexual orientation.

Friendships

Many homosexual men and women belonged to cliques or friendship groups of from six to two dozen members. These were groups of friends who regularly got together socially, with or without an occasional other guest or two. Among the members of some cliques there was some sharing of sexual partners, and when this occurred it was seen as an expression of friendship rather than infidelity to one's partner. More important, however, the clique often took the place of the extended family, particularly for those whose homosexuality had brought about alienation or estrangement from their own families. In the cliques of longer standing and larger membership, different individuals tended to take on roles analogous to those of different family members. One might be like a mother, for example, who comforted people and gave advice; another might be a sort of mascot, humored and indulged by the others like the youngest child of a family.

Our ethnographers describe several kinds of cliques on the following pages. The first is one that formed spontaneously and went on to become the core of a larger group.

Dan and Michael, friends from high school, met Steve, a newly arrived AWOL Marine, at a North Beach gay bar. The three soon became good friends, and they decided to open a gay commune for about fifteen people. They saved their money for about a year, found two more men who would agree to share expenses, and finally leased an old, Victorian, three-story house near Golden Gate Park, which they dubbed "The Pad."

Word spread throughout the gay community that The Pad's doors were open to people who needed food or a place to stay. As many as twenty-five people are sometimes "crashing" there, and sexual partners are plentiful for everybody. The original five pay most of the expenses, although donations are regularly sought. People who stay longer than a few days usually are employed and do contribute to the household.

At this time, The Pad is going strong. The landlord, gay himself, not only condones the flexible life-style of its residents; he often participates in their parties, picnics, and rounds of bar-hopping.

A quite different clique consisted of professional men and women:

Jim and Pat, who were roommates, happened to meet Randy and Carlos at a Bay Area restaurant because Carlos noticed Jim holding a book of matches from a gay bar (one of the few he'd ever been in). After some cautious preliminary conversation, it developed that neither couple had any other good gay friends in the area, and they began to get together socially. Eventually the group expanded as one or the other would meet another gay person in the professions. Its membership stabilized at twelve—a lesbian couple, three gay male couples, and four other gay men. Although Cora and Francene, the two lesbians, sometimes go out on dates with other members of the clique, there is no sexual activity among the different members, only between the established partners.

The essential purpose of this unique clique of persons is a stable, informal, intimate group membership. As Jan states: "We love each other." The activities of the group, or subgroups of the clique, include about every form of social, interpersonal, and recreational activity imaginable: skiing, swimming, bridge-playing, hiking, camping, flying, partying, cooking, sewing, painting, musicales, films, plays, lectures, football, hockey, baseball, political groups, play-reading groups, dinners, retreats, Unitarian Church participation, traveling, mountain climbing, and winemaking. On any given day two or more members of the group will gather together with one or more of the others for any one or more of these activities.

A clique of lesbians, who got together initially because they feared disclosing their sexual orientation by visiting the bars and in any case disdained bars as places for sad and lonely people, began with four women who met regularly to play tennis:

The group grew as members began bringing their friends to join in the weekly game. It now numbers about thirty women, mostly professional types, ranging in age from twenty-five to sixty-five. The wide age range of the group is looked on as a benefit by all the members, although closest associations are between people near the same age.

On the group's regular meeting night everyone gathers together after work at the place where they engage in their sports activities. They play until about eight o'clock and then go to someone's house (different each week) for dinner and a party. Dinner usually consists of meat, vegetable, salad, and wine. After dinner a plate is passed, and everyone contributes a dollar. The party, which includes dancing, may last until 1:00 or 2:00 in the morning. Often the group will stay together for an entire weekend.

Each woman provides her own liquor. Her bottle is labeled with her name, and a box containing everyone's bottle is taken to the group each week. A can of coffee is kept in the box for those who don't drink. Too much drinking or the use of hard drugs is not tolerated in this group. If a woman does either of these things, she is informed that if such behavior continues she will be dropped. In the last three years smoking marijuana and hashish has become acceptable at the group's parties. Some use LSD occasionally.

Because these women are all professional, the party conversation is often quite stimulating. Their discussions involve current medical research, literature, and politics; sometimes they read poetry. Although they are all interested in the subject of homosexuality and are able to discuss the latest research in this area, entire evenings may be spent without any reference to it. An individual's status in the group is based on her achievements. Members are admired and respected by the group if they function well in their profession.

Jealousy between members of the group is not at all evident. Because they are all friends first and foremost, no one acts in any way that might threaten a happy and stable relationship. As long as a relationship is going on, it is understood that the two people are "involved," and neither is approached by anyone else. If a breakup occurs, neither person ever talks against the ex-partner in the group. Explanations for why the relationship was terminated are never given except in private conversation with their closest friends. In the group, no one takes sides. The feeling is that each of them has tried her best and that sometimes things just do not work out.

In addition to belonging to friendship groups such as these, of course, most homosexual respondents had friends and acquaintances at work, among other patrons at their favorite bar, (less commonly) among their neighbors, and so on, just as heterosexuals do.

Social Activities

Our homosexual respondents took part in a variety of activities during their leisure time. Like heterosexuals, they enjoyed entertaining their friends at home, going out to dinner or to an occasional movie, or watching their favorite television shows. One outstanding difference between gay and heterosexual social activities, however, is the institution of the gay bar. Our ethnographic descriptions of the respondents' leisure activities accordingly begin with the bars.

Gay Bars and Restaurants

As they are for heterosexuals, bars are a place for homosexuals to eat and drink, get together with friends, be entertained, sit alone, dance—to feel a sense of community. In addition, as has already been described, gay bars are a setting in which to find new sexual partners. Beyond these ends, the gay bar has a more central place in the homosexual community than does a bar for heterosexuals. The gay bar is one place where homosexuals can relax and enjoy themselves without having to hide their sexual orientation (as many do, at least in some contexts, all day). The bar is also a clearinghouse for information, where people find out what has become of old friends, what activities are coming up, when homophile organization meetings take place, and generally, the news in the gay community.

At the time of our study, the atmosphere in many of the Bay Area's eighty-odd gay bars was casual and friendly. One ethnographer remarked:

People in gay bars seem to drink beer more than anything else, even when hard liquor is available. Some of the customers I have questioned say that it's too expensive to drink other things because they spend so much time cruising and seeing friends in the bars. Others state that hard liquor would leave them impotent later if they got too drunk. Two men said they thought beer is especially "masculine," and five said that if another man wants to buy you a drink, beer is cheaper than something more elaborate. Also, if they want to leave with someone, a beer is easier either to finish quickly or leave behind. In addition, beer is more quickly served—that benefits the customers and management both.

Most of the city's dozen or so gay restaurants had complete bars on their premises. When food was not being served, these establishments were known as gay bars, and some were quite popular late-evening drinking spots. Many of the smaller bars served snacks because a liquor-food license was easier to obtain than one restricted to drinking. Since many persons in the gay community go out to eat alone, these bar-restaurants (many serving good food at relatively low prices) enjoyed a large and frequently loyal clientele.

A new restaurant in the Russian Hill area opened a month ago. It has a good menu and elegant surroundings. The dining room is separate from the bar with its loud music, cruising, and drinking activities. In other places the bar is usually an integral part of the restaurant. Early in the evening the nearby Polk Street crowd could be found cruising in the bar, which had taken on a neighborhood bar appearance. It was the first bar of that kind that I had seen in the city.

During weekdays and daytimes the Jumbo serves a crowd of people who work in the large corporations located in skyscrapers just a few blocks away. When meals are not being served, the eating areas are partly cleared away, and the restaurant becomes essentially a gay bar.

Gay restaurants were located in various parts of the city, about half of them in the North Beach, Embarcadero, or Fisherman's Wharf areas. They could seat 25 to 125 diners, and many specialized in weekend brunches. Some charged no more than three dollars for a dinner, even the more elegant places. Their regular, large clientele also might have appreciated the fact that most of the owners, on the premises during open hours, and almost all of the employees were gay themselves. Relations between them and the customers tended to be relaxed and familiar.

Almost all gay bars provided music, live or recorded, that was so loud as to preclude much conversation. The style was popular, tending (at least in 1970) toward soul music, as well as occasional songs that seemed to have a special relevance, such as "Strangers in the Night." An ethnographer commented:

Conversations, intimacy, subject matter, and (I suppose) background and intelligence are not cues that are important in the gay bar. It is what and whom the homosexual sees. The visual cue is the important one. Tonight in The Bar I observed four couples leave together at first meeting without saying more than ten words. Their eyes scanned each other, a few movements closer, one instance of fondling; all the while Aretha Franklin was singing out of the phonograph at a million decibels. I swear the ice in my drink melted from the friction produced by the sound waves.

In years past, a bar would have been busted if it allowed patrons to dance on the premises, but at the time of our study many gay bars permitted dancing. Dance bars attracted large crowds of young people; hundreds might come over a five-hour period on a weekend night. Our ethnographers described such bars:

El Sombrero is reminiscent of the L.A. go-go dance halls of the early sixties. Strobe lights, flashing colored lights, ultraviolet lighting, and fluorescent paint splotched on the walls in abstract patterns and visually "exciting" colors. The music is very loud, coming from both jukebox and phonograph. Everyone is stylishly dressed. The youthful men here are not really hip; most are without beards, have very long hair and wear scruffy clothes. On the tiny dance floor the dancing is wild when rock dances are played, with some fifty people gyrating away. (During slow dances, couples may not touch each other for fear of legal repercussions, so they usually face each other about a foot apart.) Some couples arrive together, others hook up to one another early in the evening, others dance together from time to time. Almost everyone dances. Some good-looking young men are obviously in high demand. I noticed a couple of hustlers come in and linger around the door, looking for a trick. Many other men drank together or alone, standing around the walls. The waiters and bartenders were all in their early twenties, handsome and sexily dressed—tight pants and open shirts. The bar volume of drinks was immense tonight; at times it was almost impossible to get to the men's room, a constant difficulty for this ethnographer. People really put themselves into the dancing. Even the much older men appeared graceful on the dance floor.

[In another bar:] Tonight, as before, there is the acrid smell of marijuana in the air. Joints are regularly passed around. Some dope pushing occurs too. The place is just packed. This is the smallest bar with the most customers in the entire city. I swear it takes twenty minutes to get from front to rear on a week-end night. Dancing in the rear is roughly equivalent to coming out of the tunnel from the grandstands of a football game with a hundred thousand others; the dance movements are mostly involuntary, caused by the jostling of others. Although dancing is not supposed to be permitted here, the management allows it.

The Dance Hall is the largest and most popular of the city's gay bars. It has three bars and two dance floors, one so designated, one impromptu. Jukebox music sometimes, but most of the night, phonograph music played by an in-residence disc jockey. The customers look like a page out of *Gentlemen's Quarterly,* everyone well-dressed, handsome, and somewhat aloof. A lot of cruising, but very few matchups. I am struck by the narcissism in the air of this particular bar. Couples dance but rarely look at each other. Those on the dance floor are obviously aware of others looking at them and are also apparently cruising while they are dancing. Dancing is lively and popular. Just about everyone is asked to dance. I was even asked twice, and I went to the floor once to see what it was like. My impression was that I was in a high-school gym class on a rainy day doing running-in-place. So many people!

Live entertainment included the same variety as to be found in ordinary nightclubs, and it sometimes attracted tourists as well as members of the gay community. Our ethnographers described a variety of entertainments:

The Room is a fairly popular bar among Tenderloin residents and working-class San Francisco homosexuals. The waitresses are mostly lesbians, friendly and maternal, and the drinks strong. Two kinds of entertainment tonight: topless male dancers and female impersonators. The dancers are young and muscle-bound, though somewhat effeminate, men who dance along the full length of the runway, twisting and gyrating. All are dressed in tight leotards, accentuating bulging genitals. The female impersonators, not half as good as others in town, sing popular rock numbers, interspersed with comedy routines. Many black customers are here, and the place is bustling, reminiscent of a pub. Many couples are present. Hustlers come and go from their work on Market Street and seem to have good relationships with the dancers, waitresses, and bartenders.

The Silver Pen had the funniest and most sophisticated show of all those I've visited in the past several weeks. The stars of the show are known throughout the gay community and in gay circles around the country. The pianist and choreographer are delightful. The comedy, impersonators, and routines are superb. After the bar closes, the back showroom becomes an after-hours coffeehouse, entered on another street by another entrance. Several straight couples and persons were here tonight to see the show.

The Night Club has been known for years in San Francisco as a first-rate nightclub. Gays and straights come here after dinner in the North Beach area to listen, be entertained, and join in a good floor show. The showroom is intimate, friendly, and is almost always packed. Many of the bartenders and waiters and waitresses here are not gay, and at times it is almost impossible to tell it is a gay bar. This is one of the city's few gay bars where gay men *and* women congregate regularly.

Operating a gay bar entailed more than the usual number of risks. The police and the Alcoholic Beverages Control (ABC) knew which bars were gay and gave them more scrutiny than they did other bars. Thus the owners were especially careful to observe the licensing regulations— closing hours (mentioned above), maximum number of persons permitted, minimum age of customers, etc. In addition there were other hazards connected with the illegality of homosexuality. Hence the rules against patrons' touching one another and the custom of nonverbal solicitation. Anyone who made a direct proposition might find that he was talking to an undercover ABC agent. These agents regularly patrolled the bars. Excerpts from their reports illustrate the kinds of things they looked for:

On two occasions the inspector observed Patrons #1 and #2 holding hands. This lasted for approximately one minute on each occasion. On three separate occasions, the cocktail waitress told them to stop what they were doing. They complied with the request but then started holding hands again. . . .

Patron: "Why don't we go out and park for a while?"
Investigator: "What do you have in mind?"
Patron: "I'm the homosexual type myself."

The patron and officer left the area in the patron's auto. The patron made advances, kissing the officer several times. The two then returned to the bar where the patron was arrested.

The police kept records of arrests made for homosexual activity or drunkenness in or near the gay bars, and a bar in whose neighborhood "too many" arrests occurred could be cited as a disorderly place and threatened with loss of licensure. To help prevent this, in addition to enforcing the no-touching rule, bar employees made an extra effort to get to know the clientele. When the atmosphere was a friendly one, customers were more likely to heed their admonitions.

Jack, a bouncer and ID checker at the Cyprus, who was helpful night after night in pointing out the essential elements of street cruising to me while we stood outside the bar, would grill young men about their ages upon entering the bar, telling each one of them how important it was to keep the gay bars open and how the fuzz would bust the bar sure as hell at the very least provocation.

At the X Club, young persons who are or appear to be under the minimum drinking age are told to leave quickly by the rear exit when "the word goes out" in the bar.

I was surprised the first night I visited the Meeting Place and saw uniformed patrolmen of the Brinks variety roaming around the place keeping everything cool. Not too much drinking, moving around, no touching or groping, and no cheek-to-cheek dancing. It was like a combination high-school chaperoned dance and prison social activity.

One Friday evening, I took along a close female friend. We decided to dance. All went well until we embraced during a slow dance and we noticed we were the only two people on the floor (the last fast dance there must have been sixty). Soon a waiter came over and said, "No slow dancing." We asked why. He said: "Well, it's legal, but we can't permit it for you when the gays can't." Jane and I felt very foolish.

Gay bar employees' friendliness also served to enhance the "belongingness" of the clientele and to foster patrons' enjoyment:

Johnny was strikingly handsome and intelligent. He could turn on "faggoty" mannerisms to amuse the customers, who were very fond of him. He carried his tray with the grace of a ballet artist, laughing, joking, calling a nickname here, a "Happy birthday" there. He was in graduate school in the area to earn his master's degree in engineering.

Fred had to be the most flamboyantly flirtatious waiter on the city's gay scene. Several nights he was observed going out of the bar, twice apparently to have sex with a customer. The manager stated he was only docked for the time, since no other employee could ferret out a cop or an ABC man better than Fred.

An ID checker at a North Beach "hip" bar stated: "I know all these guys are pretty much here for one purpose, more or less. It is understood. We hire guys who themselves have some sex appeal. It's not like the Bunnies; we want everyone to turn on. We're here for that purpose too. Sex is the great leveler. It would only be better if we were all nude. That's the thing with the baths; we're all the same in that sense. Nothing to hide here but the fact that everybody's somewhat scared they might not find what they want."

Stan, a straight bartender with twenty years' experience, said: "I've worked a lot of places and I think I like this place the best. These guys savor their nights here; it really means something to them. I put on my best servant hat when I serve them. They respect me and I them. It sometimes reminds me of when I was in Korea and we went to the USO or someplace. The gays here really enjoy themselves; they tip well and are gracious. Shame they get so few breaks."

The manager of an East Bay bar remarked, "You know, many of us not only are in this business for the money, but also because what we're doing is a service for so many guys who live pretty lonely here. I tell my guys, 'Be good to these people. In a country where they get so much shit all the time, they deserve to have a good time when they come here.' To see some of the people who come into here, you'd think they never had a friend. If they can smile for a few hours, all the better."

Gay bar employees varied from the flirtatious Fred to the sympathetic Stan, and the bars themselves varied too, each tending to cater to a particular clientele. While all bars emphasized youthfulness, playing currently popular music and using dim lighting to conceal wrinkles and other signs of aging, their ambiance was quite diverse. Examples of the different types of bars appear in our ethnographers' reports:

The Wild One is strictly a leather bar. It is located in a highly industrial area of the city right down by the bay. Everyone in the place is wearing leather in some fashion—boots, jackets, pants, shirts, gloves, hats, etc. It's extremely popular, as one can readily tell by the dozens of very expensive motorcycles parked in front of the place. The bar does not permit dancing, and dancing would not be appropriate to this apparently stoic crowd. The crowd at the Wild One is usually older than at other bars, ages ranging from late twenties to middle fifties. Two or three times a week there is a leather drawing at the bar, with the management raffling leather goods to customers who pick up their tickets at the door. The very loud jukebox has popular rock numbers, but mostly country and western selections. Tonight the place was like a longshoremen's bar during a strike. Dozens of leather-clad men jostling, yelling, groping, cruising, carrying motorcycle helmets. Like the other "masculine" bars, there is a lot of drink buying here, always someone shaking your hand or slapping your back. The sound of revving cycles and their exhaust filtered through the bar throughout the evening. What a crowd! But as raucous as the place is, it is friendly. The rough-looking attire and costumes are incongruent with the warm and friendly persons I've met there. The S and M connotation of the leather crowd is pretty much a myth.

A newly opened bar caters to the "muscle beach" or "he-man" gay community type. It's a converted bar-restaurant, L-shaped, painted almost entirely black with various iridescent signs and murals on the walls that fluoresce when ultraviolet lights play on them. A college instructor customer I spoke with tonight said that the he-man scene and the stud and leather scenes are frequented more by older gays than younger. "As the years wear on, we've got to attract other guys by means other than youthful good looks. Therefore we add some particular attracting factor like leather, or weight lifting." The customers are mainly in their thirties and early forties. All appear huge, wearing silk or transparent shirts, and pants that appear to be out of an Italian movie, at least two sizes too small. Surprising to me on my two visits were the number of "nellie" or "she" types in the bar. This appeared very incongruous: solid, large, muscular males using feminine gestures and manners of speaking; almost like a parody. Music was older rock and very loud. Once in a while a couple would dance. Magazines about muscular men were sold behind the bar, which served beer and wine. Cruising is not as apparent and furtive; it goes on but at a more casual pace. Two young men, both of whom could have been professional football players by their appearance, spent an hour or so talking about local gyms and health clubs and YMCAs that cater to their gay group. Both of these men turned out to be hairdressers.

The Purple Zebra in the East Bay is a "mixed" bar, a favorite gathering place for both men and women in the area, particularly people from the various campus communities. The bar, which is associated with a good restaurant, is frequented by many gay couples of both sexes. This is one of the few bars I have visited where the men and women mix freely and are overtly friendly and accepting of each other. From time to time the couples sit together and even share partners. The bar is noted for heavy drinking, even though none of the customers appear to be alcoholics.

Among the young and the hip the Rancho is a favorite gay bar for drinking and dancing by gays and straights alike. Last night I met some thirty young people who had gone there for the music, dancing, drinking, and general camaraderie of the place. The straight people, who usually come in groups or in couples, mixed freely with the gay men. Five or six lesbian couples came in during the evening to dance and meet each other. The place was packed as usual, some 125 people there at a time. Several of the young straight people I spoke with said they came to the bar because it was hip, free, and fun. They liked the flexibility and frivolity. Some of those I talked to were into campus and radical politics, and felt some identification with the gay movement, referring to gay people as their brothers and sisters.

The Martini Club is a neighborhood bar in the Lake District of Oakland. It is small, charming, and usually quiet. Situated on a corner and serving meals for a few hours in the evening, this bar is usually full of the same dozen or so people each night, gays of both sexes. Often it appears like a Steinbeck setting: talk about sports, local politics, the local gay scene, each other's problems and families. Everyone knew one another from hours and hours of drinking together. There was the freedom here to sit and get drunk, something rarely seen in many other gay bars. There was some switching of couples and the usual sorts of jealousies arising from this. I became known in the bar as "the egghead," readily accepted by the patrons after a week or so. To the outsider the bar would not be readily identifiable as a gay bar. In fact, several of the local residents were widows and widowers who came in regularly.

A unique bar in the North Beach area is Celeste's. Right here in the middle of a million tourist traps, some gay, on the district's main thoroughfare, this bar attracts a local clientele interested in each other and in the opera. The owner-bartender is a late-middle-aged woman who has been known in the area by beat, hip, gay, and straight, mostly young, people for more than a decade. The bar is small, garnished with dozens of objets d'art, and opera music is played regularly. It's reminiscent of the Kerouac beat scene of the middle and late fifties. Usually it is sparsely filled with gays, several lesbians, and many intellectual sorts. Cruising is minimal.

There are fifteen gay bars in the Bay Area which cater mostly to lesbians. Two of them actually refuse to admit males to the premises, usually with the explanation that "tonight is ladies' night." The higher the percentage of female customers, the more apt it is that a male customer (straight or gay) will be made to feel unwelcome. There have been instances in which heterosexual men, attempting to make social or sexual advances to female customers, have been evicted by the management or even by a cooperative policeman. Unlike homosexual men, whose cruising interests may lead them to make a large number of contacts with others standing around the bar, lesbians often sit at a table or in a booth in couples or with groups of friends, seemingly not interested in a new face and sometimes anxious to keep their partners from entering conversations with persons they do not know. They tend to avoid contact with those whose social or sexual interests are not known, and until they are sure that the person does not represent a threat to their own relationship, she is viewed as an intruder. Rather than an arena in which to find new partners, the gay bar provides lesbians with an opportunity to relax in a comfortable social setting with a partner and to keep up with what's going on in the gay world.

Entrance to the Wooden Vessel, a private club located beneath a large night-club in the North Beach district, is gained by a steep set of stairs leading from the sidewalk past a large sign warning that only members will be admitted. A guard, hired from a private agency, is posted at the door and admits only those with membership cards, who are permitted to bring one or two guests. The screening is no empty ritual. If the guests "just don't look good" they (as well as the member who brought them) are apt to be turned away. And if the member objects or persists in trying to enter, his membership card may be revoked. At all times, proper behavior in keeping with "the rules of good taste" is empha-sized. Since persons under twenty-one are admitted, no alcohol is served—only soft drinks, coffee, snacks, and early-morning breakfasts. The possession of drugs on the premises is considered grounds for revocation of one's member-ship. A strict and constant self-imposed surveillance probably accounts for the fact that during the three years of its operation, not one arrest has occurred inside or in the immediate vicinity of the club. This particular after-hours spot has become popular with large numbers of younger—eighteen to twenty-five—homosexuals. Some come to cruise, others to distinguish themselves as "stars" by their dancing abilities, but most just to sit around and talk about the evening of drinking and cruising.

Since dancing academies require neither business nor dancing licenses, the owners opened the Wooden Vessel as a dancing academy. There is a dance teacher on the payroll, and practice sessions are held nightly during the week. This fictitious arrangement was discussed beforehand with the police, who sug-gested several ways that the owners could circumvent local ordinances. It is not an isolated instance of such cooperation, and its result, a quasi-legal status for a gay business, reflects the spirit of compromise between the gay community and the authorities of the surrounding culture.

Relationships between gay bars and the community were also made smoother by the Tavern Guild, an organization of gay bar owners, man-agers, and employees. It was founded in 1961 originally for discussing mutual problems, but when, in the next year, the president of the guild was arrested twice in trying to help patrons who he thought were being illegally questioned by the police, the organization decided instead that its aim should be to combat discriminatory practices and harassment by the ABC and the police. The Tavern Guild retained an attorney and established a working relationship with a local bail bondsman, who was directed to look through the docket of arrests every morning. The bondsman bailed out whoever was arrested in or near a gay bar and was reimbursed by the Tavern Guild. If the individual in question could not afford his own attorney, the organization's attorney defended him. Besides an interest in the welfare of the person who had been arrested, the Tavern Guild also had a vital stake in the matter. Each arrest successfully countered by the attorney helped to keep the bar open a little longer and gave credence to complaints of harassment.

Over the years, and not without considerable effort on the part of the Tavern Guild, the harassment of gay bars has been eliminated almost entirely. At the time of our study, no gay bar was known to make payoffs to police officers (a usual occurrence in such places as Los Angeles and Chicago). Entrapment by the police or ABC agents had virtually stopped. In fact, the ABC director had asked that he be informed of any incidents of entrapment brought to the attention of any member of the Tavern Guild. New ABC regulations, policies, and court decisions had been printed in the Tavern Guild newsletter, and complete copies of the ABC rules and regulations had been obtained for use by the organization.

The Tavern Guild also functioned as a trade association. Its code of conduct provided discipline for any member bar allowing criminal activities (usually drug sales) to take place. It helped find work for unemployed bartenders and maintained a fund to help support them. Workers in the member bars, all nonunion employees, were provided health and life insurance through the guild's group insurance plan. In many instances the insurance fees were paid by the bar owners themselves.

Parties

Parties in the Bay Area homosexual community took varied forms. At some, cruising and sexual activity took place, but this was less likely when the party was a planned event, such as cocktails and dinner or to honor someone's birthday, or when mostly couples were in attendance—true especially of lesbians' parties. (Parties were nevertheless favorite cruising locales for those homosexual women who ever cruised.) Spur-of-the-moment "happenings," however, could involve a great deal of it. Our ethnographers attended several kinds of parties whose descriptions follow. First is a typical "happening," which illustrates the sexual exuberance homosexual men may display.

Gary and Frank had been bar-hopping and were wondering if their roommate, Dennis, had returned home. When they called him, he said he had just got home with two male hustlers and three fruit-flies (women who hang around gay bars) and that the group of them had some "hash." He suggested they bring some friends to join in the fun. Gary and Frank ran into two young gay men along Union Square and invited them to come with them to turn on. By the time they got home, five neighbors had also come over. Three were gay; the other two were a straight teenage couple who knew the life-styles of the hosts and other guests. Most of those present had already had some beer or wine. The conversation was humorous and somewhat political. Just when the second pipe of hashish was being lit, the doorbell rang. Everyone scurried to hide the contraband, and Dennis, opening the door, greeted three friends—a lesbian couple and a young gay man—who were enthusiastically invited in.

Soon people began to dance to records, in various partner combinations. As the party grew more boisterous and hilarious, one of the men suggested they all take off their clothes and invited one and all, one at a time, to "an ecstatic sexual experience." Gary and Dennis took him up on the offer, and as the other guests watched, giggling, the straight couple also began lovemaking. One of the lesbians joined them; Frank approached one of the hustlers; and before long everyone had become involved in group activity. By this time the noise of the party was carrying out to the street, and a friend telephoned to warn them that someone might call the police. They turned down the record player and people drifted off to sleep. Near dawn the lesbian couple went out and stole some oranges for everyone's breakfast.

A quite different party, to which some eighty women were invited, was given to celebrate the birthday of a well-known lesbian activist:

The party was held in a spacious suburban house. Most of the women, like the hostess and Paula, the guest of honor, were in their thirties or forties, neatly dressed in slacks, and most came with one or two friends. A bar on the patio provided every kind of liquor; three male bartenders had been hired for the occasion. Everyone who arrived was given a stick-on name tag, and the woman who was handing them out would apply them either above or on one's left breast, depending on how well she knew the guests. The people who came lived all over the Bay Area, and many had not seen each other since Paula's last birthday party. Most people were quite friendly with one another, although a few couples kept to themselves—I got the idea some people were sensitive about seeing an ex-partner there with a new lover—and after the buffet dinner at nine o'clock, dancing began. Most people had left by two; those who remained were somewhat drunk. Except for some embracing and kissing on the dance floor, there was little sexual activity.

Another example of a smaller suburban party demonstrates the ease with which homosexual men and women may "pass for straight":

Frank and Carlos had invited two other homosexual friends to come early to the party, and they were still swimming when the other guests arrived—twelve married couples, a lesbian couple (one of whom taught at the same school as Frank and Carlos), and three gay men with female dates. None of the heterosexual guests knew any of the others were gay; Frank and Carlos had represented themselves as friends whose fiancées were killed in a car crash. Carlos set up a portable bar while Frank lit the charcoal. People moved about and talked freely, usually about political or educational issues. After dinner, an elegant shish kebab with wine and freshly ground coffee, it began to get cold and people moved indoors for liqueurs around the fireplace. Four couples decided to play bridge and some of the rest played charades. Most people left by ten, since they had to work the next day. The lesbian couple remained; the gay men took their dates home and returned. Then they all began to drink beer, listen to rock music, and joke about the straight couples who had been there. Everyone was invited to join Carlos and Frank on their vacation in Hawaii.

Some parties are in sharp contrast to the "happening" type:

To honor a friend who was leaving for Europe, the hostess invited a dozen female couples and a few single women to her modest Peninsula house. The guests, mostly in their late twenties, represented all kinds of occupations, and all except for one "masculine-looking" girl, a horse trainer, could have passed for straight women. This party never got off the ground. Couples would sit and quietly talk to each other, two here on the sofa, two others in the kitchen. Nobody moved around or mixed with others much. It seemed that most of the guests took the opportunity to show their fidelity to their partners by not talking to anyone they didn't know. A few people danced, people would light each other's cigarettes, but only within a given couple. Occasionally the dancers would kiss each other, and one woman remarked, "I guess we came here just so other people can see us neck." Although things didn't break up until about 1:00, and people had been drinking pretty steadily, it remained a quiet, inhibited gathering.

Gay organizations also sponsored social events. One of the most extravagant was the Tavern Guild picnic, held at a private site. For a five-dollar ticket one could have his fill of food and drink.

By 5:00 P.M., there were about nine hundred people milling around the large picnic area containing beautiful shade trees, numerous picnic tables, an open-air stage where a rock band was playing, a refreshment stand operated by the owners of the property, and a large swimming pool. Only a handful were women; I was told that women don't enjoy these picnics because of the men's drunkenness and carnality. Around the swimming pool, tanned young men in skintight trunks paraded around and frolicked, throwing each other into the water, doing mediocre swan dives, shouting loudly to their friends on the sidelines. A group from a drag bar, many of them wearing heavy makeup, set up their own special table beside the pool. It was covered with a white linen cloth and set with fine silver and crystal. Their repast consisted of chicken cooked in wine, caviar, and rolls, all washed down by champagne kept cool in a silver ice bucket. Near the bandstand were congregated a number of men dressed in leather shorts or pants, leather vests, boots, and motorcycle hats. One of the "leather boys" got into a fight with a member of the band and was observed sitting on the ground in tears, but this was the only fight that occurred despite the large numbers present. There was really no overt sexual behavior, either—just some friendly hugging and kissing. Presumably people who were cruising at the picnic found privacy up the hill by the pool or in the men's rooms. When a couple returned from one of these areas, there would be good-natured teasing: "How was it, Joe?" or "It's my turn with 'her' next, George." No one seemed to take offense at such taunts. The overall mood was one of hilarity.

Motorcycle Clubs

Another kind of social activity which homosexual men enjoyed was belonging to a "bike club." The Bay Area had about a dozen such clubs, some of which were limited to men who owned their own motorcycles and others which also allowed "buddies"—people who didn't own a machine but would ride behind on someone else's. The bike clubs charged dues, and membership in most was, like college fraternities, limited to those who were recommended by one member and personally accepted by all the others. Bike club members should not be confused with the "leather crowd," people who espouse a tough, supermasculine image and often enjoy fetishistic or sadomasochistic sex. The bikers did wear leather clothing (to protect themselves from abrasion in case of accident), but in most bike clubs the purpose was recreational—they simply enjoyed riding motorcycles together. In the larger clubs, money from dues was used to defray expenses at periodic "runs." An ethnographer describes one such run:

Participants met at 10:00 A.M. at the Levee, a bike bar, for drinks and a bite to eat. People sign in at the bar and are given a run badge and a map. People do not know the destination of the run until they are given the map. They talk about it for days beforehand, wondering where they will be going. The route is chosen for its scenic beauty. Freeway driving is avoided at all costs.

Today's was a "poker" run, with as many stops along the way as there are cards in a poker hand. At each stop, indicated by a chalk mark in the road, a participant gets an envelope containing a playing card, and the envelopes collected along the way are not opened until the final contact point is reached and then by the road captain of the club.

The lunch stop was on the maintenance workers' parking lot of the San Francisco airport. Covered tables containing chicken, beans, soft drinks, beer, coffee, and rolls had been set up by the time the riders arrived. After lunch, the participants signed in, and the run captains opened the envelopes. The cards inside were scored as a poker hand for each person and added to the individual score sheets for the day.

After the lunch tables were cleared and packed away, the parking lot was set up for various contests: a slalom course, sharp turns, riding on a plank, riding as slowly as possible for a hundred yards, stopping with the front wheel or the back wheel on a particular line, and riding in as many concentric circles around a marker as possible in one minute. One event was a quiz on driving regulations for motorcyclists.

By 5:00 P.M. people started leaving the area for the Ramrod bar for the evening's activities. All of the participants had been given a chit for a free drink. Awards were given out for the winners in each class. People who had won awards in previous runs were given a handicap so that the same people would not be the winners. By 10:00 P.M., most of the participants began leaving the bar, exhausted by the day's activities.

These descriptions of the Bay Area "scene" illustrate the style of the San Francisco gay community in 1970. It is from this social milieu that we obtained the respondents who made our study possible.

Appendix B / Elaboration of Typology Procedures

In our exploratory cluster analyses, run on randomly selected thirds of the male homosexual sample for whom we had complete data on all thirteen criterion variables, a hierarchical agglomerative clustering algorithm was used to define existing clusters in the homosexual male samples (Ward, 1963; Veldman, 1967). This method computes a "distance" value between each pair of persons in the sample, and successively clusters individuals together based on their similarity across the thirteen criterion variables. Each variable had been standardized before the random one-third replicates were chosen, so that each of the thirteen variables had equal weights in the computations of this one-dimensional distance function. The cluster analysis was run several times over the separate random subgroups and also with minor variations, such as recording outliers (i.e., extreme values on the thirteen variables) and subsets of the original thirteen variables. The cluster analysis program yielded solutions with successively smaller numbers of groups, finally resulting in two very large groups. We routinely examined the profiles of group means for various solutions, from the stage which contained fifteen groups down to the stage which contained only two. The profiles of the various clusters at each stage were plotted on transparent paper. We were thus able to examine the computer-defined groups by superimposing profiles of group means on the thirteen criterion variables.

Cluster analysis is a very subjective analytical technique and is used for a wide variety of research goals (Anderberg, 1973; Blashfield, 1977). There were numerous reasonable cluster solutions at which we could have finally arrived. However, the male homosexual clusters (based on the thirteen variables) that seemed most reasonable to us involved five major types of clusters. An examination of the cluster profiles showed that only six of the thirteen variables distinguished the five clusters. The other cluster variables seemed only to be responsible for minor variations between clusters. For example, the respondents' standings on the homosexual-heterosexual continuum and level of overtness seemed to differentiate three small clusters of respondents which otherwise looked very similar to each other. Since these two variables played no part in defining the other clusters, we decided to collapse these three male clusters into one larger cluster. Subsequently we performed cluster analysis with only the "discriminating" subset of variables. In general, the same groups emerged as they did when all thirteen variables were included, but this time the groups were more sharply defined. Subjective decisions like these greatly influence whatever cluster analytic solutions emerge and may have caused our final results to differ from those which other researchers might reach using the same data set.

Although we were satisfied with the five types which emerged and believed that the labels for each type had empirical as well as theoretical meaning, we were not satisfied with the assignment of respondents to groups simply on the basis of the cluster analysis results. Inevitably there were respondents who fell on the boundary between two (or more) groups. The cluster analysis algorithm routinely computed the group membership for these respondents. In other cases, although the label that we had assigned to a type fit the members of that cluster in general, there were some members who did not have one of the distinguishing characteristics of that group, although they were especially similar to group members on other variables. For example, the initial Close-Coupled cluster included a few respondents who were currently having a homosexual affair but who were not classifed as being "married" (a critical variable in our interpretation of the group) because they were not living with their current sexual partner. In the face of these ambiguities, which were understandable given the nature of the cluster analysis algorithm, we decided to invoke theoretical considerations in assigning members to types. The cluster analysis had taken us most of the distance to our goal, but we formulated the rules for group membership on this last step.

These membership criteria, based on the groups which emerged and reemerged in many cluster analyses, permitted us to define five mutually exclusive groups of homosexual males. Using these definitions, we know that each member of a particular group has the defining characteristics of the entire group. Our groups, while mutually exclusive, are not exhaustive: approximately a quarter of all the male homosexuals (and subsequently of the lesbian respondents) were unclassifiable according to our revised typology-definition criteria; thus the homosexual typology which emerged was considerably more "pure" than the final solution from the cluster analysis.

The analysis of the homosexual women was carried out according to the same procedures. Because of the smaller numbers of female respondents, we were not able to construct random cross-validation subsamples as we did with their male counterparts. Exploratory hierarchical cluster analysis was done using the same thirteen criterion variables used with the males. Although the five female subgroups (or "types") correspond to the male "types," it should be noted that the criteria used in assigning men to a given subgroup sometimes differ from those for their female counterparts. In addition, it should be remembered that the men's and the women's standard scores were based upon the scores of the male and the female groups respectively. Thus, an "asexual" male, for example, may be actually quite different from his female counterpart. Although classified as "asexual" in comparison to other males, he could be far more sexually involved than the "asexual" female whose scores were compared with other females, who generally tended to have fewer sexual partners and to cruise far less frequently than their male counterparts.

Appendix C / Tables

The tables in this Appendix present the data which were the basis for the findings presented in the chapters of this book. Because the information they offer is fairly detailed, we chose to include them here rather than to intersperse them in the text, where they might detract from the reader's ease in seeing the "picture" each chapter attempted to draw.

Our data come, for the most part, from three kinds of variables: those pertaining to dimensions of sexual experience, to social adjustment, and to psychological adjustment. Some variables apply only to the homosexual respondents and others to both the homosexual and the heterosexual respondents. Some variables are "continuous"—i.e., they measure characteristics for which people's scores can be ranged along a continuum, such as age. Others are "discrete," meaning that the various answers people might give constitute categories that are entirely separate from one another, such as political affiliation. The tables concerning sexual experience do not include information about our homosexual "types," since the analysis of these data was what provided the basis for drawing up the typology. The first three tables are also different; they present descriptive information about our samples, as outlined in the chapter, "Methods of Investigation." A few other tables, showing data derived from other kinds of analyses than are detailed below, are different as well. Despite all these differences, we have tried to make the format of the tables as uniform as possible, so that they may be more easily read.

In each table, data are first presented about males and then about females, and finally about the males in our Chicago pilot study (where comparable data are available). For column headings we use the same abbreviations as in the text, e.g., "WHM" stands for "white homosexual males," "BHTF" stands for "black heterosexual females," etc. The top half of the table shows percentages for the variable of interest, broken down by race and sexual orientation. That is, it shows what percent of the people in each of our sex-race-sexual orientation categories gave each of the responses listed.

The lower half of the table presents (where applicable) comparisons which show whether the size of the differences in the percentages in the top half is "significant." (Pilot study data are not included in these comparisons.) The analytical methods used for testing these differences are multiple regression for continuous variables and chi-square analysis for discrete variables. The bottom half of the table thus answers, separately for males and for females, the following questions:

1. Are the responses of the black homosexual males (or females) as a whole on this variable different from those of the white homosexual males (or females) as a whole?
2. Are the responses of the members of any one of the homosexual subgroups or "types" different from those of the homosexual males (or females) as a whole?
3. Are the responses of the homosexual males (or females) as a whole different from those of the heterosexual males (or females) as a whole?
4. Are the responses of the members of any one of the homosexual subgroups different from those of the heterosexual males (or females) as a whole?

Obviously, for variables which pertain only to homosexual respondents, there can be no comparison with the heterosexuals. Bearing this in mind, one can interpret figures in the lower half of the table as follows:

For continuous variables, we present the results in two steps. In the homosexual comparisons, step 1 analyzes a set of demographic variables for their power in predicting scores on the variable in question. The R-squared reported for this step shows the extent to which scores on the variable in question are related to variations in these demographic characteristics (age, education, and occupational level). At step 2, question #1 above is addressed by adding the variable Race to the demographic variables; the R-squared for step 2 shows how much being black is related to scores on the variable of interest when the other demographic variables are taken into account. Thus, the difference in magnitude between the R-squared of step 1 and the R-squared of step 2 is due to the direct relation between Race and the variable in question. (If there is little or no difference between the two, then we can infer that Race has little or no relationship with the variable.) We also report the unstandardized regression coefficient, or b value, for Race. The b value shows how well we can estimate scores on the variable in question statistically. If the difference between blacks and whites is statistically significant—probably not due only to chance—the extent of this significance is indicated by asterisks after the b value. One asterisk (*) means that the probability value is .05 or less—that is, that the odds are no more than 5 out of 100 that the difference shown is due just to chance. Two asterisks (**) denote a probability level of .01 or less, and three, a probability level of .001 or less (i.e., the odds are only 1 out of 1000 that the difference is due to chance). If the b value is positive, it means that blacks tended to score higher than whites on the variable of interest, and if it is negative, blacks tended to score lower, when age, education, and occupational level are statistically controlled. The top half of the table shows the score assigned to each of the responses listed. For example, if the first response listed is "0: Never," and the BHM-WHM b value is negative, this means that the black males were less likely than the white males to have had the experience described in the table. However, if no asterisks follow the b value, it means that this tendency is not statistically significant (i.e., it is probably due to chance). Tables pertaining to continuous, sexual experience variables present only this first regression.

The second regression in each table is similar but not exactly the same. The variables entered in the first step include Race this time; the R-squared for step 1 in this regression therefore shows the extent to which variations in scores on the variable of interest are related to differences in age, education, occupational level, and race. In step 2, variables that are entered concern whether a respondent belongs to one or another of the five homosexual subgroups or types. Thus, the R-squared for step 2 shows to what extent membership in one or another of the types is related to scores on the variable of interest when all the demographic variables entered in step 1 are taken into account. The b value is presented for each of the types. Where, for example, the b value for only one of these types has one or more asterisks by it, the reader can see that only the members of this subgroup differed significantly from the homosexual males (or females) as a whole on the variable in question; if the b value here should be positive, it would mean that the members of this subgroup tended to score higher.

The third and fourth regressions are shown for variables where it was possible to compare homosexual and heterosexual respondents. In the third regression, step 1 includes the same four demographic variables as in the second regression, and step 2 adds sexual orientation. Thus, differences between the R-squared of step 1 and the R-squared of step 2 are due to being homosexual when age, race, education, and occupational level are taken into account. Where the b value is significant, this shows that the homosexual males (or females) as a whole are meaningfully different from the heterosexual males (or females) as a whole on the variable in question; in other words, their mean score was significantly different from the heterosexuals'—higher, if the b is positive, and lower if it is negative.

The fourth regression shows whether members of any of the homosexual subgroups differ from the heterosexual males (or females) as a whole. It is just like the second regression except that it compares subgroup mean (i.e., average) scores with heterosexual mean scores instead of homosexual ones. Thus, for example, if only the Close-Coupleds and Functionals have statistically significant b values in this part of the table and if these bs are positive, it means that members of these two groups tended to score higher than the heterosexual mean but that the Open-Coupleds, Dysfunctionals, and Asexuals scored about the same as the heterosexuals.

For variables that are discrete rather than continuous in nature, the table presents chi-square values that compare black homosexual males (or females) as a whole with white homosexual males (or females) as a whole, each homosexual subgroup with the homosexual males (or females) as a whole, homosexual males (or females) as a whole with heterosexual males (or females) as a whole, and each homosexual subgroup with the heterosexual males (or females) as a whole. In these analyses we do not take demographic variables into account because it is too difficult to control for them when the variable of interest is a discrete one. In addition, the meaning of the chi-square values that result is harder to interpret than is the meaning of the b value in a regression, because one would ideally need much more comprehensive cross-tabulations in order to assess what the chi-square signifies. Nevertheless, it seemed of more value to us to present tables concerning these discrete variables in a form parallel to that used for the continuous ones. In this way the reader can draw inferences from the tables in much the same fashion for the two kinds of variables.

Finally, as noted on pages 46–47, from time to time throughout the book we have pointed out differences between males and females. Because this was not a major focus of our study, the tables do not include information about these differences. The reader can be assured, however, that every such difference that is reported was tested in exactly the same ways as described above—by multiple regression analysis for continuous variables and by chi-square analysis for discrete variables—and that all differences between males and females reported in the text were significant with a probability level of .05 or better.

TABLE 2.1 / Recruitment Pool: Number of Potential Homosexual Respondents by Recruiting Source, Age, and Educational Level

Education:[a]	WHM (N=3538)			BHM (N=316)			WHF (N=675)			BHF (N=110)		
	HS	SC	C	HS	SC	C	HS	SC	C	HS	SC	C
Public Advertising												
Age: 25 or less	55	115	52	6	7	1	12	19	8	3	2	1
26–35	61	96	187	1	9	5	9	20	23	3	0	3
36–45	33	68	119	2	2	1	4	7	13	0	0	1
46 or more	14	27	87	0	0	1	5	4	8	0	0	0
[% of total pool]		[26%]			[11%]			[20%]			[12%]	
Bars & Nightclubs												
Age: 25 or less	116	161	62	16	37	7	35	32	15	5	7	3
26–35	93	123	157	19	19	8	20	23	34	5	5	6
36–45	41	62	94	0	0	1	9	7	11	0	1	0
46 or more	23	21	41	0	2	1	5	5	9	0	0	0
[% of total pool]		[28%]			[35%]			[30%]			[29%]	
Personal Contacts												
Age: 25 or less	56	105	33	31	23	3	33	42	21	11	5	1
26–35	47	64	3	11	13	9	18	27	39	3	12	5
36–45	24	42	87	10	5	1	12	17	28	3	13	3
46 or more	11	20	36	1	0	0	9	11	14	2	3	0
[% of total pool]		[17%]			[34%]			[40%]			[56%]	

Baths

Age										
25 or less	20	26	13	0	1	1	0			0
26–35	17	30	46	1	0	0	1			0
36–45	11	14	42	0	0	2	0			0
46 or more	7	6	17	0	0	0	0			0
[% of total pool]		[7%]			[2%]					

Organizations[b]

Age										
25 or less	19	31	7	2	2	0	5	12	7	1
26–35	20	23	42	0	6	1	2	7	13	0
36–45	15	12	25	0	0	0	3	4	9	2
46 or more	7	6	15	0	0	0	0	2	3	0
[% of total pool]		[6%]			[4%]			[10%]		[4%]

Mailing Lists[b]

Age										
25 or less	5	14	7	0	1	0	0			0
26–35	8	28	39	0	3	0	0			0
36–45	12	13	30	0	0	0	0			0
46 or more	8	12	24	0	0	0	0			0
[% of total pool]		[6%]			[1%]					

Private Bars

Age										
25 or less	23	25	12	4	8	0	0	0	0	0
26–35	20	30	30	1	3	4	0	0	0	0
36–45	8	17	21	0	0	0	0	0	0	0
46 or more	5	6	8	0	0	0	0	0	0	0
[% of total pool]		[6%]			[6%]			[0%]		[0%]

TABLE 2.1—(Continued)

Education:[a]	WHM (N=3538)			BHM (N=316)			WHF (N=675)			BHF (N=110)		
	HS	SC	C	HS	SC	C	HS	SC	C	HS	SC	C
Public Places												
Age: 25 or less	22	21	11	4	9	0	0	0	0	0	0	0
26–35	9	11	13	2	5	2	0	0	0	0	0	0
36–45	5	12	13	1	0	0	0	0	0	0	0	0
46 or more	6	5	9	0	0	1	0	0	0	0	0	0
[% of total pool]		[4%]			[8%]			[0%]			[0%]	
		[100%]			[101%]			[100%]			[101%]	

[a] Education was trichotomized as follows: HS = high-school diploma or less; SC = some college but no degree; C = undergraduate degree or more.
[b] The number of females recruited from organizations was combined with the number recruited from mailing lists because relatively few were recruited from either source.

TABLE 2.2 / **Description of Final Samples**

	WHM	BHM	WHF	BHF	WHTM	BHTM	WHTF	BHTF	Pilot Study
Source[a]:	(N=575)	(N=111)	(N=229)	(N=64)					
Public advertising	14%	14%	21%	16%					
Bars & nightclubs	20	32	29	17					
Personal contacts	14	37	36	63					
Baths	14	2	0	0					
Organizations	9	4	9	5					
Mailing lists	9	4	2	0					
Private bars	9	5	0	0					
Public places	9	4	0	0					
Age:	(N=575)	(N=111)	(N=229)	(N=64)	(N=284)	(N=53)	(N=101)	(N=39)	(N=458)
25 or less	24%	43%	26%	27%	25%	49%	27%	49%	29%
26–35	25	49	28	39	25	51	25	51	44
36–45	26	8	24	28	24	0	24	0	19
46 or more	25	10	21	8	25	0	25	0	8
(average)	(36.97)	(27.20)	(35.17)	(32.47)	(36.30)	(26.45)	(35.70)	(26.26)	(31.15)
Education:	(N=575)	(N=111)	(N=229)	(N=64)	(N=284)	(N=53)	(N=101)	(N=39)	(N=458)
High school or less	25%	27%	23%	27%	25%	32%	25%	28%	26%
Some college	33	52	31	55	33	40	33	46	33
College degree or more	42	21	45	19	42	28	42	26	41
(average[b])	3.62	3.14	3.70	3.14	3.59	3.17	3.36	3.13	3.51

TABLE 2.2—(Continued)

	WHM	BHM	WHF	BHF	WHTM	BHTM	WHTF	BHTF	Pilot Study
Occupational Level:	(N=546)	(N=105)	(N=220)	(N=58)	(N=261)	(N=49)	(N=85)	(N=30)	(N=445)
Unskilled	4%	8%	10%	0%	4%	6%	0%	4%	6%
Semiskilled	10	14	14	10	10	27	17	30	10
Skilled	17	30	31	43	15	20	34	27	15
Semiprof/Small Business	39	22	21	26	33	22	25	10	25
Prof-Manag I[c]	26	25	26	16	29	22	24	27	41
Prof-Manag II	5	2	7	5	8	2	1	3	3
Occupational Field:	(N=545)	(N=101)	(N=220)	(N=63)	(N=261)	(N=50)	(N=86)	(N=33)	
Hairdressers, designers, decorators, etc. (typically "feminine" fields)	8%	4%	3%	0%	5%	2%	0%	0%	
Skilled crafts, technical, engineering (typically "masculine" fields)	10	12	13	5	25	36	6	6	
Positions of public trust	12	14	23	21	17	10	19	27	
Other	80	70	61	74	53	52	75	77	
With Whom Currently Living?	(N=575)	(N=111)	(N=229)	(N=64)	(N=284)	(N=51)	(N=229)	(N=39)	(N=457)
Parents	3%	2%	1%	3%	5%	6%	2%	5%	10%
Same-sex roommate	50	64	53	50	5	12	7	3	43
Alone	37	29	26	22	18	22	13	13	41
Other (spouse and/or children, opposite-sex roommate, etc.)	10	5	20	25	72	60	78	79	6

Proportion of Neighbors Who Are Homosexual

	(N=505)	(N=83)	(N=191)	(N=44)	(N=173)	(N=10)	(N=69)	(N=14)
	28%	23%	56%	43%	71%	50%	57%	86%
None	37	41	27	25	24	50	38	14
Only a few	17	13	6	5	4	0	3	0
Less than half	10	11	5	7	1	0	1	0
About half	4	1	2	2	0	0	1	0
More than half	3	6	1	0	0	0	0	0
Most	2	5	1	2	0	0	0	0
All								

Proportion of Neighbors Known by Name

	(N=574)	(N=111)	(N=229)	(N=64)	(N=282)	(N=52)	(N=101)	(N=39)
	15%	28%	15%	27%	10%	2%	6%	18%
None	47	41	39	45	39	50	30	44
Only a few	9	8	10	9	12	25	8	13
Less than half	8	4	7	2	13	10	10	8
About half	5	4	4	0	6	2	4	0
More than half	9	5	12	5	10	6	20	13
Most	8	11	12	12	10	6	23	5
All								

Percent of Life Spent in Bay Area

	(N=575)	(N=111)	(N=229)	(N=64)	(N=282)	(N=53)	(N=101)	(N=39)
	22%	28%	24%	28%	18%	19%	17%	10%
0 to 9.9%	16	31	15	14	13	24	13	13
10 to 19.9%	19	14	10	12	13	17	5	10
20 to 29.9%	12	5	10	12	7	9	12	0
30 to 39.9%	10	3	10	6	5	8	8	5
40 to 49.9%	11	11	14	14	15	14	21	34
50 to 99.9%	10	8	17	14	29	9	24	28
100%								

TABLE 2.2—(Continued)

Religious Preference	WHM	BHM	WHF	BHF	WHTM	BHTM	WHTF	BHTF	Pilot Study
	(N=574)	(N=111)	(N=228)	(N=64)	(N=284)	(N=53)	(N=101)	(N=39)	(N=457)
Protestant	28%	39%	19%	36%	27%	53%	40%	74%	36%
Roman Catholic	13	21	14	17	19	11	17	13	21
Jewish	2	0	4	2	3	0	3	0	5
Other	21	10	14	12	10	11	14	10	5
Agnostic or atheist	37	31	48	33	41	25	27	3	33

[a] The heterosexual respondents were drawn by means of a stratified random sampling procedure (see p. 000).

[b] A score of 3 on this variable means some college education and a score of 4, a bachelor's degree.

[c] An occupation designated "Prof-Manag I" involves less supervisory responsibility, fiscal authority, professional training, etc., than one designated "Prof-Manag II."

TABLE 2.3 / Comparison of Homosexual and Heterosexual Samples on Age, Education, and Occupational Level[a]

Comparison	Age eta^2	Education eta^2	Occupational Level eta^2
WHM–WHTM	.0006	.0000	.0018
BHM–BHTM	.0040	.0000	.0023
WHF–WHTF	.0004	.0103	.0058
BHF–BHTF	.1394***	.0000	.0112
WHM–WHF	.0047	.0004	.0012
BHM–BHF	.1125***	.0000	.0034
WHTM–WHTF	.0004	.0043	.0199**
BHTM–BHTF	.0005	.0002	.0000
WHM–BHM	.0902***	.0124**	.0156***
WHF–BHF	.0117	.0221*	.0031
WHTM–BHTM	.0864***	.0091	.0334
WHTF–BHTF	.1330***	.0062	.0074

* p < .05.
** p < .01.
*** p < .001.
[a] Based on the response distributions in Table 2.2.

TABLE 3.1 / Significant Correlations Between Selected Sexual Experience Items and Age[a]

	WHM	BHM	WHF	BHF
1 Homosexual-heterosexual rating	.18***	.18*		
2 Extrafamilial overtness		−.16*		
3 Level of sexual activity	−.23***	.23**	−.35***	−.31**
4 Amount of cruising	−.24***			
5 Proportion of cruising done in:				
—bars				
—baths	.28***	.21*		
—streets	−.17***			
—private parties		.21*		
—public parks	−.09*			
—beaches	−.24***			
—tearooms	.08*			
—movie theaters	.08*			
6 Time spent with partner	−.30***	−.18*		

TABLE 3.1—(Continued)

	WHM	BHM	WHF	BHF
7 Extent of cruising worries about:				
—being refused				
—partner's unwelcome requests				
—making conversation	−.11**	−.20*		
—venereal disease				
—adequate sexual performance				
—being robbed or rolled				
—being caught by police	.18***			
—being publicly exposed	.09*			
8 Proportion of partners whom R paid for sex ..	.27***	.17*		
9 Number of sexual partners in past year	−.15***		−.30***	−.39***
10 Currently involved in homosexual affair			.20***	
11 Sex appeal (homosexual)	−.35***	−.19*		
12 Sexual repertoire	−.42***	−.28**	−.39***	
13 Frequency of:				
—body-rubbing	−.26***		−.43***	−.34**
—performing manual-genital	−.26***		−.40***	
—receiving manual-genital	−.31***		−.42***	
—performing oral-genital	−.15***		−.27***	
—receiving oral-genital	−.27***		−.25***	
—performing anal intercourse	−.30***			
—receiving anal intercourse	−.24***			
14 Proportion of homosexual sex spent:				
—performing fellatio	.34***			
—receiving fellatio	.13***			
15 Level of sexual interest			−.23***	
16 Extent of sexual problems in:				
—P's failure to respond to R's requests ..				
—finding a partner	.14***	−.17*	.14*	
—responding to partner's requests	−.09*		.14*	−.24*
—frequency of sexual contact	.10**			
—getting/maintaining erection	.16***			
—partner's lack of orgasm	.13***			
—maintaining affection for partner	−.16***			
—premature ejaculation				
—concerns about sexual adequacy				
—respondent's lack of orgasm				
17 Extent of regret about homosexuality				

* p < .05.
** p < .01.
*** p < .001.
a In Tables 3.1, 3.2, and 3.3, blank spaces after various items indicate correlations that were not statistically significant.

TABLE 3.2 / **Significant Correlations Between Selected Sexual Experience Items and Education**

	WHM	BHM	WHF	BHF
1 Homosexual-heterosexual rating				−.27*
2 Extrafamilial overtness	−.24***	−.17*	−.17**	
3 Level of sexual activity				−.27*
4 Amount of cruising				
5 Proportion of cruising done in:				
—bars	.09*			
—baths	.08*	.27**		
—streets	−.19***			
—private parties				
—public parks				
—beaches				
—tearooms				
—movie theaters	−.08*			
6 Time spent with partner		−.21*		
7 Extent of cruising worries about:				
—being refused	.11**			
—partner's unwelcome requests				
—making conversation				
—venereal disease				
—adequate sexual performance				
—being robbed or rolled				
—being caught by police	.18***			
—being publicly exposed	.21***			
8 Proportion of partners whom R paid for sex				
9 Number of sexual partners in past year				
10 Currently involved in homosexual affair				
11 Sex appeal (homosexual)		−.24**		
12 Sexual repertoire	.07*			
13 Frequency of:				
—body-rubbing			−.19*	−.24*
—performing manual-genital				
—receiving manual-genital		−.18*		
—performing oral-genital				
—receiving oral-genital				
—performing anal intercourse				
—receiving anal intercourse				
14 Proportion of homosexual sex spent:				
—performing fellatio				
—receiving fellatio				
15 Level of sexual interest	.07*			

TABLE 3.2—(*Continued*)

	WHM	BHM	WHF	BHF
16 Extent of sexual problems in:				
—P's failure to respond to R's requests ..				
—finding a partner			.13*	
—responding to partner's requests				
—frequency of sexual contact				
—getting/maintaining erection				
—partner's lack of orgasm				
—maintaining affection for partner				
—premature ejaculation				
—concerns about sexual adequacy				
—respondent's lack of orgasm				
17 Extent of regret about homosexuality	.14***		.14*	

* p < .05.
** p < .01.
*** p < .001.

TABLE 3.3 / Significant Correlations Between Selected Sexual Experience Items and Occupational Level

	WHM	BHM	WHF	BHF
1 Homosexual-heterosexual rating				
2 Extrafamilial overtness	−.28***			−.31**
3 Level of sexual activity				
4 Amount of cruising........................		.23**		
5 Proportion of cruising done in:				
—bars	.08*			
—baths	.11**			
—streets	−.19***			
—private parties	.08*			
—public parks	−.13**			
—beaches...........................		.20*		
—tearooms				
—movie theaters.....................				
6 Time spent with partner				
7 Extent of cruising worries about:				
—being refused				
—partner's unwelcome requests				
—making conversation				
—venereal disease				
—adequate sexual performance				

TABLE 3.3—*(Continued)*

	WHM	BHM	WHF	BHF
—being robbed or rolled	.10*			
—being caught by police	.08*			
—being publicly exposed	.08*			
8 Proportion of partners whom R paid for sex . .				
9 Number of sexual partners in past year				
10 Currently involved in homosexual affair	−.09*			
11 Sex appeal (homosexual)		−.22***		
12 Sexual repertoire				
13 Frequency of:				
—body-rubbing	−.17***		−.20**	
—performing manual-genital				
—receiving manual-genital				
—performing oral-genital				
—receiving oral-genital				
—performing anal intercourse		.24**		
—receiving anal intercourse				
14 Proportion of homosexual sex spent:				
—performing fellatio				
—receiving fellatio	.09*			
15 Level of sexual interest			−.18**	
16 Extent of sexual problems in:				
—P's failure to respond to R's requests . .				
—finding a partner		−.19*	.14*	
—responding to partner's requests				
—frequency of sexual contact				
—getting/maintaining erection				
—partner's lack of orgasm	.08*			
—maintaining affection for partner				
—premature ejaculation				
—concerns about sexual adequacy				
—respondent's lack of orgasm	−.07*			
17 Extent of regret about homosexuality				

* $p < .05$.
** $p < .01$.
*** $p < .001$.

TABLE 3.4 / **Homosexual-Heterosexual Continuum: Behaviors**

		WHM	BHM	WHF	BHF	Pilot Study
Current Kinsey Rating		(N=575)	(N=111)	(N=228)	(N=64)	
6: 6		74%	62%	68%	61%	
5: 5		18	23	19	17	
4: 4		3	11	5	5	
0–3: 0–3		5	4	8	17	
	R^2	b			R^2	b
Demographics	.02		Demographics		.01	
BHM–WHM	.02	−.03	BHF–WHF		.03	−.21*
Ever HT Coitus?		(N=573)	(N=110)	(N=229)	(N=64)	(N=458)
0: No		36%	27%	17%	12%	37%
1: Yes		64	73	83	88	63
	R^2	b			R^2	b
Demographics	.00		Demographics		.02	
BHM–WHM	.01	.05	BHF–WHF		.02	.03
Any HT Coitus in Past Year?		(N=573)	(N=110)	(N=229)	(N=64)	(N=458)
0: No		86%	78%	76%	67%	82%
1: Yes		14	22	24	33	18
	R^2	b			R^2	b
Demographics	.05		Demographics		.08	
BHM–WHM	.05	—[a]	BHF–WHF		.08	.05
Ever Receive HT Oral-Genital?		(N=574)	(N=111)	(N=229)	(N=64)	
0: No		54%	60%	36%	30%	
1: Yes		46	40	64	70	
	R^2	b			R^2	b
Demographics	.02		Demographics		.04	
BHM–WHM	.02	—[a]	BHF–WHF		.04	.11
Ever Perform HT Oral-Genital?		(N=574)	(N=111)	(N=229)	(N=64)	
0: No		67%	78%	39%	58%	
1: Yes		33	22	61	42	
	R^2	b			R^2	b
Demographics	.02		Demographics		.03	
BHM–WHM	.02	.02	BHF–WHF		.04	.26

TABLE 3.4—(Continued)

		WHM	BHM	WHF	BHF	Pilot Study
Ever Receive HT Masturbation?		(N=573)	(N=111)	(N=229)	(N=64)	
0: No		60%	60%	30%	36%	
1: Yes		40	40	70	64	
	R^2	b			R^2	b
Demographics	.02			Demographics	.04	
BHM–WHM	.02	−.06		BHF–WHF	.04	.12
Ever Perform HT Masturbation?		(N=574)	(N=111)	(N=227)	(N=64)	
0: No		65%	62%	29%	20%	
1: Yes		35	38	71	80	
	R^2	b			R^2	b
Demographics	.03			Demographics	.03	
BHM–WHM	.04	−.13		BHF–WHF	.03	.10
How Often Reached Orgasm in HT Sex?		(N=383)	(N=81)	(N=198)	(N=58)	
0: Never		8%	5%	33%	33%	
1–5: Sometimes		41	32	59	62	
6: Always		51	63	8	5	
	R^2	b			R^2	b
Demographics	.00			Demographics	.02	
BHM–WHM	.02	−.36**		BHF–WHF	.03	.13
Comparison of H and HT Experiences: Competence		(N=378)	(N=81)	(N=192)	(N=56)	
More competent in H sex		18%	21%	14%	11%	
Equally competent in H and HT		5	9	3	7	
More competent in HT sex		1	1	0	0	
Other response		1	0	1	0	
No mention of competence		75	69	82	82	
	X^2				X^2	
BHM–WHM	3.47c			BHF–WHF	2.88c	

TABLE 3.4—(Continued)

	WHM	BHM	WHF	BHF	Pilot Study
Comparison of H and HT					
Experiences: Feeling States[b]	(N=376)	(N=81)	(N=190)	(N=56)	
Less guilt in H sex	1%	4%	4%	2%	
Fear of pregnancy in HT sex	2	6	4	5	
Idea of HT sex repulsive	1	1	1	2	
More positive feelings with H sex	62	53	50	57	
Neither experience more positive	7	11	6	11	
More positive feelings with HT sex	4	5	5	5	
No mention of feeling states	23	20	30	18	

X^2

BHM–WHM   10.59[c]   BHF–WHF   6.09[c]

* $p < .05$.
** $p < .01$.

[a] F is too small for program to compute; difference is not significant.

[b] Respondents could give more than one answer to this question, so column percents may add up to more than 100%; this inflates the chi-square, but not substantially.

[c] Does not meet the conventional expected frequency rule for chi-square; collapsing categories would obscure our analytic focus.

TABLE 3.5 / Homosexual-Heterosexual Continuum: Feelings

		WHM	BHM	WHF	BHF	Pilot Study
Current Kinsey Rating:		(N=575)	(N=111)	(N=229)	(N=64)	
6: 6		58%	45%	50%	62%	
5: 5		28	31	28	12	
4: 4		8	16	12	9	
0–3: 0–3		6	8	10	17	
	R^2	b			R^2	b
Demographics	.05		Demographics	.04		
BHM–WHM	.05	−.04	BHF–WHF	.04	−.02	
Ever HT Sex Dreams?		(N=574)	(N=110)	(N=229)	(N=64)	
0: No		67%	58%	45%	59%	
1: Yes		33	42	55	41	
	R^2	b			R^2	b
Demographics	.02		Demographics	.03		
BHM–WHM	.02	.03	BHF–WHF	.04	−.07	
Ever HT Masturbatory Fantasy?		(N=571)	(N=111)	(N=228)	(N=64)	(N=427)
0: No		77%	73%	62%	77%	72%
1: Yes		23	27	38	23	28
	R^2	b			R^2	b
Demographics	.02		Demographics	.08		
BHM–WHM	.02	−.01	BHF–WHF	.09	−.05	
Ever HT Sexual Arousal?		(N=575)	(N=111)	(N=229)	(N=64)	
0: No		28%	16%	21%	20%	
1: Yes		72	84	79	80	
	R^2	b			R^2	b
Demographics	.03		Demographics	.03		
BHM–WHM	.03	.25	BHM–WHM	.03	−.11	

TABLE 3.6 / **Homosexual-Heterosexual Continuum: Behaviors and Feelings**

		WHM	BHM	WHF	BHF	Pilot Study
Exclusively Homosexual?		(N=575)	(N=111)	(N=228)	(N=64)	(N=458)
0: No		45%	59%	55%	47%	49%
1: Yes		55	41	45	53	51
	R^2	b			R^2	b
Demographics	.04		Demographics		.02	
BHM–WHM	.04	−.06	BHF–WHF		.03	−.23
Any Discrepancy Between Feelings and Behavior?		(N=575)	(N=111)	(N=228)	(N=64)	
0: No		68%	67%	62%	70%	
1: Yes		32	33	38	30	
	R^2	b			R^2	b
Demographics	.05		Demographics		.02	
BHM–WHM	.05	−.03	BHF–WHF		.02	−.03
Nature of Discrepancy Between Feelings and Behavior		(N=184)	(N=37)	(N=87)	(N=19)	
0: Behavior more H than feelings		76%	84%	75%	37%	
1: Feelings more H than behavior		24	16	25	63	
	R^2	b			R^2	b
Demographics	.03		Demographics		.04	
BHM–WHM	.04	−.04	BHF–WHF		.13	.18**

** $p < .01$.

TABLE 3.7 / Kinsey Behavior Ratings by HT Sexual Behavior Items: Males

Kinsey Behavior Rating:	WHM				BHM			
	6	5	4	0–3	6	5	4	0–3
Ever Receive HT Masturbation?	(N=424)	(N=104)	(N=17)	(N=28)	(N=69)	(N=26)	(N=12)	(N=4)
No	70%	31%	29%	25%	59%	69%	42%	50%
Yes	30	69	71	75	41	31	58	50
Ever Perform HT Masturbation?	(N=425)	(N=104)	(N=17)	(N=28)	(N=69)	(N=26)	(N=12)	(N=4)
No	75%	41%	41%	18%	70%	54%	50%	25%
Yes	25	59	59	82	30	46	50	75
Ever Receive HT Oral-Genital?	(N=425)	(N=104)	(N=17)	(N=28)	(N=69)	(N=26)	(N=12)	(N=4)
No	65%	26%	12%	14%	64%	65%	33%	25%
Yes	35	74	88	86	36	35	67	75
Ever Perform HT Oral-Genital?	(N=425)	(N=104)	(N=17)	(N=28)	(N=69)	(N=26)	(N=12)	(N=4)
No	79%	36%	35%	18%	84%	62%	67%	100%
Yes	21	64	65	82	16	38	33	0
Ever HT Coitus?	(N=424)	(N=104)	(N=17)	(N=28)	(N=68)	(N=26)	(N=12)	(N=4)
No	48%	7%	0%	0%	35%	15%	17%	0%
Yes	52	93	100	100	65	85	83	100
Any HT Coitus in Past Year?	(N=424)	(N=104)	(N=17)	(N=28)	(N=68)	(N=26)	(N=12)	(N=4)
No	98%	66%	29%	11%	89%	65%	58%	50%
Yes	2	34	71	89	10	35	42	50
How Often Reached Orgasm in HT Sex?	(N=241)	(N=97)	(N=17)	(N=28)	(N=44)	(N=23)	(N=10)	(N=4)
Never	12%	1%	0%	0%	2%	13%	0%	0%
Sometimes	33	53	65	54	32	30	40	25
Always	55	46	35	46	66	57	60	75

TABLE 3.8 / Kinsey Feelings Ratings by HT Sexual Feelings Items: Males

Kinsey Feelings Rating:	WHM				BHM			
	6	5	4	0–3	6	5	4	0–3
Ever HT Sex Dreams?	(N=336)	(N=157)	(N=45)	(N=36)	(N=50)	(N=33)	(N=18)	(N=9)
No	80%	56%	44%	28%	72%	61%	28%	33%
Yes	20	44	56	72	28	39	72	67
Ever HT Masturbatory Fantasy?	(N=70)	(N=74)	(N=37)	(N=32)	(N=11)	(N=16)	(N=12)	(N=6)
No	63%	32%	19%	16%	64%	25%	25%	17%
Yes	37	68	81	84	36	75	75	83
Ever HT Sexual Arousal?	(N=336)	(N=158)	(N=45)	(N=36)	(N=50)	(N=34)	(N=18)	(N=9)
No	40%	15%	2%	6%	24%	12%	11%	0%
Yes	60	85	98	94	76	88	89	100

TABLE 3.9 / Kinsey Behavior Ratings by HT Sexual Behavior Items: Females

Kinsey Behavior Rating:	WHF				BHF			
	6	5	4	0–3	6	5	4	0–3
Ever Receive HT Masturbation?	(N=153)	(N=44)	(N=12)	(N=17)	(N=39)	(N=11)	(N=3)	(N=11)
No	37%	14%	0%	12%	28%	9%	33%	0%
Yes	63	86	100	88	72	91	67	100
Ever Perform HT Masturbation?	(N=154)	(N=44)	(N=12)	(N=18)	(N=39)	(N=11)	(N=3)	(N=11)
No	33%	25%	17%	17%	46%	36%	33%	0%
Yes	67	75	83	83	54	64	67	100
Ever Receive HT Oral-Genital?	(N=154)	(N=44)	(N=12)	(N=18)	(N=39)	(N=11)	(N=3)	(N=11)
No	44%	30%	8%	0%	38%	27%	33%	0%
Yes	56	70	92	100	62	73	67	100
Ever Perform HT Oral-Genital?	(N=154)	(N=44)	(N=12)	(N=18)	(N=39)	(N=11)	(N=3)	(N=11)
No	47%	30%	25%	0%	69%	54%	33%	27%
Yes	53	70	75	100	31	46	67	73
Ever HT Coitus?	(N=154)	(N=44)	(N=12)	(N=18)	(N=39)	(N=11)	(N=3)	(N=11)
No	23%	7%	0%	0%	15%	9%	33%	0%
Yes	77	93	100	100	85	91	67	100
Any HT Coitus in Past Year?	(N=154)	(N=44)	(N=12)	(N=18)	(N=39)	(N=11)	(N=3)	(N=11)
No	92%	61%	33%	11%	90%	54%	33%	9%
Yes	8	39	67	89	10	46	67	91
How Often Reached Orgasm in HT Sex?	(N=124)	(N=43)	(N=12)	(N=18)	(N=35)	(N=10)	(N=2)	(N=11)
Never	36%	37%	8%	11%	46%	20%	0%	9%
Sometimes	53	58	92	89	51	70	50	91
Always	10	5	0	0	3	10	50	0

TABLE 3.10 / Kinsey Feelings Ratings by HT Sexual Feelings Items: Females

Kinsey Feelings Rating:	WHF				BHF			
	6	5	4	0–3	6	5	4	0–3
Ever HT Sex Dreams?	(N=114)	(N=64)	(N=27)	(N=24)	(N=40)	(N=8)	(N=6)	(N=10)
No	66%	25%	26%	25%	75%	38%	17%	40%
Yes	34	75	74	75	25	62	83	60
Ever HT Masturbatory Fantasy?	(N=114)	(N=64)	(N=27)	(N=23)	(N=40)	(N=8)	(N=6)	(N=10)
No	81%	50%	37%	35%	85%	75%	67%	50%
Yes	19	50	63	65	15	25	33	50
Ever HT Sexual Arousal?	(N=114)	(N=64)	(N=27)	(N=24)	(N=40)	(N=8)	(N=6)	(N=10)
No	38%	9%	0%	0%	28%	0%	33%	0%
Yes	62	91	100	100	72	100	67	100

TABLE 4 / Overtness

		WHM	BHM	WHF	BHF	Pilot Study
FAMILIAL						
Mother (If Living)		(N=513)	(N=97)	(N=199)	(N=59)	(N=422)
0: Neither knows nor suspects		38%	29%	32%	27%	39%
1: Suspects		21	20	19	15	20
2: Knows		42	52	49	58	41

	R^2	b			R^2	b
Demographics	.06			Demographics	.03	
BHM–WHM	.06	.04		BHF–WHF	.03	.05

		WHM	BHM	WHF	BHF	Pilot Study
Father (If Living)		(N=476)	(N=84)	(N=167)	(N=51)	(N=347)
0: Neither knows nor suspects		53%	44%	46%	47%	47%
1: Suspects		16	17	17	12	14
2: Knows		31	39	37	41	40

	R^2	b			R^2	b
Demographics	.04			Demographics	.00	
BHM–WHM	.04	.02		BHF–WHF	.00	—[a]

		WHM	BHM	WHF	BHF	
Siblings		(N=434)	(N=88)	(N=165)	(N=54)	
0: None know		49%	43%	38%	35%	
1–49: Less than half know		6	12	6	13	
50–99: Most know		11	12	12	13	
100: All know		33	33	44	39	

	R^2	b			R^2	b
Demographics	.04			Demographics	.01	
BHM–WHM	.04	3.27		BHF–WHF	.01	—[a]

		WHM	BHM	WHF	BHF	
Cousins		(N=533)	(N=107)	(N=202)	(N=62)	
0: None know		66%	49%	78%	48%	
1: Few know		19	28	12	32	
2: Less than half know		3	0	0	2	
3: Most know		2	4	0	2	
4: All know		10	19	9	16	

	R^2	b			R^2	b
Demographics	.01			Demographics	.02	
BHM–WHM	.02	2.01**		BHF–WHF	.04	2.68**

TABLE 4—(Continued)

		WHM	BHM	WHF	BHF	Pilot Study
Other Adult Relatives		(N=548)	(N=106)	(N=211)	(N=61)	
0: None know		67%	46%	67%	44%	
1: Few know		18	28	18	30	
2: Less than half know		2	2	1	2	
3: About half know		2	3	1	3	
4: Most know		11	21	14	21	
	R^2	b			R^2	b
Demographics	.02		Demographics		.03	
BHM–WHM	.04	2.43**	BHF–WHF		.05	2.36*
Summary: Familial Overtness		(N=407)	(N=78)	(N=133)	(N=46)	
0–1: Relatively low		22%	28%	32%	30%	
2–5: Moderate		43	36	29	26	
6–13: Relatively high		35	29	39	43	
	R^2	b			R^2	b
Demographics	.03		Demographics		.02	
BHM–WHM	.04	.43*	BHF–WHF		.03	.50

EXTRAFAMILIAL

		WHM	BHM	WHF	BHF	Pilot Study
Employer		(N=419)	(N=93)	(N=164)	(N=57)	
0: Neither knows nor suspects		53%	66%	68%	60%	
1: Suspects		18	11	17	24	
2: Knows		29	23	15	16	
	R^2	b			R^2	b
Demographics	.05		Demographics		.02	
BHM–WHM	.06	−.13*	BHF–WHF		.02	.05
Fellow Workers		(N=505)	(N=104)	(N=197)	(N=60)	
0: None know		31%	38%	48%	37%	
1: Few know		31	32	28	35	
2: Less than half know		6	4	6	8	
3: About half know		3	2	4	7	
4: Most know		29	24	15	13	
	R^2	b			R^2	b
Demographics	.07		Demographics		.04	
BHM–WHM	.08	−1.99*	BHF–WHF		.04	.65

TABLE 4—*(Continued)*

		WHM	BHM	WHF	BHF	Pilot Study
Heterosexual Friends		(N=564)	(N=111)	(N=219)	(N=62)	
0: None know		21%	19%	16%	18%	
1: Few know		27	28	30	32	
2: Less than half know		6	5	8	5	
3: About half know		6	7	6	6	
4: Most know		29	40	39	39	
	R^2	b			R^2	b
Demographics	.05		Demographics		.04	
BHM–WHM	.05	−.40	BHF–WHF		.04	.36
Neighbors		(N=571)	(N=109)	(N=222)	(N=63)	
0: None know		49%	44%	63%	59%	
1: Few know		28	31	21	11	
2: Less than half know		5	5	4	3	
3: About half know		5	1	2	3	
4: Most know		14	18	11	14	
	R^2	b			R^2	b
Demographics	.02		Demographics		.01	
BHM–WHM	.02	.48	BHF–WHF		.01	.69
Summary: Extrafamilial Overtness		(N=572)	(N=111)	(N=223)	(N=64)	
0: Relatively low		33%	33%	33%	33%	
1–3: Moderate		33	33	33	33	
4–7: Relatively high		33	32	34	34	
	R^2	b			R^2	b
Demographics	.07		Demographics		.03	
BHM–WHM	.07	−.08	BHF–WHF		.03	.03
Correlation Between Familial and Extrafamilial Overtness		.39***	.50***	.40***	.40**	

* $p < .05$.
** $p < .01$.
*** $p < .001$.

a F is too small for program to compute; difference is not significant.

TABLE 5 / **Level of Sexual Activity**

Frequency of H Sexual Activity in Past Year	**WHM**	**BHM**	**WHF**	**BHF**	**Pilot Study**
	(N=574)	(N=111)	(N=228)	(N=64)	(N=458)
0: Not at all	3%	0%	8%	3%	0%
1: Once or a few times	3	1	6	9	4
2: Every other month	3	1	5	0	3
3: Once a month	7	3	10	8	8
4: 2–3 times a month	17	13	20	14	15
5: Once a week	22	17	20	9	20
6: 2–3 times a week	30	42	19	39	33
7: 4–6 times a week	13	16	9	11	11
8: 7 times a week or more	4	7	4	6	6

	R^2	b			R^2	b
Demographics	.07			Demographics	.14	
BHM–WHM	.08	.21*		BHF–WHF	.14	.23

* $p < .05$.

TABLE 6 / Cruising

	WHM	BHM	WHF	BHF	Pilot Study
Cruising in Past Year	(N=573)	(N=111)	(N=229)	(N=64)	
0: Not at all	16%	14%	83%	83%	
1: Once a month or less	21	22	12	8	
2: A few times a month	20	27	3	5	
3: Once or twice a week	28	15	1	5	
4: More than twice a week	15	23	1	0	

	R^2	b		R^2	b
Demographics	.04		Demographics	.04	
BHM–WHM	.04	−.05	BHF–WHF	.04	.02

Incidence of Cruising at Specific Locales in Past Year

Ever Cruised at Bars?	(N=574)	(N=111)	(N=229)	(N=64)	
0: No	34%	24%	83%	84%	
1: Yes	66	76	17	16	

	R^2	b		R^2	b
Demographics	.07		Demographics	.04	
BHM–WHM	.07	.01	BHF–WHF	.04	−.01

Ever Cruised at Baths?	(N−574)	(N=111)			
0: No	46%	52%			
1: Yes	54	47			

	R^2	b
Demographics	.01	
BHM–WHM	.01	−.03

Ever Cruised on the Street?	(N=573)	(N=111)	(N=229)	(N=64)	
0: No	51%	36%	100%	92%	
1: Yes	48	63	0	9	

	R^2	b		R^2	b
Demographics	.08		Demographics	.02	
BHM–WHM	.08	.03	BHF–WHF	.06	.04***

Ever Cruised at Private Parties?	(N=574)	(N=111)	(N=229)	(N=64)	
0: No	56%	47%	92%	84%	
1: Yes	44	53	8	16	

	R^2	b		R^2	b
Demographics	.05		Demographics	.02	
BHM–WHM	.05	.02	BHF–WHF	.03	.04

TABLE 6—(Continued)

		WHM	BHM	WHF	BHF	Pilot Study
Ever Cruised in Parks?		(N=573)	(N=111)	(N=229)	(N=64)	
0: No		70%	64%	100%	97%	
1: Yes		30	36	0	3	
	R^2	b			R^2	b
Demographics	.03			Demographics	.02	
BHM–WHM	.03	−.00		BHF–WHF	.03	.01
Ever Cruised on Beaches?		(N=573)	(N=111)	(N=229)	(N=64)	
0: No		70%	74%	99%	97%	
1: Yes		30	26	1	3	
	R^2	b			R^2	b
Demographics	.08			Demographics	.02	
BHM–WHM	.09	−.06*		BHF–WHF	.02	.01
Ever Cruised in Public Rest Rooms?		(N=574)	(N=111)	(N=229)	(N=64)	
0: No		78%	81%	100%	100%	
1: Yes		22	19	0	0	
	R^2	b				
Demographics	.00					
BHM–WHM	.02	−.02				
Ever Cruised in Movie Theaters?		(N=574)	(N=111)	(N=229)	(N=64)	
0: No		85%	82%	100%	97%	
1: Yes		15	18	0	3	
	R^2	b			R^2	b
Demographics	.01			Demographics	.01	
BHM–WHM	.01	.02		BHF–WHF	.03	.02*
If Cruised in Past Year: Frequency of Cruising		(N=484)	(N=96)	(N=40)	(N=11)	
0: Once a month or less		25%	25%	68%	45%	
1: A few times a month		23	31	20	27	
2: Once or twice a week		34	18	7	27	
3: More than twice a week		18	26	5	0	
	R^2	b			R^2	b
Demographics	.01			Demographics	.07	
BHM–WHM	.01	−.02		BHF–WHF	.10	.15

TABLE 6—(*Continued*)

	WHM	BHM	WHF	BHF	Pilot Study
If Cruised in a Specific Locale in Past Year: Frequency of Cruising There					
How Often Cruised at Bars?	(N=378)	(N=84)	(N=39)	(N=10)	
1–2: Once a month or less	32%	21%	61%	50%	
3: A few times a month	15	18	13	10	
4: Once or twice a week	42	39	26	40	
5: More than twice a week	11	21	0	0	

	R^2	b		R^2	b
Demographics	.06		Demographics	.07	
BHM–WHM	.06	.07	BHF–WHF	.08	.18

How Often Cruised at Baths?	(N=309)	(N=53)			
1–2: Once a month or less	64%	74%			
3: A few times a month	21	15			
4: Once or twice a week	14	11			
5: More than twice a week	1	0			

	R^2	b
Demographics	.00	
BHM–WHM	.01	−.13

How Often Cruised on the Street?	(N=281)	(N=71)	(N=1)	(N=5)	
1–2: Once a month or less	45%	37%	0%	20%	
3: A few times a month	16	11	0	20	
4: Once or twice a week	19	22	0	40	
5: More than twice a week	20	30	100	20	

	R^2	b		R^2	b
Demographics	.02		Demographics	.72	
BHM–WHM	.03	.19	BHF–WHF	.74	−.22

How Often Cruised at Private Parties?	(N=250)	(N=59)	(N=19)	(N=10)	
1–2: Once a month or less	78%	71%	90%	60%	
3: A few times a month	16	19	5	20	
4: Once or twice a week	6	8	5	20	
5: More than twice a week	0	2	0	0	

	R^2	b		R^2	b
Demographics	.00		Demographics	.33	
BHM–WHM	.01	.08	BHF–WHF	.42	.26

TABLE 6—(Continued)

	WHM	BHM	WHF	BHF	Pilot Study
How Often Cruised in Parks?	(N=170)	(N=40)	(N=1)	(N=2)	
1–2: Once a month or less	57%	57%	0%	100%	
3: A few times a month	16	13	0	0	
4: Once or twice a week	18	23	100	0	
5: More than twice a week	9	7	0	0	

	R^2	b		R^2	b
Demographics	.02		Demographics	1.00	
BHM–WHM	.02	.01	BHF–WHF	1.00	—[a]

	WHM	BHM	WHF	BHF
How Often Cruised on Beaches?	(N=169)	(N=29)	(N=2)	(N=2)
Once a month or less	70%	79%	50%	100%
A few times a month	10	14	50	0
Once or twice a week	18	3	0	0
More than twice a week	3	3	0	0

	R^2	b		R^2	b
Demographics	.04		Demographics	1.00	
BHM–WHM	.05	−.14	BHF–WHF	1.00	—[a]

	WHM	BHM
How Often Cruised in Public Rest Rooms?	(N=128)	(N=21)
1–2: Once a month or less	49%	52%
3: A few times a month	16	9
4: Once or twice a week	23	29
5: More than twice a week	12	10

	R^2	b
Demographics	.00	
BHM–WHM	.00	.13

	WHM	BHM	WHF	BHF
How Often Cruised in Movie Theaters?	(N=83)	(N=20)	(N=10)	(N=2)
1–2: Once a month or less	69%	70%	0%	50%
3: A few times a month	14	5	100	50
4: Once or twice a week	16	25	0	0
5: More than twice a week	1	0	0	0

	R^2	b		R^2	b
Demographics	.03		Demographics	1.00	
BHM–WHM	.03	.01	BHF–WHF	1.00	—[a]

TABLE 6—(Continued)

	WHM	BHM	WHF	BHF	Pilot Study
If Cruised in Past Year: Proportion of Cruising Time Spent in Specific Locales					
Cruising Time at Bars	(N=485)	(N=96)	(N=40)	(N=11)	
0: None of the time	22%	12%	2%	9%	
1–32: Less than one-third of the time	45	52	2	45	
33–100: One-third of the time or more	33	35	95	46	

	R^2	b		R^2	b
Demographics	.01		Demographics	.00	
BHM–WHM	.01	1.25	BHF–WHF	.35	−20.83***

	WHM	BHM
Cruising Time at Baths	(N=485)	(N=96)
0: None of the time	36%	45%
1–32: Less than one-third of the time	49	49
33–100: One-third of the time or more	14	6

	R^2	b
Demographics	.09	
BHM–WHM	.09	−1.43

	WHM	BHM	WHF	BHF
Cruising Time on the Street	(N=484)	(N=96)	(N=40)	(N=11)
0: None of the time	42%	26%	98%	55%
1–32: Less than one-third of the time	45	55	2	36
33–100: One-third of the time or more	14	19	0	9

	R^2	b		R^2	b
Demographics	.06		Demographics	.04	
BHM–WHM	.07	1.87	BHF–WHF	.31	6.26***

	WHM	BHM	WHF	BHF
Cruising Time at Private Parties	(N=485)	(N=96)	(N=40)	(N=11)
0: None of the time	48%	39%	52%	9%
1–32: Less than one-third of the time	48	55	23	45
33–100: One-third of the time or more	4	6	25	45

	R^2	b		R^2	b
Demographics	.01		Demographics	.03	
BHM–WHM	.02	1.58*	BHF–WHF	.19	11.73**

TABLE 6—(Continued)

	WHM	BHM	WHF	BHF	Pilot Study
Cruising Time in Parks	(N=484)	(N=96)	(N=40)	(N=11)	
0: None of the time	65%	58%	97%	82%	
1–32: Less than one-third of the time	31	42	3	18	
33–100: One-third of the time or more	4	0	0	0	

	R^2	b			R^2	b
Demographics	.01			Demographics	.05	
BHM–WHM	.01	$-.74$		BHF–WHF	.07	.69

	WHM	BHM	WHF	BHF	Pilot Study
Cruising Time on Beaches	(N=484)	(N=96)	(N=40)	(N=11)	
0: None of the time	65%	70%	95%	82%	
1–32: Less than one-third of the time	32	30	5	18	
33–100: One-third of the time or more	3	0	0	0	

	R^2	b			R^2	b
Demographics	.06			Demographics	.09	
BHM–WHM	.08	$-2.09***$		BHF–WHF	.11	.71

	WHM	BHM
Cruising Time in Public Rest Rooms	(N=485)	(N=96)
0: None of the time	74%	78%
1–32: Less than one-third of the time	22	22
33–100: One-third of the time or more	4	0

	R^2	b
Demographics	.02	
BHM–WHM	.02	$-.64$

	WHM	BHM	WHF	BHF	Pilot Study
Cruising Time in Movie Theaters	(N=485)	(N=96)	(N=40)	(N=11)	
0: None of the time	83%	79%	97%	82%	
1–32: Less than one-third of the time	16	21	0	18	
33–100: One-third of the time or more	1	0	2	0	

	R^2	b			R^2	b
Demographics	.01			Demographics	.03	
BHM–WHM	.01	.98		BHF–WHF	.15	1.45*

TABLE 6—(Continued)

	WHM	BHM	WHF	BHF	Pilot Study
When Cruising, Does R More Often Approach or Wait for the Other to Approach?	(N=484)	(N=96)	(N=40)	(N=11)	
0: R usually approaches	28%	19%	43%	27%	
1: R sometimes approaches, sometimes waits	31	32	23	46	
2: R usually waits to be approached	41	49	35	27	

	R^2	b		R^2	b
Demographics	.01		Demographics	.07	
BHM–WHM	.01	.07	BHF–WHF	.07	.04

Why Use This Cruising Style?[b]	(N=329)	(N=64)	(N=28)	(N=6)
I tend to be aggressive	8%	11%	14%	17%
Partner might not approach me	12	5	7	17
It just works best	5	14	25	50
I am too shy to approach	21	17	25	17
They might turn me down	20	27	14	0
Safer to wait for approach	14	25	7	0
Want to be sure it's mutual	5	2	0	17
Other reasons	17	27	14	17

	X^2			X^2
BHM–WIIM	12.71		BHF–WHF	6.28

Where Does Sex Usually Take Place?	(N=481)	(N=96)	(N=35)	(N=11)
Respondent's residence	49%	48%	54%	27%
Partner's residence	29	40	29	36
Somewhere else	22	12	17	36

	X^2			X^2
BHM–WHM	6.57[*]		BHF–WHF	2.87[c]

How Much Time is Usually Spent with Partner?	(N=481)	(N=96)	(N=33)	(N=11)
0–2: An hour or less	21%	7%	3%	0%
3: One or two hours	15	16	9	0
4: Several hours	20	12	3	9
5: All night	41	62	62	91
6: All weekend	2	4	24	0

	R^2	b		R^2	b
Demographics	.11		Demographics	.10	
BHM–WHM	.12	.10	BHF–WHF	.10	−.03

TABLE 6—*(Continued)*

	WHM	BHM	WHF	BHF	Pilot Study
Frequency of Specific Worries While Cruising					

Being Refused by Prospective Partner

	WHM (N=486)	BHM (N=96)	WHF (N=38)	BHF (N=11)
0: Never worry	17%	21%	21%	18%
1: Rarely worry	24	26	18	18
2: Sometimes worry	29	35	26	27
3: Often worry	29	18	34	36

	R^2	b		R^2	b
Demographics	.01		Demographics	.01	
BHM–WHM	.02	−.10	BHF–WHF	.08	.32

Having Partner Want to Do Sexual Things R Doesn't Want to Do

	WHM (N=486)	BHM (N=96)	WHF (N=39)	BHF (N=11)
0: Never worry	24%	25%	61%	54%
1: Rarely worry	48	42	26	27
2: Sometimes worry	23	26	13	18
3: Often worry	4	6	0	0

	R^2	b		R^2	b
Demographics	.00		Demographics	.10	
BHM–WHM	.00	—[a]	BHF–WHF	.10	—[a]

Having Difficulty Conversing

	WHM (N=486)	BHM (N=96)	WHF (N=39)	BHF (N=11)
0: Never worry	25%	34%	36%	27%
1: Rarely worry	32	44	26	18
2: Sometimes worry	28	15	26	45
3: Often worry	14	7	13	9

	R^2	b		R^2	b
Demographics	.01		Demographics	.05	
BHM–WHM	.03	−.23***	BHF–WHF	.05	.65

Catching Venereal Disease

	WHM (N=486)	BHM (N=96)	WHF (N=39)	BHF (N=11)	Pilot Study (N=458)
0: Never worry	34%	25%	74%	54%	19%
1: Rarely worry	34	36	13	27	26
2: Sometimes worry	22	21	10	18	32
3: Often worry	11	18	3	0	33

	R^2	b		R^2	b
Demographics	.01		Demographics	.04	
BHM–WHM	.01	.96	BHF–WHF	.05	.98

TABLE 6—*(Continued)*

		WHM	BHM	WHF	BHF	Pilot Study
Performing Inadequately Sexually		(N=486)	(N=96)	(N=39)	(N=11)	
0: Never worry		35%	45%	46%	27%	
1: Rarely worry		41	44	26	64	
2: Sometimes worry		20	10	15	9	
3: Often worry		4	1	13	0	
	R^2	b			R^2	b
Demographics	.01			Demographics	.11	
BHM–WHM	.02	−.14**		BHF–WHF	.13	−.15
Being Robbed or Rolled		(N=486)	(N=96)	(N=39)	(N=11)	(N=458)
0: Never worry		39%	52%	92%	64%	9%
1: Rarely worry		42	31	5	27	22
2: Sometimes worry		15	8	3	9	34
3: Often worry		4	8	0	0	35
	R^2	b			R^2	b
Demographics	.04			Demographics	.06	
BHM–WHM	.04	.13		BHF–WHF	.13	.16
Being Caught by the Police		(N=486)	(N=96)	(N=39)	(N=11)	(N=458)
0: Never worry		44%	67%	82%	73%	25%
1: Rarely worry		32	18	13	27	25
2: Sometimes worry		15	9	3	0	26
3: Often worry		9	6	3	0	23
	R^2	b			R^2	b
Demographics	.08			Demographics	.03	
BHM–WHM	.08	−.10		BHF–WHF	.04	.05
Having One's Homosexuality Publicly Exposed		(N=486)	(N=96)	(N=39)	(N=11)	(N=458)
0: Never worry		51%	71%	67%	54%	10%
1: Rarely worry		36	22	20	18	19
2: Sometimes worry		8	6	10	18	27
3: Often worry		4	1	3	9	44
	R^2	b			R^2	b
Demographics	.05			Demographics	.02	
BHM–WHM	.06	−.10*		BHF–WHF	.06	.19

* $p < .05$.
** $p < .01$.
*** $p < .001$.
[a] F is too small for program to compute; difference is not significant.
[b] Respondents could give more than one answer to this question, so column percents may add up to more than 100%; this inflates the chi-square, but not substantially.
[c] For the females, the conventional expected frequency rule for chi-square is not met; collapsing categories would obscure our analytic focus.

TABLE 7 / Sexual Partnerships

	WHM	BHM	WHF	BHF	Pilot Study
Number of Homosexual Partners Ever	(N=574)	(N=111)	(N=227)	(N=64)	(N=458)
0: 1	0%	0%	3%	5%	
1: 2	0	0	9	5	.
2: 3–4	1	2	15	14	1%[a]
3: 5–9	2	4	31	30	3
4: 10–14	3	5	16	9	4
5: 15–24	3	6	10	16	5
6: 25–49	8	6	8	11	8
7: 50–99	9	18	5	8	12
8: 100–249	15	15	1	2	20
9: 250–499	17	11	1	2	13
10: 500–999	15	14	0	0	14
11: 1000 or more	28	19	0	0	20

	R^2	b		R^2	b
Demographics	.09		Demographics	.04	
BHM–WHM	.09	−.11	BHF–WHF	.05	.17

	WHM	BHM	WHF	BHF	
Proportion of Opposite Race Partners	(N=574)	(N=111)	(N=227)	(N=64)	
0: None	22%	2%	72%	22%	
1–3: Half or less	78	31	27	48	
4–6: More than half	0	67	1	30	

	R^2	b		R^2	b
Demographics	.04		Demographics	.01	
BHM–WHM	.61	1.47***	BHF–WHF	.28	.89***

	WHM	BHM	WHF	BHF	
Proportion of Partners Who Were Strangers	(N=574)	(N=111)	(N=225)	(N=64)	(N=458)
0: None	1%	5%	62%	56%	6%
1–3: Half or less	20	43	32	38	26
4–6: More than half	79	51	6	6	68

	R^2	b		R^2	b
Demographics	.01		Demographics	.02	
BHM–WHM	.05	−.42***	BHF–WHF	.02	−.13

TABLE 7—(Continued)

		WHM	BHM	WHF	BHF	Pilot Study
Proportion of Partners for Whom R Had Some Affection		(N=573)	(N=111)	(N=226)	(N=64)	(N=456)
0: None		2%	2%	1%	3%	2%
1–3: Half or less		71	66	18	36	78
4–6: More than half		27	32	81	61	20
	R^2	b			R^2	b
Demographics	.02		Demographics		.04	
BHM–WHM	.02	.90	BHF–WHF		.07	−.36**

		WHM	BHM	WHF	BHF	Pilot Study
Proportion of Partners with Whom R Had Sex Only Once		(N=572)	(N=111)	(N=225)	(N=64)	(N=458)
0: None		1%	4%	38%	41%	3%
1–3: Half or less		29	59	51	55	40
4–6: More than half		70	38	12	5	57
	R^2	b			R^2	b
Demographics	.04		Demographics		.01	
BHM–WHM	.09	−.46***	BHF–WHF		.02	−.14

		WHM	BHM	WHF	BHF	
Proportion of Partners Whom R Did Not See Socially Again		(N=572)	(N=111)	(N=226)	(N=64)	
0: None		2%	6%	54%	45%	
1–3: Half or less		37	48	31	41	
4–6: More than half		61	46	15	14	
	R^2	b			R^2	b
Demographics	.04		Demographics		.01	
BHM–WHM	.05	−.19*	BHF–WHF		.01	.78

		WHM	BHM	WHF	BHF	Pilot Study
Proportion of Partners with Whom R Would Associate Socially		(N=574)	(N=111)	(N=225)	(N=64)	(N=457)
0: None		1%	2%	1%	0%	2%
1–3: Half or less		23	12	4	3	34
4–6: More than half		76	86	95	97	64
	R^2	b			R^2	b
Demographics	.03		Demographics		.00	
BHM–WHM	.04	.15	BHF–WHF		.00	.03

TABLE 7—(*Continued*)

	WHM	BHM	WHF	BHF	Pilot Study
Proportion of Partners Who Were Willing to Give Their Addresses and/or Phone Numbers	(N=574)	(N=111)	(N=226)	(N=64)	
0: None	2%	0%	3%	6%	
1–3: Half or less	35	30	5	6	
4–6: More than half	63	70	92	88	

	R^2	b		R^2	b
Demographics	.15		Demographics	.01	
BHM–WHM	.15	−.06	BHF–WHF	.01	−.17

	WHM	BHM	WHF	BHF	
Proportion of Partners Who Told a Fair Amount About Themselves	(N=574)	(N=111)	(N=225)	(N=64)	
0: None	1%	0%	0%	5%	
1–3: Half or less	48	48	9	9	
4–6: More than half	51	52	90	86	

	R^2	b		R^2	b
Demographics	.09		Demographics	.00	
BHM–WHM	.09	−.20	BHF–WHF	.02	−.19

	WHM	BHM	WHF	BHF	
Proportion of Partners Whom R Told a Fair Amount About Self	(N=574)	(N=111)	(N=226)	(N=64)	
0: None	2%	3%	1%	5%	
1–3: Half or less	63	63	25	41	
4–6: More than half	35	34	74	55	

	R^2	b		R^2	b
Demographics	.06		Demographics	.02	
BHM–WHM	.06	−.11	BHF–WHF	.06	−.48***

	WHM	BHM	WHF	BHF	Pilot Study
Proportion of Partners Who Were Older Than R	(N=572)	(N=111)	(N=226)	(N=64)	(N=456)
0: None	6%	3%	13%	9%	4%
1–3: Half or less	65	43	53	47	54
4–6: More than half	29	54	34	44	42

	R^2	b		R^2	b
Demographics	.17		Demographics	.12	
BHM–WHM	.18	.23***	BHF–WHF	.12	−.97

TABLE 7—(Continued)

		WHM	BHM	WHF	BHF	Pilot Study
Proportion of Partners Who Were Younger Than R		(N=573)	(N=111)	(N=225)	(N=64)	(N=455)
0: None		5%	15%	19%	15%	8%
1–3: Half or less		55	62	51	59	71
4–6: More than half		39	23	30	25	20
	R^2	b			R^2	b
Demographics	.19			Demographics	.10	
BHM–WHM	.19	−.11		BHF–WHF	.10	−.66
Proportion of Partners Who Were 16 or Younger (When R was 21 or Older)		(N=565)	(N=106)	(N=224)	(N=64)	
0: None		75%	86%	97%	94%	
1–3: Half or less		25	14	3	6	
4–6: More than half		0	0	0	0	
	R^2	b			R^2	b
Demographics	.01			Demographics	.00	
BHM–WHM	.01	−.56		BHF–WHF	.01	.26
Proportion of Partners Who Paid R for Sex		(N=574)	(N=111)	(N=225)	(N=64)	(N=458)
0: None		75%	62%	100%	88%	79%
1–3: Half or less		25	37	0	12	20
4–6: More than half		0	1	0	0	1
	R^2	b			R^2	b
Demographics	.03			Demographics	.01	
BHM–WHM	.04	.08*		BHF–WHF	.10	.08***
Proportion of Partners Whom R Paid for Sex		(N=574)	(N=111)	(N=225)	(N=64)	(N=458)
0: None		72%	84%	100%	94%	81%
1–3: Half or less		27	15	0	6	18
4–6: More than half		1	1	0	0	1
	R^2	b			R^2	b
Demographics	.07			Demographics	.01	
BHM–WHM	.07	−.00		BHF–WHF	.04	.03***

TABLE 7—(Continued)

		WHM	BHM	WHF	BHF	Pilot Study
Number of Homosexual Partners in Past Year		(N=572)	(N=110)	(N=228)	(N=64)	(N=458)
0: None		3%	0%	8%	6%	0%
1: 1–2		8	10	63	53	7
2: 3–5		10	12	16	23	13
3: 6–10		12	14	7	11	15
4: 11–19		12	5	3	2	12
5: 20–50		27	28	3	3	28
6–7: 51 or more		28	32	0	2	25
	R^2	b			R^2	b
Demographics	.03			Demographics	.10	
BHM–WHM	.03	−.03		BHF–WHF	.10	.07

Physical Characteristics Preferred in Sexual Partners[b]	(N=555)	(N=99)	(N=194)	(N=56)	
"Masculine"	27%	26%	6	2%	
"Feminine"	1	1	13	4	
Genitalia	29	18	0	0	
Buttocks	6	8	3	11	
Face, hair, eyes	35	46	42	45	
Age	15	9	5	0	
Body hair	21	10	3	7	
Musculature	24	9	9	4	
Breasts	0	0	29	45	
Chest	3	1	0	0	
Hips	1	0	3	13	
Height	26	37	23	25	
Body type, frame	69	72	68	52	
	X^2			X^2	
BHM–WHM	32.81***[c]		BHF–WHF	27.02***[c]	

		WHM	BHM	WHF	BHF	Pilot Study
Number of Affairs Ever		(N=572)	(N=111)	(N=229)	(N=64)	(N=458)
0: 0		9%	7%	4%	2%	8%
1: 1		17	23	10	17	15
2: 2		16	18	21	23	24
3: 3		20	22	23	19	20
4: 4		13	10	12	14	10
5: 5		8	6	11	9	8
6–87: 6		16	13	29	16	15
	R^2	b			R^2	b
Demographics	.02			Demographics	.07	
BHM–WHM	.02	−.05		BHF–WHF	.08	.19

TABLE 7—(*Continued*)

		WHM	BHM	WHF	BHF	Pilot Study
R's Age at Beginning of First Affair		(N=521)	(N=102)	(N=220)	(N=63)	
0: 19 or younger		31%	43%	40%	43%	
1: 20–23		33	40	36	32	
2: 24 or older		36	17	24	25	
(Mean age)		(23)	(21)	(22)	(22)	
	R^2	b			R^2	b
Demographics	.14		Demographics		.07	
BHM–WHM	.14	−.02	BHF–WHF		.07	.01
R's Age Compared with Partner's at Beginning of First Affair		(N=520)	(N=102)	(N=220)	(N=63)	
0: R was younger		60%	74%	60%	59%	
1: Same age		15	9	17	17	
2: R was older		25	17	23	24	
	R^2	b			R^2	b
Demographics	.08		Demographics		.02	
BHM–WHM	.08	.01	BHF–WHF		.03	−.01
Discrepancy Between Ages of R and Partner at Beginning of First Affair		(N=520)	(N=103)	(N=220)	(N=63)	
0: No discrepancy		15%	9%	17%	17%	
1: 1–2 years		22	21	35	21	
2: 3–5 years		24	20	20	22	
3: 6–10 years		22	26	15	27	
4: More than 10 years		16	23	12	13	
	R^2	b			R^2	b
Demographics	.00		Demographics		.02	
BHM–WHM	.01	.73*	BHF–WHF		.02	.30
Did R and Partner Live Together (First Affair)?		(N=521)	(N=103)	(N=220)	(N=63)	
0: No		47%	42%	35%	59%	
1: Yes		52	58	65	41	
	R^2	b			R^2	b
Demographics	.00		Demographics		.02	
BHM–WHM	.00	−.02	BHF–WHF		.05	.10**

TABLE 7—*(Continued)*

	WHM	BHM	WHF	BHF	Pilot Study
Was R in Love with Partner (First Affair)?	(N=521)	(N=102)	(N=219)	(N=64)	
0: No	22%	21%	10%	14%	
1: Yes	78	79	90	86	

	R^2	b		R^2	b
Demographics	.00		Demographics	.03	
BHM–WHM	.00	−.02	BHF–WHF	.03	.01

Comparison of Social Positions of R and Partner (First Affair)	(N=520)	(N=102)	(N=220)	(N=63)	
0: R's social position lower	26%	39%	18%	29%	
1: Same	55	44	68	36	
2: R's social position higher	19	17	14	35	

	R^2	b		R^2	b
Demographics	.06		Demographics	.03	
BHM–WHM	.06	.01	BHF–WHF		—[d]

Duration of First Affair	(N=521)	(N=103)	(N=220)	(N=63)	
0–1: 3 months or less	16%	12%	9%	3%	
2–3: 4–11 months	24	22	18	22	
4: 1–3 years	38	48	42	48	
5: 4–5 years	10	11	17	21	
6: More than 5 years	12	8	14	6	

	R^2	b		R^2	b
Demographics	.07		Demographics	.06	
BHM–WHM	.09	.27**	BHF–WHF	.06	.04

Who Initiated Breakup of First Affair?	(N=470)	(N=86)	(N=195)	(N=53)	
Respondent	40%	41%	38%	40%	
Partner	35	30	44	42	
Mutual	15	12	12	9	
No indication	10	17	6	9	

	X^2		X^2
BHM–WHM	4.69	BHF–WHF	.86

TABLE 7—(Continued)

	WHM	BHM	WHF	BHF	Pilot Study
Reason for Breakup of First Affair	(N=470)	(N=86)	(N=195)	(N=53)	
Factors beyond control	29%	30%	13%	13%	
Relationship unsatisfying	23	24	24	26	
Relationship too weak	16	14	11	13	
Romantic involvement with someone else	14	13	31	21	
Sexual involvement with other(s)	4	3	3	0	
Forced apart by others	2	3	5	11	
Other response	10	12	12	11	
No indication	1	0	2	4	

X^2
BHM–WHM 2.82 X^2 BHF–WHF 5.82

	WHM	BHM	WHF	BHF	
How R Felt When First Affair Ended	(N=468)	(N=88)	(N=191)	(N=50)	
0: Extremely upset, unhappy	44%	45%	43%	48%	
1: A little upset, unhappy	12	11	5	12	
2: Both unhappy and relieved	33	27	34	24	
3: Very relieved it was over	11	16	17	16	

X^2
BHM–WHM 2.50 X^2 BHF–WHF 4.20

What R Got Out of First Affair

	WHM	BHM	WHF	BHF	
Positive Changes in Self[b]	(N=128)	(N=32)	(N=72)	(N=20)	
Greater maturity	30%	44%	24%	40%	
Self-insight	26	25	35	40	
Became a better or more complete person	25	19	19	20	
Higher aspirations, broader horizons	18	9	17	10	
More self-confident, more self-accepting	13	19	24	15	
Other changes	3	6	6	5	

X^2
BHM–WHM 4.09 X^2 BHF–WHF 2.55

TABLE 7—(Continued)

	WHM	BHM	WHF	BHF	Pilot Study
What R Got Out of First Affair					
Other Things[b]	(N=520)	(N=103)	(N=220)	(N=62)	
Love, warmth, friendship	62%	46%	64%	52%	
Sexual satisfaction	25	18	27	26	
Learned about keeping relationships going	8	9	4	7	
Peace, happiness	16	16	13	16	
Negative response	12	10	16	31	
Material things	5	7	2	0	
Other response	18	16	17	18	

X^2 BHM–WHM 3.82 X^2 BHF–WHF 8.39

What Partner Got Out of First Affair					
Positive Changes in Self[b]	(N=61)	(N=15)	(N=44)	(N=11)	
Greater maturity	31%	40%	25%	27%	
Self-insight	23	20	23	45	
Became a better or more complete person	25	27	27	18	
Higher aspirations, broader horizons	16	0	14	9	
More self-confident, more self-accepting	11	13	23	18	
Other changes	3	7	5	0	

X^2 BHM–WHM 3.25 X^2 BHF–WHF 2.66

Other Things[b]	(N=485)	(N=89)	(N=213)	(N=60)	
Love, warmth, friendship	64%	63%	67%	58%	
Sexual satisfaction	36	30	24	23	
Learned about keeping relationships going	2	3	2	5	
Peace, happiness	12	21	16	12	
Negative response	0	0	0	0	
Material things	8	3	6	10	
Other response	9	3	9	12	

X^2 BHM–WHM 11.66* X^2 BHF–WHF 4.54

TABLE 7—*(Continued)*

	WHM	BHM	WHF	BHF	Pilot Study
How First Affair Differed from Subsequent Affairs[b]	(N=471)	(N=87)	(N=194)	(N=64)	
Had a lot to learn	39%	38%	32%	40%	
More superficial relationship	13	11	17	17	
R more positively involved	11	11	14	12	
More complete relationship	9	5	9	6	
Different sexually	9	8	8	2	
R less involved	7	8	4	2	
Not very different	6	5	3	4	
R more negatively involved	4	8	7	4	

$$X^2$$
BHM–WHM 3.50   BHF–WHF X^2 5.08

How First Affair Changed R

	WHM	BHM	WHF	BHF	
Positive Changes in Self[b]	(N=221)	(N=52)	(N=113)	(N=28)	
Greater maturity	43%	54%	33%	43%	
A better or more complete person	29	35	28	14	
Self-confidence, self-acceptance	21	13	25	54	
Self-insight	20	8	14	11	
Higher aspirations, goals	10	2	14	11	
Other changes	6	10	11	9	

$$X^2$$
BHM–WHM 10.34   BHF–WHF X^2 11.37*

	WHM	BHM	WHF	BHF	
Other Things[b]	(N=471)	(N=87)	(N=194)	(N=64)	
Learned about keeping a relationship going	17%	14%	11%	6%	
Learned about gay life	13	14	6	8	
More committed to one's homosexuality	9	8	18	13	
Negative change	5	4	9	5	
More afraid to get involved again	14	9	14	12	
Other response	14	9	10	5	

$$X^2$$
BHM–WHM 2.14   BHF–WHF X^2 2.87

TABLE 7—(*Continued*)

		WHM	BHM	WHF	BHF	Pilot Study
Is R Currently Involved in Homosexual Affair?		(N=574)	(N=111)	(N=229)	(N=63)	(N=458)
0: No		49%	42%	28%	30%	54%
1: Yes		51	58	72	70	46
	R^2	b			R^2	b
Demographics	.00			Demographics	.03	
BHM–WHM	.00	.03		BHF–WHF	.04	−.04
Is Current Affair the First?		(N=295)	(N=64)	(N=165)	(N=45)	
0: No		85%	77%	86%	78%	
1: Yes		15	23	14	22	
	R^2	b			R^2	b ·
Demographics	.06			Demographics	.04	
BHM–WHM	.06	.00		BHF–WHF	.04	.04
R's Age at Beginning of Current Affair		(N=250)	(N=49)	(N=146)	(N=36)	
0: 25 or younger		28%	55%	41%	31%	
1: 26–32		25	41	17	42	
2: 33 or older		47	4	42	28	
(Mean age)		(33)	(26)	(32)	(30)	
	R^2	b			R^2	b
Demographics	.59			Demographics	.73	
BHM–WHM	.59	−.05		BHF–WHF	.73	.05
R's Age Compared with Partner's (Current Affair)		(N=250)	(N=49)	(N=146)	(N=36)	
0: R is younger		38%	57%	44%	47%	
1: Same age		5	10	10	3	
2: R is older		57	33	47	50	
	R^2	b			R^2	b
Demographics	.14			Demographics	.13	
BHM–WHM	.14	.04		BHF–WHF	.14	−.09

TABLE 7—(Continued)

	WHM	BHM	WHF	BHF	Pilot Study
Discrepancy Between Ages of R and Partner (Current Affair)	(N=250)	(N=49)	(N=146)	(N=36)	
0: No discrepancy	5%	10%	10%	3%	
1: 1–2 years	22	25	23	31	
2: 3–5 years	21	25	33	19	
3: 6–10 years	23	20	19	28	
4: More than 10 years	28	20	16	19	

	R^2	b		R^2	b
Demographics	.19		Demographics	.12	
BHM–WHM	.19	.25	BHF–WHF	.13	.54

	WHM	BHM	WHF	BHF	
Do R and Partner Live Together (Current Affair)?	(N=250)	(N=49)	(N=146)	(N=36)	
0: No	34%	41%	20%	25%	
1: Yes	66	59	80	75	

	R^2	b		R^2	b
Demographics	.00		Demographics	.02	
BHM–WHM	.01	.03	BHF–WHF	.03	.04

	WHM	BHM	WHF	BHF	
Is R in Love with Partner (Current Affair)?	(N=250)	(N=49)	(N=145)	(N=35)	
0: No	16%	18%	14%	29%	
1: Yes	84	82	86	71	

	R^2	b		R^2	b
Demographics	.01		Demographics	.01	
BHM–WHM	.01	.02	BHF–WHF	.05	.10*

	WHM	BHM	WHF	BHF	
Comparison of Social Positions of R and Partner (Current Affair)	(N=250)	(N=49)	(N=145)	(N=36)	
0: R's social position lower	14%	43%	14%	28%	
1: Same	64	39	72	56	
2: R's social position higher	22	18	14	17	

	R^2	b		R^2	b
Demographics	.12		Demographics	.04	
BHM–WHM	.13	.07	BHF–WHF	.04	.03

TABLE 7—(Continued)

	WHM	BHM	WHF	BHF	Pilot Study
Duration of Current Affair	(N=249)	(N=49)	(N=146)	(N=35)	
0–1: 3 months or less	10%	6%	9%	9%	
2–3: 4–11 months	18	45	20	28	
4: 1–3 years	28	35	40	37	
5: 4–5 years	12	6	16	14	
6: More than 5 years	31	8	15	11	

	R^2	b		R^2	b
Demographics	.22		Demographics	.18	
BHM–WHM	.22	−.05	BHF–WHF	.19	−.02

What R Is Getting Out of Current Affair

Positive Changes in Self[b]

	WHM	BHM	WHF	BHF
	(N=60)	(N=11)	(N=50)	(N=15)
A better or more complete person	38%	45%	32%	40%
Self-insight	22	9	16	40
Self-confidence, self-acceptance	18	18	22	13
Greater maturity	17	27	22	13
Higher aspirations, broader horizons	13	36	26	13
Other changes	7	0	2	0

	X^2		X^2
BHM–WHM	4.06	BHF–WHF	2.28

What R Is Getting Out of Current Affair

Other Things[b]

	WHM	BHM	WHF	BHF
	(N=249)	(N=45)	(N=142)	(N=34)
Love, warmth, friendship	79%	71%	78%	59%
Sexual satisfaction	26	20	21	18
Peace, happiness	25	27	27	26
Material things	11	7	5	3
Learning about keeping relationships going	5	9	4	0
Negative response	4	4	9	12
Other response	7	2	8	9

	X^2		X^2
BHM–WHM	11.58	BHF–WHF	5.81

TABLE 7—(Continued)

	WHM	BHM	WHF	BHF	Pilot Study
What Partner Is Getting Out of Current Affair					
Positive Changes in Self[b]	(N=74)	(N=14)	(N=51)	(N=11)	
A better or more complete person	28%	36%	31%	36%	
Higher aspirations, broader horizons	24	14	18	27	
Greater maturity	23	21	22	18	
Self-insight	22	14	29	18	
Self-confidence, self-acceptance	9	21	29	9	
Other changes	4	7	2	0	

$$X^2$$
BHM–WHM 7.32[e] $$X^2$$ BHF–WHF 3.97

	WHM	BHM	WHF	BHF	Pilot Study
Other Things[b]	(N=242)	(N=43)	(N=141)	(N=31)	
Love, warmth, friendship	79%	60%	77%	68%	
Sexual satisfaction	21	14	18	16	
Peace, happiness	24	26	27	26	
Material things	13	5	9	10	
Learning about keeping relationships going	4	7	2	3	
Negative response	3	7	9	13	
Other response	8	2	5	3	

$$X^2$$
BHM–WHM 7.18[e] $$X^2$$ BHF–WHF 2.23

	WHM	BHM	WHF	BHF	Pilot Study
How Current Affair Differs From Previous Affairs[b]	(N=173)	(N=39)	(N=104)	(N=25)	
More complete relationship	64%	54%	62%	68%	
R more positively involved	23	23	23	25	
Different sexually	18	13	13	8	
R more mature	13	36	14	24	
R less involved	9	0	8	8	
More superficial relationship	2	5	6	0	
Not very different	2	3	3	8	
R more negatively involved	1	0	3	4	

$$X^2$$
BHM–WHM 18.03[*c] $$X^2$$ BHF–WHF 3.88[c]

TABLE 7—(Continued)

	WHM	BHM	WHF	BHF	Pilot Study
If Currently Involved: Is R "Coupled" with Partner?	(N=295)	(N=64)	(N=165)	(N=45)	
0: No	44%	50%	33%	36%	
1: Yes	56	50	67	64	

	R^2	b			R^2	b
Demographics	.01			Demographics	.01	
BHM–WHM	.01	−.02		BHF–WHF	.01	−.02

	WHM	BHM	WHF	BHF	
Is R Currently "Coupled"?	(N=575)	(N=111)	(N=229)	(N=64)	
0: No	71%	71%	52%	54%	
1: Yes	29	29	48	46	

	R^2	b			R^2	b
Demographics	.00			Demographics	.01	
BHM–WHM	.00	.01		BHF–WHF	.02	−.04

Importance of Permanent Living Arrangement with Homosexual Partner at Beginning of R's Homosexual Career	WHM	BHM	WHF	BHF	
	(N=575)	(N=111)	(N=228)	(N=64)	
Not important at all	33%	32%	21%	22%	
Nice, but not important	19	17	11	27	
Somewhat important	12	15	14	17	
Very important	22	29	28	16	
The most important thing in life	15	6	26	19	

	R^2	b			R^2	b
Demographics	.01			Demographics	.02	
BHM–WHM	.01	−.09		BHF–WHF	.03	−.20

Importance of Permanent Living Arrangement with Homosexual Partner, Currently	WHM	BHM	WHF	BHF	Pilot (N=456)
	(N=575)	(N=111)	(N=229)	(N=64)	(N=456)
0: Not important at all	20%	18%	14%	12%	15%
1: Nice, but not important	13	15	8	9	27
2: Somewhat important	20	29	17	20	21
3: Very important	30	26	35	34	27
4: The most important thing in life	17	12	24	23	10

	R^2	b			R^2	b
Demographics	.01			Demographics	.01	
BHM–WHM	.02	−.09		BHF–WHF	.01	−.04

TABLE 7—*(Continued)*

		WHM	BHM	WHF	BHF	Pilot Study
If Coupled: Do R and Partner Combine Incomes?		(N=153)	(N=28)	(N=91)	(N=26)	
0: No, kept separate		44%	29%	29%	31%	
1: Some kept separate, some combined		9	32	14	15	
2: Yes, all combined		47	39	57	54	
	R^2	b			R^2	b
Demographics	.03			Demographics	.09	
BHM–WHM	.03	−.03		BHF–WHF	.09	−.03

		WHM	BHM	WHF	BHF	
If Coupled: Who Earns More?		(N=164)	(N=32)	(N=105)	(N=29)	
0: Only partner has income		2%	6%	3%	3%	
1: Partner earns more		32	47	28	41	
2: Incomes are equal		18	3	17	3	
3: R earns more		43	38	42	45	
4: Only R has income		5	6	10	7	
	R^2	b			R^2	b
Demographics	.15			Demographics	.04	
BHM–WHM	.15	.06		BHF–WHF	.05	−.15

		WHM	BHM	WHF	BHF	
If Coupled: Effect of Income Disparity (If Any) on Relationship		(N=124)	(N=27)	(N=62)	(N=24)	
No effect indicated		22%	26%	26%	21%	
Negative effect		2	4	6	4	
Positive effect		5	0	3	4	
Relationship not affected		68	70	65	67	
		X^2			X^2	
BHM–WHM		2.28[c]		BHF–WHF	3.41[c]	

		WHM	BHM	WHF	BHF	
If Coupled: Who Does the Housework?		(N=163)	(N=32)	(N=103)	(N=28)	
0: Partner		18%	9%	23%	14%	
1: Shared equally		61	69	58	71	
2: Respondent		20	22	18	14	
	R^2	b			R^2	b
Demographics	.05			Demographics	.01	
BHM–WHM	.05	−.00		BHF–WHF	.01	.03

TABLE 7—(Continued)

		WHM	BHM	WHF	BHF	Pilot Study
If Coupled: Who Does the Household Shopping?		(N=164)	(N=32)	(N=110)	(N=28)	
0: Partner		16%	22%	20%	21%	
1: Shared equally		44	44	51	72	
2: Respondent		39	34	29	7	
	R^2	b			R^2	b
Demographics	.01		Demographics		.02	
BHM–WHM	.01	−.03	BHF–WHF		.04	−.13
If Coupled: Who Does Household Repairs?		(N=156)	(N=30)	(N=101)	(N=27)	
0: Partner		26%	37%	22%	26%	
1: Shared equally		36	47	42	30	
2: Respondent		37	17	37	44	
	R^2	b			R^2	b
Demographics	.01		Demographics		.04	
BHM–WHM	.03	−.18*	BHF–WHF		.04	.02
If Coupled: Who Keeps Household Accounts?		(N=157)	(N=27)	(N=101)	(N=27)	
0: Partner		28%	37%	35%	48%	
1: Shared equally		30	41	32	33	
2: Respondent		42	22	34	18	
	R^2	b			R^2	b
Demographics	.04		Demographics		.03	
BHM–WHM	.05	−.08	BHF–WHF		.07	.21*
If Coupled: Who Does the Cooking?		(N=162)	(N=32)	(N=108)	(N=29)	
0: Partner		35%	19%	39%	24%	
1: Shared equally		28	38	32	48	
2: Respondent		37	44	30	28	
	R^2	b			R^2	b
Demographics	.00		Demographics		.00	
BHM–WHM	.02	.15	BHF–WHF		.01	.04
If Coupled: Do R and Partner Share All Roles Equally?		(N=140)	(N=29)	(N=88)	(N=24)	
0: No		91%	83%	91%	96%	
1: Yes		9	17	9	4	
	R^2	b			R^2	b
Demographics	.04		Demographics		.05	
BHM–WHM	.04	−.01	BHF–WHF		.06	−.01

TABLE 7—(Continued)

	WHM	BHM	WHF	BHF	Pilot Study

If Coupled: Does R Do All the "Feminine" Tasks?

	WHM	BHM	WHF	BHF
	(N=155)	(N=34)	(N=102)	(N=28)
0: No	93%	82%	94%	96%
1: Yes	7	18	6	4

	R^2	b		R^2	b
Demographics	.01		Demographics	.03	
BHM–WHM	.03	.05	BHF–WHF	.03	−.01

If Coupled: Does Partner Do All the "Feminine" Tasks?

	WHM	BHM	WHF	BHF
	(N=154)	(N=32)	(N=102)	(N=28)
0: No	94%	97%	96%	93%
1: Yes	6	3	4	7

	R^2	b		R^2	b
Demographics	.02		Demographics	.04	
BHM–WHM	.02	.01	BHF–WHF	.04	.01

If Coupled: Does R Do All the "Masculine" Tasks?

	WHM	BHM	WHF	BHF
	(N=159)	(N=28)	(N=95)	(N=25)
0: No	76%	93%	81%	88%
1: Yes	24	7	19	12

	R^2	b		R^2	b
Demographics	.01		Demographics	.04	
BHM–WHM	.04	−.10*	BHF–WHF	.04	−.02

If Coupled: Does Partner Do All the "Masculine" Tasks?

	WHM	BHM	WHF	BHF
	(N=149)	(N=26)	(N=93)	(N=25)
0: No	91%	92%	94%	88%
1: Yes	9	8	6	12

	R^2	b		R^2	b
Demographics	.02		Demographics	.01	
BHM–WHM	.02	−.01	BHF–WHF	.03	.05

* $p < .05$.
** $p < .01$.
*** $p < .001$.

[a] One percent of the pilot study respondents reported "fewer than five" partners.

[b] Respondents could give more than one answer to this question, so column percents may add up to more than 100%; this inflates the chi-square, but not substantially.

[c] Does not meet the conventional expected frequency rule for chi-square; collapsing categories would obscure our analytic focus.

[d] Number of cases in some cells was too low to allow for valid analysis.

[e] For the males, the conventional expected frequency rule for chi-square is not met; collapsing categories would obscure our analytic focus.

TABLE 8 / Sex Appeal

	WHM	BHM	WHF	BHF	Pilot Study
Self-Rating of Homosexual Sex Appeal	(N=574)	(N=111)	(N=227)	(N=63)	(N=458)
0: Definitely below average	4%	1%	3%	0%	7%
1: A bit below average	12	7	10	10	21
2: Average	34	38	38	29	23
3: A bit above average	35	41	33	38	41
4: Definitely above average	16	14	17	24	9

	R^2	b			R^2	b
Demographics	.11			Demographics	.01	
BHM–WHM	.11	−.01		BHF–WHF	.02	.13

TABLE 9 / Sexual Techniques

	WHM	BHM	WHF	BHF	Pilot Study
Number of Different Homosexual Activities in Past Year	(N=571)	(N=110)	(N=225)	(N=63)	
0: 0	3%	1%	8%	5%	
1: 1	1	1	3	2	
2: 2	4	1	11	5	
3: 3	3	2	9	8	
4: 4	7	7	39	22	
5: 5	19	14	29	57	
6: 6 (males only)	38	39			
7: 7 (males only)	24	35			

	R^2	b		R^2	b
Demographics	.19		Demographics	.14	
WHM–BHM	.19	−.04	WHF–BHF	.16	.24*

Incidence of Sexual Techniques in Past Year

	WHM	BHM	WHF	BHF	
Body-Rubbing	(N=575)	(N=111)	(N=228)	(N=64)	
0: No	59%	47%	54%	23%	
1: Yes	41	53	46	77	

	R^2	b		R^2	b
Demographics	.05		Demographics	.05	
WHM–BHM	.05	.02	WHF–BHF	.09	.13***

	WHM	BHM	WHF	BHF	
Masturbating Partner	(N=574)	(N=110)	(N=226)	(N=64)	
0: No	17%	9%	21%	12%	
1: Yes	83	91	79	88	

	R^2	b		R^2	b
Demographics	.07		Demographics	.15	
WHM–BHM	.07	.00	WHF–BHF	.16	.04

	WHM	BHM	WHF	BHF	
Being Masturbated by Partner	(N=574)	(N=111)	(N=227)	(N=64)	
0: No	15%	12%	18%	11%	
1: Yes	85	88	82	89	

	R^2	b		R^2	b
Demographics	.08		Demographics	.24	
BHM–WHM	.08	−.02	BHF–WHF	.24	.01

TABLE 9—(*Continued*)

		WHM	BHM	WHF	BHF	Pilot Study
Performing Oral-Genital		(N=575)	(N=111)	(N=228)	(N=63)	
0: No		5%	11%	22%	20%	
1: Yes		95	89	78	80	
	R^2	b			R^2	b
Demographics	.03			Demographics	.04	
BHM–WHM	.04	−.04**		BHF–WHF	.04	.01
Receiving Oral-Genital		(N=573)	(N=111)	(N=228)	(N=64)	
0: No		6%	4%	25%	16%	
1: Yes		94	96	75	84	
	R^2	b			R^2	b
Demographics	.07			Demographics	.04	
BHM–WHM	.08	−.01		BHF–WHF	.05	.04
Performing Anal Intercourse		(N=575)	(N=111)			
0: No		22%	10%			
1: Yes		78	90			
	R^2	b				
Demographics	.15					
BHM–WHM	.15	−.00				
Receiving Anal Intercourse		(N=574)	(N=111)			
0: No		33%	22%			
1: Yes		67	78			
	R^2	b				
Demographics	.11					
BHM–WHM	.11	.00				

Frequency of Sexual Techniques in Past Year

		WHM	BHM	WHF	BHF	
Body-Rubbing		(N=575)	(N=111)	(N=228)	(N=64)	
0: Never		59%	47%	54%	23%	
1: Once or a few times		20	18	10	9	
2–4: More than a few times		16	17	17	28	
5–7: Once a week or more		6	18	19	39	
	R^2	b			R^2	b
Demographics	.07			Demographics	.20	
BHM–WHM	.09	.37**		BHF–WHF	.21	.32

TABLE 9—(Continued)

	WHM	BHM	WHF	BHF	Pilot Study
Masturbating Partner	(N=574)	(N=110)	(N=226)	(N=64)	
0: Never	17%	9%	21%	12%	
1: Once or a few times	22	19	19	16	
2–4: More than a few times	35	39	28	25	
5–7: Once a week or more	26	42	40	47	

	R^2	b		R^2	b
Demographics	.08		Demographics	.16	
BHM–WHM	.08	.07	BHF–WHF	.16	.18

	WHM	BHM	WHF	BHF	
Being Masturbated by Partner	(N=574)	(N=111)	(N=227)	(N=64)	
0: Never	15%	12%	18%	11%	
1: Once or a few times	23	16	11	16	
2–4: More than a few times	36	36	31	23	
5–7: Once a week or more	26	36	40	50	

	R^2	b		R^2	b
Demographics	.08		Demographics	.16	
BHM–WHM	.10	.08	BHF–WHF	.16	—[a]

	WHM	BHM	WHF	BHF	
Performing Oral-Genital	(N=575)	(N=111)	(N=228)	(N=63)	
0: Never	5%	11%	22%	20%	
1: Once or a few times	7	7	16	14	
2–4: More than a few times	34	30	34	22	
5–7: Once a week or more	54	53	28	42	

	R^2	b		R^2	b
Demographics	.02		Demographics	.08	
BHM–WHM	.02	−.12	BHF–WHF	.09	.31

	WHM	BHM	WHF	BHF	
Receiving Oral-Genital	(N=573)	(N=111)	(N=228)	(N=64)	
0: Never	6%	4%	25%	16%	
1: Once or a few times	6	5	12	16	
2–4: More than a few times	35	28	36	27	
5–7: Once a week or more	53	63	26	42	

	R^2	b		R^2	b
Demographics	.08		Demographics	.05	
BHM–WHM	.08	−.03	BHF–WHF	.07	.36*

	WHM	BHM	
Performing Anal Intercourse	(N=575)	(N=111)	
0: Never	22%	10%	
1: Once or a few times	16	11	
2–4: More than a few times	40	37	
5–7: Once a week or more	22	42	

	R^2	b
Demographics	.12	
BHM–WHM	.14	.34**

TABLE 9—*(Continued)*

	WHM	BHM	WHF	BHF	Pilot Study
Receiving Anal Intercourse	(N=574)	(N=111)			
Never	33%	22%			
Once or a few times	18	20			
More than a few times	30	32			
Once a week or more	19	26			
R^2	b				
Demographics .06					
BHM–WHM .07	.18				
Favorite Sexual Activity	(N=552)	(N=108)	(N=210)	(N=59)	
Body-rubbing	3%	2%	12%	24%	
Masturbating partner	0	0	0	2	
Being masturbated by partner	1	0	16	5	
Mutual masturbation	2	1	13	7	
Performing oral-genital	2	3	6	0	
Receiving oral-genital	27	18	20	29	
Mutual oral-genital	14	8	20	24	
Performing anal intercourse	26	44			
Receiving anal intercourse	5	11			
Self-masturbation	5	3	1	0	
Favorite technique is heterosexual	2	5	4	5	
Other response	13	5	8	5	
X^2				X^2	
BHM–WHM 28.70***[b]			BHF–WHF 17.08*[b]		

* $p < .05$.
** $p < .01$.
*** $p < .001$.
[a] F is too small for program to compute; difference is not significant.
[b] Does not meet the conventional expected frequency rule for chi-square; collapsing categories would obscure our analytic focus.

TABLE 10 / Level of Sexual Interest

		WHM	BHM	WHF	BHF	Pilot Study
Frequency of Sexual Thoughts		(N=575)	(N=111)	(N=229)	(N=64)	(N=458)
0: Not at all		2%	0%	8%	3%	1%
1: Not very much		16	24	29	23	35
2: Some		44	40	42	44	59
3: Quite a bit		37	36	21	30	4
	R^2	b			R^2	b
Demographics	.01			Demographics	.08	
BHM–WHM	.01	−.03		BHF–WHF	.09	.11
Importance of Sex		(N=575)	(N=111)	(N=229)	(N=64)	(N=458)
0: Unimportant		1%	0%	2%	2%	0%
1: Not very important		12	19	24	19	12
2: Fairly important		47	55	47	48	61
3: Very important		40	26	27	31	27
	R^2	b			R^2	b
Demographics	.01			Demographics	.02	
BHM–WHM	.02	−.07		BHF–WHF	.02	.66
Summary Measure of Interest Level		(N=575)	(N=111)	(N=229)	(N=64)	
0–3: Relatively low		22%	29%	42%	36%	
4–6: Moderate		42	50	34	33	
7–10: Relatively high		37	21	24	31	
	R^2	b			R^2	b
Demographics	.01			Demographics	.05	
BHM–WHM	.01	−.13		BHF–WHF	.06	.22

TABLE 11 / Sexual Problems

	WHM	BHM	WHF	BHF	Pilot Study
Are the Following a Problem in Sexual Life?					

Partner's Failure to Respond to Sexual Requests

	(N=575)	(N=111)	(N=228)	(N=64)
0: No	19%	27%	50%	47%
1: Yes	81	73	50	53

	R^2	b			R^2	b
Demographics	.00		Demographics		.01	
BHM–WHM	.00	−.04	BHF–WHF		.01	.01

Finding a Suitable Partner

	(N=575)	(N=110)	(N=229)	(N=64)
0: No	24%	37%	54%	44%
1: Yes	76	63	46	56

	R^2	b			R^2	b
Demographics	.01		Demographics		.01	
BHM–WHM	.02	−.06*	BHF–WHF		.02	.55

Responding to Partner's Sexual Requests

	(N=575)	(N=111)	(N=229)	(N=64)
0: No	33%	34%	58%	53%
1: Yes	67	66	42	47

	R^2	b			R^2	b
Demographics	.01		Demographics		.00	
BHM–WHM	.01	−.02	BHF–WHF		.01	.01

Lack of Frequency

	(N=574)	(N=111)	(N=229)	(N=64)
0: No	32%	41%	48%	33%
1: Yes	68	59	52	67

	R^2	b			R^2	b
Demographics	.01		Demographics		.01	
BHM–WHM	.01	−.04	BHF–WHF		.02	.07

Difficulty in Getting or Maintaining an Erection

	(N=575)	(N=111)
0: No	40%	63%
1: Yes	60	37

	R^2	b
Demographics	.02	
BHM–WHM	.04	−.10***

TABLE 11—*(Continued)*

		WHM	BHM	WHF	BHF	Pilot Study
Lack of Orgasm on Part of Partner		(N=573)	(N=110)	(N=229)	(N=64)	
0: No		39%	57%	57%	67%	
1: Yes		61	43	43	33	
	R^2	b			R^2	b
Demographics	.01			Demographics	.00	
BHM–WHM	.02	−.08**		BHF–WHF	.02	−.07
Maintaining Affection for Sexual Partner		(N=575)	(N=111)	(N=228)	(N=64)	
0: No		42%	49%	69%	55%	
1: Yes		58	51	31	45	
	R^2	b			R^2	b
Demographics	.02			Demographics	.01	
BHM–WHM	.03	−.08**		BHF–WHF	.02	.07
"Coming" Too Fast		(N=575)	(N=111)			
0: No		44%	52%			
1: Yes		56	48			
	R^2	b				
Demographics	.00					
BHM–WHM	.01	−.06*				
Concern That You Are Not Sexually Adequate		(N=574)	(N=110)	(N=229)	(N=64)	
0: No		48%	65%	62%	63%	
1: Yes		52	35	38	37	
	R^2	b			R^2	b
Demographics	.01			Demographics	.01	
BHM–WHM	.03	−.10***		BHF–WHF	.01	−.17
Lack of Orgasm		(N−572)	(N=111)	(N=228)	(N=64)	
0: No		53%	55%	54%	47%	
1: Yes		47	45	46	53	
	R^2	b			R^2	b
Demographics	.00			Demographics	.02	
BHM–WHM	.00	−.01		BHF–WHF	.02	.05

TABLE 11—(*Continued*)

	WHM	BHM	WHF	BHF	Pilot Study

To What Extent Are the Following a Problem in Sexual Life?

Partner's Failure to Respond to Sexual Requests

		WHM (N=575)	BHM (N=111)	WHF (N=228)	BHF (N=64)
0: Not at all		19%	27%	50%	47%
1: Very little		53	45	32	34
2: Somewhat		25	24	13	17
3: Very much		3	4	5	2

	R^2	b			R^2	b
Demographics	.00			Demographics	.00	
BHM–WHM	.00	−.03		BHF–WHF	.00	−.01

Finding a Suitable Partner

		(N=575)	(N=110)	(N=229)	(N=64)
0: Not at all		24%	37%	54%	44%
1: Very little		29	23	10	17
2: Somewhat		29	28	18	20
3: Very much		18	12	18	19

	R^2	b			R^2	b
Demographics	.03			Demographics	.01	
BHM–WHM	.03	−.12*		BHF–WHF	.02	.11

Responding to Partner's Sexual Requests

		(N=575)	(N=111)	(N=229)	(N=64)
0: Not at all		33%	34%	58%	53%
1: Very little		46	43	27	28
2: Somewhat		18	19	12	14
3: Very much		3	4	3	5

	R^2	b			R^2	b
Demographics	.01			Demographics	.00	
BHM–WHM	.01	−.02		BHF–WHF	.01	.06

Lack of Frequency

		(N=574)	(N=111)	(N=229)	(N=64)
0: Not at all		32%	41%	48%	33%
1: Very little		31	32	22	31
2: Somewhat		26	23	18	25
3: Very much		11	4	11	11

	R^2	b			R^2	b
Demographics	.02			Demographics	.01	
BHM–WHM	.02	−.08		BHF–WHF	.01	.08

TABLE 11—(Continued)

	WHM	BHM	WHF	BHF	Pilot Study
Difficulty in Getting or Maintaining an Erection	(N=575)	(N=111)			
0: Not at all	40%	63%			
1: Very little	37	27			
2: Somewhat	19	9			
3: Very much	4	1			

	R^2	b
Demographics	.04	
BHM–WHM	.05	−.15**

	WHM	BHM	WHF	BHF	
Lack of Orgasm on Part of Partner	(N=573)	(N=110)	(N=229)	(N=64)	
0: Not at all	39%	57%	57%	67%	
1: Very little	47	32	30	28	
2: Somewhat	12	9	10	3	
3: Very much	2	2	3	2	

	R^2	b		R^2	b
Demographics	.02		Demographics	.00	
BHM–WHM	.03	−.06	BHF–WHF	.02	−.11

	WHM	BHM	WHF	BHF	
Maintaining Affection for Sexual Partner	(N=575)	(N=111)	(N=228)	(N=64)	
0: Not at all	42%	49%	69%	55%	
1: Very little	32	23	14	17	
2: Somewhat	19	22	13	19	
3: Very much	7	5	4	9	

	R^2	b		R^2	b
Demographics	.02		Demographics	.01	
BHM–WHM	.03	−.12*	BHF–WHF	.03	.14*

	WHM	BHM	WHF	BHF	
"Coming" Too Fast	(N=575)	(N=111)			
0: Not at all	44%	52%			
1: Very little	28	26			
2: Somewhat	22	17			
3: Very much	6	5			

	R^2	b
Demographics	.00	
BHM–WHM	.01	−.10

TABLE 11—(*Continued*)

		WHM	BHM	WHF	BHF	Pilot Study
Concern That You Are Not Sexually Adequate		(N=574)	(N=110)	(N=229)	(N=64)	
0: Not at all		48%	65%	62%	63%	
1: Very little		28	23	19	16	
2: Somewhat		19	10	17	16	
3: Very much		5	2	3	5	
	R^2	b			R^2	b
Demographics	.00			Demographics	.01	
BHM–WHM	.02	−.17***		BHF–WHF	.01	—[a]
Lack of Orgasm		(N=572)	(N=111)	(N=228)	(N=64)	
0: Not at all		53%	55%	54%	47%	
1: Very little		33	32	25	37	
2: Somewhat		11	12	14	11	
3: Very much		3	1	7	5	
	R^2	b			R^2	b
Demographics	.01			Demographics	.02	
BHM–WHM	.01	−.02		BHF–WHF	.02	.04
Venereal Disease from Homosexual Contacts		(N=575)	(N=110)	(N=229)	(N=64)	
0: Never		38%	34%	100%	98%	
1–2: Once or twice		34	39	0	2	
3–87: Three or more times		28	27	0	0	
	R^2	b			R^2	b
Demographics	.00			Demographics	.01	
BHM–WHM	.00	.05		BHF–WHF	.03	.96*

* $p < .05$.
** $p < .01$.
*** $p < .001$.
[a] F is too small for program to compute; difference is not significant.

TABLE 12 / Acceptance of Homosexuality

		WHM	BHM	WHF	BHF	Pilot Study
Amount of Regret		(N=575)	(N=111)	(N=229)	(N=64)	(N=458)
0: None		49%	59%	64%	73%	45%
1: Very little		24	21	20	17	24
2: Some		21	18	14	9	20
3: A great deal		6	3	2	0	10
	R^2	b			R^2	b
Demographics	.02			Demographics	.04	
BHM–WHM	.03	−.07		BHF–WHF	.05	−.07

	WHM	BHM	WHF	BHF
Reason for Regret[a]	(N=289)	(N=45)	(N=82)	(N=17)
Societal rejection, punitiveness	44%	42%	46%	65%
Cannot have children	32	22	24	12
Fewer life options than HTs	15	11	18	12
Feelings of loneliness	14	18	8	0
Other	44	3	49	41

$$X^2$$
BHM–WHM 2.91   BHF–WHF 2.45[b]

		WHM	BHM	WHF	BHF	Pilot Study
Ever Considered Discontinuing Homosexual Activity?		(N=575)	(N=111)	(N=229)	(N=64)	(N=458)
0: No		71%	75%	62%	70%	60%
1: Yes		29	25	38	30	40
	R^2	b			R^2	b
Demographics	.04			Demographics	.04	
BHM–WHM	.04	.06*		BHF–WHF	.04	.02

		WHM	BHM	WHF	BHF	Pilot Study
If Considered Giving Up Homosexuality, Ever Attempted?		(N=166)	(N=26)	(N=84)	(N=19)	(N=184)
0: No		37%	61%	25%	42%	38%
1: Yes		63	39	75	58	62
	R^2	b			R^2	b
Demographics	.02			Demographics	.04	
BHM–WHM	.04	−.63**		BHF–WHF	.04	−.03

TABLE 12—(Continued)

	WHM	BHM	WHF	BHF	Pilot Study
If Attempted to Give Up Homosexuality, Number of Attempts	(N=105)	(N=10)	(N=63)	(N=11)	
1: 1	53%	30%	70%	73%	
2: 2	23	40	16	9	
3–87: 3 or more	24	30	14	18	

	R^2	b		R^2	b
Demographics	.03		Demographics	.03	
BHM–WHM	.03	.37	BHF–WHF	.03	−.06

Means by Which Attempt Made to Stop Being Homosexual[a]	(N=105)	(N=11)	(N=65)	(N=11)
Less H sociosexual involvement	39%	45%	26%	55%
More HT sociosexual involvement	28	82	66	45
Sought professional help	18	9	12	18
Tried to stop H feelings	24	27	5	27
HT marriage	14	0	20	0
Other	9	18	0	0

X^2		X^2	
BHM–WHM 7.89[c]		BHF–WHF 10.15[c]	

To What Extent Has the Following Been a Problem?

Engaging in Activities You Have Been Raised to Believe Are Wrong or Immoral	(N=575)	(N=111)	(N=229)	(N=63)
0: Not at all	72%	55%	81%	64%
1: Very little	19	27	9	16
2: Somewhat	5	13	6	14
3: Very much	4	5	4	6

	R^2	b		R^2	b
Demographics	.04		Demographics	.02	
BHM–WHM	.04	.08	BHF–WHF	.05	.15*

338 / Homosexualities

TABLE 12—(Continued)

	WHM	BHM	WHF	BHF	Pilot Study
Agreement That Homosexuality Is an Emotional Disorder	(N=573)	(N=111)	(N=225)	(N=64)	
0: Strongly disagree	43%	39%	44%	42%	
1: Disagree	30	34	33	38	
2: Agree	22	21	16	19	
3: Strongly agree	5	6	7	2	

	R^2	b		R^2	b
Demographics	.00		Demographics	.01	
BHM–WHM	.00	.24	BHF–WHF	.02	−.05

	WHM	BHM	WHF	BHF	
How Upset if Child Became Homosexual?	(N=570)	(N=111)	(N=226)	(N=64)	
0: Not at all	51%	56%	49%	52%	
1: Very little	25	17	20	25	
2: Some	18	18	24	18	
3: Much	7	8	9	9	

	R^2	b		R^2	b
Demographics	.01		Demographics	.03	
BHM–WHM	.01	—[d]	BHF–WHF	.03	−.03

	WHM	BHM	WHF	BHF	
Want Magic HT Pill at Birth?	(N=569)	(N=109)	(N=228)	(N=63)	
0: No	72%	76%	84%	89%	
1: Yes	28	23	16	11	

	R^2	b		R^2	b
Demographics	.01		Demographics	.01	
BHM–WHM	.01	.01	BHF–WHF	.01	.02

	WHM	BHM	WHF	BHF	Pilot
Want Magic HT Pill Today?	(N=574)	(N=109)	(N=229)	(N=64)	(N=432)
0: No	86%	87%	95%	94%	76%
1: Yes	14	13	5	6	24

	R^2	b		R^2	b
Demographics	.01		Demographics	.01	
BHM–WHM	.01	.01	BHF–WHF	.01	−.01

* $p < .05$.
** $p < .01$.

[a] Respondents could give more than one answer to this question, so column percents may add up to more than 100%; this inflates the chi-square, but not substantially.

[b] For the females, the conventional expected frequency rule for chi-square is not met; collapsing categories would obscure our analytic focus.

[c] Does not meet the conventional expected frequency rule for chi-square; collapsing categories would obscure our analytic focus.

[d] F is too small for program to compute; difference is not significant.

Variable	2	3	4	5	6	7	8	9	10	11	12	13	14	15	16
1 Homosexual-heterosexual rating	13	14	−02	−01	08	−04	04	−06	04	03	−02	−15	06	06	12
2 Extrafamilial overtness		12	07	−09	−06	−01	−00	−09	04	−05	−13	−21	11	−04	03
3 Level of sexual activity			31	−04	−04	−03	−03	04	−08	−03	01	−08	45	28	22
4 Amount of cruising				34	29	22	22	24	22	23	23	14	58	−17	−18
5 Extent of cruising worries					75	63	66	67	63	68	68	63	24	−10	−08
6 Worry about being refused						44	58	37	45	37	33	28	20	−07	−06
7 Worry about partner's unwelcome requests							35	35	42	31	25	25	13	−11	−11
8 Worry about making conversation								25	43	28	26	24	17	−05	−08
9 Worry about venereal disease									28	42	48	39	18	−04	−04
10 Worry about adequate sexual performance										34	26	25	15	−10	−10
11 Worry about being robbed or rolled											51	50	15	−07	−04
12 Worry about being caught by police												58	18	−04	−00
13 Worry about being publicly exposed													07	−04	01
14 Number of sexual partners in past year														−19	−24
15 Currently involved in homosexual affair															60
16 Currently "coupled"															
17 Sex appeal (homosexual)															
18 Sexual repertoire															
19 Level of sexual interest															
20 Extent of sexual problems															
21 Problem with P's failure to respond															
22 Problem with finding a partner															
23 Problem with responding to P's requests															
24 Problem with frequency of sexual contact															
25 Problem with getting/maintaining erection															
26 Problem with partner's lack of orgasm															
27 Problem with maintaining affection for partner															
28 Problem with premature ejaculation															
29 Problem with concerns about sexual adequacy															
30 Problem with respondent's lack of orgasm															
31 Regret about homosexuality															
32 Race															
33 Age															
34 Education															
35 Occupational level															

17	18	19	20	21	22	23	24	25	26	27	28	29	30	31	32	33	34	35
-12	08	-03	-04	-04	-04	02	02	05	-05	-08	-04	05	01	-04	-07	19	-00	-00
01	04	06	-03	01	-03	02	-06	-01	-04	03	-01	-05	03	-13	-01	-04	-23	23
24	50	22	-34	-08	-43	-12	-36	-16	-07	-06	-14	-24	-13	-17	17	-23	01	01
13	30	26	05	04	-00	03	-03	03	01	19	02	-02	03	-04	08	-23	-04	03
-14	11	12	40	20	30	26	23	18	17	27	13	23	23	18	-07	08	18	-05
-09	11	10	34	16	26	18	25	12	16	22	11	18	22	10	-05	-00	11	-00
-03	06	-00	26	12	15	32	06	07	11	15	11	12	13	07	02	-07	-06	04
-06	13	10	28	13	24	14	20	07	12	24	10	14	15	10	-11	-07	-01	06
-05	12	07	16	16	11	15	10	03	03	11	02	08	09	11	08	01	03	03
-13	10	00	45	16	28	26	22	37	17	23	09	41	37	13	-10	01	08	-02
-19	04	12	27	13	23	11	15	13	12	16	13	17	13	14	-03	20	04	-08
-13	01	12	17	09	15	11	08	09	12	14	07	04	08	12	-12	20	17	-11
-09	02	11	23	12	16	11	13	14	07	16	09	13	09	23	-11	12	20	-15
15	34	24	-06	02	-06	-03	-15	03	03	09	-08	-12	05	-06	05	-14	-02	00
07	14	01	-19	00	-31	-08	-14	-10	-03	-13	-01	-08	-10	-11	05	01	00	01
05	08	-01	-17	03	-29	-10	-08	-08	-03	-11	-02	-07	-11	-12	01	04	03	-07
	24	09	-18	-06	-23	-06	-20	-10	-05	01	-05	-20	-08	-12	04	-33	00	03
		12	-14	-02	-23	-02	-20	-11	-08	07	-01	-08	-06	-10	11	-42	05	-00
			-03	01	-07	-10	05	00	-00	04	-05	-05	00	-01	-08	-01	08	-03
				52	66	48	59	54	56	51	42	62	54	31	-11	06	04	03
					28	25	30	18	36	18	11	23	23	12	-04	02	02	03
						21	50	28	30	23	16	33	24	27	-10	13	04	00
							15	17	19	16	16	26	19	18	-00	-08	00	03
								19	26	13	15	27	27	14	-10	12	05	00
									19	23	13	41	37	11	-17	20	05	-05
										23	20	22	30	10	-12	15	05	-07
											16	20	24	20	-03	-13	-00	01
												18	-04	09	-06	02	-04	05
													33	27	-13	02	07	-01
														13	-02	04	04	06
															-09	03	14	-07

Variable	2	3	4	5	6	7	8	9	10	11	12	13	14	15	16
1 Homosexual-heterosexual rating	18	27	12	08	05	11	12	04	03	08	01	01	-20	34	28
2 Extrafamilial overtness		15	07	01	-03	07	13	-05	07	-01	-11	-11	13	08	13
3 Level of sexual activity			04	-01	-05	-01	03	-00	-02	05	00	-04	30	49	30
4 Amount of cruising				76	65	55	62	48	47	52	50	57	29	-12	-09
5 Extent of cruising worries					88	72	80	61	73	58	50	75	27	-18	-11
6 Worry about being refused						45	69	48	62	39	38	60	28	-25	-16
7 Worry about partner's unwelcome requests							58	44	58	45	31	40	15	-09	-06
8 Worry about making conversation								29	55	43	23	46	26	-10	-05
9 Worry about venereal disease									33	35	28	48	13	-10	-09
10 Worry about adequate sexual performance										29	09	34	13	-18	-09
11 Worry about being robbed or rolled											35	55	21	-00	02
12 Worry about being caught by police												69	19	-07	-06
13 Worry about being publicly exposed													18	-05	-04
14 Number of sexual partners in past year														-04	-15
15 Currently involved in homosexual affair															61
16 Currently "coupled"															
17 Sex appeal (homosexual)															
18 Sexual repertoire															
19 Level of sexual interest															
20 Extent of sexual problems															
21 Problem with P's failure to respond															
22 Problem with finding a partner															
23 Problem with responding to P's requests															
24 Problem with frequency of sexual contact															
25 Problem with partner's lack of orgasm															
26 Problem with maintaining affection for partner															
27 Problem with concerns about sexual adequacy															
28 Problem with respondent's lack of orgasm															
29 Regret about homosexuality															
30 Race															
31 Age															
32 Education															
33 Occupational level															

17	18	19	20	21	22	23	24	25	26	27	28	29	30	31	32	33
−06	14	−14	−16	−01	−18	−08	−07	02	−07	−09	−21	−04	−09	08	−10	03
−05	14	01	−09	01	−10	04	−04	−01	−08	−08	−14	−04	01	−04	−16	15
30	55	23	−32	−20	−29	−21	−31	04	−00	−28	−23	−03	12	−36	−08	02
−00	13	20	18	16	18	11	02	10	07	15	11	04	13	−13	−14	10
−07	09	19	30	17	25	16	14	13	11	27	25	09	04	−16	−10	24
−09	08	20	28	18	27	11	17	13	06	24	24	08	02	−13	12	11
−05	09	10	20	07	11	14	04	13	15	20	14	04	03	−17	−30	21
−05	11	13	19	19	16	10	03	14	08	15	12	05	03	−13	−03	22
−01	06	17	22	01	22	18	12	02	06	21	25	−07	05	02	−18	09
−07	03	10	27	12	19	11	17	13	07	29	23	04	−01	−04	−07	30
−04	06	11	15	02	12	11	04	06	11	14	13	04	17	−22	−12	06
−02	06	14	12	10	08	08	02	05	08	10	12	25	01	06	02	−09
−02	03	14	20	14	17	11	11	00	08	18	18	11	07	−01	04	−01
15	41	34	−02	−03	01	−05	−08	04	07	−11	09	01	11	−32	−06	07
20	31	−04	−32	−15	−48	−04	−22	−05	−03	−25	−29	06	−02	16	03	04
03	18	−13	−35	−12	−43	−06	−21	−12	−15	−21	−33	−01	−03	−11	−04	02
	17	11	−19	−13	−15	01	−20	−11	01	−29	−07	−05	11	−03	01	−06
		35	−19	−12	−22	−10	−13	07	−09	−14	−13	00	15	−36	−07	−00
			05	03	07	−03	13	−03	−00	−02	03	03	10	−22	−06	06
				55	69	58	63	47	48	61	66	24	08	03	01	−02
					23	23	44	35	07	24	20	13	−00	06	02	−02
						29	30	19	32	35	47	10	04	10	10	−10
							27	08	37	32	27	13	07	05	01	−00
								25	08	31	32	09	06	03	−05	03
									10	15	28	09	−10	02	04	−01
										11	26	12	14	05	−04	−04
											36	22	−02	−11	−04	05
												16	01	−04	06	04
													−08	−03	16	−13

TABLE 13.3 / **Loadings in Four-Factor Orthogonal Structure: Males**

	Factor 1	Factor 2	Factor 3	Factor 4
Homosexual-Heterosexual Continuum	.007	−.030	−.099	−.122
Overtness	.025	−.140	−.200	.003
Level of Sexual Activity	−.244	−.001	−.703	−.329
Cruising				
Amount of cruising	.038	.310	−.587	.220
Extent of cruising worry	.272	1.033	−.065	.037
Worry: being refused	.295	.592	−.137	.043
Worry: making conversation	.254	.497	−.133	.046
Worry: performing adequately	.450	.442	−.120	.054
Worry: partner's requests	.207	.492	−.094	.080
Worry: being arrested	.040	.681	.023	.010
Worry: venereal disease	.062	.625	−.062	.018
Worry: being rolled or robbed	.160	.641	.011	.033
Worry: public exposure	.095	.630	.119	−.005
Sexual Partnerships				
Number of partners	−.036	.208	−.716	.256
Currently involved	−.112	−.029	−.003	−.758
Currently coupled	−.099	−.012	.057	−.765
Sex Appeal	−.142	−.123	−.301	−.059
Sexual Techniques	−.082	.109	−.546	−.175
Level of Sexual Interest	−.039	.129	−.262	.014
Sexual Problems				
Extent of problems	1.080	.123	.102	.083
Problem: responding to partner	.403	.145	.031	.026
Problem: partner not responding	.464	.089	−.002	−.077
Problem: lack of frequency	.481	.113	.250	.103
Problem: lack of orgasm	.517	.074	−.036	.054
Problem: partner's lack of orgasm	.499	.039	−.002	−.028
Problem: finding a partner	.542	.163	.264	.328
Problem: activities immoral	.313	.090	.062	.080
Problem: sexual adequacy	.579	.083	.139	.008
Problem: maintaining affection	.413	.152	−.122	.092
Problem: premature ejaculation	.292	.069	.079	−.020
Problem: erectile difficulties	.484	.048	.023	.051
Acceptance of Homosexuality	.261	.147	.170	.108

TABLE 13.4 / Loadings in Four-Factor Orthogonal Structure: Females

	Factor 1	Factor 2	Factor 3	Factor 4
Homosexual-Heterosexual Continuum	.119	−.068	.480	−.101
Overtness	.027	−.039	.178	.083
Level of Sexual Activity	−.005	−.118	.479	.627
Cruising				
Amount of cruising	.794	.057	−.006	.125
Extent of cruising worry	1.027	.127	−.037	.023
Worry: being refused	.811	.115	−.149	.053
Worry: making conversation	.742	.088	.035	.057
Worry: performing adequately	.625	.158	−.052	−.034
Worry: partner's requests	.684	.107	.052	.001
Worry: being arrested	.498	.060	−.020	.079
Worry: venereal disease	.562	.102	−.076	.043
Worry: being rolled or robbed	.589	.081	.077	.048
Worry: public exposure	.726	.088	−.009	.014
Sexual Partnerships				
Number of partners	.258	−.037	−.160	.641
Currently involved	−.153	−.026	.814	.187
Currently coupled	−.066	−.152	.694	−.053
Sex Appeal	−.072	−.117	.085	.352
Sexual Techniques	.092	−.051	.281	.641
Level of Sexual Interest	.168	.039	−.136	.471
Sexual Problems				
Extent of problems	.144	1.093	−.280	−.097
Problem: responding to partner	.098	.504	−.034	−.101
Problem: partner not responding	.116	.444	−.082	.126
Problem: lack of frequency	.064	.493	−.207	−.160
Problem: lack of orgasm	.167	.503	−.351	−.010
Problem: partner's lack of orgasm	.072	.408	−.008	.045
Problem: finding a partner	.179	.461	−.483	−.086
Problem: activities immoral	−.039	.325	.020	.006
Problem: sexual adequacy	.213	.473	−.183	−.245
Problem: maintaining affection	.058	.388	−.078	.057
Acceptance of Homosexuality	.050	.278	.042	.006

TABLE 13.5 / Description of Typology: Males

	Close-Coupleds	Open-Coupleds	Functionals	Dysfunctionals	Asexuals	Row Totals
Typology Criterion Scores[a]						
Coupled	yes	yes	no	no	no	
Regret	—	—	≤X̄+.5SD	$\left[\begin{array}{c} >\bar{X}+.5SD \end{array}\right]^{c}$	—	
Sexual problems	<X̄	>X̄[b]	≤X̄+.5SD	>X̄	—	
Number of partners	<X̄	>X̄[b]	>X̄	>X̄[b]	<X̄	
Amount of cruising	<X̄	>X̄[b]	—	—	<X̄	
Sexual activity	—	—	>X̄	>X̄[b]	<X̄	
Assignment to Typology						
Number of respondents	67	120	102	86	110	485
Percent of all respondents*	10	18	15	12	16	71%
Percent of all classifiable respondents*	14	25	21	18	23	101%

[a] Noncriterion variables are indicated by dashes.
[b] For this group, members had to achieve this score on at least one but not necessarily all of the noted variables.
[c] For this group, members had to score no less than the mean on one of these items and no less than .5SD above the mean on the other.

* 201 of the 686 male respondents (29%) could not be classified.

TABLE 13.6 / **Description of Typology: Females**

	Close-Coupleds	Open-Coupleds	Functionals	Dysfunctionals	Asexuals	Row Totals
Typology Criterion Scores[a]						
Coupled	yes	yes	no	no	no	
Regret	—	—	$<\overline{X}$	$>\overline{X}$	—	
Sexual problems	$<\overline{X}$	$>\overline{X}^b$	$<\overline{X}+.5SD$	$>\overline{X}+.5SD$ [c]	—	
Number of partners	$<\overline{X}$	$>\overline{X}^b$	—	—	$<\overline{X}$	
Amount of cruising	$<\overline{X}$	$>\overline{X}^b$	—	—	$<\overline{X}$	
Sexual activity	—	—	$>\overline{X}-.3SD$	$>\overline{X}-.3SD$	$<\overline{X}-.3SD$	
Sex appeal	—	—	$>\overline{X}-.3SD$	$<\overline{X}+.3SD$	—	

[a] Noncriterion variables are indicated by dashes.
[b] For this group, members had to achieve this score on at least one but not necessarily all of the noted variables.
[c] For this group, members had to score greater than the mean on one of these items and greater than .5SD above the mean on the other.

Assignment to Typology						Row Totals
Number of respondents	81	51	30	16	33	211
Percent of all respondents*	28	17	10	5	11	71%
Percent of all classifiable respondents*	38	24	14	8	16	100%

* 82 of the 293 female respondents (28%) could not be classified.

TABLE 13.7 / Regressions Involving Major Sexual Experience Items

Homosexual-Heterosexual Rating

			Males		Females	
			Types–$\overline{HX}$ N=463		Types–$\overline{HX}$ N=204	
			R^2	$\underline{b}$	R^2	$\underline{b}$
1	Demographics[a]		.03		.04	
2	[types–$\overline{HX}$]		.08		.16	
		H_1–$\overline{HX}$		.15		.46***
		H_2–$\overline{HX}$		.16		.35**
		H_3–$\overline{HX}$		.13		.03
		H_4–$\overline{HX}$		-.06		-.41*
		H_5–$\overline{HX}$		-.38***		-.43**

Extrafamilial Overtness

			Males		Females	
			Types–$\overline{HX}$ N=462		Types–$\overline{HX}$ N=204	
			R^2	$\underline{b}$	R^2	$\underline{b}$
1	Demographics[a]		.06		.03	
2	[types–$\overline{HX}$]		.10		.06	
		H_1–$\overline{HX}$		.16		-.02
		H_2–$\overline{HX}$		.03		.30
		H_3–$\overline{HX}$		.21*		-.02
		H_4–$\overline{HX}$		-.07		-.12
		H_5–$\overline{HX}$		-.34***		-.14

Level of Sexual Activity

			Males		Females	
			Types–$\overline{HX}$ N=463		Types–$\overline{HX}$ N=204	
			R^2	$\underline{b}$	R^2	$\underline{b}$
1	Demographics[a]		.12		.19	
2	[types–$\overline{HX}$]		.55		.56	
		H_1–$\overline{HX}$		.33***		.30***
		H_2–$\overline{HX}$		.28***		.36****
		H_3–$\overline{HX}$		.67***		.61***
		H_4–$\overline{HX}$		.09		.12
		H_5–$\overline{HX}$		-1.38***		-1.40***

Amount of Cruising

Types-HX N=463			R²	b		Types-HX N=204			R²	b
1	Demographics[a]		.09			1	Demographics[a]		.09	
2	[types-HX]		.40			2	[types-HX]		.18	
		H_1–HX		-.86***				H_1–HX		-.26**
		H_2–HX		.20**				H_2–HX		.33***
		H_3–HX		.82***				H_3–HX		.30*
		H_4–HX		.41***				H_4–HX		-.15
		H_5–HX		-.57***				H_5–HX		-.21

Extent of Cruising Worries

Types-HX N=463			R²	b		Types-HX N=204			R²	b
1	Demographics[a]		.03			1	Demographics[a]		.09	
2	[types-HX]		.17			2	[types-HX]		.19	
		H_1–HX		-.68***				H_1–HX		-.33***
		H_2–HX		.29***				H_2–HX		.32**
		H_3–HX		-.16				H_3–HX		.20
		H_4–HX		.60***				H_4–HX		.06
		H_5–HX		-.05				H_5–HX		-.24

Worry About Being Refused

Types-HX N=463			R²	b		Types-HX N=204			R²	b
1	Demographics[a]		.02			1	Demographics[a]		.08	
2	[types-HX]		.10			2	[types-HX]		.17	
		H_1–HX		-.44***				H_1–HX		-.33***
		H_2–HX		.17*				H_2–HX		.16
		H_3–HX		-.15				H_3–HX		.32*
		H_4–HX		.48				H_4–HX		.11
		H_5–HX		-.06				H_5–HX		-.26

TABLE 13.7—(Continued)

Males

Worry About Partner's Unwelcome Requests

Types-HX N=463			R^2	b
	1	Demographics[a]	.02	
	2	[types-HX]	.09	
		H_1-HX		-.45***
		H_2-HX		.13
		H_3-HX		-.11
		H_4-HX		.44***
		H_5-HX		-.01

Worry About Making Conversation

Types-HX N=463			R^2	b
	1	Demographics[a]	.05	
	2	[types-HX]	.11	
		H_1-HX		-.40***
		H_2-HX		.14
		H_3-HX		-.10
		H_4-HX		.37***
		H_5-HX		-.01

Worry About Venereal Disease

Types-HX N=463			R^2	b
	1	Demographics[a]	.01	
	2	[types-HX]	.05	
		H_1-HX		-.37***
		H_2-HX		.21*
		H_3-HX		-.06

Females

Worry About Partner's Unwelcome Requests

Types-HX N=204			R^2	b
	1	Demographics[a]	.06	
	2	[types-HX]	.12	
		H_1-HX		-.24*
		H_2-HX		.27*
		H_3-HX		.20
		H_4-HX		-.10
		H_5-HX		-.13

Worry About Making Conversation

Types-HX N=204			R^2	b
	1	Demographics[a]	.06	
	2	[types-HX]	.16	
		H_1-HX		-.29**
		H_2-HX		.41***
		H_3-HX		.17
		H_4-HX		-.08
		H_5-HX		-.20

Worry About Venereal Disease

Types-HX N=204			R^2	b
	1	Demographics[a]	.06	
	2	[types-HX]	.10	
		H_1-HX		-.18
		H_2-HX		.10
		H_3-HX		.26*

			R² (N=463)	b (N=463)	R² (N=204)	b (N=204)
		H₄–H̄X		.24*		−.07
		H₅–H̄X		−.02		−.11

Worry About Adequate Sexual Performance

Types–H̄X			R² (N=463)	b (N=463)	R² (N=204)	b (N=204)
	1	Demographics[a]	.03		.07	
	2	[types–H̄X]	.16		.14	
		H₁–H̄X		−.52***		−.32***
		H₂–H̄X		.11		.18
		H₃–H̄X		−.20*		.04
		H₄–H̄X		.69***		.32
		H₅–H̄X		−.08		−.23

Worry About Being Robbed or Rolled

Types–H̄X			R² (N=463)	b (N=463)	R² (N=204)	b (N=204)
	1	Demographics[a]	.03		.07	
	2	[types–H̄X]	.15		.09	
		H₁–H̄X		−.66***		−.16
		H₂–H̄X		.30***		.22
		H₃–H̄X		−.12		−.01
		H₄–H̄X		.47***		.11
		H₅–H̄X		.00		−.15

Worry About Being Caught by Police

Types–H̄X			R² (N=463)	b (N=463)	R² (N=204)	b (N=204)
	1	Demographics[a]	.04		.02	
	2	[types–H̄X]	.09		.07	
		H₁–H̄X		−.43***		−.10
		H₂–H̄X		.29***		.18*
		H₃–H̄X		.06		−.10
		H₄–H̄X		.19		.11
		H₅–H̄X		−.11		−.09

TABLE 13.7—(Continued)

Males

Worry About Being Publicly Exposed

Types–$\overline{HX}$ N=463

		R^2	b
1	Demographics[a]	.04	
2	[types–$\overline{HX}$]	.10	
	H$_1$–$\overline{HX}$		−.39***
	H$_2$–$\overline{HX}$		.24**
	H$_3$–$\overline{HX}$		−.19*
	H$_4$–$\overline{HX}$		.32***
	H$_5$–$\overline{HX}$		.02

Number of Sexual Partners in Past Year

Types–$\overline{HX}$ N=463

		R^2	b
1	Demographics[a]	.03	
2	[types–$\overline{HX}$]	.61	
	H$_1$–$\overline{HX}$		−1.10***
	H$_2$–$\overline{HX}$		.23***
	H$_3$–$\overline{HX}$		1.10***
	H$_4$–$\overline{HX}$		.64***
	H$_5$–$\overline{HX}$		−.88***

Currently Involved in Homosexual Affair

Types–$\overline{HX}$ N=463

		R^2	b
1	Demographics[a]	.01	
2	[types–$\overline{HX}$]	.42	
	H$_1$–$\overline{HX}$		.77***
	H$_2$–$\overline{HX}$		.77***
	H$_3$–$\overline{HX}$		−.40***

Females

Worry About Being Publicly Exposed

Types–$\overline{HX}$ N=204

		R^2	b
1	Demographics[a]	.06	
2	[types–$\overline{HX}$]	.11	
	H$_1$–$\overline{HX}$		−.14
	H$_2$–$\overline{HX}$		.32**
	H$_3$–$\overline{HX}$		−.00
	H$_4$–$\overline{HX}$		−.09
	H$_5$–$\overline{HX}$		−.10

Number of Sexual Partners in Past Year

Types–$\overline{HX}$ N=204

		R^2	b
1	Demographics[a]	.10	
2	[types–$\overline{HX}$]	.33	
	H$_1$–$\overline{HX}$		−.51***
	H$_2$–$\overline{HX}$		.18
	H$_3$–$\overline{HX}$		.66***
	H$_4$–$\overline{HX}$		.45*
	H$_5$–$\overline{HX}$		−.78***

Currently Involved in Homosexual Affair

Types–$\overline{HX}$ N=204

		R^2	b
1	Demographics[a]	.05	
2	[types–$\overline{HX}$]	.56	
	H$_1$–$\overline{HX}$		.66***
	H$_2$–$\overline{HX}$		.66***
	H$_3$–$\overline{HX}$		−.11

Appendix C / 353

		N = 463 R^2	N = 463 b	N = 204 R^2	N = 204 b
H₄–H$\overline{X}$			−.64***		−.08
H₅–H$\overline{X}$			−.50***		−1.14***

Currently "Coupled"

Types–H$\overline{X}$ N = 463 Types–H$\overline{X}$ N = 204

		N = 463 R^2	N = 463 b	N = 204 R^2	N = 204 b
1	Demographics[a] [types–H$\overline{X}$]	.01		.02	
2	H₁–H$\overline{X}$	1.00	1.32***	1.00	1.20***
	H₂–H$\overline{X}$		1.32***		1.20***
	H₃–H$\overline{X}$		−.88***		−.80***
	H₄–H$\overline{X}$		−.88***		−.80***
	H₅–H$\overline{X}$		−.88***		−.80***

Sex Appeal (Homosexual)

Types–H$\overline{X}$ N = 463 Types–H$\overline{X}$ N = 204

		N = 463 R^2	N = 463 b	N = 204 R^2	N = 204 b
1	Demographics[a] [types–H$\overline{X}$]	.13		.04	
2	H₁–H$\overline{X}$	.18	.09	.20	.05
	H₂–H$\overline{X}$		.08		.03
	H₃–H$\overline{X}$		.31***		.86***
	H₄–H$\overline{X}$		−.24**		−.48*
	H₅–H$\overline{X}$		−.25**		−.46**

Sexual Repertoire

Types–H$\overline{X}$ N = 463 Types–H$\overline{X}$ N = 204

		N = 463 R^2	N = 463 b	N = 204 R^2	N = 204 b
1	Demographics[a] [types–H$\overline{X}$]	.19		.18	
2	H₁–H$\overline{X}$	.31	.09	.37	.28**
	H₂–H$\overline{X}$		.19*		.31**
	H₃–H$\overline{X}$		.23**		.33*
	H₄–H$\overline{X}$		.23**		.08
	H₅–H$\overline{X}$		−.74***		−1.00***

TABLE 13.7—(Continued)

Level of Sexual Interest

	Males		Females	
	R^2	b	R^2	b
Types–H$\overline{X}$ (Males N=463, Females N=204)				
1 Demographics[a]	.02		.06	
2 [types–H$\overline{X}$]	.07		.12	
H$_1$–H$\overline{X}$		−.11		−.26*
H$_2$–H$\overline{X}$		−.02		.04
H$_3$–H$\overline{X}$		.03***		.48**
H$_4$–H$\overline{X}$		.02		−.02
H$_5$–H$\overline{X}$		−.32***		−.24

Extent of Sexual Problems

	Males		Females	
	R^2	b	R^2	b
Types–H$\overline{X}$ (Males N=463, Females N=204)				
1 Demographics[a]	.02		.02	
2 [types–H$\overline{X}$]	.37		.45	
H$_1$–H$\overline{X}$		−.87***		−.90***
H$_2$–H$\overline{X}$		.15		.29
H$_3$–H$\overline{X}$		−.60***		−.65***
H$_4$–H$\overline{X}$		.94***		1.00***
H$_5$–H$\overline{X}$		.37***		.51***

Problem with Partner's Failure to Respond to Respondent's Requests

	Males		Females	
	R^2	b	R^2	b
Types–H$\overline{X}$ (Males N=463, Females N=204)				
1 Demographics[a]	.01		.01	
2 [types–H$\overline{X}$]	.09		.13	
H$_1$–H$\overline{X}$		−.38***		−.43***
H$_2$–H$\overline{X}$		.25**		.24
H$_3$–H$\overline{X}$		−.30***		−.45**

		N=463 R²	N=463 b	N=204 R²	N=204 b
	H_4-$\overline{HX}$		.40***		.52*
	H_5-$\overline{HX}$		.03		.12

Problem with Finding a Partner

Types-$\overline{HX}$ N=463   Types-$\overline{HX}$ N=204

Step	Variable	N=463 R^2	N=463 b	N=204 R^2	N=204 b
1	Demographics[a]	.04		.01	
2	[types-$\overline{HX}$]	.33		.32	
	H_1-$\overline{HX}$		-.87***		-.78***
	H_2-$\overline{HX}$		-.10		-.22
	H_3-$\overline{HX}$		-.37***		-.26
	H_4-$\overline{HX}$		.62***		.61
	H_5-$\overline{HX}$		.72***		.65

Problem with Responding to Partner's Requests

Types-$\overline{HX}$ N=463   Types-$\overline{HX}$ N=204

Step	Variable	N=463 R^2	N=463 b	N=204 R^2	N=204 b
1	Demographics[a]	.01		.01	
2	[types-$\overline{HX}$]	.09		.15	
	H_1-$\overline{HX}$		-.46***		-.38***
	H_2-$\overline{HX}$		.10		.24
	H_3-$\overline{HX}$		-.25**		-.62***
	H_4-$\overline{HX}$		.48***		.42*
	H_5-$\overline{HX}$		.13		.34*

Problem with Frequency of Sexual Contact

Types-$\overline{HX}$ N=463   Types-$\overline{HX}$ N=204

Step	Variable	N=463 R^2	N=463 b	N=204 R^2	N=204 b
1	Demographics[a]	.02		.01	
2	[types-$\overline{HX}$]	.17		.16	
	H_1-$\overline{HX}$		-.42***		-.46***
	H_2-$\overline{HX}$		.09		.04
	H_3-$\overline{HX}$		-.53***		-.50***
	H_4-$\overline{HX}$		.41***		.72***
	H_5-$\overline{HX}$		.45***		.29

TABLE 13.7—(Continued)

		Males		Females	

Problem with Partner's Lack of Orgasm

Types-HX N=463		R^2	b	Types-HX N=204		R^2	b
1	Demographics[a]	.02		1	Demographics[a]	.01	
2	[types-HX]	.10		2	[types-HX]	.12	
	H₁–HX		-.36***		H₁–HX		-.47***
	H₂–HX		.13		H₂–HX		.09
	H₃–HX		-.17		H₃–HX		-.08
	H₄–HX		.52***		H₄–HX		.64***
	H₅–HX		.12		H₅–HX		-.17

Problem with Maintaining Affection for Partner

Types-HX N=463		R^2	b	Types-HX N=204		R^2	b
1	Demographics[a]	.03		1	Demographics[a]	.04	
2	[types-HX]	.14		2	[types-HX]	.13	
	H₁–HX		-.60***		H₁–HX		-.47***
	H₂–HX		.08		H₂–HX		.13
	H₃–HX		-.11		H₃–HX		-.13
	H₄–HX		.60***		H₄–HX		.48*
	H₅–HX		.02		H₅–HX		-.01

Problem with Concerns About Sexual Adequacy

Types-HX N=463		R^2	b	Types-HX N=204		R^2	b
1	Demographics[a]	.02		1	Demographics[a]	.02	
2	[types-HX]	.17		2	[types-HX]	.28	
	H₁–HX		-.28**		H₁–HX		-.58***
	H₂–HX		.00		H₂–HX		-.02
	H₃–HX		-.51***		H₃–HX		-.63***

		b		b
H₄–HX̄		.66***		.65***
H₅–HX̄		.13		.57***

Problem with Respondent's Lack of Orgasm

	R²	b	R²	b
Types–HX̄	N=463		N=204	
1 Demographics[a]	.01		.03	
2 [types–HX̄]	.13		.23	
H₁–HX̄		-.51***		-.60***
H₂–HX̄		.07		-.22
H₃–HX̄		-.24**		-.28*
H₄–HX̄		.64***		.74***
H₅–HX̄		.04		.36*

Regret About Homosexuality

	R²	b	R²	b
Types–HX̄	N=463		N=204	
1 Demographics[a]	.05		.11	
2 [types–HX̄]	.31		.27	
H₁–HX̄		-.43***		-.21*
H₂–HX̄		-.09		.07
H₃–HX̄		-.64***		-.76***
H₄–HX̄		.91***		1.03***
H₅–HX̄		.26***		-.13

Race

	R²	b	R²	b
Types–HX̄	N=485		N=211	
1 Demographics	—[b]		—[b]	
2 [types–HX̄]	.03		.01	
H₁–HX̄		.05		-.35
H₂–HX̄		-.01		.15
H₃–HX̄		.09**		.02
H₄–HX̄		.04		.12
H₅–HX̄		-.09**		.07

TABLE 13.7—(Continued)

Males

Age — Types-HX N=485

		R² (—ᵇ)	b
1	Demographics	.05	
2	[types-HX]		
	H_1–H$\overline{X}$		1.52
	H_2–H$\overline{X}$		-.80
	H_3–H$\overline{X}$		-3.65***
	H_4–H$\overline{X}$		-1.06
	H_5–H$\overline{X}$		3.99***

Education — Types-HX N=485

		R² (—ᵇ)	b
1	Demographics	.01	
2	[types-HX]		
	H_1–H$\overline{X}$		-.03
	H_2–H$\overline{X}$		.02
	H_3–H$\overline{X}$		-.27
	H_4–H$\overline{X}$		.31*
	H_5–H$\overline{X}$		-.04

Occupational Level — Types-HX N=463

		R² (—ᵇ)	b
1	Demographics	.01	
2	[types-HX]		
	H_1–H$\overline{X}$		.13
	H_2–H$\overline{X}$		.07
	H_3–H$\overline{X}$		.10
	H_4–H$\overline{X}$		.03
	H_5–H$\overline{X}$		.06

Females

Age — Types-HX N=211

		R² (—ᵇ)	b
1	Demographics	.14	
2	[types-HX]		
	H_1–H$\overline{X}$		.56
	H_2–H$\overline{X}$		-3.04*
	H_3–H$\overline{X}$		-1.36
	H_4–H$\overline{X}$		-4.39*
	H_5–H$\overline{X}$		8.24***

Education — Types-HX N=211

		R² (—ᵇ)	b
1	Demographics	.01	
2	[types-HX]		
	H_1–H$\overline{X}$		-.11
	H_2–H$\overline{X}$		-.09
	H_3–H$\overline{X}$		-.26
	H_4–H$\overline{X}$		.13
	H_5–H$\overline{X}$		.32

Occupational Level — Types-HX N=204

		R² (—ᵇ)	b
1	Demographics	.01	
2	[types-HX]		
	H_1–H$\overline{X}$		.04
	H_2–H$\overline{X}$		.14
	H_3–H$\overline{X}$		-.09
	H_4–H$\overline{X}$		.13
	H_5–H$\overline{X}$		.15

* $p < .05$. ** $p < .01$. *** $p < .001$.

a Variables entered in step 1 are age, education, occupational level, and race.

b In order to discern the absolute demographic differences among the homosexual subgroups, demographic adjustments are not made in this regression.

TABLE 14.1 / "How many times have you changed employment in the last five years, excluding military service?"

	WHM	BHM	WHTM	BHTM	WHF	BHF	WHTF	BHTF (Pilot Study)
	N=547	N=106	N=264	N=50	N=220	N=63	N=86	N=33
	%	%	%	%	%	%	%	%
0: Never	42	22	48	26	30	27	45	24
1: Once	18	25	21	38	26	24	16	24
2: Twice	12	24	8	16	12	24	15	27
3-7: Three or more times	28	29	23	20	32	25	24	25

Males

Comparison	N	Step	Variable(s)	R^2	b
BHM–WHM	648	1	Demographics[a]	.16	
		2	BHM–WHM	.16	-.21*
Types–$H\overline{X}$	461	1	Demographics[b]	.18	
		2	[types–$H\overline{X}$]	.19	
			H_1–$H\overline{X}$		.02
			H_2–$H\overline{X}$		-.18
			H_3–$H\overline{X}$		.04
			H_4–$H\overline{X}$		.20
			H_5–$H\overline{X}$		-.08
HM–HTM	957	1	Demographics[b]	.18	
		2	HM–HTM	.18	.10

Females

Comparison	N	Step	Variable(s)	R^2	b
BHF–WHF	276	1	Demographics[a]	.20	
		2	BHF–WHF	.20	-.05
Types–$H\overline{X}$	203	1	Demographics[b]	.22	
		2	[types–$H\overline{X}$]	.23	
			H_1–$H\overline{X}$		-.25
			H_2–$H\overline{X}$		.07
			H_3–$H\overline{X}$		.19
			H_4–$H\overline{X}$		-.20
			H_5–$H\overline{X}$		.20
HF–HTF	391	1	Demographics[b]	.18	
		2	HF–HTF	.20	.25**

* p < .05.
** p < .01.
[a] Variables entered in step 1 are age, education, and occupational level.
[b] Variables entered in step 1 are age, education, occupational level, and race.

TABLE 14.2 / Job Satisfaction

	WHM	BHM	WHTM	BHTM	WHF	BHF	WHTF	BHTF	Pilot Study
	N=488	N=100	N=226	N=45	N=195	N=63	N=78	N=31	N=458
	%	%	%	%	%	%	%	%	%
0–4: Relatively low	29	30	31	47	25	40	27	16	20
5–7: Moderate	41	42	46	33	41	38	37	45	40
8–10: Relatively high	30	28	23	20	34	22	36	39	40

Males

Comparison	N	Step	Variable(s)	R^2	b
BHM–WHM	583	1	Demographics[a]	.06	
		2	BHM–WHM	.06	.12
Types–$\overline{HX}$	410	1	Demographics[b]	.07	
		2	[types–$\overline{HX}$]	.09	
			H_1–$\overline{HX}$		.36
			H_2–$\overline{HX}$		.17
			H_3–$\overline{HX}$		.32
			H_4–$\overline{HX}$		−.46
			H_5–$\overline{HX}$		−.38
HM–HTM	849	1	Demographics[b]	.09	
		2	HM–HTM	.09	.21*

Females

Comparison	N	Step	Variable(s)	R^2	b
BHF–WHF	251	1	Demographics[a]	.05	
		2	BHF–WHF	.07	−.42*
Types–$\overline{HX}$	188	1	Demographics[b]	.10	
		2	[types–$\overline{HX}$]	.11	
			H_1–$\overline{HX}$		.08
			H_2–$\overline{HX}$		−.27
			H_3–$\overline{HX}$		.66
			H_4–$\overline{HX}$		−.04
			H_5–$\overline{HX}$		−.44
HF–HTF	356	1	Demographics[b]	.06	
		2	HF–HTF	.07	−.17

* $p < .05$
[a] Variables entered in step 1 are age, education, and occupational level.
[b] Variables entered in step 1 are age, education, occupational level, and race.

TABLE 14.3 / "Has your homosexuality had any effect upon your career?"

	WHM	BHM	WHF	BHF Pilot Study
	N=557	N=108	N=224	N=63
	%	%	%	%
0: Very harmful	9	2	3	0
1: Somewhat harmful	19	10	13	6
2: No effect	61	72	76	89
3: Somewhat helpful	9	11	4	5
4: Very helpful	2	5	3	0

Males

Comparison	N	Step	Variable(s)	R^2	b
BHM–WHM	649	1	Demographics[a]	.05	
		2	BHM–WHM	.05	.09*
Types–H$\overline{X}$	461	1	Demographics[b]	.06	
		2	[types–H$\overline{X}$]	.10	
			H$_1$–H$\overline{X}$		.19*
			H$_2$–H$\overline{X}$		−.04
			H$_3$–H$\overline{X}$		.13
			H$_4$–H$\overline{X}$		−.30***
			H$_5$–H$\overline{X}$		.01

Females

Comparison	N	Step	Variable(s)	R^2	b
BHF–WHF	277	1	Demographics[a]	.02	
		2	BHF–WHF	.02	.03
Types–H$\overline{X}$	204	1	Demographics[b]	.04	
		2	[types–H$\overline{X}$]	.05	
			H$_1$–H$\overline{X}$		.02
			H$_2$–H$\overline{X}$		−.02
			H$_3$–H$\overline{X}$		−.07
			H$_4$–H$\overline{X}$		.07
			H$_5$–H$\overline{X}$		.00

* $p < .05$.
*** $p < .001$.
[a] Variables entered in step 1 are age, education, and occupational level.
[b] Variables entered in step 1 are age, education, occupational level, and race.

TABLE 14.4 / "Why do you say that [that homosexuality has affected your career]?"[a]

	WHM	BHM	WHF	BHF Pilot Study
	N=214	N=29	N=52	N=7
	%	%	%	%
I lost or almost lost my job because of it	21	7	29	14
If you're homosexual you lose out on promotion, doing what you want to do, etc.	17	17	8	0
It makes me so tense or fearful that I can't do my best on the job	15	3	15	14
Being homosexual makes me especially (or better) qualified for my particular work	10	10	15	14
Being homosexual helped me get ahead because of my homosexual contacts	9	28	4	0
Other negative effects	8	14	10	14
Other positive effects	7	7	4	14
Some other kind of effect	22	17	19	43

Males

Comparison	N	X^2
WH–BH	269	13.35*
H_1–H†	198	5.35ᵇ
H_2–H†	198	7.00
H_3–H†	198	5.39ᵇ
H_4–H†	198	10.90
H_5–H†	198	8.28

Females

Comparison	N	X^2
WH–BH	‡	‡
H_1–H†	46	3.78ᵇ
H_2–H†	46	5.89ᵇ
H_3–H†	‡	‡
H_4–H†	‡	‡
H_5–H†	‡	‡

* $p < .05$.
† Excluding the subgroup being compared.
‡ Relevant cases were too few to permit meaningful comparison.
a Respondents could give more than one answer to this question, so column percentages may add up to more than 100%; this inflates the chi-square, but not substantially.
b Does not meet the conventional expected frequency rule for chi-square; collapsing categories would obscure our analytic focus.

TABLE 15.1 / "How religious in the conventional sense would you say you are—very religious, moderately religious, not too religious, or not at all religious?"

	WHM	BHM	WHTM	BHTM	WHF	BHF	WHTF	BHTF	Pilot Study
	N=575	N=111	N=284	N=53	N=229	N=64	N=101	N=39	N=458
	%	%	%	%	%	%	%	%	%
0: Not at all religious	51	30	44	24	55	27	34	5	23
1: Not too religious	28	35	30	51	26	36	25	15	22
2: Moderately religious	16	30	21	23	16	33	33	56	32
3: Very religious	6	5	5	2	3	5	9	23	23

Males

Comparison	N	Step	Variable(s)	R^2	b
BHM–WHM	651	1	Demographics[a]	.01	
		2	BHM–WHM	.02	.18***
Types–$\overline{HX}$	463	1	Demographics[b]	.02	
		2	[types–$\overline{HX}$]	.02	
			H_1–$\overline{HX}$		.09
			H_2–$\overline{HX}$		−.05
			H_3–$\overline{HX}$		−.07
			H_4–$\overline{HX}$		.09
			H_5–$\overline{HX}$		−.07
HM–HTM	961	1	Demographics[b]	.02	
		2	HM–HTM	.03	−.04

Females

Comparison	N	Step	Variable(s)	R^2	b
BHF–WHF	277	1	Demographics[a]	.03	
		2	BHF–WHF	.08	.25***
Types–$\overline{HX}$	204	1	Demographics[b]	.09	
		2	[types–$\overline{HX}$]	.12	
			H_1–$\overline{HX}$		.09
			H_2–$\overline{HX}$		−.15
			H_3–$\overline{HX}$		−.24
			H_4–$\overline{HX}$		.03
			H_5–$\overline{HX}$		.27
HF–HTF	392	1	Demographics[b]	.11	
		2	HF–HTF	.19	−.30***

*** $p < .001$.
[a] Variables entered in step 1 are age, education, and occupational level.
[b] Variables entered in step 1 are age, education, occupational level, and race.

TABLE 15.2 / "How often, on the average, have you attended religious functions of any kind during the last three months (including religious services and church activities)?"

	WHM	BHM	WHTM	BHTM	WHF	BHF	WHTF	BHTF	Pilot Study
	N=575	N=111	N=284	N=53	N=229	N=64	N=101	N=39	N=458
	%	%	%	%	%	%	%	%	%
0: Not at all	69	54	57	49	75	69	63	36	53
1: Less than once a month	13	13	16	28	12	11	12	10	7
2: About once a month	4	7	5	11	6	2	3	5	9
3: A few times a month	3	9	7	11	2	5	9	23	9
4: About once a week	6	13	12	0	3	11	9	21	16
5: Twice a week or more	4	4	3	0	2	3	4	5	6

Males

Comparison	N	Step	Variable(s)	R^2	b
BHM-WHM	651	1	Demographics[a]	.00	
		2	BHM-WHM	.02	.26***
Types-HX	463	1	Demographics[b]	.02	
		2	[types-HX]	.05	
			H_1-HX		-.07
			H_2-HX		-.37**
			H_3-HX		.05
			H_4-HX		.00
			H_5-HX		.39**
HM-HTM	961	1	Demographics[b]	.01	
		2	HM-HTM	.02	-.12*

Females

Comparison	N	Step	Variable(s)	R^2	b
BHF-WHF	277	1	Demographics[a]	.01	
		2	BHF-WHF	.02	.20*
Types-HX	204	1	Demographics[b]	.03	
		2	[types-HX]	.08	
			H_1-HX		-.15
			H_2-HX		-.16
			H_3-HX		-.48*
			H_4-HX		.46
			H_5-HX		.32
HF-HTF	392	1	Demographics[b]	.04	
		2	HF-HTF	.10	-.38***

			Demographics[b]	
Types–HT$\overline{X}$	773	1	Demographics[b]	.03
		2	[types–HT$\overline{X}$]	.04
			H$_1$–HT$\overline{X}$	−.02
			H$_2$–HT$\overline{X}$	−.29
			H$_3$–HT$\overline{X}$	.16
			H$_4$–HT$\overline{X}$	.10
			H$_5$–HT$\overline{X}$	.39
Types–HT$\overline{X}$	319	1	Demographics[b]	.05
		2	[types–HT$\overline{X}$]	.16
			H$_1$–HT$\overline{X}$	−1.15***
			H$_2$–HT$\overline{X}$	−1.15***
			H$_3$–HT$\overline{X}$	−1.49***
			H$_4$–HT$\overline{X}$	− .50
			H$_5$–HT$\overline{X}$	− .66*

* $p < .05$.
** $p < .01$.
*** $p < .001$.
[a] Variables entered in step 1 are age, education, and occupational level.
[b] Variables entered in step 1 are age, education, occupational level, and race.

TABLE 15.3 / "How do you feel your homosexuality has affected your religiousness in the conventional sense—has it strengthened it very much, strengthened it somewhat, weakened it somewhat, or weakened it very much?"

	WHM	BHM	WHF	BHF	Pilot Study
	N=575	N=111	N=229	N=64	N=457
	%	%	%	%	%
0: Weakened very much	24	12	10	3	12
1: Weakened somewhat	15	19	14	30	19
2: No effect	50	55	71	61	48
3: Strengthened somewhat	8	11	3	3	13
4: Strengthened very much	3	4	2	3	8

Males

Comparison	N	Step	Variable(s)	R^2	b
BHM-WHM	651	1	Demographics[a]	.00	
		2	BHM-WHM	.01	.14*
Types-$\overline{\text{HX}}$	463	1	Demographics[b]	.02	
		2	[types-$\overline{\text{HX}}$]	.03	
			H_1-$\overline{\text{HX}}$		.13
			H_2-$\overline{\text{HX}}$		.02
			H_3-$\overline{\text{HX}}$		.00
			H_4-$\overline{\text{HX}}$		-.06
			H_5-$\overline{\text{HX}}$		-.09

Females

Comparison	N	Step	Variable(s)	R^2	b
BHF-WHF	277	1	Demographics[a]	.01	
		2	BHF-WHF	.01	—[c]
Types-$\overline{\text{HX}}$	204	1	Demographics[b]	.01	
		2	[types-$\overline{\text{HX}}$]	.04	
			H_1-$\overline{\text{HX}}$		.04
			H_2-$\overline{\text{HX}}$		.16
			H_3-$\overline{\text{HX}}$		.20
			H_4-$\overline{\text{HX}}$		-.27
			H_5-$\overline{\text{HX}}$		-.12

* $p < .05$.
a Variables entered in step 1 are age, education, and occupational level.
b Variables entered in step 1 are age, education, occupational level, and race.
c F is too small for program to compute; difference is not significant.

TABLE 16.1 / "Do you consider yourself a Democrat, Republican, or Independent?"

	WHM	BHM	WHTM	BHTM	WHF	BHF	WHTF	BHTF	Pilot Study
	N=572	N=110	N=283	N=53	N=228	N=64	N=100	N=39	N=453
	%	%	%	%	%	%	%	%	%
Democrat	36	49	36	49	47	53	41	77	38
Republican	17	3	21	4	10	0	23	3	32
Independent	42	45	38	34	31	42	30	20	30
Other	6	3	5	13	12	5	6	0	0

Males

Comparison	N	X^2
WH–BH	682	18.28***
H_1–H†	485	1.67
H_2–H†	485	1.21
H_3–H†	485	3.67
H_4–H†	485	.18
H_5–H†	485	3.73
H–HT	1018	3.66

Females

Comparison	N	X^2
WH–BH	292	10.82*
H_1–H†	210	3.82
H_2–H†	210	8.27*
H_3–H†	210	2.23[a]
H_4–H†	210	3.49[a]
H_5–H†	210	4.50[a]
H–HT	431	13.63**

* $p < .05$.
** $p < .01$.
*** $p < .001$.
† Excluding the subgroup being compared.
[a] Does not meet the conventional expected frequency rule for chi-square; collapsing categories would obscure our analytic focus.

TABLE 16.2 / "On most issues of the day would you call yourself conservative, moderately conservative, moderately liberal, or liberal?"

	WHM	BHM	WHTM	BHTM	WHF	BHF	WHTF	BHTF	Pilot Study
	N=575	N=111	N=284	N=53	N=229	N=64	N=101	N=39	
	%	%	%	%	%	%	%	%	
0: Conservative	8	9	10	4	3	5	17	3	
1: Moderately conservative	12	4	19	0	12	9	15	3	
2: Moderately liberal	25	22	25	15	27	31	33	38	
3: Liberal	50	61	44	77	52	50	36	56	
4: Radical	6	4	2	4	6	5	0	0	

Males

Comparison	N	Step	Variable(s)	R^2	b
BHM–WHM	651	1	Demographics[a]	.06	
		2	BHM–WHM	.06	.06
Types–$\overline{HX}$	463	1	Demographics[b]	.06	
		2	[types–$\overline{HX}$]	.07	
			H_1–$\overline{HX}$		.08
			H_2–$\overline{HX}$		-.17
			H_3–$\overline{HX}$		.07
			H_4–$\overline{HX}$		-.06
			H_5–$\overline{HX}$		.07
HM–HTM	961	1	Demographics[b]	.08	
		2	HM–HTM	.09	.09**

Females

Comparison	N	Step	Variable(s)	R^2	b
BHF–WHF	277	1	Demographics[a]	.05	
		2	BHF–WHF	.05	.01
Types–$\overline{HX}$	204	1	Demographics[b]	.08	
		2	[types–$\overline{HX}$]	.10	
			H_1–$\overline{HX}$		-.01
			H_2–$\overline{HX}$		-.10
			H_3–$\overline{HX}$		.26
			H_4–$\overline{HX}$		-.04
			H_5–$\overline{HX}$		-.11
HF–HTF	392	1	Demographics[b]	.08	
		2	HF–HTF	.13	.25***

** $p < .01$.
*** $p < .001$.
[a] Variables entered in step 1 are age, education, and occupational level.
[b] Variables entered in step 1 are age, education, occupational level, and race.

TABLE 16.3 / Political Involvement

	WHM	BHM	WHTM	BHTM	WHF	BHF	WHTF	BHTF	Pilot Study
	N=565	N=106	N=275	N=53	N=223	N=62	N=99	N=39	N=439
	%	%	%	%	%	%	%	%	%
0-4: Relatively low	23	37	25	47	31	27	27	26	71
5-6: Moderate	38	38	35	25	32	37	35	31	18
7-9: Relatively high	39	25	40	28	37	36	38	43	11

Males

Comparison	N	Step	Variable(s)	R^2	b
BHM-WHM	638	1	Demographics[a]	.19	
		2	BHM-WHM	.19	-.09
Types-H$\overline{X}$	453	1	Demographics[b]	.20	
		2	[types-H$\overline{X}$]	.20	
			H_1-H$\overline{X}$		.14
			H_2-H$\overline{X}$		-.06
			H_3-H$\overline{X}$		-.16
			H_4-H$\overline{X}$		.19
			H_5-H$\overline{X}$		-.10
HM-HTM	940	1	Demographics[b]	.20	
		2	HM-HTM	.20	—[c]

Females

Comparison	N	Step	Variable(s)	R^2	b
BHF-WHF	269	1	Demographics[a]	.15	
		2	BHF-WHF	.15	.18
Types-H$\overline{X}$	198	1	Demographics[b]	.22	
		2	[types-H$\overline{X}$]	.23	
			H_1-H$\overline{X}$		.04
			H_2-H$\overline{X}$		.32
			H_3-H$\overline{X}$		-.08
			H_4-H$\overline{X}$		-.45
			H_5-H$\overline{X}$		.17
HF-HTF	382	1	Demographics[b]	.17	
		2	HF-HTF	.17	-.12

[a] Variables entered in step 1 are age, education, and occupational level.
[b] Variables entered in step 1 are age, education, occupational level, and race.
[c] F is too small for program to compute; difference is not significant.

TABLE 16.4 / "Has your homosexuality affected you politically in any way?"

Pilot Study

	WHM	BHM	WHF	BHF
	N=575	N=111	N=227	N=64
	%	%	%	%
0: No	58	84	82	88
1: Yes	42	16	18	12

Males

Comparison	N	Step	Variable(s)	R^2	b
BHM–WHM	651	1	Demographics[a]	.04	
		2	BHM–WHM	.08	−.15***
Types–$\overline{HX}$	463	1	Demographics[b]	.08	
		2	[types–$\overline{HX}$]	.09	
			H_1–$\overline{HX}$		.01
			H_2–$\overline{HX}$		−.04
			H_3–$\overline{HX}$		.01
			H_4–$\overline{HX}$		.04
			H_5–$\overline{HX}$		−.04

Females

Comparison	N	Step	Variable(s)	R^2	b
BHF–WHF	275	1	Demographics[a]	.03	
		2	BHF–WHF	.03	−.03
Types–$\overline{HX}$	203	1	Demographics[b]	.03	
		2	[types–$\overline{HX}$]	.04	
			H_1–$\overline{HX}$		−.03
			H_2–$\overline{HX}$		−.05
			H_3–$\overline{HX}$		.03
			H_4–$\overline{HX}$		−.00
			H_5–$\overline{HX}$		.06

*** $p < .001$.

[a] Variables entered in step 1 are age, education, and occupational level.

[b] Variables entered in step 1 are age, education, occupational level, and race.

TABLE 16.5 / **Political Effects of Being Homosexual: Effect on Liberalism**

	WHM	BHM	WHF	BHF	Pilot Study
	N=575	N=111	N=227	N=64	
	%	%	%	%	
Made me less liberal	0	13	15	0	
Made me more liberal	34	0	0	11	
No effects concerning liberalism	8	4	3	2	
No effects at all	58	84	81	87	

Males

Comparison	N	X^2
WH–BH	686	25.99***
H_1–H[†]	485	.36
H_2–H[†]	485	.94
H_3–H[†]	485	3.25
H_4–H[†]	485	4.43
H_5–H[†]	485	4.66

Females

Comparison	N	X^2
WH–BH	291	1.12
H_1–H[†]	210	2.30
H_2–H[†]	210	1.06
H_3–H[†]	210	1.21
H_4–H[†]	210	.56
H_5–H[†]	210	1.13

*** $p < .001$.
[†] Excluding the subgroup being compared.

TABLE 16.6 / Political Effects of Being Homosexual: Effect on Confidence

	WHM	BHM	WHF	BHF	Pilot Study
	N=568	N=111	N=227	N=64	
	%	%	%	%	
More confident in present system	1	0	0	0	
Less confident in present system	21	6	8	9	
Other relevant response	15	7	6	3	
No effect concerning confidence	5	3	4	0	
No effects at all	59	84	82	88	

Males

Comparison	N	X^2
WH–BH	679	25.26***
H_1–H†	479	1.79
H_2–H†	479	1.72
H_3–H†	479	.24
H_4–H†	479	3.66
H_5–H†	479	2.68

Females

Comparison	N	X^2
WH–BH	291	2.90
H_1–H†	210	2.95
H_2–H†	210	1.17
H_3–H†	210	.85
H_4–H†	210	.43
H_5–H†	210	1.06

*** p < .001.
† Excluding the subgroup being compared.

TABLE 16.7 / Political Effects of Being Homosexual: Effect on Activism

	WHM N=574 (%)	BHM N=111 (%)	WHF N=227 (%)	BHF N=64 (%)
Made me less active	5	1	1	2
Made me more active	17	7	9	8
No effect concerning activism	20	8	7	3
No effects at all	58	84	82	87

Males

Comparison	N	X^2
WH–BH	685	25.98***
H₁–H†	484	5.16
H₂–H†	484	5.41
H₃–H†	484	3.09
H₄–H†	484	9.19*
H₅–H†	484	1.34

Females

Comparison	N	X^2
WH–BH	291	1.78
H₁–H†	210	2.66
H₂–H†	210	.89
H₃–H†	210	2.21
H₄–H†	210	2.97
H₅–H†	210	7.09

* $p < .05$.
*** $p < .001$.
† Excluding the subgroup being compared.

TABLE 17.1 / "Have you ever been married?"

	WHM	BHM	WHTM	BHTM	WHF	BHF	WHTF	BHTF	Pilot Study
	N=575	N=111	N=284	N=53	N=229	N=64	N=101	N=39	N=458
	%	%	%	%	%	%	%	%	%
0: No	80	87	26	49	65	53	27	31	83
1: Yes	20	13	74	51	35	47	73	69	17

Males

Comparison	N	Step	Variable(s)	R^2	b
BHM–WHM	651	1	Demographics[a]	.04	
		2	BHM–WHM	.04	−.01
Types–$\overline{HX}$	463	1	Demographics[b]	.05	
		2	[types–$\overline{HX}$]	.06	
			H_1–$\overline{HX}$		.05
			H_2–$\overline{HX}$		−.05
			H_3–$\overline{HX}$		−.00
			H_4–$\overline{HX}$		−.03
			H_5–$\overline{HX}$		.03
HM–HTM	961	1	Demographics[b]	.05	
		2	HM–HTM	.32	−.54***

Females

Comparison	N	Step	Variable(s)	R^2	b
BHF–WHF	277	1	Demographics[a]	.12	
		2	BHF–WHF	.14	.17*
Types–$\overline{HX}$	204	1	Demographics[b]	.10	
		2	[types–$\overline{HX}$]	.14	
			H_1–$\overline{HX}$		−.02
			H_2–$\overline{HX}$		−.12
			H_3–$\overline{HX}$		.15*
			H_4–$\overline{HX}$		.10
			H_5–$\overline{HX}$		−.11
HF–HTF	392	1	Demographics[b]	.13	
		2	HF–HTF	.24	−.36***
Types–$\overline{HTX}$	319	1	Demographics[b]	.14	
		2	[types–$\overline{HTX}$]	.26	
			H_1–$\overline{HTX}$		−.38***
			H_2–$\overline{HTX}$		−.48***

H_3-HTX̄	-.21*
H_4-HTX̄	-.25*
H_5-HTX̄	-.48***

* $p < .05$.
*** $p < .001$.
[a] Variables entered in step 1 are age, education, and occupational level.
[b] Variables entered in step 1 are age, education, occupational level, and race.

TABLE 17.2 / "How many times have you been married?"

	WHM	BHM	WHTM	BHTM	WHF	BHF	WHTF	BHTF	Pilot Study
	N=116	N=14	N=211	N=27	N=80	N=30	N=74	N=27	N=79
	%	%	%	%	%	%	%	%	%
1: Once	85	100	85	81	72	77	78	81	91
2-7: Two or more times	15	0	15	19	28	23	22	19	9

Males

Comparison	N	Step	Variable(s)	R^2	b
BHM-WHM	128	1	Demographics[a]	.03	
		2	BHM-WHM	.04	-.16
Types-H$\overline{X}$	92	1	Demographics[b]	.04	
		2	[types-H$\overline{X}$]	.05	
			H$_1$-H$\overline{X}$		-.04
			H$_2$-H$\overline{X}$		.00
			H$_3$-H$\overline{X}$		-.05
			H$_4$-H$\overline{X}$		-.03
			H$_5$-H$\overline{X}$		.11
HM-HTM	356	1	Demographics[b]	.02	
		2	HM-HTM	.03	-.06

Females

Comparison	N	Step	Variable(s)	R^2	b
BHF-WHF	104	1	Demographics[a]	.13	
		2	BHF-WHF	.14	-.06
Types-H$\overline{X}$	74	1	Demographics[b]	.18	
		2	[types-H$\overline{X}$]	.24	
			H$_1$-H$\overline{X}$		-.03
			H$_2$-H$\overline{X}$		-.18
			H$_3$-H$\overline{X}$		.32*
			H$_4$-H$\overline{X}$		.01
			H$_5$-H$\overline{X}$		-.13
HF-HTF	188	1	Demographics[b]	.11	
		2	HF-HTF	.12	-.04
Types-HT$\overline{X}$	158	1	Demographics[b]	.14	
		2	[types-HT$\overline{X}$]	.16	
			H$_1$-HT$\overline{X}$		-.04
			H$_2$-HT$\overline{X}$		-.19

H_3–HT$\overline{X}$	.29
H_4–HT$\overline{X}$	–.02
H_5–HT$\overline{X}$	–.04

* $p < .05$.

[a] Variables entered in step 1 are age, education, and occupational level.

[b] Variables entered in step 1 are age, education, occupational level, and race.

TABLE 17.3 / "How old were you when you got married [the first time]?"

	WHM	BHM	WHTM	BHTM	WHF	BHF	WHTF	BHTF	Pilot Study
	N=116	N=14	N=210	N=27	N=80	N=30	N=74	N=27	N=80
	%	%	%	%	%	%	%	%	%
1-19: 19 or younger	16	29	7	30	49	43	26	48	14
20-22: 20-22	30	43	30	48	29	33	34	33	38
23-25: 23-25	23	21	26	11	10	13	27	11	22
26-87: 26 or older	31	7	37	11	12	11	13	8	26

Males

Comparison	N	Step	Variable(s)	R^2	b
BHM-WHM	128	1	Demographics[a]	.26	
		2	BHM-WHM	.26	-.79
Types-$\overline{HX}$	92	1	Demographics[b]	.25	
		2	[types-$\overline{HX}$]	.37	
			H_1-$\overline{HX}$		-2.42*
			H_2-$\overline{HX}$		-1.92
			H_3-$\overline{HX}$		.00
			H_4-$\overline{HX}$		1.85
			H_5-$\overline{HX}$		2.49**
HM-HTM	355	1	Demographics[b]	.26	
		2	HM-HTM	.27	-.78
Types-$\overline{HTX}$	319	1	Demographics[b]	.26	
		2	[types-$\overline{HTX}$]	.31	
			H_1-$\overline{HTX}$		-3.04*

Females

Comparison	N	Step	Variable(s)	R^2	b
BHF-WHF	104	1	Demographics[a]	.16	
		2	BHF-WHF	.16	.90
Types-$\overline{HX}$	74	1	Demographics[b]	.18	
		2	[types-$\overline{HX}$]	.21	
			H_1-$\overline{HX}$		-.02
			H_2-$\overline{HX}$		-.14
			H_3-$\overline{HX}$		-1.69
			H_4-$\overline{HX}$		1.45
			H_5-$\overline{HX}$		.39
HF-HTF	188	1	Demographics[b]	.19	
		2	HF-HTF	.21	-1.12*

H_2–HTX̄	−2.55*
H_3–HTX̄	−.94
H_4–HTX̄	1.15
H_5–HTX̄	1.87

* $p < .05$.
** $p < .01$.
[a] Variables entered in step 1 are age, education, and occupational level.
[b] Variables entered in step 1 are age, education, occupational level, and race.

TABLE 17.4 / "How would you rate this [first] marriage—very happy, moderately happy, moderately unhappy, or very unhappy?"

	WHM	BHM	WHTM	BHTM	WHF	BHF	WHTF	BHTF Pilot Study
	N=115	N=14	N=210	N=27	N=80	N=29	N=74	N=27
	%	%	%	%	%	%	%	%
0: Very unhappy	18	0	9	11	36	41	9	26
1: Moderately unhappy	25	21	11	33	22	38	14	15
2: Moderately happy	42	64	34	30	34	14	31	22
3: Very happy	15	14	46	26	8	7	46	37

Males

Comparison	N	Step	Variable(s)	R^2	b
BHM–WHM	127	1	Demographics[a]	.01	
		2	BHM–WHM	.03	.36
Types–$\overline{HX}$	91	1	Demographics[b]	.05	
		2	[types–$\overline{HX}$]	.11	
			H_1–$\overline{HX}$		.40
			H_2–$\overline{HX}$		−.32
			H_3–$\overline{HX}$		−.00
			H_4–$\overline{HX}$		−.18
			H_5–$\overline{HX}$		.10

Females

Comparison	N	Step	Variable(s)	R^2	b
BHF–WHF	103	1	Demographics[a]	.07	
		2	BHF–WHF	.08	−.23
Types–$\overline{HX}$	74	1	Demographics[b]	.13	
		2	[types–$\overline{HX}$]	.15	
			H_1–$\overline{HX}$		.17
			H_2–$\overline{HX}$		.03
			H_3–$\overline{HX}$		.21
			H_4–$\overline{HX}$		−.35
			H_5–$\overline{HX}$		−.06

		Demographics		HF–HTF		Demographics[b]		
		HM–HTM	.00			HF–HTF	.03	
	2		.08	−.58***			.21	−.97***
				18?	1			
					2			

*** p < .001.
[a] Variables entered in step 1 are age, education, and occupational level.
[b] Variables entered in step 1 are age, education, occupational level, and race.

TABLE 17.5 / "How often (have/did) you (had/have) intercourse or sexual relations with your (husband/wife) during the first year of your [first] marriage?"

	WHM	BHM	WHTM	BHTM	WHF	BHF	WHTF	BHTF (Pilot Study)
	N=116	N=14	N=208	N=27	N=80	N=30	N=74	N=27
	%	%	%	%	%	%	%	%
0: Never	9	0	0	0	10	3	0	0
1: Less than once a month	4	0	1	4	6	13	3	0
2: < once a week, ≥ once a month	8	0	3	4	10	13	5	4
3: 1–1.9 times a week	10	7	10	0	19	10	9	4
4: 2–3.9 times a week	31	50	30	26	30	17	36	22
5: 4–5.9 times a week	19	21	32	33	14	13	27	26
6: 6 or more times a week	18	21	24	33	11	30	19	44

Males

Comparison	N	Step	Variable(s)	R^2	b
BHM–WHM	118	1	Demographics[a]	.00	
		2	BHM–WHM	.02	.47
Types–$\overline{HX}$	84	1	Demographics[b]	.02	
		2	[types–$\overline{HX}$]	.02	
			H₁–$\overline{HX}$		.16
			H₂–$\overline{HX}$		−.07
			H₃–$\overline{HX}$		.11
			H₄–$\overline{HX}$		−.16
			H₅–$\overline{HX}$		.04

Females

Comparison	N	Step	Variable(s)	R^2	b
BHF–WHF	95	1	Demographics[a]	.03	
		2	BHF–WHF	.03	.18
Types–$\overline{HX}$	68	1	Demographics[b]	.08	
		2	[types–$\overline{HX}$]	.15	
			H₁–$\overline{HX}$		−.44
			H₂–$\overline{HX}$		−.66
			H₃–$\overline{HX}$		.27
			H₄–$\overline{HX}$		.77
			H₅–$\overline{HX}$		.06

			Demographics		
	2	HM–HTM	.01	.04	−.43**

			Demographics[b]		
1	2	HF–HTF	.01	.10	−.85***

** $p < .01$.
*** $p < .001$.
[a] Variables entered in step 1 are age, education, and occupational level.
[b] Variables entered in step 1 are age, education, occupational level, and race.

TABLE 17.6 / "How often (have/did) you (had/have) intercourse or sexual relations with your (husband/wife) during the last year of your [first] marriage?"

	WHM	BHM	WHTM	BHTM	WHF	BHF	WHTF	BHTF (Pilot Study)
	N=97	N=11	N=182	N=25	N=52	N=27	N=71	N=22
	%	%	%	%	%	%	%	%
0: Never	29	0	7	4	31	26	8	5
1: Less than once a month	21	18	5	8	13	19	10	5
2: < once a week, ≥ once a month	18	18	18	16	31	11	18	5
3: 1–1.9 times a week	13	27	32	20	15	22	25	23
4: 2–3.9 times a week	10	27	26	16	6	11	27	36
5: 4–5.9 times a week	5	9	7	32	2	7	10	14
6: 6 or more times a week	4	0	3	4	2	4	1	14

Males

Comparison	N	Step	Variable(s)	R^2	b
BHM–WHM	98	1	Demographics[a]	.08	
		2	BHM–WHM	.09	.47
Types–$\overline{HX}$	72	1	Demographics[b]	.07	
		2	[types–$\overline{HX}$]	.09	
			H_1–$\overline{HX}$		–.24
			H_2–$\overline{HX}$		.36
			H_3–$\overline{HX}$		.28
			H_4–$\overline{HX}$		–.24
			H_5–$\overline{HX}$		–.16
HM–HTM	298	1	Demographics[b]	.14	
		2	HM–HTM	.19	–.77***

Females

Comparison	N	Step	Variable(s)	R^2	b
BHF–WHF	69	1	Demographics[a]	.01	
		2	BHF–WHF	.02	.42
Types–$\overline{HX}$	47	1	Demographics[b]	.08	
		2	[types–$\overline{HX}$]	.14	
			H_1–$\overline{HX}$		.31
			H_2–$\overline{HX}$		–.63
			H_3–$\overline{HX}$		.44
			H_4–$\overline{HX}$		–.10
			H_5–$\overline{HX}$		–.02
HF–HTF	146	1	Demographics[b]	.07	
		2	HF–HTF	.22	–1.30***

*** p < .001.
a Variables entered in step 1 are age, education, and occupational level.
b Variables entered in step 1 are age, education, occupational level, and race.

TABLE 17.7 / "During sexual relations in your [first] marriage, how often (do/did) you think about having sex with (men/women, referring to same sex)?"

	WHM	BHM	WHF	BHF	Pilot Study
	N=106	N=14	N=72	N=29	N=76
	%	%	%	%	%
0: Never	28	36	40	48	46
1: Rarely	17	7	13	7	24
2: Sometimes	22	36	25	3	20
3: Often	33	21	22	41	10

Males

Comparison	N	Step	Variable(s)	R^2	b
BHM–WHM	118	1	Demographics[a]	.05	
		2	BHM–WHM	.05	−.13
Types–HX	84	1	Demographics[b]	.07	
		2	[types–HX]	.10	
			H_1–HX		−.24
			H_2–HX		.32
			H_3–HX		.28
			H_4–FX		−.13
			H_5–HX		−.23

Females

Comparison	N	Step	Variable(s)	R^2	b
BHF–WHF	95	1	Demographics[a]	.06	
		2	BHF–WHF	.06	.10
Types–HX	68	1	Demographics[b]	.10	
		2	[types–HX]	.13	
			H_1–HX		.04
			H_2–HX		.28
			H_3–HX		.30
			H_4–HX		−.34
			H_5–HX		−.29

[a] Variables entered in step 1 are age, education, and occupational level.
[b] Variables entered in step 1 are age, education, occupational level, and race.

TABLE 17.8 / "Before you got married [the first time], did you tell your (husband/wife) that you were homosexual?"

	WHM	BHM	WHF	BHF	Pilot Study
	N=116	N=14	N=80	N=30	N=80
	%	%	%	%	%
Yes	33	14	22	13	30
No	49	86	28	57	52
Was not homosexual then	15	0	48	23	18
Spouse knew without being told	3	0	2	7	0

Males

Comparison	N	X^2
WH–BH	130	7.07
H_1–H†	94	6.46
H_2–H†	94	.68
H_3–H†	94	1.04
H_4–H†	94	1.14
H_5–H†	94	4.61

Females

Comparison	N	X^2
WH–BH	110	10.31*
H_1–H†	75	5.18
H_2–H†	75	1.62
H_3–H†	75	.87
H_4–H†	‡	‡
H_5–H†	75	1.84

* $p < .05$.
† Excluding the subgroup being compared.
‡ Relevant cases were too few to permit meaningful comparison.

TABLE 17.9 / "What did you tell (her/him) you were going to do about it [your homosexuality] after you were married?"

	WHM	BHM	WHF	BHF	Pilot Study
	N=42	N=2	N=19	N=6	N=23
	%	%	%	%	%
Nothing	52	100	53	67	0
Quit entirely	21	0	26	0	8
Try to cut down	7	0	0	0	22
Go on as before	19	0	21	33	70

Males

Comparison	N	X^2
WH–BH		‡
H_1–H†		‡
H_2–H†		‡
H_3–H†		‡
H_4–H†		‡
H_5–H†	37	3.10

Females

Comparison	N	X^2
WH–BH		‡
H_1–H†		‡
H_2–H†		‡
H_3–H†		‡
H_4–H†		‡
H_5–H†		‡

† Excluding the subgroup being compared.
‡ Relevant cases were too few to permit meaningful comparison.

TABLE 17.10 / "How long (have you been/were you) married [the first time]?"

	WHM	BHM	WHTM	BHTM	WHF	BHF	WHTF	BHTF	Pilot Study
	N=116	N=14	N=210	N=27	N=80	N=30	N=74	N=27	N=27
	%	%	%	%	%	%	%	%	%
0: Less than a year	9	7	7	0	21	3	1	7	7
1: 1–2 years	24	36	17	30	28	27	16	22	22
2: 3–5 years	23	43	17	41	19	50	18	30	30
3: 6–10 years	18	14	18	26	15	17	23	30	30
4: 11 years or longer	25	0	41	4	18	3	42	11	11

Males

Comparison	N	Step	Variable(s)	R^2	b
BHM–WHM	128	1	Demographics[a]	.31	
		2	BHM–WHM	.31	.05
Types–$\overline{\text{HX}}$	92	1	Demographics[b]	.32	
		2	[types–$\overline{\text{HX}}$]	.36	
			H_1–$\overline{\text{HX}}$		.44
			H_2–$\overline{\text{HX}}$		−.15
			H_3–$\overline{\text{HX}}$		−.04
			H_4–$\overline{\text{HX}}$		−.33
			H_5–$\overline{\text{HX}}$		.08
HM–HTM	355	1	Demographics[b]	.32	
		2	HM–HTM	.38	−.65***

Females

Comparison	N	Step	Variable(s)	R^2	b
BHF–WHF	104	1	Demographics[a]	.04	
		2	BHF–WHF	.05	.35
Types–$\overline{\text{HX}}$	74	1	Demographics[b]	.09	
		2	[types–$\overline{\text{HX}}$]	.12	
			H_1–$\overline{\text{HX}}$		−.21
			H_2–$\overline{\text{HX}}$		−.01
			H_3–$\overline{\text{HX}}$		−.23
			H_4–$\overline{\text{HX}}$		.14
			H_5–$\overline{\text{HX}}$		.31
HF–HTF	188	1	Demographics[b]	.07	
		2	HF–HTF	.23	−1.05***

*** $p < .001$.
[a] Variables entered in step 1 are age, education, and occupational level.
[b] Variables entered in step 1 are age, education, occupational level, and race.

TABLE 17.11 / "Did homosexuality have anything to do with this [end of first marriage]?"

	WHM	BHM	WHF	BHF	Pilot Study
	N=97	N=13	N=72	N=27	
	%	%	%	%	
0: No	46	77	46	59	
1: Yes	54	23	54	41	

Males

Comparison	N	Step	Variable(s)	R^2	b
BHM–WHM	108	1	Demographics[a]	.02	
		2	BHM–WHM	.06	−.31*
Types–$\overline{HX}$	78	1	Demographics[b]	.06	
		2	[types–$\overline{HX}$]	.18	
			H_1–$\overline{HX}$		.13
			H_2–$\overline{HX}$		.09
			H_3–$\overline{HX}$		.12
			H_4–$\overline{HX}$		.00
			H_5–$\overline{HX}$		−.34**

Females

Comparison	N	Step	Variable(s)	R^2	b
BHF–WHF	95	1	Demographics[a]	.00	
		2	BHF–WHF	.01	−.13
Types–$\overline{HX}$	70	1	Demographics[b]	.02	
		2	[types–$\overline{HX}$]	.11	
			H_1–$\overline{HX}$		.14
			H_2–$\overline{HX}$		.25
			H_3–$\overline{HX}$		−.09
			H_4–$\overline{HX}$		−.17
			H_5–$\overline{HX}$		−.13

* $p < .05$.
** $p < .01$.
[a] Variables entered in step 1 are age, education, and occupational level.
[b] Variables entered in step 1 are age, education, occupational level, and race.

TABLE 17.12 / "In what way was homosexuality a cause [of the breakup of your first marriage]?"[a]

	WHM N=50 %	BHM N=2 %	WHF N=36 %	BHF N=11 %
Homosexual involvement	48	100	69	73
Uninterested in heterosexual sex	20	50	33	27
Spouse found out I was homosexual	18	0	0	18
Unable to satisfy my spouse sexually	10	50	3	0

Males

Comparison	N	X^2
WH–BH	‡	‡
H_1–H†	37	6.95
H_2–H†	37	3.08
H_3–H†	‡	‡
H_4–H†	‡	‡
H_5–H†	‡	‡

Females

Comparison	N	Pilot Study X^2
WH–BH	51	6.45
H_1–H†	38	1.08
H_2–H†	38	2.86
H_3–H†	‡	‡
H_4–H†	‡	‡
H_5–H†	‡	‡

† Excluding the subgroup being compared.
‡ Relevant cases were too few to permit meaningful comparison.
[a] Respondents could give more than one answer to this question, so column percentages may add up to more than 100%; this inflates the chi-square, but not substantially.

TABLE 17.13 / "How many children (have you had/did you have) in this [first] marriage?"

	WHM	BHM	WHTM	BHTM	WHF	BHF	WHTF	BHTF	Pilot Study
	N=116	N=14	N=210	N=26	N=80	N=30	N=74	N=27	N=80
	%	%	%	%	%	%	%	%	%
0: None	50	29	34	27	50	27	31	26	30
1: One	25	50	22	31	29	40	19	33	25
2: Two	15	21	26	27	6	13	15	22	26
3: Three	5	0	10	15	6	3	26	4	15
4–6: Four or more	5	0	8	0	9	17	9	15	4

Males

Comparison	N	Step	Variable(s)	R^2	b
BHM–WHM	128	1	Demographics[a]	.02	
		2	BHM–WHM	.03	.20
Types–$\overline{HX}$	92	1	Demographics[b]	.01	
		2	[types–$\overline{HX}$]	.06	
			H_1–$\overline{HX}$		.14
			H_2–$\overline{HX}$		–.14
			H_3–$\overline{HX}$		.28
			H_4–$\overline{HX}$		–.40
			H_5–$\overline{HX}$		.12
HM–HTM	354	1	Demographics[b]	.07	
		2	HM–HTM	.11	–.60***

Females

Comparison	N	Step	Variable(s)	R^2	b
BHF–WHF	104	1	Demographics[a]	.06	
		2	BHF–WHF	.12	.80**
Types–$\overline{HX}$	74	1	Demographics[b]	.18	
		2	[types–$\overline{HX}$]	.21	
			H_1–$\overline{HX}$		–.04
			H_2–$\overline{HX}$		–.48
			H_3–$\overline{HX}$		.15
			H_4–$\overline{HX}$		.55
			H_5–$\overline{HX}$		–.18
HF–HTF	188	1	Demographics[b]	.05	
		2	HF–HTF	.10	–.64**

** $p < .01$.
*** $p < .001$.
[a] Variables entered in step 1 are age, education, and occupational level.
[b] Variables entered in step 1 are age, education, occupational level, and race.

TABLE 17.14 / **Number of Natural, Adopted, and Stepchildren (12 Years of Age or Older) Who Definitely Know About or Suspect R's Homosexuality**

	Pilot Study			
	WHM	BHM	WHF	BHF
	N=46	N=2	N=29	N=16
	%	%	%	%
0: None	61	100	38	13
1: One	24	0	34	50
2: Two	15	0	21	31
3–54: Three or more	0	0	7	6

Males

Comparison	N	Step	Variable(s)	R^2	b
BHM–WHM	47	1	Demographics[a]	.06	
		2	BHM–WHM	.07	−.37
Types–$\overline{HX}$	36	1	Demographics[b]	.12	
		2	[types–$\overline{HX}$]	.42	
			H_1–$\overline{HX}$		.05
			H_2–$\overline{HX}$		.71**
			H_3–$\overline{HX}$		.34
			H_4–$\overline{HX}$		−.57
			H_5–$\overline{HX}$		−.53*

Females

Comparison	N	Step	Variable(s)	R^2	b
BHF–WHF	39	1	Demographics[a]	.14	
		2	BHF–WHF	.14	.07
Types–$\overline{HX}$	24	1	Demographics[b]	.09	
		2	[types–$\overline{HX}$]	.19	
			H_1–$\overline{HX}$		−.01
			H_2–$\overline{HX}$		−.65
			H_3–$\overline{HX}$		.39
			H_4–$\overline{HX}$		.75
			H_5–$\overline{HX}$		−.48

* $p < .05$.
** $p < .01$.
[a] Variables entered in step 1 are age, education, and occupational level.
[b] Variables entered in step 1 are age, education, occupational level, and race.

	WHM	BHM	WHF	BHF	Pilot Study
	N=14	N=0	N=16	N=12	
	%	%	%	%	
R told	36	0	25	33	
Spouse told	29	0	6	8	
Children were told by others	7	0	19	8	
Children discovered on own (guessed, surmised)	29	0	44	50	
Other response	0	0	6	0	

Males

Comparison	N	X^2
WH–BH	‡	‡
H₁–H†	‡	‡
H₂–H†	‡	‡
H₃–H†	‡	‡
H₄–H†	‡	‡
H₅–H†	‡	‡

Females

Comparison	N	X^2
WH–BH	28	1.54
H₁–H†	‡	‡
H₂–H†	‡	‡
H₃–H†	‡	‡
H₄–H†	‡	‡
H₅–H†	‡	‡

† Excluding the subgroup being compared.
‡ Relevant cases were too few to permit meaningful comparison.

TABLE 17.16 / "How has this knowledge or suspicion [of your homosexuality] affected your relationship with them [your children aged 12 or older]?" Child(ren)'s Overall Reaction

	WHM	BHM	WHF	BHF	Pilot Study
	N=17	N=0	N=18	N=14	
	%	%	%	%	X^2
No reaction indicated	71	0	61	71	3.27
Tolerant, understanding	29	0	6	14	‡
Negative reaction (shock, horror, etc.)	0	0	11	7	‡
Worry, fears for my welfare	0	0	11	0	‡
Indifference, didn't care, no particular reaction	0	0	6	7	‡
Some other reaction	0	0	6	0	‡

Males

Comparison	N	X^2
WH–BH		‡
H_1–H†		‡
H_2–H†		‡
H_3–H†		‡
H_4–H†		‡
H_5–H†		‡

Females

Comparison	N	X^2
WH–BH	32	3.27
H_1–H†		‡
H_2–H†		‡
H_3–H†		‡
H_4–H†		‡
H_5–H†		‡

† Excluding the subgroup being compared.
‡ Relevant cases were too few to permit meaningful comparison.

TABLE 17.17 / "How has this knowledge or suspicion [of your homosexuality] affected your relationship with them [your children aged 12 or older]?" Effect on Relationship

	WHM N=17 %	BHM N=0 %	WHF N=18 %	BHF N=14 %
No effect	76	0	78	79
Strengthened relationship	12	0	11	21
Weakened relationship	6	0	0	0
Destroyed relationship	0	0	6	0
Other changes in relationship	6	0	6	0

Males

Comparison	N	X^2
WH–BH	‡	‡
H_1–H†	‡	‡
H_2–H†	‡	‡
H_3–H†	‡	‡
H_4–H†	‡	‡
H_5–H†	‡	‡

Females — Pilot Study

Comparison	N	X^2
WH–BH	32	2.09
H_1–H†	‡	‡
H_2–H†	‡	‡
H_3–H†	‡	‡
H_4–H†	‡	‡
H_5–H†	‡	‡

† Excluding the subgroup being compared.
‡ Relevant cases were too few to permit meaningful comparison.

TABLE 18.1 / "How many good, close friends do you have—that is, people you can talk to or go to for help about relatively intimate matters?"

	WHM	BHM	WHTM	BHTM	WHF	BHF	WHTF	BHTF	Pilot Study
	N=575	N=111	N=284	N=53	N=229	N=64	N=101	N=39	N=457
	%	%	%	%	%	%	%	%	%
0: None	2	4	6	11	2	8	7	3	3
1: One	6	14	7	15	4	12	3	15	7
2: Two	10	9	15	17	6	17	14	26	9
3: Three	14	16	19	9	19	17	17	28	17
4: Four	13	17	13	19	14	11	14	15	16
5: Five	14	12	12	11	14	11	17	3	18
6-98: Six or more	41	28	28	18	41	24	28	10	30

Males

Comparison	N	Step	Variable(s)	R^2	b
BHM–WHM	649	1	Demographics[a]	.02	
		2	BHM–WHM	.03	–.48
Types–$\overline{HX}$	463	1	Demographics[b]	.02	
		2	[types–$\overline{HX}$]	.04	
			H_1–$\overline{HX}$		–.15
			H_2–$\overline{HX}$		1.00*
			H_3–$\overline{HX}$		–.17
			H_4–$\overline{HX}$		.11
			H_5–$\overline{HX}$		–.79
HM–HTM	959	1	Demographics[b]	.02	
		2	HM–HTM	.03	.62***

Females

Comparison	N	Step	Variable(s)	R^2	b
BHF–WHF	277	1	Demographics[a]	.02	
		2	BHF–WHF	.03	–.65
Types–$\overline{HX}$	204	1	Demographics[b]	.02	
		2	[types–$\overline{HX}$]	.08	
			H_1–$\overline{HX}$		–.60
			H_2–$\overline{HX}$		–.45
			H_3–$\overline{HX}$		2.60***
			H_4–$\overline{HX}$		–1.02
			H_5–$\overline{HX}$		–.53
HF–HTF	392	1	Demographics[b]	.04	
		2	HF–HTF	.06	.84***

Types–HTX	773	1	Demographics[b]	.03	
		2	[types–HTX]	.05	
				H_1–$\overline{HTX}$	1.46
				H_2–$\overline{HTX}$	2.52***
				H_3–$\overline{HTX}$	1.34*
				H_4–$\overline{HTX}$	1.58*
				H_5–$\overline{HTX}$	.93

Types–HTX	319	1	Demographics[b]	.05	
		2	[types–HTX]	.12	
				H_1–$\overline{HTX}$	1.37*
				H_2–$\overline{HTX}$	1.50*
				H_3–$\overline{HTX}$	4.59***
				H_4–$\overline{HTX}$	.93
				H_5–$\overline{HTX}$	1.39

* $p < .05$.
*** $p < .001$.
[a] Variables entered in step 1 are age, education, and occupational level.
[b] Variables entered in step 1 are age, education, occupational level, and race.

TABLE 18.2 / Proportion of Friends Who Are Male/Female

	WHM	BHM	WHTM	BHTM	WHF	BHF	WHTF	BHTF (Pilot Study)
	N=572	N=111	N=282	N=51	N=227	N=63	N=98	N=39
	%	%	%	%	%	%	%	%
0: All friends female	0	0	1	0	15	22	6	10
1–49: More female than male friends	5	4	14	45	68	60	63	64
50: As many female as male friends	4	5	17	12	6	5	18	10
51–99: More male than female friends	62	67	58	33	10	11	12	15
100: All friends male	29	24	11	10	1	2	0	0

Males

Comparison	N	Step	Variable(s)	R^2	b
BHM–WHM	648	1	Demographics[a]	.00	
		2	BHM–WHM	.00	—[c]
Types–$\overline{\text{HX}}$	463	1	Demographics[b]	.01	
		2	[types–$\overline{\text{HX}}$]	.03	
			H_1–$\overline{\text{HX}}$		.96
			H_2–$\overline{\text{HX}}$		.90
			H_3–$\overline{\text{HX}}$		3.95*
			H_4–$\overline{\text{HX}}$		-.90
			H_5–$\overline{\text{HX}}$		-4.91**
HM–HTM	954	1	Demographics[b]	.01	
		2	HM–HTM	.16	9.05***

Females

Comparison	N	Step	Variable(s)	R^2	b
BHF–WHF	274	1	Demographics[a]	.02	
		2	BHF–WHF	.02	.51
Types–$\overline{\text{HX}}$	202	1	Demographics[b]	.03	
		2	[types–$\overline{\text{HX}}$]	.05	
			H_1–$\overline{\text{HX}}$		.52
			H_2–$\overline{\text{HX}}$		-5.39
			H_3–$\overline{\text{HX}}$		-2.30
			H_4–$\overline{\text{HX}}$		1.69
			H_5–$\overline{\text{HX}}$		5.48
HF–HTF	386	1	Demographics[b]	.01	
		2	HF–HTF	.04	-4.06***

Types–HT$\overline{X}$	768	1	Demographics[b]	.05	
		2	[types–HT$\overline{X}$]	.18	
			H$_1$–HT$\overline{X}$		21.44***
			H$_2$–HT$\overline{X}$		21.29***
			H$_3$–HT$\overline{X}$		24.29***
			H$_4$–HT$\overline{X}$		19.38***
			H$_5$–HT$\overline{X}$		15.50***

* $p < .05$.
** $p < .01$.
*** $p < .001$.
[a] Variables entered in step 1 are age, education, and occupational level.
[b] Variables entered in step 1 are age, education, occupational level, and race.
[c] F is too small for program to compute; difference is not significant.

TABLE 18.3 / Proportion of Same-Sex Friends Who Are Homosexual

	WHM	BHM	WHTM	BHTM	WHF	BHF	WHTF	BHTF (Pilot Study)
	N=570	N=111	N=280	N=51	N=226	N=62	N=98	N=39
	%	%	%	%	%	%	%	%
0: None	3	4	84	86	6	8	98	90
1-50: Less than half	18	18	15	14	29	39	2	10
51-99: More than half	35	37	0	0	40	35	0	0
100: All	44	41	1	0	25	18	0	0

Males

Comparison	N	Step	Variable(s)	R^2	b
BHM-WHM	646	1	Demographics[a]	.02	
		2	BHM-WHM	.02	-.30
Types-H$\overline{X}$	460	1	Demographics[b]	.03	
		2	[types-H$\overline{X}$]	.10	
			H_1-H$\overline{X}$		-1.94
			H_2-H$\overline{X}$		7.16**
			H_3-H$\overline{X}$		6.66*
			H_4-H$\overline{X}$		1.68
			H_5-H$\overline{X}$		-13.55***
HM-HTM	950	1	Demographics[b]	.00	
		2	HM-HTM	.67	37.74***
Types-HT$\overline{X}$	764	1	Demographics[b]	.34	
		2	[types-HT$\overline{X}$]	.73	

Females

Comparison	N	Step	Variable(s)	R^2	b
BHF-WHF	272	1	Demographics[a]	.02	
		2	BHF-WHF	.05	-7.15***
Types-H$\overline{X}$	201	1	Demographics[b]	.03	
		2	[types-H$\overline{X}$]	.08	
			H_1-H$\overline{X}$		4.05
			H_2-H$\overline{X}$		12.04**
			H_3-H$\overline{X}$		2.92
			H_4-H$\overline{X}$		-11.39
			H_5-H$\overline{X}$		-7.63
HF-HTF	384	1	Demographics[b]	.03	
		2	HF-HTF	.53	31.15***
Types-HT$\overline{X}$	313	1	Demographics[b]	.22	
		2	[types-HT$\overline{X}$]	.61	

$H_1-HT\overline{X}$	72.55***	$H_1-HT\overline{X}$	60.97***
$H_2-HT\overline{X}$	81.53***	$H_2-HT\overline{X}$	68.72***
$H_3-HT\overline{X}$	81.20***	$H_3-HT\overline{X}$	60.01***
$H_4-HT\overline{X}$	75.70***	$H_4-HT\overline{X}$	45.18***
$H_5-HT\overline{X}$	61.23***	$H_5-HT\overline{X}$	48.96***

* $p < .05$.
** $p < .01$.
*** $p < .001$.
[a] Variables entered in step 1 are age, education, and occupational level.
[b] Variables entered in step 1 are age, education, occupational level, and race.

TABLE 18.4 / "As you think about men and women in general, how would your attitudes or feelings toward them differ?"[a]

	WHM	BHM	WHTM	BHTM	WHF	BHF	WHTF	BHTF Pilot Study
	N=543	N=106	N=248	N=51	N=203	N=61	N=99	N=35
	%	%	%	%	%	%	%	%
I can't/don't look on men as sexual partners	1	1	32	49	22	48	1	3
I can't/don't look on women as sexual partners	33	47	0	0	0	0	15	31
More at ease with men	31	26	21	20	18	20	25	17
More at ease with women	11	8	9	12	26	23	22	6
Men easier to get emotionally involved with	3	3	1	0	0	0	0	3
Women easier to get emotionally involved with	1	2	2	4	13	10	1	0
Men better psychologically than women	31	22	15	8	13	11	28	11
Women better psychologically than men	4	2	5	14	26	36	7	3
Some other difference	14	8	23	18	16	8	12	14
There is no difference	12	14	49	10	11	5	42	17

Males

Comparison	N	X^2
WH–BH	980	16.80*
H_1–H[†]	689	4.88
H_2–H[†]	689	5.26

Females

Comparison	N	X^2
WH–BH	417	18.80*
H_1–H[†]	297	9.35
H_2–H[†]	297	5.78

H$_3$–H[†]	689	5.98	H$_3$–H[†]	297	3.04
H$_4$–H[†]	689	6.57	H$_4$–H[†]	297	2.90
H$_5$–H[†]	689	15.01	H$_5$–H[†]	297	12.51
H–HT	1441	409.10***	H–HT	612	154.61***

* $p < .05$.
*** $p < .001$.
[†] Excluding the subgroup being compared.
[a] Respondents could give more than one answer to this question, so column percentages may add up to more than 100%; this inflates the chi-square, but not substantially.

TABLE 19.1 / "What proportion of your leisure time do you spend alone?"

	WHM	BHM	WHF	BHF	Pilot Study
	N=575	N=111	N=229	N=64	
	%	%	%	%	
0: None	5	5	8	9	
1: Only a small amount	33	34	50	41	
2: Less than half	19	25	15	19	
3: About half	19	9	10	9	
4: More than half	11	11	6	8	
5: Most	12	13	11	11	
6: All	1	3	1	3	

Males

Comparison	N	Step	Variable(s)	R^2	b
BHM–WHM	651	1	Demographics[a]	.01	
		2	BHM–WHM	.01	.08
Types–HX	463	1	Demographics[b]	.01	
		2	[types–HX]	.24	
			H_1–HX		-.94***
			H_2–HX		-.59***
			H_3–HX		-.05
			H_4–HX		.47***
			H_5–HX		1.11***

Females

Comparison	N	Step	Variable(s)	R^2	b
BHF–WHF	277	1	Demographics[a]	.02	
		2	BHF–WHF	.03	.10
Types–HX	204	1	Demographics[b]	.03	
		2	[types–HX]	.25	
			H_1–HX		-.52**
			H_2–HX		-.68***
			H_3–HX		-.44
			H_4–HX		.14
			H_5–HX		1.51***

** $p < .01$.
*** $p < .001$.
[a] Variables entered in step 1 are age, education, and occupational level.
[b] Variables entered in step 1 are age, education, occupational level, and race.

TABLE 19.2 / "How many evenings per week do you spend at home?"

	WHM	BHM	WHF	BHF Pilot Study
	N=574	N=111	N=228	N=64
	%	%	%	%
0: Less than one a month	1	2	0	0
1: One a month	0	0	0	0
2: Two nights a month	1	0	1	0
3: One night a week	5	4	4	3
4: Two nights a week	10	13	11	13
5: Three nights a week	18	17	13	9
6: Four nights a week	24	27	15	17
7: Five nights a week	27	31	29	34
8: Six nights a week	10	3	18	9
9: Every night	5	4	10	14

Males

Comparison	N	Step	Variable(s)	R^2	b
BHM-WHM	650	1	Demographics[a]	.02	
		2	BHM-WHM	.02	-.03
Types-HX	463	1	Demographics[b]	.02	
		2	[types-HX]	.13	
			H_1-HX		.62***
			H_2-HX		.36***
			H_3-HX		-.90***
			H_4-HX		-.31*
			H_5-HX		.24

Females

Comparison	N	Step	Variable(s)	R^2	b
BHF-WHF	276	1	Demographics[a]	.06	
		2	BHF-WHF	.06	.07
Types-HX	203	1	Demographics[b]	.07	
		2	[types-HX]	.22	
			H_1-HX		.70***
			H_2-HX		.43*
			H_3-HX		-.68**
			H_4-HX		-1.22***
			H_5-HX		.77**

* $p < .05$.
** $p < .01$.
*** $p < .001$.
[a] Variables entered in step 1 are age, education, and occupational level.
[b] Variables entered in step 1 are age, education, occupational level, and race.

TABLE 19.3 / Contact with Friends

	WHM	BHM	WHF	BHF	Pilot Study
	N=575	N=111	N=229	N=64	
	%	%	%	%	
0–8: Relatively low	28	23	33	31	
9–11: Moderate	32	45	38	39	
12–15: Relatively high	40	32	29	30	

Males

Comparison	N	Step	Variable(s)	R^2	b
BHM–WHM	651	1	Demographics[a]	.06	
		2	BHM–WHM	.06	−.11
Types–HX	463	1	Demographics[b]	.07	
		2	[types–HX]	.13	
			H_1–HX		−.31
			H_2–HX		−.05
			H_3–HX		1.51***
			H_4–HX		−.24
			H_5–HX		−.91***

Females

Comparison	N	Step	Variable(s)	R^2	b
BHF–WHF	277	1	Demographics[a]	.04	
		2	BHF–WHF	.04	−.08
Types–HX	204	1	Demographics[b]	.04	
		2	[types–HX]	.14	
			H_1–HX		−.50
			H_2–HX		−.23
			H_3–HX		1.73***
			H_4–HX		.31
			H_5–HX		−1.31**

** p < .01.
*** p < .001.
[a] Variables entered in step 1 are age, education, and occupational level.
[b] Variables entered in step 1 are age, education, occupational level, and race.

TABLE 19.4 / "How often in the last 12 months have you gone to the movies?"

	WHM	BHM	WHF	BHF
Pilot Study	N=575	N=111	N=229	N=64
	%	%	%	%
0: Never	4	1	6	6
1: Special occasions	35	41	45	48
2: Once a month	23	23	26	30
3: Two or three times a month	24	19	17	9
4: Once a week	11	15	5	5
5: Two or more times a week	3	2	0	2

Males

Comparison	N	Step	Variable(s)	R^2	b
BHM–WHM	651	1	Demographics[a]	.04	
		2	BHM–WHM	.04	–.06
Types–$\overline{HX}$	463	1	Demographics[b]	.05	
		2	[types–$\overline{HX}$]	.06	
			H_1–$\overline{HX}$		–.16
			H_2–$\overline{HX}$		.07
			H_3–$\overline{HX}$		.13
			H_4–$\overline{HX}$		.11
			H_5–$\overline{HX}$		–.14

Females

Comparison	N	Step	Variable(s)	R^2	b
BHF–WHF	277	1	Demographics[a]	.09	
		2	BHF–WHF	.09	–.07
Types–$\overline{HX}$	204	1	Demographics[b]	.12	
		2	[types–$\overline{HX}$]	.13	
			H_1–$\overline{HX}$		–.06
			H_2–$\overline{HX}$		.11
			H_3–$\overline{HX}$		.05
			H_4–$\overline{HX}$		.12
			H_5–$\overline{HX}$		–.22

[a] Variables entered in step 1 are age, education, and occupational level.
[b] Variables entered in step 1 are age, education, occupational level, and race.

TABLE 19.5 / "How often in the last 12 months have you seen live theater?"

	WHM	BHM	WHF	BHF	Pilot Study
	N=575	N=111	N=229	N=64	
	%	%	%	%	
0: Never	11	13	21	22	
1: Special occasions	53	60	62	62	
2: Once a month	24	16	13	11	
3: Two or three times a month	9	7	3	5	
4: Once a week	2	2	0	0	
5: Two or more times a week	1	2	0	0	

Males

Comparison	N	Step	Variable(s)	R^2	b
BHM–WHM	651	1	Demographics[a]	.04	
		2	BHM–WHM	.04	−.05
Types–$\overline{HX}$	463	1	Demographics[b]	.04	
		2	[types–$\overline{HX}$]	.06	
			H_1–$\overline{HX}$		.02
			H_2–$\overline{HX}$		.11
			H_3–$\overline{HX}$		.18*
			H_4–$\overline{HX}$		−.05
			H_5–$\overline{HX}$		−.26**

Females

Comparison	N	Step	Variable(s)	R^2	b
BHF–WHF	277	1	Demographics[a]	.07	
		2	BHF–WHF	.07	−.02
Types–$\overline{HX}$	204	1	Demographics[b]	.10	
		2	[types–$\overline{HX}$]	.11	
			H_1–$\overline{HX}$		−.08
			H_2–$\overline{HX}$		.08
			H_3–$\overline{HX}$		.01
			H_4–$\overline{HX}$		.12
			H_5–$\overline{HX}$		−.13

* $p < .05$.
** $p < .01$.
a Variables entered in step 1 are age, education, and occupational level.
b Variables entered in step 1 are age, education, occupational level, and race.

TABLE 19.6 / "How often in the last 12 months have you gone to concerts?"

	WHM	BHM	WHF	BHF Pilot Study
	N=575	N=111	N=229	N=64
	%	%	%	%
0: Never	30	26	48	28
1: Special occasions	46	46	38	56
2: Once a month	14	16	10	14
3: Two or three times a month	5	4	2	2
4: Once a week	3	4	1	0
5: Two or more times a week	1	3	0	0

Males

Comparison	N	Step	Variable(s)	R^2	b
BHM-WHM	650	1	Demographics[a]	.05	
		2	BHM-WHM	.06	.08
Types-$\overline{HX}$	463	1	Demographics[b]	.07	
		2	[types-$\overline{HX}$]	.08	
			H_1-$\overline{HX}$		.02
			H_2-$\overline{HX}$		.02
			H_3-$\overline{HX}$		.16
			H_4-$\overline{HX}$		-.16
			H_5-$\overline{HX}$		-.04

Females

Comparison	N	Step	Variable(s)	R^2	b
BHF-WHF	277	1	Demographics[a]	.08	
		2	BHF-WHF	.10	.14*
Types-$\overline{HX}$	204	1	Demographics[b]	.14	
		2	[types-$\overline{HX}$]	.15	
			H_1-$\overline{HX}$		-.12
			H_2-$\overline{HX}$		-.09
			H_3-$\overline{HX}$		.10
			H_4-$\overline{HX}$		.12
			H_5-$\overline{HX}$		-.01

* $p < .05$.
[a] Variables entered in step 1 are age, education, and occupational level.
[b] Variables entered in step 1 are age, education, occupational level, and race.

TABLE 19.7 / "How often in the last 12 months have you gone to sporting events?"

	WHM	BHM	WHF	BHF Pilot Study
	N=575	N=111	N=229	N=64
	%	%	%	%
0: Never	69	43	56	44
1: Special occasions	23	34	33	36
2: Once a month	5	9	6	9
3: Two or three times a month	1	9	3	6
4: Once a week	1	4	1	3
5: Two or more times a week	0	1	1	2

Males

Comparison	N	Step	Variable(s)	R^2	b
BHM–WHM	650	1	Demographics[a]	.03	
		2	BHM–WHM	.07	.26***
Types–$\overline{HX}$	462	1	Demographics[b]	.09	
		2	[types–$\overline{HX}$]	.10	
			H_1–$\overline{HX}$		−.01
			H_2–$\overline{HX}$		−.05
			H_3–$\overline{HX}$		.05
			H_4–$\overline{HX}$		.10
			H_5–$\overline{HX}$		−.10

Females

Comparison	N	Step	Variable(s)	R^2	b
BHF–WHF	277	1	Demographics[a]	.03	
		2	BHF–WHF	.04	.13
Types–$\overline{HX}$	204	1	Demographics[b]	.06	
		2	[types–$\overline{HX}$]	.07	
			H_1–$\overline{HX}$		.12
			H_2–$\overline{HX}$		.07
			H_3–$\overline{HX}$		.08
			H_4–$\overline{HX}$		−.14
			H_5–$\overline{HX}$		−.12

*** $p < .001$.
[a] Variables entered in step 1 are age, education, and occupational level.
[b] Variables entered in step 1 are age, education, occupational level, and race.

TABLE 19.8 / "How often in the last 12 months have you participated in sports or game activities?"

	WHM	BHM	WHF	BHF
				Pilot Study
	N=575	N=111	N=229	N=64
	%	%	%	%
0: Never	62	46	49	41
1: Special occasions	18	25	16	30
2: Once a month	7	9	13	9
3: Two or three times a month	4	10	9	8
4: Once a week	3	4	7	8
5: Two or more times a week	6	5	7	5

Males

Comparison	N	Step	Variable(s)	R^2	b
BHM-WHM	651	1	Demographics[a]	.04	
		2	BHM-WHM	.04	.07
Types-HX	463	1	Demographics[b]	.03	
		2	[types-HX]	.04	
			H_1-HX		-.19
			H_2-HX		.00
			H_3-HX		-.13
			H_4-HX		.19
			H_5-HX		.12

Females

Comparison	N	Step	Variable(s)	R^2	b
BHF-WHF	277	1	Demographics[a]	.03	
		2	BHF-WHF	.03	-.05
Types-HX	204	1	Demographics[b]	.02	
		2	[types-HX]	.04	
			H_1-HX		-.14
			H_2-HX		.29
			H_3-HX		.17
			H_4-HX		-.05
			H_5-HX		-.27

[a] Variables entered in step 1 are age, education, and occupational level.
[b] Variables entered in step 1 are age, education, occupational level, and race.

TABLE 19.9 / "How often in the last 12 months have you gone to bars?"

	WHM	BHM	WHF	BHF
	N=575	N=111	N=228	N=64
	%	%	%	%
0: Never	9	0	15	11
1: Special occasions	18	6	27	25
2: Once a month	11	5	16	11
3: Two or three times a month	13	24	14	20
4: Once a week	20	17	17	25
5: Two or more times a week	29	47	11	8

Males

Comparison	N	Step	Variable(s)	R^2	b
BHM-WHM	651	1	Demographics[a]	.06	
		2	BHM-WHM	.07	.28**
Types-$\overline{HX}$	463	1	Demographics[b]	.07	
		2	[types-$\overline{HX}$]	.13	
			H_1-$\overline{HX}$		-.56***
			H_2-$\overline{HX}$		-.06
			H_3-$\overline{HX}$		.52***
			H_4-$\overline{HX}$		.52***
			H_5-$\overline{HX}$		-.42**

Females

Comparison	N	Step	Variable(s)	R^2	b
BHF-WHF	276	1	Demographics[a]	.07	
		2	BHF-WHF	.07	-.01
Types-$\overline{HX}$	203	1	Demographics[b]	.10	
		2	[types-$\overline{HX}$]	.13	
			H_1-$\overline{HX}$		-.28
			H_2-$\overline{HX}$		.32
			H_3-$\overline{HX}$		.11
			H_4-$\overline{HX}$		.24
			H_5-$\overline{HX}$		-.39

** p < .01.
*** p < .001.
[a] Variables entered in step 1 are age, education, and occupational level.
[b] Variables entered in step 1 are age, education, occupational level, and race.

TABLE 19.10 / **"How often in the last 12 months have you gone to baths?"**

	WHM	BHM	WHF	BHF	Pilot Study
	N=573	N=111			N=456
	%	%			%
0: Never	38	44			69
1: Special occasions	31	32			16
2: Once a month	13	13			9
3: Two or three times a month	11	5			6
4: Once a week	6	5			0
5: Two or more times a week	2	1			0

Males

Comparison	N	Step	Variable(s)	R^2	b
BHM–WHM	649	1	Demographics[a]	.00	
		2	BHM–WHM	.01	−.16*
Types–HX̄	462	1	Demographics[b]	.00	
		2	[types–HX̄]	.16	
			H_1–HX̄		−.66***
			H_2–HX̄		.12
			H_3–HX̄		.52***
			H_4–HX̄		.64***
			H_5–HX̄		−.62***

* $p < .05$.
*** $p < .001$.
[a] Variables entered in step 1 are age, education, and occupational level.
[b] Variables entered in step 1 are age, education, occupational level, and race.

TABLE 19.11 / "Do you currently belong to any homophile organizations?"

	WHM	BHM	WHF	BHF	Pilot Study
	N=575	N=111	N=229	N=64	
	%	%	%	%	
0: No	76	87	79	92	
1: Yes	24	13	21	8	

Males

Comparison	N	Step	Variable(s)	R^2	b
BHM–WHM	651	1	Demographics[a]	.03	
		2	BHM–WHM	.03	−.04
Types–$\overline{HX}$	463	1	Demographics[b]	.03	
		2	[types–$\overline{HX}$]	.04	
			H_1–$\overline{HX}$		−.03
			H_2–$\overline{HX}$		.01
			H_3–$\overline{HX}$		.08*
			H_4–$\overline{HX}$		−.04
			H_5–$\overline{HX}$		−.02

Females

Comparison	N	Step	Variable(s)	R^2	b
BHF–WHF	277	1	Demographics[a]	.03	
		2	BHF–WHF	.04	−.05
Types–$\overline{HX}$	204	1	Demographics[b]	.04	
		2	[types–$\overline{HX}$]	.05	
			H_1–$\overline{HX}$		−.02
			H_2–$\overline{HX}$		.02
			H_3–$\overline{HX}$		−.01
			H_4–$\overline{HX}$		.01
			H_5–$\overline{HX}$		−.01

[a] Variables entered in step 1 are age, education, and occupational level.
[b] Variables entered in step 1 are age, education, occupational level, and race.

TABLE 19.12 / "How often in the last 12 months have you involved yourself in homophile organizations [if R belongs to any]?"

	WHM	BHM	WHF	BHF	Pilot Study
	N=140	N=14	N=48	N=5	
	%	%	%	%	
0: Never	15	7	8	0	
1: Special occasions	24	36	23	20	
2: Once a month	16	21	15	60	
3: Two or three times a month	16	7	23	0	
4: Once a week	12	7	19	0	
5: Two or more times a week	17	21	12	20	

Males

Comparison	N	Step	Variable(s)	R^2	b
BHM–WHM	143	1	Demographics[a]	.03	
		2	BHM–WHM	.03	−.05
Types–H$\overline{\text{X}}$	106	1	Demographics[b]	.03	
		2	[types–H$\overline{\text{X}}$]	.06	
			H$_1$–H$\overline{\text{X}}$		.25
			H$_2$–H$\overline{\text{X}}$		.31
			H$_3$–H$\overline{\text{X}}$		.07
			H$_4$–H$\overline{\text{X}}$		−.15
			H$_5$–H$\overline{\text{X}}$		−.48

Females

Comparison	N	Step	Variable(s)	R^2	b
BHF–WHF	49	1	Demographics[a]	.09	
		2	BHF–WHF	.10	−.22
Types–H$\overline{\text{X}}$	30	1	Demographics[b]	.20	
		2	[types–H$\overline{\text{X}}$]	.42	
			H$_1$–H$\overline{\text{X}}$		−.19
			H$_2$–H$\overline{\text{X}}$		−.18
			H$_3$–H$\overline{\text{X}}$		2.05*
			H$_4$–H$\overline{\text{X}}$		−.49
			H$_5$–H$\overline{\text{X}}$		−1.19

* $p < .05$.
[a] Variables entered in step 1 are age, education, and occupational level.
[b] Variables entered in step 1 are age, education, occupational level, and race.

TABLE 20.1 / "Other than for traffic offenses, have you ever been arrested or picked up by the police?"

	WHM	BHM	WHTM	BHTM	WHF	BHF	WHTF	BHTF	Pilot Study
	N=575	N=111	N=284	N=53	N=229	N=64	N=101	N=39	N=458
	%	%	%	%	%	%	%	%	%
0: No	51	65	69	58	75	75	91	90	67
1: Yes	49	35	31	42	25	25	9	10	33

Males

Comparison	N	Step	Variable(s)	R^2	b
BHM–WHM	651	1	Demographics[a]	.07	
		2	BHM–WHM	.08	−.05
Types–$H\overline{X}$	463	1	Demographics[b]	.07	
		2	[types–$H\overline{X}$]	.09	
			H_1–$H\overline{X}$		−.10
			H_2–$H\overline{X}$		−.04
			H_3–$H\overline{X}$		.05
			H_4–$H\overline{X}$		.13**
			H_5–$H\overline{X}$		−.05
HM–HTM	961	1	Demographics[b]	.04	
		2	HM–HTM	.06	.07***
Types–$H T\overline{X}$	773	1	Demographics[b]	.07	
		2	[types–$H T\overline{X}$]	.08	
			H_1–$H T\overline{X}$		−.02
			H...$H T\overline{X}$		.01

Females

Comparison	N	Step	Variable(s)	R^2	b
BHF–WHF	277	1	Demographics[a]	.04	
		2	BHF–WHF	.04	−.02
Types–$H\overline{X}$	204	1	Demographics[b]	.05	
		2	[types–$H\overline{X}$]	.06	
			H_1–$H\overline{X}$		.05
			H_2–$H\overline{X}$		−.06
			H_3–$H\overline{X}$		.04
			H_4–$H\overline{X}$		−.04
			H_5–$H\overline{X}$		.01
HF–HTF	392	1	Demographics[b]	.04	
		2	HF–HTF	.08	.09***

(H₃–HTX̄)	.10
H₄–HTX̄	.18***
H₅–HTX̄	.04

** p < .01.
*** p < .001.
[a] Variables entered in step 1 are age, education, and occupational level.
[b] Variables entered in step 1 are age, education, occupational level, and race.

TABLE 20.2 / "How many times has this happened [being arrested or picked up by police]?"

	WHM	BHM	WHTM	BHTM	WHF	BHF	WHTF	BHTF	Pilot Study
	N=282	N=39	N=89	N=22	N=56	N=16	N=9	N=4	N=150
	%	%	%	%	%	%	%	%	%
1: Once	61	59	54	27	70	69	56	75	66
2: Twice	19	18	20	36	9	0	22	25	22
3: Three times	9	10	13	14	7	6	0	0	5
4–98: Four or more times	11	13	13	23	14	25	22	0	7

Males

Comparison	N	Step	Variable(s)	R^2	b
BHM–WHM	651	1	Demographics[a]	.02	
		2	BHM–WHM	.02	−.12
Types–HX̄	463	1	Demographics[b]	.03	
		2	[types–HX̄]	.04	
			H_1–HX̄		−.43
			H_2–HX̄		−.23
			H_3–HX̄		.44*
			H_4–HX̄		.06
			H_5–HX̄		.17
HM–HTM	961	1	Demographics[b]	.02	
		2	HM–HTM	.02	.03
Types–HTX̄	773	1	Demographics[b]	.02	
		2	[types–HTX̄]	.03	
			H_1–HTX̄		−.68
			H_2–HTX̄		−.52
			H_3–HTX̄		.12
			H_4–HTX̄		−.24
			H_5–HTX̄		−.06

Females

Comparison	N	Step	Variable(s)	R^2	b
BHF–WHF	276	1	Demographics[a]	.04	
		2	BHF–WHF	.04	−.05
Types–HX̄	203	1	Demographics[b]	.04	
		2	[types–HX̄]	.05	
			H_1–HX̄		.33
			H_2–HX̄		−.26
			H_3–HX̄		.10
			H_4–HX̄		−.41
			H_5–HX̄		.24
HF–HTF	391	1	Demographics[b]	.04	
		2	HF–HTF	.05	.18

TABLE 20.3 / **Number of Times Arrested or Picked Up in Connection with Homosexuality**

	WHM	BHM	WHF	BHF	Pilot Study
	N=574	N=111	N=229	N=64	N=458
	%	%	%	%	%
0: Never	70	88	96	95	78
1-87: One or more times	30	12	4	5	22

Males

Comparison	N	Step	Variable(s)	R^2	b
BHM-WHM	650	1	Demographics[a]	.05	
		2	BHM-WHM	.05	—[c]
Types-H$\overline{X}$	463	1	Demographics[b]	.03	
		2	[types-H$\overline{X}$]	.06	
			H$_1$-H$\overline{X}$		-.25*
			H$_2$-H$\overline{X}$		-.06
			H$_3$-H$\overline{X}$		.28**
			H$_4$-H$\overline{X}$		.20
			H$_5$-H$\overline{X}$		-.17

Females

Comparison	N	Step	Variable(s)	R^2	b
BHF-WHF	277	1	Demographics[a]	.02	
		2	BHF-WHF	.02	-.00
Types-H$\overline{X}$	204	1	Demographics[b]	.04	
		2	[types-H$\overline{X}$]	.04	
			H$_1$-H$\overline{X}$		-.01
			H$_2$-H$\overline{X}$		.02
			H$_3$-H$\overline{X}$		-.00
			H$_4$-H$\overline{X}$		-.03
			H$_5$-H$\overline{X}$		.01

[a] Variables entered in step 1 are age, education, and occupational level.
[b] Variables entered in step 1 are age, education, occupational level, and race.

* $p < .05$.
** $p < .01$.
[a] Variables entered in step 1 are age, education, and occupational level.
[b] Variables entered in step 1 are age, education, occupational level, and race.
[c] F is too small for program to compute; difference is not significant.

TABLE 20.4 / "Have you ever been booked, i.e., a record made of it [being arrested or picked up by police]?"

	WHM	BHM	WHTM	BHTM	WHF	BHF	WHTF	BHTF	Pilot Study
	N=572	N=111	N=283	N=53	N=227	N=63	N=101	N=38	
	%	%	%	%	%	%	%	%	
0: No	60	74	76	66	83	81	94	95	
1: Yes	40	26	24	34	17	19	6	5	

Males

Comparison	N	Step	Variable(s)	R^2	b
BHM-WHM	649	1	Demographics[a]	.06	
		2	BHM-WHM	.07	-.04
Types-H$\overline{X}$	462	1	Demographics[b]	.06	
		2	[types-H$\overline{X}$]	.08	
			H_1-H$\overline{X}$		-.04
			H_2-H$\overline{X}$		-.01
			H_3-H$\overline{X}$		.04
			H_4-H$\overline{X}$		.12**
			H_5-H$\overline{X}$		-.11*
HM-HTM	958	1	Demographics[b]	.04	
		2	HM-HTM	.06	.07***
Types-HT$\overline{X}$	771	1	Demographics[b]	.06	
		2	[types-HT$\overline{X}$]	.07	
			H_1-HT$\overline{X}$		.03
			H_2-HT$\overline{X}$		.05
			H_3-HT$\overline{X}$		.08
			H_4-HT$\overline{X}$		.17**
			H_5-HT$\overline{X}$		-.01

Females

Comparison	N	Step	Variable(s)	R^2	b
BHF-WHF	274	1	Demographics[a]	.03	
		2	BHF-WHF	.03	-.01
Types-H$\overline{X}$	202	1	Demographics[b]	.03	
		2	[types-H$\overline{X}$]	.03	
			H_1-H$\overline{X}$		.03
			H_2-H$\overline{X}$		-.04
			H_3-H$\overline{X}$		.06
			H_4-H$\overline{X}$		-.04
			H_5-H$\overline{X}$		-.01
HF-HTF	388	1	Demographics[b]	.03	
		2	HF-HTF	.06	.06***

TABLE 20.5 / **Number of Times Booked by Police in Connection with Homosexuality**

	WHM	BHM	WHF	BHF	Pilot Study
	N=573	N=111	N=229	N=64	
	%	%	%	%	
0: None	76	90	98	97	
1-87: One or more	24	10	2	3	

Males

Comparison	N	Step	Variable(s)	R²	b
BHM-WHM	650	1	Demographics[a]	.04	
		2	BHM-WHM	.04	—[c]
Types-H$\overline{X}$	463	1	Demographics[b]	.02	
		2	[types-H$\overline{X}$]	.05	
			H_1-H$\overline{X}$		-.18
			H_2-H$\overline{X}$		-.01
			H_3-H$\overline{X}$		.23*
			H_4-H$\overline{X}$		.16
			H_5-H$\overline{X}$		-.20*

Females

Comparison	N	Step	Variable(s)	R²	b
BHF-WHF	277	1	Demographics[a]	.00	
		2	BHF-WHF	.00	-.00
Types-H$\overline{X}$	204	1	Demographics[b]	.01	
		2	[types-H$\overline{X}$]	.02	
			H_1-H$\overline{X}$		.01
			H_2-H$\overline{X}$		.01
			H_3-H$\overline{X}$		-.01
			H_4-H$\overline{X}$		-.02
			H_5-H$\overline{X}$		.01

** $p < .01$.
*** $p < .001$.
[a] Variables entered in step 1 are age, education, and occupational level.
[b] Variables entered in step 1 are age, education, occupational level, and race.

* $p < .05$.
[a] Variables entered in step 1 are age, education, and occupational level.
[b] Variables entered in step 1 are age, education, occupational level, and race.
[c] F is too small for program to compute; difference is not significant.

TABLE 20.6 / "Have you ever been convicted?"

	WHM	BHM	WHTM	BHTM	WHF	BHF	WHTF	BHTF	Pilot Study
	N=575	N=111	N=283	N=53	N=229	N=64	N=101	N=39	N=457
	%	%	%	%	%	%	%	%	%
0: No	75	85	88	75	90	88	97	97	91
1: Yes	25	15	12	25	10	12	3	3	9

Males

Comparison	N	Step	Variable(s)	R^2	b
BHM–WHM	651	1	Demographics[a]	.06	
		2	BHM–WHM	.06	−.03
Types–$\overline{\text{HX}}$	463	1	Demographics[b]	.04	
		2	[types–$\overline{\text{HX}}$]	.06	.05***
			H_1–$\overline{\text{HX}}$		−.04
			H_2–$\overline{\text{HX}}$		−.02
			H_3–$\overline{\text{HX}}$		.04
			H_4–$\overline{\text{HX}}$		.08*
			H_5–$\overline{\text{HX}}$		−.06
HM–HTM	960	1	Demographics[b]	.03	
		2	HM–HTM	.05	.05***
Types–$\overline{\text{HTX}}$	772	1	Demographics[b]	.05	
		2	[types–$\overline{\text{HTX}}$]	.06	
			H_1–$\overline{\text{HTX}}$		−.01
			H_2–$\overline{\text{HTX}}$		.00
			H_3–$\overline{\text{HTX}}$		.05
			H_4–$\overline{\text{HTX}}$		.09
			H_5–$\overline{\text{HTX}}$		−.02

Females

Comparison	N	Step	Variable(s)	R^2	b
BHF–WHF	277	1	Demographics[a]	.02	
		2	BHF–WHF	.02	.01
Types–$\overline{\text{HX}}$	204	1	Demographics[b]	.01	
		2	[types–$\overline{\text{HX}}$]	.01	
			H_1–$\overline{\text{HX}}$		.02
			H_2–$\overline{\text{HX}}$		−.02
			H_3–$\overline{\text{HX}}$		.01
			H_4–$\overline{\text{HX}}$		−.03
			H_5–$\overline{\text{HX}}$		.01
HF–HTF	392	1	Demographics[b]	.03	
		2	HF–HTF	.05	.04**

TABLE 20.7 / **Number of Convictions Related to Homosexuality**

	WHM	BHM	WHF	BHF	Pilot Study
	N=575	N=111	N=229	N=64	
	%	%	%	%	
0: None	85	93	99	100	
1–87: One or more	15	7	1	0	

Males

Comparison	N	Step	Variable(s)	R^2	b
BHM–WHM	651	1	Demographics[a]	.05	
		2	BHM–WHM	.05	−.03
Types–$\overline{HX}$	463	1	Demographics[b]	.04	
		2	[types–$\overline{HX}$]	.06	
			H_1–$\overline{HX}$		−.10
			H_2–$\overline{HX}$		−.03
			H_3–$\overline{HX}$		.11*
			H_4–$\overline{HX}$		.11
			H_5–$\overline{HX}$		−.09

Females

Comparison	N	Step	Variable(s)	R^2	b
BHF–WHF	277	1	Demographics[a]	.00	
		2	BHF–WHF	.01	−.00
Types–$\overline{HX}$	204	1	Demographics[b]	.01	
		2	[types–$\overline{HX}$]	.02	
			H_1–$\overline{HX}$		.01
			H_2–$\overline{HX}$		−.00
			H_3–$\overline{HX}$		−.00
			H_4–$\overline{HX}$		−.00
			H_5–$\overline{HX}$		−.00

* p < .05.
a Variables entered in step 1 are age, education, and occupational level.
b Variables entered in step 1 are age, education, occupational level, and race.

TABLE 20.8 / "How many times has money been illegally demanded of you by the police (or persons believed to be police) for reasons related to your homosexuality?"

	WHM	BHM	WHF	BHF	Pilot Study BHF
	N=575	N=110	N=229	N=64	
	%	%	%	%	
0: Never	94	96	100	100	
1–87: One or more times	6	4	0	0	

Females[c]

Males

Comparison	N	Step	Variable(s)	R^2	b
BHM–WHM	651	1	Demographics[a]	.01	
		2	BHM–WHM	.01	−.03
Types–$\overline{\text{HX}}$	463	1	Demographics[b]	.02	
		2	[types–$\overline{\text{HX}}$]	.03	
			H_1–$\overline{\text{HX}}$		−.15
			H_2–$\overline{\text{HX}}$		−.12
			H_3–$\overline{\text{HX}}$		−.12
			H_4–$\overline{\text{HX}}$		.62**
			H_5–$\overline{\text{HX}}$		−.23

** $p < .01$.

[a] Variables entered in step 1 are age, education, and occupational level.

[b] Variables entered in step 1 are age, education, occupational level, and race.

[c] F is too small for program to compute; difference is not significant.

TABLE 20.9 / Number of Times Rolled or Robbed in Connection with Homosexuality

	WHM	BHM	WHF	BHF	Pilot Study
	N=574	N=110	N=229	N=64	N=458
	%	%	%	%	%
0: Never	62	79	98	95	65
1–87: One or more times	38	21	2	5	35

Males

Comparison	N	Step	Variable(s)	R^2	b
BHM–WHM	650	1	Demographics[a]	.09	
		2	BHM–WHM	.09	.02
Types–HX̄	463	1	Demographics[b]	.08	
		2	[types–HX̄]	.10	
			H_1–HX̄		−.75*
			H_2–HX̄		−.03
			H_3–HX̄		−.10
			H_4–HX̄		.72*
			H_5–HX̄		.16

Females

Comparison	N	Step	Variable(s)	R^2	b
BHF–WHF	277	1	Demographics[a]	.01	
		2	BHF–WHF	.02	.04*
Types–HX̄	204	1	Demographics[b]	.02	
		2	[types–HX̄]	.02	
			H_1–HX̄		.03
			H_2–HX̄		.00
			H_3–HX̄		.04
			H_4–HX̄		−.04
			H_5–HX̄		−.03

* $p < .05$.
a Variables entered in step 1 are age, education, and occupational level.
b Variables entered in step 1 are age, education, occupational level, and race.

TABLE 20.10 / Number of Times Someone Has Threatened Exposure of Homosexuality in Order to Get Something of Value

	WHM	BHM	WHF	BHF Pilot Study
	N=575	N=110	N=229	N=64
	%	%	%	%
0: Never	85	87	77	86
1–87: One or more times	15	13	23	14

Males

Comparison	N	Step	Variable(s)	R^2	b
BHM–WHM	651	1	Demographics[a]	.01	
		2	BHM–WHM	.01	−.14
Types–$\overline{HX}$	463	1	Demographics[b]	.02	
		2	[types–$\overline{HX}$]	.03	
			H_1–$\overline{HX}$		1.17**
			H_2–$\overline{HX}$		−.20
			H_3–$\overline{HX}$		−.14
			H_4–$\overline{HX}$		−.56
			H_5–$\overline{HX}$		−.26

Females

Comparison	N	Step	Variable(s)	R^2	b
BHF–WHF	277	1	Demographics[a]	.02	
		2	BHF–WHF	.03	.36
Types–$\overline{HX}$	204	1	Demographics[b]	.03	
		2	[types–$\overline{HX}$]	.05	
			H_1–$\overline{HX}$		.72
			H_2–$\overline{HX}$		.09
			H_3–$\overline{HX}$		−.51
			H_4–$\overline{HX}$		.13
			H_5–$\overline{HX}$		−.42

** $p < .01$.
[a] Variables entered in step 1 are age, education, and occupational level.
[b] Variables entered in step 1 are age, education, occupational level, and race.

TABLE 20.11 / "What did they [persons threatening to expose homosexuality] want from you?"

	WHM	BHM	WHF	BHF	Pilot Study
	N=88	N=13	N=52	N=9	
	%	%	%	%	%
Money or material goods	62	69	10	11	
Sexual favors	11	15	15	11	
To keep me from breaking up our relationship	10	0	25	67	
Other demand	16	15	50	11	

Males

Comparison	N	X^2
WH–BH	101	1.57
H_1–H†	70	5.07
H_2–H†	70	.55
H_3–H†	70	4.43
H_4–H†	‡	‡
H_5–H†	70	4.36

Females

Comparison	N	X^2
WH–BH	‡	‡
H_1–H†	49	.81
H_2–H†	49	.48
H_3–H†	‡	‡
H_4–H†	‡	‡
H_5–H†	‡	‡

† Excluding the subgroup being compared.
‡ Relevant cases were too few to permit meaningful comparison.

TABLE 21.1 / "How would you rate your health at present? Is it excellent, good, fair, or poor?"

	WHM	BHM	WHTM	BHTM	WHF	BHF	WHTF	BHTF	Pilot Study
	N=575	N=111	N=284	N=53	N=229	N=64	N=101	N=39	N=458
	%	%	%	%	%	%	%	%	%
0: Poor	2	2	2	2	1	3	1	0	1
1: Fair	11	6	11	4	10	22	9	18	10
2: Good	42	47	36	34	44	47	46	54	44
3: Excellent	45	45	51	60	45	28	44	28	45

Males

Comparison	N	Step	Variable(s)	R^2	b
BHM–WHM	651	1	Demographics[a]	.01	
		2	BHM–WHM	.01	.03
Types–$\overline{HX}$	463	1	Demographics[b]	.01	
		2	[types–$\overline{HX}$]	.03	
			H_1–$\overline{HX}$		.11
			H_2–$\overline{HX}$		–.01
			H_3–$\overline{HX}$		.13
			H_4–$\overline{HX}$		–.01
			H_5–$\overline{HX}$		–.22**
HM–HTM	961	1	Demographics[b]	.02	
		2	HM–HTM	.03	–.03
Types–$\overline{HTX}$	773	1	Demographics[b]	.02	
		2	[types–$\overline{HTX}$]	.04	
			H_1–$\overline{HTX}$		.02
			H–$\overline{HTX}$		.13

Females

Comparison	N	Step	Variable(s)	R^2	b
BHF–WHF	277	1	Demographics[a]	.01	
		2	BHF–WHF	.04	–.14*
Types–$\overline{HX}$	204	1	Demographics[b]	.03	
		2	[types–$\overline{HX}$]	.05	
			H_1–$\overline{HX}$		.08
			H_2–$\overline{HX}$		–.04
			H_3–$\overline{HX}$		.10
			H_4–$\overline{HX}$		.02
			H_5–$\overline{HX}$		–.16
HF–HTF	392	1	Demographics[b]	.04	
		2	HF–HTF	.04	–.02

H_3–HTX	.03
H_4–HT$\overline{X}$	–.12
H_5–HT$\overline{X}$	–.29**

* $p < .05$.
** $p < .01$.
[a] Variables entered in step 1 are age, education, and occupational level.
[b] Variables entered in step 1 are age, education, occupational level, and race.

TABLE 21.2 / Psychosomatic Symptoms

	WHM	BHM	WHTM	BHTM	WHF	BHF	WHTF	Pilot Study BHTF
	N=575	N=111	N=284	N=53	N=229	N=64	N=101	N=39
	%	%	%	%	%	%	%	%
0-1: Relatively low	28	26	34	62	26	14	25	5
2-5: Moderate	39	36	40	19	38	33	34	31
6-18: Relatively high	33	38	26	19	36	53	41	64

Males

Comparison	N	Step	Variable(s)	R^2	b
BHM–WHM	651	1	Demographics[a]	.03	
		2	BHM–WHM	.03	-.04
Types–H$\overline{X}$	463	1	Demographics[b]	.02	
		2	[types–H$\overline{X}$]	.07	
			H$_1$–H$\overline{X}$		-.51
			H$_2$–H$\overline{X}$		.26
			H$_3$–H$\overline{X}$		-1.08***
			H$_4$–H$\overline{X}$		.14
			H$_5$–H$\overline{X}$		1.19
HM–HTM	961	1	Demographics[b]	.03	
		2	HM–HTM	.05	.48***
Types–HT$\overline{X}$	773	1	Demographics[b]	.03	
		2	[types–HT$\overline{X}$]	.07	
			H$_1$–HT$\overline{X}$		.83
			H$_2$–HT$\overline{X}$		1.64***

Females

Comparison	N	Step	Variable(s)	R^2	b
BHF–WHF	277	1	Demographics[a]	.04	
		2	BHF–WHF	.07	.92***
Types–H$\overline{X}$	204	1	Demographics[b]	.07	
		2	[types–H$\overline{X}$]	.10	
			H$_1$–H$\overline{X}$		-.49
			H$_2$–H$\overline{X}$		.91
			H$_3$–H$\overline{X}$		-1.07
			H$_4$–H$\overline{X}$		.16
			H$_5$–H$\overline{X}$		.49
HF–HTF	392	1	Demographics[b]	.09	
		2	HF–HTF	.09	—[c]

$H_3-H\overline{T}\overline{X}$	.33
$H_4-H\overline{T}\overline{X}$	1.52**
$H_5-H\overline{T}\overline{X}$	2.41***

** $p < .01$.
*** $p < .001$.
[a] Variables entered in step 1 are age, education, and occupational level.
[b] Variables entered in step 1 are age, education, occupational level, and race.
[e] F is too small for program to compute; difference is not significant.

TABLE 21.3 / "Taking things altogether, how would you say you are feeling these days? Very happy, pretty happy, not too happy, or very unhappy?"

	WHM	BHM	WHTM	BHTM	WHF	BHF	WHTF	BHTF (Pilot Study)
	N=575	N=111	N=284	N=53	N=229	N=63	N=101	N=39
	%	%	%	%	%	%	%	%
0: Very unhappy	3	2	1	0	2	3	1	3
1: Not too happy	14	18	11	4	16	22	10	10
2: Pretty happy	55	61	67	53	57	59	57	61
3: Very happy	28	19	20	43	25	16	32	26

Males

Comparison	N	Step	Variable(s)	R^2	b
BHM–WHM	651	1	Demographics[a]	.01	
		2	BHM–WHM	.01	−.07
Types–HX̄	463	1	Demographics[b]	.00	
		2	[types–HX̄]	.14	
			H₁–HX̄		.40***
			H₂–HX̄		.10
			H₃–HX̄		.17**
			H₄–HX̄		−.34***
			H₅–HX̄		−.33***
HM–HTM	961	1	Demographics[b]	.01	
		2	HM–HTM	.01	−.02
Types–HTX̄	773	1	Demographics[b]	.01	
		2	[types–HTX̄]	.11	
			H₁–HX̄		.22*
			H₂–HX̄		−.09

Females

Comparison	N	Step	Variable(s)	R^2	b
BHF–WHF	276	1	Demographics[a]	.02	
		2	BHF–WHF	.03	−.09
Types–HX̄	203	1	Demographics[b]	.04	
		2	[types–HX̄]	.11	
			H₁–HX̄		.29***
			H₂–HX̄		−.02
			H₃–HX̄		.11
			H₄–HX̄		−.26
			H₅–HX̄		−.12
HF–HTF	391	1	Demographics[b]	.03	
		2	HF–HTF	.04	−.08*
Types–HTX̄	318	1	Demographics[b]	.04	
		2	[types–HTX̄]	.09	
			H₁–HTX̄		.14
			H₂–HTX̄		−.15

H_3–H$\overline{X}$	−.03		H_3–HT$\overline{X}$	−.03
H_4–H$\overline{X}$	−.52***		H_4–HT$\overline{X}$	−.38*
H_5–H$\overline{X}$	−.50***		H_5–HT$\overline{X}$	−.27

* $p < .05$.
** $p < .01$.
*** $p < .001$.
[a] Variables entered in step 1 are age, education, and occupational level.
[b] Variables entered in step 1 are age, education, occupational level, and race.

Appendix C / **433**

TABLE 21.4 / "Looking back, would you say that you are happier now than you were five years ago or less happy now?"

	WHM	BHM	WHTM	BHTM	WHF	BHF	WHTF	BHTF	Pilot Study
	N=575	N=111	N=283	N=53	N=229	N=64	N=101	N=39	N=458
	%	%	%	%	%	%	%	%	%
0: Less happy now	16	26	14	8	13	16	11	13	19
1: The same	14	5	19	43	12	17	23	20	10
2: Happier now	70	69	67	49	75	67	66	67	70

Males

Comparison	N	Step	Variable(s)	R^2	b
BHM–WHM	651	1	Demographics[a]	.03	
		2	BHM–WHM	.04	−.12**
Types–$\mathrm{H\overline{X}}$	463	1	Demographics[b]	.06	
		2	[types–$\mathrm{H\overline{X}}$]	.10	
			$\mathrm{H_1}$–$\mathrm{H\overline{X}}$		.29***
			$\mathrm{H_2}$–$\mathrm{H\overline{X}}$		−.03
			$\mathrm{H_3}$–$\mathrm{H\overline{X}}$		.10
			$\mathrm{H_4}$–$\mathrm{H\overline{X}}$		−.17*
			$\mathrm{H_5}$–$\mathrm{H\overline{X}}$		−.20**
HM–HTM	960	1	Demographics[b]	.04	
		2	HM–HTM	.04	.01
Types–$\mathrm{HT\overline{X}}$	772	1	Demographics[b]	.05	
		2	[types–$\mathrm{HT\overline{X}}$]	.08	
			$\mathrm{H_1}$–$\mathrm{HT\overline{X}}$		.34**

Females

Comparison	N	Step	Variable(s)	R^2	b
BHF–WHF	277	1	Demographics[a]	.08	
		2	BHF–WHF	.09	−.06
Types–$\mathrm{H\overline{X}}$	204	1	Demographics[b]	.06	
		2	[types–$\mathrm{H\overline{X}}$]	.10	
			$\mathrm{H_1}$–$\mathrm{H\overline{X}}$		.21**
			$\mathrm{H_2}$–$\mathrm{H\overline{X}}$		−.03
			$\mathrm{H_3}$–$\mathrm{H\overline{X}}$		.11
			$\mathrm{H_4}$–$\mathrm{H\overline{X}}$		−.23
			$\mathrm{H_5}$–$\mathrm{H\overline{X}}$		−.06
HF–HTF	392	1	Demographics[b]	.06	
		2	HF–HTF	.06	.01
Types–$\mathrm{HT\overline{X}}$	319	1	Demographics[b]	.04	
		2	[types–$\mathrm{HT\overline{X}}$]	.07	
			$\mathrm{H_1}$–$\mathrm{HT\overline{X}}$		.22*

$H_2-HT\overline{X}$	.03	$H_2-HT\overline{X}$	.02
$H_3-HT\overline{X}$	.16	$H_3-HT\overline{X}$	.13
$H_4-HT\overline{X}$	-.10	$H_4-HT\overline{X}$	-.16
$H_5-HT\overline{X}$	-.15	$H_5-HT\overline{X}$	-.06

* $p < .05$.
** $p < .01$.
*** $p < .001$.
[a] Variables entered in step 1 are age, education, and occupational level.
[b] Variables entered in step 1 are age, education, occupational level, and race.

TABLE 21.5 / Exuberance

	WHM	BHM	WHTM	BHTM	WHF	BHF	WHTF	BHTF
								Pilot Study
	N=575	N=111	N=284	N=53	N=229	N=64	N=101	N=39
	%	%	%	%	%	%	%	%
0–7: Relatively low	29	29	35	23	28	22	21	23
8–9: Moderate	32	30	38	47	31	33	32	31
10–12: Relatively high	39	41	27	30	41	45	47	46

Males

Comparison	N	Step	Variable(s)	R^2	b
BHM–WHM	651	1	Demographics[a]	.02	
		2	BHM–WHM	.02	−.08
Types–$H\overline{X}$	463	1	Demographics[b]	.03	
		2	[types–$H\overline{X}$]	.09	
			H_1–$H\overline{X}$		.47*
			H_2–$H\overline{X}$		.17
			H_3–$H\overline{X}$		.76***
			H_4–$H\overline{X}$		−.92***
			H_5–$H\overline{X}$		−.48*
HM–HTM	961	1	Demographics[b]	.03	
		2	HM–HTM	.04	.22**
Types–$HT\overline{X}$	773	1	Demographics[b]	.05	
		2	[types–$HT\overline{X}$]	.10	
			H_1–$HT\overline{X}$		.88**

Females

Comparison	N	Step	Variable(s)	R^2	b
BHF–WHF	277	1	Demographics[a]	.05	
		2	BHF–WHF	.05	.11
Types–$H\overline{X}$	204	1	Demographics[b]	.06	
		2	[types–$H\overline{X}$]	.13	
			H_1–$H\overline{X}$		.45
			H_2–$H\overline{X}$		.23
			H_3–$H\overline{X}$		1.08**
			H_4–$H\overline{X}$		−1.58***
			H_5–$H\overline{X}$		−.17
HF–HTF	392	1	Demographics[b]	.03	
		2	HF–HTF	.03	−.13
Types–$HT\overline{X}$	319	1	Demographics[b]	.03	
		2	[types–$HT\overline{X}$]	.07	
			H_1–$HT\overline{X}$		.39

$H_2-HT\overline{X}$	.56*
$H_3-HT\overline{X}$	1.14***
$H_4-HT\overline{X}$	-.54
$H_5-HT\overline{X}$	-.06

$H_2-HT\overline{X}$	.26
$H_3-HT\overline{X}$	1.03*
$H_4-HT\overline{X}$	-1.45*
$H_5-HT\overline{X}$	-.35

* $p < .05$.
** $p < .01$.
*** $p < .001$.
[a] Variables entered in step 1 are age, education, and occupational level.
[b] Variables entered in step 1 are age, education, occupational level, and race.

TABLE 21.6 / Self-Acceptance

	WHM	BHM	WHTM	BHTM	WHF	BHF	WHTF	BHTF	Pilot Study
	N=575	N=111	N=284	N=53	N=229	N=64	N=100	N=39	
	%	%	%	%	%	%	%	%	
0-6: Relatively low	39	45	36	18	40	33	35	23	
7-8: Moderate	40	41	44	25	34	42	40	33	
9: Relatively high	21	14	20	57	26	25	25	44	

Males

Comparison	N	Step	Variable(s)	R^2	b
BHM-WHM	651	1	Demographics[a]	.02	
		2	BHM-WHM	.02	.04
Types-$H\overline{X}$	463	1	Demographics[b]	.03	
		2	[types-$H\overline{X}$]	.14	
			H_1-$H\overline{X}$		.75***
			H_2-$H\overline{X}$		-.03
			H_3-$H\overline{X}$		.77***
			H_4-$H\overline{X}$		-.91***
			H_5-$H\overline{X}$		-.57***
HM-HTM	961	1	Demographics[b]	.03	
		2	HM-HTM	.03	-.15*
Types-$HT\overline{X}$	773	1	Demographics[b]	.04	
		2	[types-$HT\overline{X}$]	.12	
			H_1-$HT\overline{X}$		.04

Females

Comparison	N	Step	Variable(s)	R^2	b
BHF-WHF	277	1	Demographics[a]	.01	
		2	BHF-WHF	.01	.08
Types-$H\overline{X}$	204	1	Demographics[b]	.01	
		2	[types-$H\overline{X}$]	.07	
			H_1-$H\overline{X}$		.58*
			H_2-$H\overline{X}$		-.69*
			H_3-$H\overline{X}$		.50
			H_4-$H\overline{X}$		-.64
			H_5-$H\overline{X}$		-.25
HF-HTF	392	1	Demographics[b]	.01	
		2	HF-HTF	.03	-.26*
Types-$HT\overline{X}$	319	1	Demographics[b]	.01	
		2	[types-$HT\overline{X}$]	.07	
			H_1-$HT\overline{X}$		-.07

H$_2$–HT$\overline{\text{X}}$	−.74**
H$_3$–HT$\overline{\text{X}}$	.05
H$_4$–HT$\overline{\text{X}}$	−1.60***
H$_5$–HT$\overline{\text{X}}$	−1.26***

H$_2$–HT$\overline{\text{X}}$	−1.30***
H$_3$–HT$\overline{\text{X}}$	−.15
H$_4$–HT$\overline{\text{X}}$	−1.23*
H$_5$–HT$\overline{\text{X}}$	−.43

* $p < .05$.
** $p < .01$.
*** $p < .001$.
[a] Variables entered in step 1 are age, education, and occupational level.
[b] Variables entered in step 1 are age, education, occupational level, and race.

TABLE 21.7 / "How often, if ever, during the past month have you felt very lonely?"

	WHM	BHM	WHTM	BHTM	WHF	BHF	WHTF	BHTF	Pilot Study
	N=575	N=111	N=284	N=53	N=229	N=64	N=101	N=39	N=458
	%	%	%	%	%	%	%	%	%
0: Never	26	15	31	34	40	22	31	21	22
1: Rarely	37	32	37	49	24	33	35	33	33
2: Sometimes	24	34	25	13	18	30	22	33	23
3: Often	14	19	7	4	18	16	13	13	22

Males

Comparison	N	Step	Variable(s)	R^2	b
BHM–WHM	651	1	Demographics[a]	.02	
		2	BHM–WHM	.03	.14**
Types–$\overline{HX}$	463	1	Demographics[b]	.04	
		2	[types–$\overline{HX}$]	.22	
			H_1–$\overline{HX}$		−.51***
			H_2–$\overline{HX}$		−.32***
			H_3–$\overline{HX}$		−.19*
			H_4–$\overline{HX}$		.60***
			H_5–$\overline{HX}$		.42***
HM–HTM	961	1	Demographics[b]	.02	
		2	HM–HTM	.03	.13***
Types–$\overline{HTX}$	773	1	Demographics[b]	.02	
		2	[types–$\overline{HTX}$]	.15	
			H_1–$\overline{HTX}$		−.04

Females

Comparison	N	Step	Variable(s)	R^2	b
BHF–WHF	277	1	Demographics[a]	.01	
		2	BHF–WHF	.02	.17*
Types–$\overline{HX}$	204	1	Demographics[b]	.03	
		2	[types–$\overline{HX}$]	.17	
			H_1–$\overline{HX}$		−.57***
			H_2–$\overline{HX}$		−.00
			H_3–$\overline{HX}$		−.21
			H_4–$\overline{HX}$		.10
			H_5–$\overline{HX}$		.67***
HF–HTF	392	1	Demographics[b]	.02	
		2	HF–HTF	.02	—[c]
Types–$\overline{HTX}$	319	1	Demographics[b]	.03	
		2	[types–$\overline{HTX}$]	.13	
			H_1–$\overline{HTX}$		−.47**

H_2–HT$\overline{X}$	.15	.07
H_3–HT$\overline{X}$	.29*	–.11
H_4–HT$\overline{X}$	1.07***	.17
H_5–HT$\overline{X}$	.88***	.77***

* $p < .05$.
** $p < .01$.
*** $p < .001$.
[a] Variables entered in step 1 are age, education, and occupational level.
[b] Variables entered in step 1 are age, education, occupational level, and race.
[c] F is too small for program to compute; difference is not significant.

TABLE 21.8 / "Generally speaking, are you the type of person who worries a great deal, somewhat, very little, or not at all?"

	WHM	BHM	WHTM	BHTM	WHF	BHF	WHTF	BHTF	Pilot Study
	N=574	N=111	N=284	N=53	N=229	N=64	N=101	N=39	N=458
	%	%	%	%	%	%	%	%	%
0: Not at all	4	6	5	23	3	11	1	5	2
1: Very little	25	27	32	51	24	17	26	20	24
2: Somewhat	43	41	48	24	44	42	50	44	43
3: A great deal	28	26	15	2	29	30	23	31	31

Males

Comparison	N	Step	Variable(s)	R^2	b
BHM–WHM	650	1	Demographics[a]	.02	
		2	BHM–WHM	.02	−.11*
Types–$\overline{\text{HX}}$	462	1	Demographics[b]	.03	
		2	[types–$\overline{\text{HX}}$]	.09	
			H_1–$\overline{\text{HX}}$		−.02
			H_2–$\overline{\text{HX}}$		−.03
			H_3–$\overline{\text{HX}}$		−.32***
			H_4–$\overline{\text{HX}}$		.35***
			H_5–$\overline{\text{HX}}$		.03
HM–HTM	960	1	Demographics[b]	.03	
		2	HM–HTM	.06	.16***
Types–$\overline{\text{HTX}}$	772	1	Demographics[b]	.04	
		2	[types–$\overline{\text{HTX}}$]	.11	
			H_1–$\overline{\text{HTX}}$		.47***

Females

Comparison	N	Step	Variable(s)	R^2	b
BHF–WHF	277	1	Demographics[a]	.00	
		2	BHF–WHF	.00	−.02
Types–$\overline{\text{HX}}$	204	1	Demographics[b]	.01	
		2	[types–$\overline{\text{HX}}$]	.04	
			H_1–$\overline{\text{HX}}$		−.13
			H_2–$\overline{\text{HX}}$		.08
			H_3–$\overline{\text{HX}}$		−.24
			H_4–$\overline{\text{HX}}$		.09
			H_5–$\overline{\text{HX}}$		.19
HF–HTF	392	1	Demographics[b]	.01	
		2	HF–HTF	.01	.01

H_2–HT$\overline{X}$	.47***
H_3–HT$\overline{X}$	.19
H_4–HT$\overline{X}$	.85***
H_5–HT$\overline{X}$	.53***

* $p < .05$.
*** $p < .001$.
[a] Variables entered in step 1 are age, education, and occupational level.
[b] Variables entered in step 1 are age, education, occupational level, and race.

TABLE 21.9 / Depression

	WHM	BHM	WHTM	BHTM	WHF	BHF	WHTF	BHTF	Pilot Study
	N=575	N=111	N=284	N=53	N=229	N=64	N=101	N=39	
	%	%	%	%	%	%	%	%	
0–5: Relatively low	30	29	32	57	27	27	38	33	
6–8: Moderate	33	29	39	30	35	27	29	26	
9–19: Relatively high	37	42	29	13	38	46	34	41	

Males

Comparison	N	Step	Variable(s)	R^2	b
BHM–WHM	651	1	Demographics[a]	.03	
		2	BHM–WHM	.03	–.12
Types–H$\overline{\text{X}}$	463	1	Demographics[b]	.03	
		2	[types–H$\overline{\text{X}}$]	.17	
			H_1–H$\overline{\text{X}}$		–1.88***
			H_2–H$\overline{\text{X}}$		.01
			H_3–H$\overline{\text{X}}$		–1.34***
			H_4–H$\overline{\text{X}}$		1.92***
			H_5–H$\overline{\text{X}}$		1.30***
HM–HTM	961	1	Demographics[b]	.03	
		2	HM–HTM	.04	.37**
Types–HT$\overline{\text{X}}$	773	1	Demographics[b]	.04	
		2	[types–HT$\overline{\text{X}}$]	.14	
			H_1–HT$\overline{\text{X}}$		–.72

Females

Comparison	N	Step	Variable(s)	R^2	b
BHF–WHF	277	1	Demographics[a]	.02	
		2	BHF–WHF	.02	.22
Types–H$\overline{\text{X}}$	204	1	Demographics[b]	.02	
		2	[types–H$\overline{\text{X}}$]	.10	
			H_1–H$\overline{\text{X}}$		–1.39***
			H_2–H$\overline{\text{X}}$		.53
			H_3–H$\overline{\text{X}}$		–1.15*
			H_4–H$\overline{\text{X}}$		1.16
			H_5–H$\overline{\text{X}}$		.85
HF–HTF	392	1	Demographics[b]	.04	
		2	HF–HTF	.04	.24
Types–HT$\overline{\text{X}}$	319	1	Demographics[b]	.04	
		2	[types–HT$\overline{\text{X}}$]	.10	
			H_1–HT$\overline{\text{X}}$		–.94

H_2–HT$\overline{X}$	1.17**
H_3–HT$\overline{X}$	-.17
H_4–HT$\overline{X}$	3.07***
H_5–HT$\overline{X}$	2.47***

H_2–HT$\overline{X}$	.92
H_3–HT$\overline{X}$	-.71
H_4–HT$\overline{X}$	1.50
H_5–HT$\overline{X}$	1.36

* $p < .05$.
** $p < .01$.
*** $p < .001$.
[a] Variables entered in step 1 are age, education and occupational level.
[b] Variables entered in step 1 are age, education, occupational level, and race.

TABLE 21.10 / Tension

	WHM	BHM	WHTM	BHTM	WHF	BHF	WHTF	BHTF	Pilot Study
	N=575	N=111	N=284	N=53	N=229	N=64	N=101	N=39	N=457
	%	%	%	%	%	%	%	%	%
0-2: Relatively low	28	20	31	47	37	22	40	15	12
3-4: Moderate	34	24	38	28	32	28	29	36	29
5-9: Relatively high	38	56	31	25	31	50	31	49	59

Males

Comparison	N	Step	Variable(s)	R^2	b
BHM-WHM	651	1	Demographics[a]	.08	
		2	BHM-WHM	.08	.24*
Types-$\overline{HX}$	463	1	Demographics[b]	.10	
		2	[types-$\overline{HX}$]	.15	
			H_1-$\overline{HX}$		-.81***
			H_2-$\overline{HX}$		-.09
			H_3-$\overline{HX}$		-.33
			H_4-$\overline{HX}$		.81***
			H_5-$\overline{HX}$		.42*
HM-HTM	961	1	Demographics[b]	.06	
		2	HM-HTM	.07	.24***
Types-$\overline{HTX}$	773	1	Demographics[b]	.07	
		2	[types-$\overline{HTX}$]	.13	
			H_1-$\overline{HTX}$		.29

Females

Comparison	N	Step	Variable(s)	R^2	b
BHF-WHF	277	1	Demographics[a]	.05	
		2	BHF-WHF	.08	.54***
Types-$\overline{HX}$	204	1	Demographics[b]	.09	
		2	[types-$\overline{HX}$]	.14	
			H_1-$\overline{HX}$		-.80**
			H_2-$\overline{HX}$		.21
			H_3-$\overline{HX}$		.13
			H_4-$\overline{HX}$		-.14
			H_5-$\overline{HX}$		.61
HF-HTF	392	1	Demographics[b]	.09	
		2	HF-HTF	.09	.04
Types-$\overline{HTX}$	319	1	Demographics[b]	.10	
		2	[types-$\overline{HTX}$]	.13	
			H_1-$\overline{HTX}$		-.47

H_2–H1X	1.03***
H_3–HT$\overline{X}$	.79**
H_4–HT$\overline{X}$	1.95***
H_5–HT$\overline{X}$	1.49***

H_2–HT$\overline{X}$	.55
H_3–HT$\overline{X}$	.47
H_4–HT$\overline{X}$	.22
H_5–HT$\overline{X}$	.95*

* $p < .05$.
** $p < .01$.
*** $p < .001$.
[a] Variables entered in step 1 are age, education, and occupational level.
[b] Variables entered in step 1 are age, education, occupational level, and race.

TABLE 21.11 / Paranoia

	WHM	BHM	WHTM	BHTM	WHF	BHF	WHTF	BHTF	Pilot Study
	N=575	N=111	N=284	N=53	N=229	N=64	N=101	N=39	
	%	%	%	%	%	%	%	%	
0-2: Relatively low	25	12	26	26	31	22	27	21	
3-4: Moderate	33	32	41	32	37	22	39	33	
5-9: Relatively high	42	56	33	42	32	56	34	46	

Males

Comparison	N	Step	Variable(s)	R^2	b
BHM-WHM	651	1	Demographics[a]	.07	
		2	BHM-WHM	.08	.20
Types-H$\overline{X}$	463	1	Demographics[b]	.09	
		2	[types-H$\overline{X}$]	.14	
			H_1-H$\overline{X}$		-.44*
			H_2-H$\overline{X}$		-.15
			H_3-H$\overline{X}$		-.57**
			H_4-H$\overline{X}$		.77***
			H_5-H$\overline{X}$		.39*
HM-HTM	961	1	Demographics[b]	.07	
		2	HM-HTM	.08	.15*
Types-HT$\overline{X}$	773	1	Demographics[b]	.08	
		2	[types-HT$\overline{X}$]	.11	
			H_1-HT$\overline{X}$		.09

Females

Comparison	N	Step	Variable(s)	R^2	b
BHF-WHF	277	1	Demographics[a]	.11	
		2	BHF-WHF	.15	.55****
Types-H$\overline{X}$	204	1	Demographics[b]	.21	
		2	[types-H$\overline{X}$]	.24	
			H_1-H$\overline{X}$		-.64*
			H_2-H$\overline{X}$		.23
			H_3-H$\overline{X}$		-.15
			H_4-H$\overline{X}$		.18
			H_5-H$\overline{X}$		.39
HF-HTF	392	1	Demographics[b]	.11	
		2	HF-HTF	.11	.14
Types-HT$\overline{X}$	319	1	Demographics[b]	.14	
		2	[types-HT$\overline{X}$]	.18	
			H_1-HT$\overline{X}$		.13

$H_2 - HT\overline{X}$	.50
$H_3 - HT\overline{X}$	-.05
$H_4 - HT\overline{X}$	1.24***
$H_5 - HT\overline{X}$	.90**

$H_2 - HT\overline{X}$	1.05***
$H_3 - HT\overline{X}$	.66
$H_4 - HT\overline{X}$	1.05
$H_5 - HT\overline{X}$	1.01*

* $p < .05$.
** $p < .01$.
*** $p < .001$.
[a] Variables entered in step 1 are age, education, and occupational level.
[b] Variables entered in step 1 are age, education, occupational level, and race.

TABLE 21.12 / Suicidal Feelings and Impulses

	WHM	BHM	WHTM	BHTM	WHF	BHF	WHTF	BHTF (Pilot Study)
	N=575	N=111	N=284	N=53	N=229	N=64	N=101	N=39
	%	%	%	%	%	%	%	%
0: Never imagined	26	37	43	77	25	39	36	45
1: Imagined, but never seriously considered	37	39	44	21	34	36	39	37
2: Seriously considered, but never attempted	19	4	10	0	16	8	16	3
3: Attempted at least once	18	20	3	2	25	17	10	16

Males

Comparison	N	Step	Variable(s)	R^2	b
BHM–WHM	651	1	Demographics[a]	.02	
		2	BHM–WHM	.03	−.20***
Types–$\overline{\text{HX}}$	463	1	Demographics[b]	.03	
		2	[types–$\overline{\text{HX}}$]	.03	
			H_1–$\overline{\text{HX}}$		−.00
			H_2–$\overline{\text{HX}}$		−.08
			H_3–$\overline{\text{HX}}$		−.07
			H_4–$\overline{\text{HX}}$		.13
			H_5–$\overline{\text{HX}}$		.03
HM–HTM	961	1	Demographics[b]	.04	
		2	HM–HTM	.12	.21***

Females

Comparison	N	Step	Variable(s)	R^2	b
BHF–WHF	277	1	Demographics[a]	.02	
		2	BHF–WHF	.04	−.21*
Types–$\overline{\text{HX}}$	204	1	Demographics[b]	.04	
		2	[types–$\overline{\text{HX}}$]	.07	
			H_1–$\overline{\text{HX}}$		−.22
			H_2–$\overline{\text{HX}}$		−.06
			H_3–$\overline{\text{HX}}$		−.06
			H_4–$\overline{\text{HX}}$		−.05
			H_5–$\overline{\text{HX}}$		.38*
HF–HTF	391	1	Demographics[b]	.04	
		2	HF–HTF	.06	.18**

Types–HTX	318	1	Demographics[b]	.05
		2	[types–HTX]	.09
			H_1–HTX	.13
			H_2–HTX	.28
			H_3–HTX	.29
			H_4–HTX	.30
			H_5–HTX	.72***

* $p < .05$.
** $p < .01$.
*** $p < .001$.
[a] Variables entered in step 1 are age, education, and occupational level.
[b] Variables entered in step 1 are age, education, occupational level, and race.

TABLE 21.13 / "What were the reasons you considered it [suicide]?"[a]

	WHM	BHM	WHTM	BHTM	WHF	BHF	WHTF	BHTF (Pilot Study)
	N=212	N=27	N=36	N=1	N=92	N=16	N=26	N=8
	%	%	%	%	%	%	%	%
Distress not related to homosexuality	57	52	100	100	66	88	100	100
Difficulty with sociosexual homosexual adjustment (external)	26	41	0	0	36	12	0	0
Acceptance of one's homosexuality (internal)	18	7	0	0	7	6	0	0
Other reasons	16	19	0	0	8	0	0	0

Males

Comparison	N	X^2
WH–BH	1652	6.35
H_1–$H^†$	1156	1.19
H_2–$H^†$	1156	1.34
H_3–$H^†$	1156	.55
H_4–$H^†$	1156	1.37
H_5–$H^†$	1156	3.73
H–HT	2363	58.17***

Females

Comparison	N	X^2
WH–BH	710	5.46
H_1–$H^†$	503	1.90
H_2–$H^†$	503	1.24
H_3–$H^†$	503	1.15
H_4–$H^†$	503	1.81
H_5–$H^†$	503	6.76
H–HT	1024	19.40***

*** $p < .001$.
† Excluding the subgroup being compared.
[a] Respondents could give more than one answer to this question, so column percentages may not add up to 100%; this inflates the chi-square, but not substantially.

TABLE 21.14 / "How many times have you tried it [suicide]?"

	WHM	BHM	WHTM	BHTM	WHF	BHF	WHTF	BHTF	Pilot Study
	N=575	N=111	N=284	N=53	N=229	N=64	N=101	N=38	N=458
	%	%	%	%	%	%	%	%	%
0: None	82	80	97	98	75	83	90	84	82
1: One time	11	13	2	2	18	11	7	13	12
2–87: Two or more times	7	7	1	0	7	6	3	3	6

Males

Comparison	N	Step	Variable(s)	R^2	b
BHM–WHM	651	1	Demographics[a]	.02	
		2	BHM–WHM	.02	−.09
Types–H$\overline{X}$	463	1	Demographics[b]	.04	
		2	[types–H$\overline{X}$]	.04	
			H_1–H$\overline{X}$		.07
			H_2–H$\overline{X}$		−.12
			H_3–H$\overline{X}$		.02
			H_4–H$\overline{X}$		.04
			H_5–H$\overline{X}$		−.01
HM–HTM	961	1	Demographics[b]	.02	
		2	HM–HTM	.05	.15***

Females

Comparison	N	Step	Variable(s)	R^2	b
BHF–WHF	277	1	Demographics[a]	.00	
		2	BHF–WHF	.01	−.10
Types–H$\overline{X}$	204	1	Demographics[b]	.01	
		2	[types–H$\overline{X}$]	.03	
			H_1–H$\overline{X}$		−.09
			H_2–H$\overline{X}$		.10
			H_3–H$\overline{X}$		.07
			H_4–H$\overline{X}$		−.24
			H_5–H$\overline{X}$		.17
HF–HTF	391	1	Demographics[b]	.01	
		2	HF–HTF	.01	.07

*** $p < .001$.
[a] Variables entered in step 1 are age, education, and occupational level.
[b] Variables entered in step 1 are age, education, occupational level, and race.

TABLE 21.15 / "How old were you when you tried it [suicide] the first time?"

	WHM	BHM	WHTM	BHTM	WHF	BHF	WHTF	BHTF	Pilot Study BHTF
	N=105	N=22	N=9	N=1	N=58	N=11	N=10	N=7	N=7
	%	%	%	%	%	%	%	%	%
1-17: 17 or younger	27	32	11	0	21	36	50	43	43
18-20: 18-20	25	27	11	100	21	18	10	0	0
21-25: 21-25	27	23	56	0	29	27	20	43	43
26-87: 26 or older	22	18	22	0	29	18	20	14	14

Males

Comparison	N	Step	Variable(s)	R^2	b
BHM-WHM	124	1	Demographics[a]	.32	
		2	BHM-WHM	.32	.63
Types-$\overline{HX}$	85	1	Demographics[b]	.34	
		2	[types-$\overline{HX}$]	.36	
			H_1-$\overline{HX}$		1.73
			H_2-$\overline{HX}$		.30
			H_3-$\overline{HX}$		.20
			H_4-$\overline{HX}$		.12
			H_5-$\overline{HX}$		-2.34
HM-HTM	133	1	Demographics[b]	.32	
		2	HM-HTM	.32	-.57

Females

Comparison	N	Step	Variable(s)	R^2	b
BHF-WHF	65	1	Demographics[a]	.17	
		2	BHF-WHF	.17	-.34
Types-$\overline{HX}$	46	1	Demographics[b]	.14	
		2	[types-$\overline{HX}$]	.21	
			H_1-$\overline{HX}$		1.04
			H_2-$\overline{HX}$		-2.01
			H_3-$\overline{HX}$		3.04
			H_4-$\overline{HX}$		-.22
			H_5-$\overline{HX}$		-1.84
HF-HTF	79	1	Demographics[b]	.18	
		2	HF-HTF	.18	-.39

[a] Variables entered in step 1 are age, education, and occupational level.
[b] Variables entered in step 1 are age, education, occupational level, and race.

TABLE 21.16 / "What were the reasons you tried it [suicide] the first time?"[a]

	WHM	BHM	WHTM	BHTM	WHF	BHF	WHTF	BHTF	Pilot Study
	N=105	N=22	N=8	N=1	N=57	N=11	N=10	N=7	N=75
	%	%	%	%	%	%	%	%	%
Distress not related to homosexuality	48	59	100	100	58	82	100	100	29
Difficulty with sociosexual homosexual adjustment (external)	38	46	0	0	51	0	0	0	25
Acceptance of one's homosexuality (internal)	16	9	0	0	4	9	0	0	3
Other reasons	16	9	0	0	5	9	0	0	43

Males

Comparison	N	X^2
WH–BH	1523	1.87
H_1–$H^\dagger$	1077	5.32
H_2–$H^\dagger$	1077	5.28
H_3–$H^\dagger$	1077	1.16
H_4–$H^\dagger$	1077	4.52
H_5–$H^\dagger$	1077	1.73
H–HT	2206	45.14***

Females

Comparison	N	X^2
WH–BH	664	8.27*
H_1–$H^\dagger$	474	3.84
H_2–$H^\dagger$	474	1.71
H_3–$H^\dagger$	474	4.85
H_4–$H^\dagger$	474	.36
H_5–$H^\dagger$	474	2.26
H–HT	961	15.10**

* $p < .05$.
** $p < .01$.
*** $p < .001$.
† Excluding the subgroup being compared.
a Respondents could give more than one answer to this question, so column percentages may not add up to 100%; this inflates the chi-square, but not substantially.

TABLE 21.17 / "Did this [first suicide attempt] have anything to do with the fact that you are homosexual?"

	WHM	BHM	WHF	BHF	Pilot Study
	N=105	N=22	N=68	N=11	N=78
	%	%	%	%	%
0: No	38	59	59	73	24
1: Yes	62	41	41	27	76

Males

Comparison	N	Step	Variable(s)	R^2	b
BHM–WHM	124	1	Demographics[a]	.03	
		2	BHM–WHM	.05	−.09
Types–$\overline{HX}$	85	1	Demographics[b]	.05	
		2	[types–$\overline{HX}$]	.14	
			H_1–$\overline{HX}$		−.15
			H_2–$\overline{HX}$		.04
			H_3–$\overline{HX}$		.07
			H_4–$\overline{HX}$		.23*
			H_5–$\overline{HX}$		−.19

Females

Comparison	N	Step	Variable(s)	R^2	b
BHF–WHF	65	1	Demographics[a]	.08	
		2	BHF–WHF	.10	−.08
Types–$\overline{HX}$	46	1	Demographics[b]	.21	
		2	[types–$\overline{HX}$]	.27	
			H_1–$\overline{HX}$		−.02
			H_2–$\overline{HX}$		.09
			H_3–$\overline{HX}$		−.25
			H_4–$\overline{HX}$		.29
			H_5–$\overline{HX}$		−.10

* $p < .05$.
[a] Variables entered in step 1 are age, education, and occupational level.
[b] Variables entered in step 1 are age, education, occupational level, and race.

TABLE 21.18 / "In what way [was homosexuality involved in first suicide attempt]?"

	WHM	BHM	WHF	BHF	Pilot Study
	N=65	N=9	N=23	N=3	
	%	%	%	%	%
Problems generated in a homosexual relationship (breaking up with partner, etc.)	43	33	67	33	
General homosexual adjustment (acceptance of one's homosexuality, etc.)	37	56	21	67	
Other (social, legal, parental problems, etc.)	20	11	8	0	

Males

Comparison	N	X^2
WH–BH	‡	‡
H_1–H†	‡	‡
H_2–H†	‡	‡
H_3–H†	47	1.50
H_4–H†	47	1.00
H_5–H†	‡	‡

Females

Comparison	N	X^2
WH–BH	‡	‡
H_1–H†	‡	‡
H_2–H†	‡	‡
H_3–H†	‡	‡
H_4–H†	‡	‡
H_5–H†	‡	‡

† Excluding the subgroup being compared.
‡ Relevant cases were too few to permit meaningful comparison.

TABLE 21.19 / "Were there any important changes in your private life that resulted from this [first suicide attempt]?"

	WHM	BHM	WHTM	BHTM	WHF	BHF	WHTF	BHTF Pilot Study
	N=105	N=22	N=9	N=1	N=58	N=11	N=10	N=7
	%	%	%	%	%	%	%	%
0: No	44	41	44	0	45	45	60	71
1: Yes	56	59	56	100	55	55	40	29

Males

Comparison	N	Step	Variable(s)	R^2	b
BHM-WHM	124	1	Demographics[a]	.01	
		2	BHM-WHM	.01	.01
Types-$\overline{HX}$	85	1	Demographics[b]	.00	
		2	[types-$\overline{HX}$]	.05	
			H_1-$\overline{HX}$		.14
			H_2-$\overline{HX}$		-.07
			H_3-$\overline{HX}$		.09
			H_4-$\overline{HX}$		.04
			H_5-$\overline{HX}$		-.20
HM-HTM	131	1	Demographics[b]	.02	
		2	HM-HTM	.02	-.05

Females

Comparison	N	Step	Variable(s)	R^2	b
BHF-WHF	65	1	Demographics[a]	.02	
		2	BHF-WHF	.02	—[c]
Types-$\overline{HX}$	46	1	Demographics[b]	.01	
		2	[types-$\overline{HX}$]	.06	
			H_1-$\overline{HX}$		.19
			H_2-$\overline{HX}$		.07
			H_3-$\overline{HX}$		-.02
			H_4-$\overline{HX}$		-.09
			H_5-$\overline{HX}$		-.16
HF-HTF	79	1	Demographics[b]	.02	
		2	HF-HTF	.03	.08

[a] Variables entered in step 1 are age, education, and occupational level.
[b] Variables entered in step 1 are age, education, occupational level, and race.
[c] F is too small for program to compute; difference is not significant.

TABLE 21.20 / "What were these changes [resulting in your life from your first suicide attempt]?"[a]

	WHM	BHM	WHTM	BHTM	WHF	BHF	WHTF	BHTF	Pilot Study BHTF
	N=59	N=13	N=5	N=1	N=31	N=6	N=4	N=2	N=2
	%	%	%	%	%	%	%	%	%
Got a different view, a different perspective	54	46	80	0	68	83	75	0	
Others became more compassionate toward me	12	8	0	100	10	0	0	50	
Got professional help	12	15	0	100	19	17	50	0	
Other changes	46	62	40	0	45	17	25	50	

Males

Comparison	N	X^2
WH–BH	52	.43
H_1–H[†]	‡	‡
H_2–H[†]	‡	‡
H_3–H[†]	38	1.06
H_4–H[†]	‡	‡
H_5–H[†]	‡	‡
H–HT	‡	‡

Females

Comparison	N	X^2
WH–BH	‡	‡
H_1–H[†]	‡	‡
H_2–H[†]	‡	‡
H_3–H[†]	‡	‡
H_4–H[†]	‡	‡
H_5–H[†]	‡	‡
H–HT	‡	‡

[†] Excluding the subgroup being compared.

[‡] Relevant cases were too few to permit meaningful comparison.

[a] Respondents could give more than one answer to this question, so column percentages may add up to more than 100%; this inflates the chi-square, but not substantially.

TABLE 21.21 / Number of Times Consulted Professional

	WHM	BHM	WHTM	BHTM	WHF	BHF	WHTF	BHTF	Pilot Study
	N=574	N=106	N=283	N=52	N=228	N=64	N=99	N=39	N=458
	%	%	%	%	%	%	%	%	%
0: Never	42	52	70	87	32	42	60	59	49
1: Once	28	30	18	13	26	30	19	31	28
2: Twice	16	14	8	0	18	14	11	5	12
3: Three times	9	3	3	0	14	11	6	3	6
4: Four or more times	5	1	1	0	10	3	4	3	5

Males

Comparison	N	Step	Variable(s)	R^2	b
BHM–WHM	645	1	Demographics[a]	.03	
		2	BHM–WHM	.05	−.25***
Types–HX̄	460	1	Demographics[b]	.07	
		2	[types–HX̄]	.09	
			H_1–HX̄		−.04
			H_2–HX̄		−.23*
			H_3–HX̄		−.02
			H_4–HX̄		.19
			H_5–HX̄		.10
HM–HTM	953	1	Demographics[b]	.05	
		2	HM–HTM	.12	.31***
Types–HTX̄	768	1	Demographics[b]	.01	
		2	[types–HTX̄]	.16	
			H_1–HTX̄		.58***
			H_2–HTX̄		.39**
			H_3–HTX̄		.50***

Females

Comparison	N	Step	Variable(s)	R^2	b
BHF–WHF	276	1	Demographics[a]	.01	
		2	BHF–WHF	.02	−.15
Types–HX̄	203	1	Demographics[b]	.04	
		2	[types–HX̄]	.07	
			H_1–HX̄		−.39*
			H_2–HX̄		.02
			H_3–HX̄		−.09
			H_4–HX̄		.25
			H_5–HX̄		.22
HF–HTF	389	1	Demographics[b]	.03	
		2	HF–HTF	.07	.29***
Types–HTX̄	316	1	Demographics[b]	.06	
		2	[types–HTX̄]	.11	
			H_1–HTX̄		.17
			H_2–HTX̄		.61**

H4–HTX	.8/*
H5–HTX	.71**

| H4–HTX | .82*** |
| H5–HTX | .71*** |

| H4–HTX | .8?* |
| H5–HTX | .71** |

* $p < .05$.   ** $p < .01$.   *** $p < .001$.
[a] Variables entered in step 1 are age, education, and occupational level.
[b] Variables entered in step 1 are age, education, occupational level, and race.

TABLE 21.22 / "[If you ever consulted a professional,] was it [ever] to give up your homosexuality?"

	WHM	BHM	WHF	BHF	Pilot Study
	N=334	N=56	N=156	N=37	
	%	%	%	%	
0: No	77	77	82	89	
1: Yes	23	23	18	11	

Males

Comparison	N	Step	Variable(s)	R^2	b
BHM–WHM	370	1	Demographics[a]	.03	
		2	BHM–WHM	.03	–.00
Types–HX	266	1	Demographics[b]	.04	
		2	[types–HX]	.05	
			H1–HX		–.00
			H2–HX		–.08
			H3–HX		.03
			H4–HX		.03
			H5–HX		.02

Females

Comparison	N	Step	Variable(s)	R^2	b
BHF–WHF	181	1	Demographics[a]	.00	
		2	BHF–WHF	.00	–.02
Types–HX	132	1	Demographics[b]	.02	
		2	[types–HX]	.08	
			H1–HX		–.06
			H2–HX		.01
			H3–HX		–.13
			H4–HX		–.01
			H5–HX		.19*

* $p < .05$.
[a] Variables entered in step 1 are age, education, and occupational level.
[b] Variables entered in step 1 are age, education, occupational level, and race.

TABLE 21.23 / "How old were you the first time [you consulted a professional]?"

	WHM	BHM	WHTM	BHTM	WHF	BHF	WHTF	BHTF	Pilot Study
	N=336	N=56	N=85	N=8	N=156	N=37	N=42	N=16	N=236
	%	%	%	%	%	%	%	%	%
1–18: 18 or younger	26	45	28	38	23	16	17	12	23
19–21: 19–21	24	27	20	38	23	22	19	6	29
22–29: 22–29	26	18	29	25	32	43	38	81	36
30–87: 30 or older	24	11	22	0	22	19	26	0	13

Males

Comparison	N	Step	Variable(s)	R^2	b
BHM–WHM	372	1	Demographics[a]	.41	
		2	BHM–WHM	.41	.47
Types–$H\overline{X}$	267	1	Demographics[b]	.39	
		2	[types–$H\overline{X}$]	.40	
			H_1–$H\overline{X}$		−1.08
			H_2–$H\overline{X}$		1.44
			H_3–$H\overline{X}$		−1.02
			H_4–$H\overline{X}$		−.23
			H_5–$H\overline{X}$		.88
HM–HTM	455	1	Demographics[b]	.43	
		2	HM–HTM	.43	−.92*

Females

Comparison	N	Step	Variable(s)	R^2	b
BHF–WHF	181	1	Demographics[a]	.40	
		2	BHF–WHF	.41	.97
Types–$H\overline{X}$	132	1	Demographics[b]	.42	
		2	[types–$H\overline{X}$]	.43	
			H_1–$H\overline{X}$		.30
			H_2–$H\overline{X}$		−1.21
			H_3–$H\overline{X}$		1.19
			H_4–$H\overline{X}$		.59
			H_5–$H\overline{X}$		−.87
HF–HTF	229	1	Demographics[b]	.43	
		2	HF–HTF	.44	−.93*

* $p < .05$.
[a] Variables entered in step 1 are age, education, and occupational level.
[b] Variables entered in step 1 are age, education, occupational level, and race.

TABLE 21.24 / "What was your reason for going [to a professional the first time]?"

	WHM	BHM	WHTM	BHTM	WHF	BHF	WHTF	BHTF	Pilot Study
	N=335	N=55	N=85	N=8	N=156	N=36	N=42	N=16	N=218
	%	%	%	%	%	%	%	%	%
Problems connected with homosexuality	44	53	5	0	43	39	0	0	53
Ordered or forced to go	24	13	11	12	14	14	7	6	13
Feelings of distress not connected with homosexuality	11	9	32	25	15	25	19	38	13
Other (situational or adjustment problems, etc.)	21	25	53	62	28	22	74	56	21

Males

Comparison	N	X^2
WH–BH	390	3.85
H_1–H†	275	1.59
H_2–H†	275	3.46
H_3–H†	275	.59
H_4–H†	275	3.15
H_5–H†	275	.18
H–HT	483	87.39***

Females

Comparison	N	X^2
WH–BH	192	2.35
H_1–H†	136	1.41
H_2–H†	136	6.11
H_3–H†	136	11.40**
H_4–H†	136	2.31
H_5–H†	136	6.33
H–HT	250	48.90***

** $p < .01$.
*** $p < .001$.
† Excluding the subgroup being compared.

TABLE 21.25 / "How many times did you see [the professional, the first time]?"

	WHM	BHM	WHTM	BHTM	WHF	BHF	WHTF	BHTF	Pilot Study
	N=334	N=56	N=85	N=7	N=153	N=37	N=42	N=16	N=235
	%	%	%	%	%	%	%	%	%
0: Just once	24	29	26	43	18	22	21	19	22
1: 2–5 times	22	29	24	14	16	19	21	50	19
2: 6–12 times	18	20	20	29	15	27	29	6	16
3: 13–16 times	5	0	4	0	5	3	0	0	2
4: 17–21 times	2	4	2	14	2	5	0	6	1
5: 22–49 times	12	9	6	0	16	14	10	12	15
6: 50–99 times	6	9	4	0	17	3	10	0	13
7: 100 or more times	11	2	15	0	12	8	10	6	12

Males

Comparison	N	Step	Variable(s)	R^2	b
BHM–WHM	371	1	Demographics[a]	.02	
		2	BHM–WHM	.03	−.36
Types–$\overline{HX}$	266	1	Demographics[b]	.02	
		2	[types–$\overline{HX}$]	.03	
			H_1–$\overline{HX}$		−.21
			H_2–$\overline{HX}$		.24
			H_3–$\overline{HX}$		−.13
			H_4–$\overline{HX}$		.02
			H_5–$\overline{HX}$		.07
HM–HTM	453	1	Demographics[b]	.03	
		2	HM–HTM	.03	.04

Females

Comparison	N	Step	Variable(s)	R^2	b
BHF–WHF	178	1	Demographics[a]	.04	
		2	BHF–WHF	.06	−.43
Types–$\overline{HX}$	129	1	Demographics[b]	.07	
		2	[types–$\overline{HX}$]	.12	
			H_1–$\overline{HX}$		−.31
			H_2–$\overline{HX}$		−.14
			H_3–$\overline{HX}$		.42
			H_4–$\overline{HX}$		1.24*
			H_5–$\overline{HX}$		−1.21*
HF–HTF	226	1	Demographics[b]	.05	
		2	HF–HTF	.06	.26

Types–HTX	177	1	Demographics[b]	.06
		2	[types–HTX]	.11
			H_1–HTX	.30
			H_2–HTX	.43
			H_3–HTX	1.04
			H_4–HTX	1.82*
			H_5–HTX	-.59

* $p < .05$.
[a] Variables entered in step 1 are age, education, and occupational level.
[b] Variables entered in step 1 are age, education, occupational level, and race.

TABLE 21.26 / "[The first time,] did the meetings [with the professional] help you a great deal, somewhat, very little, or not at all?"

	WHM	BHM	WHTM	BHTM	WHF	BHF	WHTF	BHTF	Pilot Study
	N=335	N=56	N=85	N=8	N=155	N=39	N=42	N=18	N=235
	%	%	%	%	%	%	%	%	%
0: Not at all	33	39	32	25	32	27	14	31	28
1: Very little	16	9	24	0	21	11	12	6	15
2: Somewhat	22	34	26	38	23	32	29	44	30
3: A great deal	28	18	19	38	25	30	45	19	27

Males

Comparison	N	Step	Variable(s)	R^2	b
BHM-WHM	371	1	Demographics[a]	.01	
		2	BHM-WHM	.01	-.08
Types-$H\overline{X}$	266	1	Demographics[b]	.01	
		2	[types-$H\overline{X}$]	.04	
			H_1-$H\overline{X}$		.33
			H_2-$H\overline{X}$		.09
			H_3-$H\overline{X}$		-.32*
			H_4-$H\overline{X}$		.14
			H_5-$H\overline{X}$		-.24
HM-HTM	454	1	Demographics[b]	.01	
		2	HM-HTM	.01	.04
Types-$HT\overline{X}$	349	1	Demographics[b]	.01	
		2	[types-$HT\overline{X}$]	.04	
			H_1-$HT\overline{X}$		.17

Females

Comparison	N	Step	Variable(s)	R^2	b
BHF-WHF	180	1	Demographics[a]	.03	
		2	BHF-WHF	.04	.16
Types-$H\overline{X}$	131	1	Demographics[b]	.02	
		2	[types-$H\overline{X}$]	.04	
			H_1-$H\overline{X}$		.16
			H_2-$H\overline{X}$		-.09
			H_3-$H\overline{X}$		-.13
			H_4-$H\overline{X}$		.29
			H_5-$H\overline{X}$		-.23
HF-HTF	228	1	Demographics[b]	.02	
		2	HF-HTF	.04	-.18

H_2–HTX	-.06
H_3–HT$\overline{X}$	-.44
H_4–H$\overline{T}$X	.00
H_5–H$\overline{T}\overline{X}$	-.38

* $p < .05$.

[a] Variables entered in step 1 are age, education, and occupational level.

[b] Variables entered in step 1 are age, education, occupational level, and race.

TABLE 21.27 / "In what ways have your contacts with professionals been helpful?"[a]

	WHM	BHM	WHTM	BHTM	WHF	BHF	WHTF	BHTF Pilot Study
	N=331	N=53	N=83	N=8	N=155	N=36	N=42	N=16
	%	%	%	%	%	%	%	%
Gained insight into self	33	32	39	62	44	50	55	38
Felt better generally	17	11	25	25	14	25	14	31
More self-accepting	16	15	5	0	19	22	14	12
Nice to communicate feelings	13	13	12	25	19	8	12	0
Accepted homosexuality more	12	9	0	0	13	17	0	0
Other benefits	22	13	16	0	12	3	7	12
Not helpful at all	24	35	29	25	15	19	12	38

Males

Comparison	N	X^2
WH–BH	1890	3.85
H_1–H†	1331	7.12
H_2–H†	1331	4.37
H_3–H†	1331	6.25
H_4–H†	1331	4.01
H_5–H†	1331	5.40
H–HT	2679	53.10***

Females

Comparison	N	X^2
WH–BH	850	4.14
H_1–H†	609	2.94
H_2–H†	609	5.81
H_3–H†	609	3.79
H_4–H†	609	8.19
H_5–H†	609	1.95
H–HT	1199	23.27***

*** $p < .001$.

† Excluding the subgroup being compared.

a Respondents could give more than one answer to this question, so column percentages may add up to more than 100%; this inflates the chi-square, but not substantially.

TABLE 21.28 / "In what ways have your contacts with professionals been a disappointment?"[a]

	WHM	BHM	WHTM	BHTM	WHF	BHF	WHTF	BHTF Pilot Study
	N=330	N=53	N=79	N=8	N=154	N=36	N=42	N=16
	%	%	%	%	%	%	%	%
Professional's manner	24	17	20	12	30	31	19	6
Distress not reduced	10	6	4	12	9	6	10	6
Learned nothing about self	8	9	6	0	4	8	2	12
Therapy is not a cure-all	8	11	13	12	9	14	14	6
Other disappointments	36	30	32	25	34	28	24	44
Not disappointing at all	29	43	30	38	28	25	36	38

Males

Comparison	N	X^2
WH–BH	1809	5.50
H_1–H†	1271	5.48
H_2–H†	1271	1.37
H_3–H†	1271	.77
H_4–H†	1271	2.95
H_5–H†	1271	10.13
H–HT	2574	33.22***

Females

Comparison	N	X^2
WH–BH	802	2.40
H_1–H†	577	10.05
H_2–H†	577	4.97
H_3–H†	577	4.48
H_4–H†	577	2.93
H_5–H†	577	.66
H–HT	1144	10.00

*** $p < .001$.
† Excluding the type being compared.
[a] Respondents could give more than one answer to this question, so column percentages may add up to more than 100%; this inflates the chi-square, but not substantially.

TABLE 22.1 / Sexual, Social, and Psychological Adjustment: Comparisons

Variable	I/II		III/IV	
F^a:	1.80*		3.88***	
	F^b	SDFC^c	F^b	SDFC^c
In love with current partner	.00	.14		
Duration of current affair	1.18	−.19		
Importance of partner at first	1.39	−.04	1.16	.20
Importance of partner currently	6.79*	.30	2.88	.04
Who does the cooking?	1.21	.33		
Who does the shopping?	1.23	−.10		
Who does the repairs?	.00	−.12		
Who keeps household accounts?	2.66	.39		
Who does the housework?	.61	−.17		
Income combined with roommate's?	1.49	−.09		
Who earns more?	1.76	.17		
Job changes in past five years	.01	−.19	.00	−.06
Satisfaction with current/last job	.00	−.20	1.93	.20
Current conventional religiosity	.02	−.16	1.56	.14
Conservative-radical rating	4.43*	.44	.78	.16
Political activity	.10	−.22	5.02*	.44
Ever been married?	4.99*	−.48	.23	.15
Total number of friends	2.49	−.19	.72	.11
Male friends who are homosexual	8.03**	−.53	3.52	−.45
Leisure time spent alone	1.52	.36	5.81*	.00
Number of evenings spent at home	1.06	−.25	7.46**	−.04
Contact with friends	2.30	−.19	15.23***	−.45
Number of times arrested/picked up	.10	.14	.79	−.01
Number of times rolled/robbed	1.82	−.19	.21	−.04
Number of times blackmailed	1.54	−.21	6.93**	.25
Current general health	1.08	.03	3.69	−.01
Psychosomatic symptoms	.21	.01	5.84*	−.09
Current general happiness	3.34	.20	23.63***	−.20
Happier now than 5 years ago	4.05*	.15	2.24	.17
Exuberance	.32	−.24	24.51***	−.23
Self-acceptance	4.33*	.05	31.53***	−.16
Loneliness	.09	−.00	22.96***	.40
Worry	.26	.40	24.05***	.28
Depression	11.93***	−.57	38.78***	.34
Tension	4.73*	−.17	6.20*	−.22
Paranoia	.11	.54	5.66*	.01
Number of times consulted professional	1.77	.13	1.04	−.33
Suicidal ideation and impulses	2.14	.07	1.30	.03

* $p < .05$. ** $p < .01$. *** $p < .001$.
a Multivariate test of significance F.
b Univariate F-tests.
c Standardized discriminant function coefficients. If the sign of the standardized discriminant function coefficients is positive, it means that the group first named tended to score higher

IV/V		I/III		II/IV		I, II/III, IV, V	
2.09**		6.17***		4.91***		10.34***	
F^b	$SDFC^c$	F^b	$SDFC^c$	F^b	$SDFC^c$	F^b	$SDFC^c$
.00	−.23	2.00	−.03	.47	.12	.04	−.17
1.28	−.07	78.35***	.76	25.00***	−.51	100.49***	.68
3.79	.33	1.40	.03	1.38	.03	.62	−.03
.38	−.05	1.05	−.04	3.93*	.04	4.74*	−.04
1.28	.28	.97	−.09	.98	.30	.13	−.10
0	.05	.05	−.06	1.14	.16	.18	−.05
1.03	.28	1.84	.15	1.71	.23	.02	−.07
4.77*	.55	2.48	−.04	.05	.09	.11	.00
5.87*	.34	.59	−.00	1.50	.01	7.95**	.11
4.47*	.33	2.11	−.24	4.89*	−.26	5.60*	.10
7.53**	.48	22.54***	.43	38.58***	−.39	89.93***	.61
4.93*	.06	38.42***	−.41	14.13***	.44	30.16***	−.42
3.13	−.14	24.01***	−.31	.76	−.17	.42	−.06
.42	.13	2.76	−.06	3.62	−.07	6.14*	.02
2.40	−.28	1.68	−.08	1.85	.02	2.22	.04
.47	−.10	1.28	.03	1.17	−.08	2.20	.02
3.14	.47	.15	−.13	.52	.14	3.39	−.06
.75	−.09	.08	−.31	.12	−.37	.40	.03
.41	−.13	4.88*	.18	20.74***	−.11	23.85***	.10
2.06	.13	2.10	.07	.85	.09	6.09*	.04
.05	−.15	2.26	−.30	9.09**	−.18	3.60	−.07
1.59	.09	.10	−.12	9.77**	−.16	6.19**	.04
2.55	.26	5.40*	−.08	41.54***	.43	39.86***	−.28
7.14**	.48	3.77	.20	11.44***	.32	.22	.04
1.49	.17	2.69	−.20	13.96***	−.03	12.85***	.06
3.94*	.05	4.60*	−.08	7.49**	−.23	6.93**	.07
3.37	−.13	.02	−.01	6.96**	.00	2.44	−.05
2.07	.10	.90	−.19	12.48**	.16	9.03**	−.19
1.38	.10	.08	.04	4.53*	−.02	1.40	−.02

nan the second-named group on the given variable; if negative, the first-named group scored lower.

TABLE 22.2 / Sexual, Social and Psychological Adjustment: Comparisons

Variable	I/II		III/IV	
F^a:	1.50		1.78	
	F^b	$SDFC^c$	F^b	$SDFC^c$
In love with current partner	4.38*	.05		
Duration of current affair	7.33**	.22		
Importance of partner at first	.13	−.10	.73	.43
Importance of partner currently	1.97	.45	1.23	−.67
Who does the cooking?	.82	.30		
Who does the shopping?	.57	−.03		
Who does the repairs?	.46	.10		
Who keeps household accounts?	1.16	−.28		
Who does the housework?	.00	−.29		
Who earns more?	.79	.15		
Job changes in past five years	4.98*	−.16	.05	−2.26
Satisfaction with current/last job	.76	.13	2.17	−1.38
Current conventional religiosity	1.20	.28	.54	−.80
Conservative-radical rating	.01	−.01	.14	−.68
Political activity	.45	−.19	.16	−.13
Ever been married?	2.48	−.29	0	.25
Total number of friends	.83	−.21	4.14*	−.97
Female friends who are homosexual	1.75	−.13	1.23	1.56
Leisure time spent alone	.18	−.19	2.28	2.36
Number of evenings spent at home	.32	.03	2.06	−1.48
Contact with friends	.10	−.11	1.96	−.28
Number of times arrested/picked up	.82	−.15	.01	−.92
Number of times blackmailed	.20	−.05	5.55*	−.74
Current general health	2.74	.00	.02	1.05
Psychosomatic symptoms	7.42**	−.34	.20	1.20
Current general happiness	7.30*	.44	2.33	1.00
Happier now than 5 years ago	3.11	.20	2.09	−2.05
Exuberance	.03	−.40	11.37**	2.84
Self-acceptance	6.65*	.42	2.78	.18
Loneliness	17.14***	−.65	2.12	1.34
Worry	4.05*	−.19	2.71	−1.45
Depression	5.20*	.49	5.66*	−.22
Tension	13.57***	.08	.01	.26
Paranoia	6.49*	−.25	.63	−.64
Number of times consulted professional	1.00	−.37	.76	.42
Suicidal ideation and impulses	.00	.37	.01	−.12

* p < .05.
** p < .01.
*** p < .001.
  [a] Multivariate test of significance F.
  [b] Univariate F-tests.
  [c] Standardized discriminant function coefficients. If the sign of the standardized discriminant function coefficient is positive, it means that the group first named tended to score higher

IV/V		I/III		II/IV		I, II/III, IV, V	
7.54**		**2.36****		**3.16****		**5.88*****	
F^b	$SDFC^c$	F^b	$SDFC^c$	F^b	$SDFC^c$	F^b	$SDFC^c$
.08	1.12	.02	−.39	2.05	−.12	1.67	.20
.44	−2.08	30.01***	.86	19.66***	−.78	80.98***	−.78
.14	−1.30	.51	−.20	.24	.41	.00	.06
.24	1.64	.67	−.30	.06	.12	.06	.34
.02	.58	1.04	.08	.77	−.19	.02	.06
.19	.89	1.94	−.19	.00	−.60	.55	.13
2.31	−1.61	.08	.08	.67	.16	.02	−.03
2.60	1.16	.18	.17	2.44	.98	.02	.06
1.17	1.99	4.39*	−.23	1.36	−.13	.67	.13
.01	.28	.65	−.07	5.18*	−.84	8.23**	−.09
8.17**	−.74	.46	.10	4.76*	−.59	24.36***	−.55
21.22***	−1.45	15.31***	−.17	24.00***	.69	14.14***	.23
1.43	−4.15	14.83***	−.17	.65	−.42	4.62*	.05
.11	−.62	.02	.05	.20	−.09	.03	−.07
3.98	−2.28	.68	.03	.07	.64	1.20	−.09
1.09	.12	1.98	.40	3.93	−.13	3.23	−.41
.03	1.17	.25	.23	2.17	−.06	1.23	−.05
.04	.09	1.82	−.05	.80	.40	5.87*	−.06
.05	1.52	.84	.16	.83	−.16	3.78	.02
1.54	2.08	1.82	−.24	5.99*	−.25	.62	.03
2.58	3.18	.05	−.13	.03	.14	.20	.11
.91	3.49	2.65	−.36	.93	.64	13.25***	.43
.73	2.45	.51	.09	.02	−.24	.14	−.10
.59	.54	.00	.23	.44	.77	.79	−.20
.13	1.42	3.51	−.09	.22	−.61	3.17	.06
1.03	−3.21	.91	−.31	.00	.12	.08	.15
.02	1.36	.97	−.32	.88	.29	3.67	.19
.15	−2.59	.34	.10	.06	−.33	1.21	.03

han the second-named group on the given variable; if negative, the first-named group scored lower.

TABLE 22.3 / **Sexual, Social, and Psychological Adjustment: Comparison**

Variable	I: Close-Coupled F^a: 2.67***		II: Open-Coupled 5.55***	
	F^b	SDFC^c	F^b	SDFC^c
Homosexual-heterosexual rating	.28	−.22	.15	−.15
Overtness	3.39	.04	.31	.21
Level of sexual activity	9.52**	.02	2.13	.13
Total amount of cruising	34.95***	.11	46.30***	.33
Extent of cruising worries	37.59***	.46	50.44***	.32
Number of sexual partners	44.99***	.39	64.68***	.38
Homosexual sex appeal	.08	.15	.06	−.07
Sexual repertoire	37.24***	.64	46.42***	.78
Level of sexual interest	13.40***	.15	.22	−.38
Extent of sexual problems	3.14	.09	1.82	.56
Regret over homosexuality	.05	−.07	.40	.29
Currently involved in affair				
In love with current partner	2.28	.34	.24	−.23
Duration of current affair	.03	.31	6.81*	.47
Importance of partner at first	.70	−.49	4.87*	.06
Importance of partner currently	.24	.65	.64	−.32
Who does the cooking?	.37	.02	.27	−.01
Who does the shopping?	.04	−.02	3.44	−.03
Who does the repairs?	.28	−.15	.08	−.21
Who keeps household accounts?	3.52	.36	.64	−.27
Who does the housework?	.01	−.10	.38	−.16
Who earns more?	.59	−.04	.98	−.13
Job changes in past five years	.44	.23	9.00**	−.21
Satisfaction with current/last job	.35	.01	2.68	−.10
Current conventional religiosity	.00	−.03	1.26	.11
Conservative-radical rating	.02	−.15	2.74	−.26
Political activity	.51	.09	.10	−.27
Ever been married?	.43	.11	.84	.10
Total number of friends	2.78	.22	2.21	−.04
Leisure time spent alone	.38	−.05	.01	.05
Number of evenings spent at home	2.30	−.38	2.15	.11
Contact with friends	.37	−.01	2.62	−.02
Number of times arrested/picked up	.00	.05	2.07	−.25
Number of times blackmailed	.17	.07	1.22	.06
Current general health	1.91	.11	4.99*	.13
Psychosomatic symptoms	1.74	−.48	13.96***	−.47
Current general happiness	1.24	.45	3.88	.27
Happier now than 5 years ago	.19	−.02	.69	.06
Exuberance	.14	−.33	.17	.15

III: Functional		IV: Dysfunctional		V: Asexual	
10.76***		5.04***		4.88***	
F^b	$SDFC^c$	F^b	$SDFC^c$	F^b	$SDFC^c$
7.07**	.04	18.64***	.49	5.82*	−.13
4.23*	.36	.09	−.13	.06	.34
14.65***	.10	3.58	.43	18.40***	−.12
70.24***	.21	31.82***	.33	31.18***	−.33
31.08***	.42	47.56***	.35	27.50***	−.24
309.59***	.90	55.35***	.46	39.35***	−.56
12.66***	−.22	.71	−.07	.16	.05
107.75***	.26	24.66***	.52	13.35***	.25
.65	−.32	3.14	−.17	3.40	−.42
1.87	.08	1.05	.36	.78	.24
8.12**	.04	2.53	.05	7.19**	−.72
3.63	−.11	9.00**	−.36	2.51	.17
4.87*	−.24	.03	.04	.00	.11
4.01*	.16	.70	−.45	1.07	−.64
.48	−.20	.16	.16	3.01	.39
.95	.02	.11	−.03	.12	−.05
.87	.07	.28	.27	.12	.12
1.30	.00	.67	.17	.32	.01
.01	−.11	2.63	.16	.40	−.09
11.16**	.09	9.07**	.06	.02	−.34
.59	−.05	3.09	.69	1.06	.12
5.16*	−.09	2.27	−.04	.03	−.26
2.52	−.19	4.70*	−.68	3.95*	−.31
.17	−.00	.18	−.01	.21	.04
4.17*	.19	3.88	−.11	8.00**	.61
.84	−.02	8.75**	−.37	.94	−.04
.43	−.01	.37	.05	.53	.11
1.33	.09	.07	−.15	.06	−.03
1.23	.19	.00	−.35	.02	−.36
.17	.01	.24	.14	.11	.03
.01	−.26	.61	.22	.15	−.05

TABLE 22.3—*(Continued)*

Variable	I: Close-Coupled		II: Open-Coupled	
F^a:	2.67***		5.55***	
	F^b	$SDFC^c$	F^b	$SDFC^c$
Self-acceptance	.86	.09	4.98*	.20
Loneliness	1.84	.08	9.23**	−.23
Worry	.59	−.07	4.20*	−.05
Depression	3.87	−.17	2.71	.20
Tension	.50	.56	2.46	.04
Paranoia	.59	−.01	5.47*	−.19
Number of times consulted professional	.81	−.04	13.37***	−.29
Suicidal ideation and impulses	.53	−.02	.61	.33

* p < .05.
** p < .01.
*** p < .001.
[a] Multivariate test of significance F.
[b] Univariate F-tests.
[c] Standardized discriminant function coefficients. If the sign of the standardized discriminant function coefficient is positive, it means that the group first named tended to score

III: Functional		IV: Dysfunctional		V: Asexual	
10.76***		5.04***		4.88***	
F^b	$SDFC^c$	F^b	$SDFC^c$	F^b	$SDFC^c$
.25	.24	.09	.20	4.00*	.72
.05	.29	.22	.17	3.74	.38
.49	−.16	.04	.15	.34	.24
.09	−.03	.01	−.14	.28	−.42
.30	.01	.59	−.03	.85	.17
.04	−.03	.00	−.13	.53	.15
.87	.01	1.49	−.10	4.68	.86
.40	−.07	.01	.16	.98	.06

higher than the second-named group on the given variable; if negative, the first-named group scored lower.

TABLE 22.4 / Percentage of Respondents in Each Homosexual Subgroup with Certain Sexual, Social, and Psychological Characteristics: Males[a]

	Close-Coupled (N=67)	Open-Coupled (N=120)	Functional (N=102)	Dysfunctional (N=86)	Asexual (N=110)
	%	%	%	%	%
The Homosexual–Heterosexual Continuum					
Exclusively or predominantly homosexual in behavior	94	96	95	92	83
Overtness					
Extrafamilial overtness is relatively high	21	20	27	21	8
Level of Sexual Activity					
Has homosexual sex at least twice a week	69	60	100	47	0
Cruising					
Cruises at least once a week	1	28	76	66	11
If cruises:					
—cruises at least once a week					
—at bars	4	28	65	51	15
—on the street	1	26	40	21	3
—makes the first approach at least half the time	51	54	71	63	49
—sometimes or often worries about					
—being able to make conversation	18	35	22	47	31
—the adequacy of his sexual performance	7	18	7	39	17
—being assaulted or robbed	0	22	10	30	16
Sexual Partnerships					
Had at least 20 homosexual partners in past year	0	61	100	90	0
Had fewer than 6 homosexual partners in past year	69	15	0	5	46
Sex Appeal					
Rates own homosexual sex appeal as below average	12	10	2	20	30
Sexual Techniques					
Used an extensive sexual repertoire in past year	63	72	74	77	38

Level of Sexual Interest

	84	80	89	87	69
Thinks somewhat or quite a bit about sexual matters	84	80	89	87	69
Sexual Problems					
Reports somewhat or very much of a problem with					
—getting partner to meet his sexual requests	13	40	15	44	33
—finding a suitable sexual partner	7	34	22	80	75
—being able to meet partner's sexual requests	7	21	10	42	38
—not having sex as often as he would like	19	38	10	53	54
—worrying about his sexual adequacy	10	23	3	46	30
—maintaining affection for partner	7	27	23	47	31
—premature ejaculation	13	34	10	35	36
—being able to reach orgasm	4	12	6	30	18
Acceptance of Homosexuality					
Does not at all regret being homosexual	69	54	78	0	37
Strongly disagrees that H is an emotional disorder	48	43	52	24	44
Wishes he had been given a magic HT pill at birth	22	24	15	50	32
Would take a magic HT pill today	1	10	6	30	18
Social Adjustment					
More than three-fourths of R's men friends are H	67	77	75	66	46
Spends little or no leisure time alone	75	60	43	26	20
Spends at least 5 evenings a week at home	64	54	19	38	47
Homosexuality has harmed R's career	12	28	16	43	23
Has been arrested (for any reason) more than twice	1	7	17	8	6
Has been assaulted or robbed on account of H	21	40	33	50	38
Psychological Adjustment					
Feels fairly happy or very happy	99	88	95	71	60
Does little or no worrying	28	30	44	8	35
Seldom or never feels lonely	84	75	70	36	50
Relatively low in self-acceptance	19	41	25	56	46
Relatively depressed	12	37	24	55	47

[a] Items were selected for this table on the basis of their theoretical salience and, where possible, male–female comparability. In addition, they had to display statistically significant intergroup differences in regression analysis and also meet a criterion of substantive significance: for any item, at least one group that was significantly different statistically had to show a difference of at least 10 percentage points from another group.

TABLE 22.5 / **Percentage of Respondents in Each Homosexual Subgroup with Certain Sexual, Social, and Psychological Characteristics: Females**[a]

	Close-Coupled (N=81) %	Open-Coupled (N=51) %	Functional (N=30) %	Dysfunctional (N=16) %	Asexual (N=33) %
The Homosexual–Heterosexual Continuum					
Exclusively homosexual in both feelings and behavior	59	57	50	19	30
Exclusively or predominantly homosexual in behavior	96	91	80	69	69
Had heterosexual coitus in past year	9	18	37	50	33
Overtness					
Familial overtness is relatively high	20	25	6	0	12
Extrafamilial overtness is relatively high	9	20	10	0	9
Level of Sexual Activity					
Has homosexual sex at least twice a week	43	51	60	31	0
Sexual Partnerships					
Had at least 20 homosexual partners in past year	0	8	10	12	0
Had fewer than 3 homosexual partners in past year	100	53	33	50	100
Sex Appeal					
Rates own homosexual sex appeal as below average	6	10	0	19	27
Sexual Techniques					
Used an extensive sexual repertoire in past year	70	84	80	81	27
Level of Sexual Interest					
Thinks somewhat or quite a bit about sexual matters	51	67	80	62	61
Sexual Problems					
Reports somewhat or very much of a problem with					
—getting partner to meet her sexual requests	7	25	7	38	24
—finding a suitable sexual partner	9	29	23	81	73
—being able to meet partner's sexual requests	6	28	0	31	27

—worrying about her sexual adequacy	5	21	7	50	39
—partner not being able to reach orgasm	4	12	10	31	9
—maintaining affection for partner	7	25	17	44	24
—being able to reach orgasm herself	4	14	10	62	39
Acceptance of Homosexuality					
Does not at all regret being homosexual	68	59	100	0	73
Social Adjustment					
Has at least 6 good, close friends	35	33	57	38	33
More than three-fourths of R's women friends are H	42	51	43	25	36
Spends little or no leisure time alone	72	73	53	19	21
Spends at least 5 evenings a week at home	73	59	37	12	69
Attends religious functions at least once a month	9	6	0	18	18
Psychological Adjustment					
Feels fairly happy or very happy	94	84	87	69	67
Relatively exuberant	47	39	60	19	30
Seldom or never feels lonely	84	61	63	62	27
Relatively depressed	23	45	33	56	39
Relatively paranoid	27	51	40	44	45
Has sought professional help to give up her homosexuality	9	12	3	19	27

[a] Items were selected for this table on the basis of their theoretical salience and, where possible, male-female comparability. In addition, they had to display statistically significant intergroup differences in regression analysis and also meet a criterion of substantive significance: for any item, at least one group that was significantly different statistically had to show a difference of at least 10 percentage points from another group. Because so few of the lesbians cruised, cruising variables are omitted.

Bibliography

Achilles, Nancy. 1967. "The Development of the Homosexual Bar As an Institution." Pp. 228–244 in John H. Gagnon and William Simon (eds.), *Sexual Deviance*. New York: Harper & Row.

Allen, Clifford. 1961a. "The Aging Homosexual." Pp. 91–95 in Isadore Rubin (ed.), *The Third Sex*. New York: New Book Co.

1961b. "When Homosexuals Marry." Pp. 58–62 in Isadore Rubin (ed.), *The Third Sex*. New York: New Book Co.

Anderberg, M. R. 1973. *Cluster Analysis for Applications*. New York: Academic Press.

Armon, Virginia. 1958. "Some Personality Variables in Overt Female Homosexuality." Ph.D. dissertation, University of Southern California.

1960. "Some Personality Variables in Overt Female Homosexuality." *Journal of Projective Techniques* 24(3):292–309.

Armstrong, C. N. 1955. "Diversities of Sex." *British Medical Journal* 4923:1173–1177.

Bass-Hass, Rita. 1968. "The Lesbian Dyad." *Journal of Sex Research* 4(3): 108–126.

Becker, A. L. 1967. "A Third Sex? Some Speculations on a Sexuality Spectrum." *Medical Proceedings* 13(4):67–74.

Bell, Alan P. 1974. "Homosexualities: Their Range and Character." Pp. 1–26 in James K. Cole and Richard Dienstbier (eds.), *Nebraska Symposium on Motivation: 1973.* Lincoln, Nebr.: University of Nebraska Press.

——— 1975a. "The Homosexual As Patient." Pp. 55–72 in Richard Green (ed.), *Human Sexuality: A Health Practitioner's Text.* Baltimore: Williams & Wilkins.

——— 1975b. "Research in Homosexuality: Back to the Drawing Board." *Archives of Sexual Behavior* 4(4):421–431.

Bergler, Edmund. 1948. "Lesbianism, Facts and Fiction." *Marriage Hygiene* 1(4):197–202.

——— 1958. *Counterfeit-Sex: Homosexuality, Impotence, Frigidity.* 2d ed. New York: Grune & Stratton.

Bertelson, David. 1970. "A Comparative Approach to the Meaning of Gay Liberation." Unpublished manuscript.

Bieber, Irving. 1969. "Homosexuality." *American Journal of Nursing* 69(12):2637–2641.

Bieber, Irving, Harvey J. Dain, Paul R. Dince, Marvin G. Drellich, Henry G. Grand, Ralph H. Gundlach, Malvina W. Kremer, Alfred H. Rifkin, Cornelia B. Wilbur, and Toby B. Bieber (Society of Medical Psychoanalysts). 1962. *Homosexuality: A Psychoanalytic Study.* New York: Basic Books.

Blashfield, Roger K. 1977. "A Guide to Cluster Analysis Software." Read at the meetings of the American Educational Research Association, New York, N.Y.

Bozarth, René, and Alfred A. Gross. 1962. "Homosexuality: Sin or Sickness? A Dialogue." *Pastoral Psychology* 13(129):35–42.

Braaten, Leif Johan, and C. Douglas Darling. 1965. "Overt and Covert Homosexual Problems Among Male College Students." *Genetic Psychology Monographs* 71(2):269–310.

Bromberg, Walter. 1965. "Sex Offense As a Disguise." *Corrective Psychiatry and Journal of Social Therapy* 11(6):293–298.

Bruce, Earle Wesley. 1942. "Comparison of Traits of the Homosexual from Tests and from Life History Materials." M.A. thesis, University of Chicago.

Bychowski, Gustav. 1961. "The Ego and the Object of the Homosexual." *International Journal of Psycho-Analysis* 42(3):255–259.

Caprio, Frank S. 1955. "Female Homosexuality." *Sexology* 21(8):494–499.

——— 1956. "Homosexual Women." *Sexology* 22(9):560–565.

Cavan, Sherri. 1966. *Liquor License: An Ethnography of Bar Behavior.* Chicago: Aldine.

Chang, Judy, and Jack Block. 1960. "A Study of Identification in Male Homosexuals." *Journal of Consulting Psychology* 24(4):307–310.

Churchill, Wainwright. 1967. *Homosexual Behavior Among Males: A Cross-Cultural and Cross-Species Investigation.* New York: Hawthorn.

Clark, Thomas R. 1975. "Homosexuality and Psychopathology in Nonpatient Males." *American Journal of Psychoanalysis* 35:163–168.

Cory, Donald Webster. 1951. *The Homosexual in America: A Subjective Approach.* New York: Greenberg.

———. 1952. "Homosexual Attitudes and Heterosexual Prejudices." *International Journal of Sexology* 5(3):151–153.

Cory, Donald Webster, and John P. LeRoy. 1963. "Homosexual Marriage." *Sexology* 29(10):660–662.

Corzine, Jay, and Richard Cole. 1977. "Cruising the Truckers: Sexual Encounters in a Highway Rest Area." *Urban Life* 6(2):171–192.

Cotton, Wayne L. 1972. "Role Playing Substitutions Among Male Homosexuals." *Journal of Sex Research* 8(4):310–323.

Curran, Desmond, and Denis Parr. 1957. "Homosexuality: An Analysis of 100 Male Cases Seen in Private Practice." *British Medical Journal* 5022: 797–801.

Dank, Barry M. 1972. "Why Homosexuals Marry Women." *Medical Aspects of Human Sexuality* 6(8):14.

David, Henry P., and William Rabinowitz. 1952. "Szondi Patterns in Epileptic and Homosexual Males." *Journal of Consulting Psychology* 16(4):247–250.

Dean, Robert B. 1967a. "Some Considerations on Promiscuity in Male Homosexuals." Unpublished manuscript.

———. 1967b. "Some MMPI and Biographical Questionnaire Correlates of Non-Institutionalized Male Homosexuals." M.A. thesis, San Jose State College.

DeLuca, Joseph N. 1966. "The Structure of Homosexuality." *Journal of Projective Techniques and Personality Assessment* 30(2):187–191.

———. 1967. "Performance of Overt Male Homosexuals and Controls on the Blacky Test." *Journal of Clinical Psychology* 23(4):497.

Dickey, Brenda A. 1961. "Attitudes Toward Sex Roles and Feelings of Adequacy in Homosexual Males." *Journal of Consulting Psychology* 25(2): 116–122.

Doidge, William Thomas. 1956. "Perceptual Differences in Male Homosexuals." Ph.D. dissertation, University of Texas.

Ellis, Albert. 1964. "The Truth About Lesbians." *Sexology* 30(10):652–655.

Erickson, Ralph J. 1961. "Male Homosexuality and Society." *Bulletin of the National Association of Secondary-School Principals* 45(November): 128–134.

Freedman, Mark J. 1967. "Homosexuality Among Women and Psychological Adjustment." Ph.D. dissertation, Case Western Reserve University.

Freund, Kurt, Ron Langevin, Richard Laws, and Michael Serber. 1974. "Femininity and Preferred Partner Age in Homosexual and Heterosexual Males." *British Journal of Psychiatry* 125(November):442–446.

Friedberg, Ronald L. 1975. "Early Recollections of Homosexuals as Indicators of Their Life Styles." *Journal of Individual Psychology* 31:196–204.

Gagnon, John H., and William Simon. 1968. "Sexual Deviance in Contemporary America." *Annals of the American Academy of Political and Social Science* 376:106–122.

Gershman, Harry. 1953. "Considerations of Some Aspects of Homosexuality." *American Journal of Psychoanalysis* 13:82–83.

Giallombardo, Rose. 1966. *Society of Women: A Study of a Women's Prison.* New York: Wiley.

Giannell, A. Steven. 1966. "Giannell's Criminosynthesis Theory Applied to Female Homosexuality." *Journal of Psychology* 64(2):213–222.

Gigl, John Lawrence. 1970. "The Overt Male Homosexual: A Primary Description of a Self-Selected Population." Ph.D. dissertation, University of Oregon.

Gilbert, S. F. 1954. "Homosexuality and Hypnotherapy." *British Journal of Medical Hypnotism* 5(3):2–7.

Greenberg, Jerrold S. 1973a. "A Study of Male Homosexuals (Predominantly College Students)." *Journal of the American College Health Association* 22(1):56–60.

1973b. "A Study of the Self-Esteem and Alienation of Male Homosexuals." *Journal of Psychology* 83:137–143.

Gundlach, Ralph H. 1967. "Research Project Report." *The Ladder* 11:2–9.

Gundlach, Ralph H., and Bernard F. Riess. 1968. "Self and Sexual Identity in the Female: A Study of Female Homosexuals." Pp. 205–231 in Bernard F. Riess (ed.), *New Directions in Mental Health*. New York: Grune & Stratton.

Harry, Joseph. 1976. "Marriage Among Gay Males: The Separation of Intimacy and Sex." Unpublished manuscript.

Hathaway, Starke R., and J. Charnley McKinley. 1943. *Minnesota Multiphasic Personality Inventory*. New York: Psychological Corporation.

Hatterer, Lawrence J. 1970. *Changing Homosexuality in the Male: Treatment for Men Troubled by Homosexuality*. New York: McGraw-Hill.

Hedblom, Jack. 1972. "The Social, Sexual, and Occupational Lives of Homosexual Women." *Sexual Behavior* 2(10):33–37.

Herman, Morris, and S. B. Wortis. 1947. "Aberrant Sex Behavior in Humans." *Annals of the New York Academy of Science* 47(5):639–645.

Hoffman, Martin. 1968. *The Gay World: Male Homosexuality and the Social Creation of Evil*. New York: Basic Books.

Hooker, Evelyn. 1957. "The Adjustment of the Male Overt Homosexual." *Journal of Projective Techniques* 21(1):18–31.

1965a. "An Empirical Study of Some Relations Between Sexual Patterns and Gender Identity in Male Homosexuals." Pp. 24–52 in John Money (ed.), *Sex Research: New Developments*. New York: Holt, Rinehart & Winston.

1965b. "Male Homosexuals and Their 'Worlds.' " Pp. 83–107 in Judd Marmor (ed.), *Sexual Inversion: The Multiple Roots of Homosexuality*. New York: Basic Books.

1967. "The Homosexual Community." Pp. 167–184 in John H. Gagnon and William Simon (eds.), *Sexual Deviance*. New York: Harper & Row.

Horowitz, Mardi J. 1964. "The Homosexual's Image of Himself." *Mental Hygiene* 48(2):197–201.

Humphreys, R. A. Laud. 1970. *The Tearoom Trade: Impersonal Sex in Public Places*. Chicago: Aldine.

1971. "New Styles in Homosexual Manliness." *TransAction* (March-April):38–46, 64, 66.

1972. *Out of the Closets: The Sociology of Homosexual Liberation*. Englewood Cliffs, N.J.: Prentice-Hall.

Hyde, H. Montgomery. 1970. *The Love That Dare Not Speak Its Name*. Boston: Little, Brown.

Jensen, Mehri Samandari. 1974. "Role Differentiation in Female Homosexual Quasi-Marital Unions." *Journal of Marriage and the Family* 36(2):360–367.

Katz, Robert L. 1967. "Church History, Attitudes, and Laws." Manuscript prepared for the National Institute of Mental Health Task Force on Homosexuality, Hebrew Union College, Cincinnati.

Kaye, Harvey E., Soll Berl, Jack Clare, Mary R. Eleston, Benjamin S. Gershwin, Patricia Gershwin, Leonard S. Kogan, Clara Torda, and Cornelia B. Wilbur. 1967. "Homosexuality in Women." *Archives of General Psychiatry* 17:626–634.

Kenyon, F. E. 1968a. "Studies in Female Homosexuality, IV. Social and Psychiatric Aspects. V. Sexual Development, Attitudes and Experiences." *British Journal of Psychiatry* 114:1337–1350.

1968b. "Studies in Female Homosexuality, VI. The Exclusively Homosexual Group." *Acta Psychiatrica Scandinavica* 44(3):224–237.

1968c. "Studies in Female Homosexuality: Psychological Test Results." *Journal of Consulting and Clinical Psychology* 32(5):510–513.

Kepner, J. 1971. "Professor Fradkin Evaluates *ONE's* '388 American Males' Study." *ONEletter* 16(10):3–5.

Kinsey, Alfred C., Wardell B. Pomeroy, and Clyde E. Martin. 1948. *Sexual Behavior in the Human Male*. Philadelphia: W. B. Saunders.

Kinsey, Alfred C., Wardell B. Pomeroy, Clyde E. Martin, and Paul H. Gebhard. 1953. *Sexual Behavior in the Human Female*. Philadelphia: W.B. Saunders.

Kirkham, George Lester. 1966. "Homosexuality and Its Alternatives in a Prison Setting." M.S. thesis, San Jose State College.

Klassen, Albert D., Jr., Eugene E. Levitt, and Colin J. Williams. Forthcoming. *American Sexual Standards*.

Knight, Edward H. 1965. "Overt Male Homosexuality." Pp. 434–461 in Ralph Slovenko (ed.), *Sexual Behavior and the Law*. Springfield, Ill.: Charles C Thomas.

Ladder, The. 1959. "DOB Questionnaire Reveals Some Facts About Lesbians." *The Ladder* 3(12):4–26.

1960. "DOB Questionnaire Reveals Some Comparisons Between Male and Female Homosexuals." *The Ladder* 4(12):4–25.

Landis, Carney, Agnes T. Landis, and M. Marjorie Bolles. 1940. *Sex in Development*. New York: P. B. Hoeber.

Leznoff, Maurice, and William A. Westley. 1956. "The Homosexual Community." *Social Problems* 3(4):257–263.

Liddicoat, Renée. 1956. "Homosexuality: Results of a Survey As Related to Various Theories." Ph.D. dissertation, University of Witwatersrand, Johannesburg.

1961. "A Study of Non-Institutionalized Homosexuals." *Journal of the National Institute of Personnel Research* 8:217–249.

Lindner, Robert. 1951. "Sex in Prison." *Complex* 6:5–20.

McCreary, John K. 1950. "Psychopathia Homosexualis." *Canadian Journal of Psychology* 4:63–74.

McGuire, Ruth Marjorie. 1966. "An Inquiry into Attitudes and Value Systems of a Minority Group: A Comparative Study of Attitudes and Value Systems of Adult Male Homosexuals with Adult Male Heterosexuals." Ph.D. dissertation, New York University.

McNeill, John J. 1976. *The Church and the Homosexual.* Kansas City: Sheed Andrews & McMeel.

Manosevitz, Martin. 1972. "The Development of Male Homosexuality." *Journal of Sex Research* 8(1):31–40.

Marmor, Judd. 1973. "Homosexuality and Cultural Value Systems." *American Journal of Psychiatry* 130(11):1208–1209.

Martin, Del, and Phyllis Lyon. 1970. *Lesbian/Woman.* San Francisco: Glide.

Myrick, Fred L. 1974a. "Attitudinal Differences Between Heterosexually and Homosexually Oriented Males and Between Covert and Overt Male Homosexuals." *Journal of Abnormal Psychiatry* 83(1):81–86.

1974b. "Homosexual Types: An Empirical Investigation." *Journal of Sex Research* 10(3):226–237.

Nacht, S., R. Diatkine, and J. Favreau. 1956. "The Ego in Perverse Relationships." *International Journal of Psychoanalysis* 37(4):404–413.

Nash, John, and Frank Hayes. 1965. "The Parental Relationships of Male Homosexuals: Some Theoretical Issues and a Pilot Study." *Australian Journal of Psychology* 17(1):35–43.

Neustatter, W. Lindesay. 1954. "Homosexuality: The Medical Aspects." *Practitioner* 172(April):364–373.

Nuehring, Elaine W., Sara Beck Fein, and Mary Tyler. 1974. "The Gay College Student: Perspectives for Mental Health Professionals." *Counseling Psychologist* 4(4):64–72.

Oberstone, Andrea Kincses, and Harriet Sukoneck. 1975. "Psychological Adjustment and Style of Life of Single Lesbians and Single Heterosexual Women." Read at the meetings of the Western Psychological Association, Sacramento, California.

Oliver, Wayne A., and Donald L. Mosher. 1968. "Psychopathology and Guilt in Heterosexual and Subgroups of Homosexual Reformatory Inmates." *Journal of Abnormal Psychology* 73(4):323–329.

Ovesey, Lionel. 1964. "The Meaning of Homosexual Trends in Therapy: A Round Table Discussion" [among Irving Bieber, Harry Gershman, Lionel Ovesey, and Frederick A. Weiss]. *American Journal of Psychoanalysis* 24(1):60–76.

Parr, Denis. 1957. "Homosexuality in Clinical Practice." *Proceedings of the Royal Society of Medicine* 50:651–654.

Philipp, E. 1968. "Homosexuality As Seen in a New Zealand City Practice." *New Zealand Medical Journal* 67(430):397–401.

Rancourt, Réjane, and Thérèse Limoges. 1967. "Homosexuality Among Women." *Canadian Nurse* 63(12):42–44.

Rechy, John. 1963. *City of Night.* New York: Grove Press.

1967. *Numbers.* New York: Grove Press.

1977. *The Sexual Outlaw: A Documentary.* New York: Grove Press.

Reuben, David R. 1969. *Everything You Always Wanted to Know About Sex— But Were Afraid to Ask.* New York: David McKay.

Riess, Bernard F., Jeanne Safer, and William Yotive. 1974. "Psychological Test Data on Female Homosexuality: A Review of the Literature." *Journal of Homosexuality* 1(1):71–85.

Roe, Anne. 1956. *The Psychology of Occupations*. New York: Wiley.

Rosenberg, Morris. 1965. *Society and the Adolescent Self-Image*. Princeton, N.J.: Princeton University Press.

Ross, H. Laurence. 1972. "Odd Couples: Homosexuals in Heterosexual Marriage." *Sexual Behavior* 2(1):42–49.

Roth, Martin, and J. R. B. Ball. 1964. "Psychiatric Aspects of Intersexuality." Pp. 395–443 in C. N. Armstrong and A. J. Marshall (eds.), *Intersexuality in Vertebrates Including Man*. London: Academic Press.

Sagarin, Edward. 1976. "Prison Homosexuality and Its Effects on Post-Prison Sexual Behavior." *Psychiatry* 39(3):245–257.

Saghir, Marcel T., and Eli Robins. 1973. *Male and Female Homosexuality: A Comprehensive Investigation*. Baltimore: Williams & Wilkins.

Sawyer, Ethel. 1965. "A Study of a Public Lesbian Community." M.A. thesis, Washington University.

Schäfer, Siegrid. 1976. "Sexual and Social Problems of Lesbians." *Journal of Sex Research* 12(1):50–69.

Schofield, Michael George. 1965. *Sociological Aspects of Homosexuality: A Comparative Study of Three Types of Homosexuals*. Boston: Little, Brown.

Scott, Peter D. 1957. "Homosexuality, with Special Reference to Classification." *Proceedings of the Royal Society of Medicine* 50(9): 659–660.

Simon, William, and John H. Gagnon. 1967. "The Lesbians: A Preliminary Overview." Pp. 247–282 in their *Sexual Deviance*. New York: Harper & Row.

Socarides, Charles W. 1968. *The Overt Homosexual*. New York: Grune & Stratton.

Sonenschein, David. 1968. "The Ethnography of Male Homosexual Relations." *Journal of Sex Research* 4(2):69–83.

Stephenson, Maylee. 1971. "Living with a Stigma: A Study of Eleven Female Homosexual Couples." M.A. thesis, University of British Columbia.

Sudman, Seymour. 1967. *Reducing the Cost of Surveys*. Chicago: Aldine.

Sykes, Gresham M. 1958. *The Society of Captives: A Study of a Maximum Security Prison*. Princeton, N.J.: Princeton University Press.

Troiden, Richard R. 1974. "Homosexual Encounters in a Highway Rest Stop." Pp. 211–228 in Erich Goode and Richard R. Troiden (eds.), *Sexual Deviance and Sexual Deviants*. New York: William Morrow.

Veldman, Donald J. 1967. *Fortran Programming for the Behavioral Sciences*. New York: Holt, Rinehart & Winston.

Ward, David A., and Gene Kassebaum. 1964. "Homosexuality: A Mode of Adaptation in a Prison for Women." *Social Problems* 12(2):159–177.

Ward, J. H., Jr. 1963. "Hierarchical Grouping to Optimize an Objective Function." *American Statistical Association Journal* 58:236–244.

Wayne, David M., M. Adams, and Lillian Rowe. 1947. "A Study of Military Prisoners at a Disciplinary Barracks Suspected of Homosexual Activities." *Military Surgeon* 101(6):499–504.

Weinberg, Martin S., and Alan P. Bell (eds.). 1972. *Homosexuality: An Annotated Bibliography*. New York: Harper & Row.

Weinberg, Martin S., and Colin J. Williams. 1974. *Male Homosexuals: Their Problems and Adaptations*. New York: Oxford University Press.

1975a. *Male Homosexuals: Their Problems and Adaptations*. Rev. ed. New York: Penguin.

1975b. "Gay Baths and the Social Organization of Impersonal Sex." *Social Problems* 23(2):124–136.

Westwood, Gordon. 1960. *A Minority: A Report on the Life of the Male Homosexual in Great Britain*. London: Longmans, Green.

Wheeler, William Marshall. 1949. "An Analysis of Rorschach Indices of Male Homosexuality." *Rorschach Research Exchange and Journal of Projective Techniques* 13(2):97–126.

Williams, Colin J., and Martin S. Weinberg. 1971. *Homosexuals and the Military: A Study of Less Than Honorable Discharge*. New York: Harper & Row.

Wilson, Marilyn L., and Roger L. Greene. 1971. "Personality Characteristics of Female Homosexuals." *Psychological Reports* 28:407–412.

Wolff, Charlotte. 1971. *Love Between Women*. New York: St. Martin's Press.

Contributors to the Study

Consultants

Virginia Armon
Frank A. Beach
Peter M. Bentler
David F. Berry
Irving Bieber
Wainwright Churchill
Robert Deisher
Manfred F. DeMartino
Albert Ellis
Ray Evans
Paul H. Gebhard *
John L. Gigl
Fred J. Goldstein
Ralph H. Gundlach
Martin Hoffman
Evelyn Hooker *
R. A. Laud Humphreys
Jens Jersild
Don Jones
Harvey E. Kaye

Albert D. Klassen, Jr.
Esme Langley
W. Dorr Legg
Ruth Marjorie McGuire
Donal MacNamara
Judd Marmor *
Esther Newton
Wardell B. Pomeroy
Lee Rainwater
Eli Robins
Hendrik M. Ruitenbeek
Edward Sagarin
Ethel Sawyer
Gunter Schmidt
Michael George Schofield
Steven Schreibstein
Marvin Siegelman
Robert J. Stoller
Clarence A. Tripp
Edward Tyler
Kenneth R. Whittemore
Colin J. Williams

* An asterisk denotes a member of the NIMH Task Force.

Project Staff:
San Francisco

Pete Amendola
Charles Anthony
Nancy Bardacke
Robert Bauer
Sandy Bazyouros
Rudy Berg
Konstantine Berlandt
Louise Boyden
Joe Breznau
Garth Burns
David Capri
Chris Carroll
Sylvester Christy
Jan Clanton
Charles Clay
Barbara Curran
Charles Dart
Beverly Davis
Gwen Dyer
Ted Eastman
Bobbey Ector
Al Edmonds
Phyllis Edwards
Thomas Edwards
Gregg Elberg
David Farmer
Sandra Fields
Tommie Flay
Gilbert Francis
Richard Frank
Atwood Gaines
Albert Gates
Jeff Gaynor
Mike Gibson
Chris Gilbert
David Gilmartin
Steve Gratch
Keith Graves
Mark Guerin
Dicky Harris
Marion Harris
John Haskett
De Henderson
Dorothy Henry
Sam Hiatt
Mary Hollis
Jamie Huberman
Vincent Huberman
Gail Hunt
William Hunt

Karen Hurn
Phil Israels
Richard Jaulus
Kim Johnson
Patrick Keilch
Fred Keip
Marge Keip
Ann King
Roger Levin
Joe Lewis
Peter Lewis
LaTonya Mabry
Pat McAdams
Robert McAdams
Ross McClaren
Steve McClave
Karen McClearey
Ted McEwen
Marilyn McGregor
Paul Mariah
Del Martin
Helen Matthews
Mike Matthews
Steve Matthews
Tom Maurer
Debigail Mazur
Edward Meng
Robert Mervyn Millar
Karen Miller
Rudy Monday
Mike Music
William Petzel
Walter Phelps
Marjorie Posner
Billie Purnell
Jerri Randall
Neil Ross
Michael St. James
Ron Schneider
Cecile Scott
Joe Scott
Arthur Seeger
Jean Shaw
Susan Sheffield
Joyce Smith
Lynn G. Smith
Frank Stefanich
Jan Stephans
Jim Stoll
Steve Stone
Gene Suttle
Dennis Sweeney
Roxanne Sweet

Lucy Turner
Hunter Tynes
Leland Upson
Greg West
Curtis Wilkins
Earl Williams
Zelina Williams
Gail Winston
Jim Wolfe
Dolores Wood
Elizabeth Wood
Joy Wood
Hobart Wright

Project Staff:
Bloomington

Dee Arden
Kimberly Arp
Scott Bailey
Lia Barnes
Susanna Barrows
Tad Baugh
Maureen Bendix
Evelyn Birky
Jim Black
Patricia Bracken
Nancy Brand
Gregg Bryant
Ray Burg
Margot Dasterman Byers
Patrick Cameron
Mary Ann Clark
Florence Conrad
Donna Cornsweet
Carolyn R. DeMeyer
Judith Dogley
Gerald Downey
Lois M. Downey
E. Drayden
Linda DuPlantis
Patrick Eckman
Sherolynn Edwards
Gregg Elberg
Anita Fleming
Donnalee Garcia
Steve Ginsberg
Barbara C. Gray
Cynthia Hales
Kirk Hammond
Helen Hofer
Diane Hopp
Diana Hoskins

Stephanie Huddle
Sandra E. Hunt
W. Hunt
Stan Hunter
Jean Inlow
Kim Johnson
Dorr Jones
Fred Ketteman
Eric P. Klassen
Teresa Klassen
Alida Jo Kornreich
Lynn Lane
Lenore Langley
Margie McDonald
Dorothy McGuire
Sara McIntosh
Rhonda Martin
R. Miller
Sue Ellen Miller
Joe Moe
Stephanie Penoff Molitor
Patricia Moore
Judith Munns
Mary Munro
Kathy Nagy
Linda Neagley
Edward Nison
Robert Norris
Eugenia Peterson
Colleen Quandt
Jan Ranck
Jim Rankin
Ann Richer
Simone Robbins
Victoria Rose
Perry Roseman
Jeffrey Rueble
David Rymph
Deborah Scaglion
Sherry Shanabarger
E. A. Shelby
Laura Sherfey
Jan Shipps
Marianne Siegmund
J. Smith
Steve Snyder
William Stang
Jacqueline Steele
Diane Steltzer
Mickey Stentz
Karen Ruse Strueh
William Tabor
Gary Tosca

Katherine Tourin
Brian Trayner
Sanford Upson
Roderick Ustanik
Marilyn Vogt
Janice Wagner
Cindy Webster

Daniel Weinberg
Sue Williams
Richard Wines
Janet Woodring
Luther Woodward
Ralph Wyman
Nancy Zaharako

Index

Abbreviations: HFs = homosexual females; HMs = homosexual males; HTFs = heterosexual females; HTMs = heterosexual males

active role, 106, 111
affairs
   of HFs, 93–102
   of HMs, 86–93, 101–2
age, average
   of heterosexual respondents, 38
   of homosexual respondents, 35
agnosticism
   among heterosexuals, 39–40
   among homosexuals, 37
Alameda County (Calif.), 27
Alcoholic Beverages Control (ABC), 253, 258, 259
Allen, Clifford, 82, 83, 161
American Psychiatric Association, 196–97
anal intercourse, 51, 107–9, 111
Anderberg, M. R., 266
Armon, Virginia, 97, 172
Armstrong, C. N., 50
arrests
   of HFs, 191–92, 193, 194
   of HMs, 188, 189, 191, 193–94
Asexual HFs
   friendships of, 176, 184
   general characteristics of, 137, 138, 226–28

and HTFs, compared, 218
leisure-time activities of, 184, 185–186
loneliness of, 209
paranoia of, 210
and tension, 210
and therapy, 213
Asexual HMs
   church attendance of, 151
   and depression, 200
   friendships of, 173–74, 182
   general characteristics of, 134, 138, 226–28
   general health of, 198, 207
   happiness of, 199
   and HTMs, compared, 218
   leisure-time activities of, 181, 182, 183, 185–86
   loneliness of, 200
   paranoia of, 201
   as parents, 164
   as partners in heterosexual marriage, 162, 163
   psychological adjustment of, 216
   psychosomatic symptoms of, 207
   self-acceptance of, 199–200, 207
   and tension, 201

Asexual HMs (*cont'd.*)
  and worry, 200, 207
asexuality among HMs, 137–38
  See also Asexual HMs
assault
  HFs as victims of, 192
  HMs as victims of, 190, 191, 193, 194
atheism
  among heterosexuals, 39–40
  among homosexuals, 37
autism, 197

bisexuals, 50
  homosexual offenses committed by, 188
blackmail
  HFs as victims of, 192–93
  HMs as victims of, 188, 190–1, 193–194
Blacky Pictures Test, 197
Blashfield, Roger K., 266
Block, Jack, 197
Bloomington (Ind.), 15
body rubbing, 108, 109–11
Bozarth, René, 196
Braaten, Leif Johan, 51, 82
Bromberg, Walter, 198
Bruce, Earle Wesley, 197
Bychowski, Gustav, 196

Ball, J. R. B., 51
Barrows, Susanna, 16
Bass-Hass, Rita, 84, 142, 172
Bay Area (San Francisco)
  acceptance of homosexual life-style in, 27–28, 45, 159, 170, 194, Appendix A *passim*
  employment opportunities for homosexuals in, 245–46
  gay bars in, 236–39, 250–59
  gay baths in, 239
  gay businesses in, 36, 246–47
  gay restaurants in, 250–59
  homophile organizations in, 15, 31–32, 261
  homosexual parties in, 259–62
  motorcycle clubs in, 262–63
  residence patterns of homosexuals in, 233–35
  "tearooms" in, 243–44
beach, as cruising locale, 74, 76
Becker, A. L., 50
Bell, Alan, 10, 23, 25, 49
Bergler, Edmund, 83, 96
Bertelson, David, 121
Bieber, Irving, 54, 55, 56, 63, 65, 82, 83, 107, 117, 122, 124, 204
bisexuality, 59, 117
  characteristics of, 55

Caprio, Frank S., 50, 82, 196
castration anxiety, 196
Cavan, Sherri, 73
Chang, Judy, 197
Chicago (Ill.), 28
Chicago pilot study, 34, 57, 270
  on affairs of HMs, 89
  on attendance of HMs at gay baths, 183
  on extrafamilial overtness of HMs, 64
  on friendships among HMs, 173
  on general health of HMs, 198
  on happiness among HMs, 199
  on HMs' regret of homosexuality, 123
  on incidence of assault and robbery among HMs, 190
  on incidence of heterosexual experience among HMs, 55
  on incidence of heterosexual marriage among HMs, 162
  interview schedule of, 22, 40
  on levels of sexual contact among HMs, 70

Functional HMs (*cont'd.*)
  and HTMs, compared, 218
  loneliness of, 200
  paranoia of, 201
  psychological adjustment of, 216
  psychosomatic symptoms of, 198–199, 208
  and tension, 201
  and therapy, 205
  and worry, 200

Gagnon, John H., 72, 121, 142, 188
gay bars, 30, 35
  cruising in, 73, 74, 75, 78, 79, 80, 236–39
  employees of, 254–55
  HFs' attendance at, 184
  as social institution of gay world, 180, 182, 250–59
  types of, 255–58
gay baths, 28, 31, 35, 182–83
  cruising in, 74, 75, 79, 239–41
gay businesses, in Bay Area, 246–47
gay liberation movement, 23, 32, 62
gay organizations, *see* homophile organizations
gay restaurants, as social institution, 250–59
Gebhard, Paul H., 22
Gershman, Harry, 196
Giallombardo, Rose, 50
Giannell, A. Steven, 50
Gigl, John L., 150
Gilbert, J. F., 50
"glory hole," 24
Gray, Barbara, 16
Greenberg, Jerrold S., 82, 107, 150
Greene, Roger L., 198
Gross, Alfred A., 196
Gundlach, Ralph H., 54, 58, 166

happiness
  of HFs and HTFs, 208–9, 215
  of HMs and HTMs, 199
Harry, Joseph, 82, 83
hashish, 249
Hathaway, Starke R., 41
Hatterer, Lawrence J., 62, 74, 83
Hayes, Frank, 50
health, general
  of HFs and HTFs, 208, 215
  of HMs and HTMs, 198, 207
Hedblom, Jack, 172, 181
Herman, Morris, 51
heterosexual(s)
  homoerotophobia of, 101, 121, 188
  view of homosexual life-style, 21, 112–13, 116, 171–72, 195, 229–31
heterosexual females (HTFs), psychological adjustment of, and HFs, compared, 196–98, 215
heterosexual males (HTMs), psychological adjustment of, and HMs, compared, 196–97, 207–8
Hoffman, Martin, 83, 180
homophile organizations, 15, 261
  in Bay Area, 27, 28, 31–32
  as social outlet, 181, 183, 185
homosexual females (HFs)
  affairs of, 94–102
  arrests of, 191–92, 193, 194
  attempts to discontinue homosexuality, 126
  cruising practices of, 79–80
  and depression, 210, 215
  effect of homosexuality on careers of, 146–47
  employment opportunities of, 245–246
  employment patterns of, 141–42, 146, 148
  friendships of, 175–79, 247–49
  gay bars and, 184, 250–59
  gay businesses and, 246–47
  general health of, 208, 215
  and HMs, compared, 24
  leisure-time activities of, 183–86, 249

homosexual males (HMs) (*con't.*)
as partners in heterosexual marriage, 160–64, 165
promiscuity as trait of, 81–82
psychological adjustment of, and HTMs, compared, 196–98, 207–8
psychosomatic symptoms of, 198–199, 207
regret of homosexuality by, 122–23, 125, 216
and religion, 37, 151–52, 153
residence patterns of, 36–37, 233–35
secrecy of, 62–63
self-acceptance of, 199–200
self-rating on Kinsey Scale and, 54–57, 60–61
self-rating on sex appeal by, 104, 105
sex partners of, 85–86
sexual activity of, 70, 72
sexual problems of, 117–18, 120
sexual techniques of, 107–9, 110–11
suicidal feelings of, 201–3, 216
and tension, 201
and therapy, 203–6, 207
types of, 49–51
as victims of assault and robbery, 190, 191, 192, 193, 194
as victims of blackmail, 188, 190–91, 193–94
as victims of extortion, 189–90, 191, 193, 194
and worry, 200
See also Asexual HMs; Close-Coupled HMs; Dysfunctional HMs; Functional HMs; Open-Coupled HMs
homosexual relationships, types of, 129–31
See also Asexual HFs; Asexual HMs; Close-Coupled HFs; Close-Coupled HMs; Dysfunctional HFs; Dysfunctional HMs; Functional HFs; Functional HMs; Open-Coupled HFs; Open-Coupled HMs
Hooker, Evelyn, 73, 84, 107, 180, 197
Humphreys, R. A., 74, 81, 150, 156

hustlers, 238, 241–42, 259, 260
Hyde, H. Montgomery, 62, 82
hysteria, 196, 197

incest, 83
independent political affiliations
HFs and HTFs and, 158–59
HMs and HTMs and, 156, 157
Indianapolis (Ind.), 15
Indiana University, 14, 16
Institute for Sex Research, 9, 10, 14, 22, 25
and Chicago pilot study, 40–41
See also Chicago pilot study
interviewers, qualifications for, 42–43

Jensen, Mehri Samandari, 84
Jewish faith
denunciation of homosexuality, 195
heterosexuals affiliated with, 39
homosexuals affiliated with, 37
Johnson, Kim, 15

Kasselbaum, Gene, 50
Katz, Robert L., 149
Kaye, Harvey E., 59, 127, 213
Kenyon, F. E., 50, 93, 142, 150, 166, 197

occupations, *see* gay businesses
oedipal conflict, as background to homosexuality, 83, 196
Oliver, Wayne A., 50
"one-night stands," 80, 82
Open-Coupled HFs
  friendships of, 175, 176
  general characteristics of, 135–36, 138, 221–23
  leisure-time activities of, 184
  paranoia, 210
  self-acceptance of, 209
  and therapy, 213
Open-Coupled HMs
  church attendance of, 151
  friendships of, 173
  general characteristics of, 133, 138, 221–23
  leisure-time activities of, 181, 182, 183, 186
  loneliness of, 200
  as parents, 164
  as partners in heterosexual marriage, 162
  and tension, 201
  and therapy, 204
  and worry, 200
"orgy room," in gay baths, 246
overtness
  of HFs, 66–67
  of HMs, 62–65, 67–68
Ovesey, Lionel, 51

paranoia
  HFs and HTFs and, 197, 210, 215
  HMs and HTMs and, 197, 201
parents
  HFs as, 168–69, 170
  HMs as, 164–65, 170
Parr, Denis, 160, 188
passive role, 106, 111
Philipp, E., 150, 161

police, harassment of homosexuals by, 27–28, 187, 188
political affiliations
  of HFs and HTFs, 158–59
  of HMs and HTMs, 155–58
pornography, 28
professional help, seeking
  HFs and HTFs, 212–14
  HMs and HTMs, 203–6
promiscuity, as homosexual trait, 81–82
Protestantism
  heterosexual affiliation with, 39
  homosexual affiliation with, 37
psychological adjustment of homosexuals and heterosexuals, compared, 196–98, 207–8, 215–16
psychopaths, homosexuals as, 196
psychosomatic symptoms
  of HFs and HTFs, 208, 215
  of HMs and HTMs, 198, 207–8
public places, as cruising locale, 241

Rabinowitz, William, 197
racial preferences in homosexual partner selection, 85, 92, 93
Rancourt, Réjane, 51, 83
rape, 230
Rechy, John, 74
religion
  changing views of, toward homosexuality, 149–50
  HFs and, 152–54
  HMs and, 151–52, 153
  See also individual faiths
Republican Party
  HFs and HTFs affiliated with, 158–159
  HMs and HTMs affiliated with, 156–158
residence patterns
  of HFs, 235
  of HMs, 233–35

rest rooms, cruising in, 74, 78
  See also "tearooms"
Reuben, David R., 196
Riess, Bernard, 58, 166, 198
robbery
  HFs as victims of, 192
  HMs as victims of, 190, 191, 193, 194
Robins, Eli, 38, 54, 55, 56, 58, 59, 63, 65, 67, 68n, 69, 70, 71, 74, 79, 82, 83, 85, 86, 98, 107, 122, 124, 127, 142, 150, 156, 160, 161, 162, 166, 170, 172, 188, 197, 198, 202, 204, 211, 213
Roe, Anne, 36
roles, sexual, 106, 111
Roman Catholicism
  heterosexuals affiliated with, 39
  homosexuals affiliated with, 37
roommate relationships, homosexual, and heterosexual marriage, compared, 83–84, 91, 102
Rorschach Test, 197
Rosenberg, Morris, 41
Ross, Laurence, 161
Roth, Martin, 51

Sagarin, Edward, 50
Saghir, Marcel T., 38, 54, 55, 56, 58, 59, 63, 65, 67, 68n, 69, 70, 71, 74, 78, 82, 83, 85, 86, 98, 107, 122, 124, 127, 142, 150, 156, 160, 161, 162, 166, 170, 172, 188, 197, 198, 202, 204, 211, 213
San Francisco County (Calif.), 27–28
  See also Bay Area (San Francisco, Calif.)
"San Francisco study," 25
San Mateo County (Calif.), 27
Santa Clara County (Calif.), 27
Sawyer, Ethel, 50
Schäfer, Siegrid, 54, 58, 59, 61, 66, 67, 127

Schofield, Michael George, 55, 56, 57, 82, 86, 89, 160, 188
Scott, Peter D., 51
self-acceptance
  of HFs and HTFs, 209, 214, 215
  of HMs and HTMs, 199–200
sexual activity
  of HFs, 71, 72
  of HMs, 70, 72
sexual roles, 106, 111
sexual techniques
  anal intercourse, 51, 107–9, 111
  cunnilingus, 109, 110, 111
  fellatio, 51, 107–9, 111
  masturbation, 107–8, 109–11
Simon, William, 72, 121, 142, 172, 188
Socarides, Charles, 196
Sonenschein, David, 84
sports
  HFs' participation in, 184
  HMs' participation in, 182
steam baths, *see* gay baths
Stentz, Mickey, 16
Stephenson, Maylee, 84
street, as cruising locale, 74, 75, 76, 78
Sudman, Seymour, 38
suicide and suicidal feelings
  HFs and HTFs and, 210–12, 215, 216
  HMs and HTMs and, 20–23, 196, 201–3, 216
Sukoneck, Harriet, 82, 97
Sykes, Gresham M., 50
Szondi Test, 197

Tavern Guild, 258–59, 261
"tearooms," as cruising locale, 32, 33, 75, 76, 243–44
Tennessee Self-Concept Scale, 197
tension
  HFs and HTFs and, 210, 215
  HMs and HTMs and, 201

Thematic Apperception Test (TAT), 197
therapy
    and HFs, 212–14, 215
    and HMs, 203–6, 207
transvestism, 196
Troiden, Richard R., 74
"tubs," *see* gay baths

Veldman, Donald J., 265
venereal disease, 78, 116
    among HFs, 119
    among HMs, 118

Ward, David, 50
Ward, J. M., Jr., 265
Wayne, David, 197

Weinberg, Martin S., 10, 25, 51, 54, 55, 57, 63, 64–65, 69, 70, 73, 74, 107, 122, 124, 142, 150, 160, 162, 172, 182–83, 188, 197, 199, 204, 239n
Westley, William A., 63, 68, 181
Westwood, Gordon, 69, 70, 142, 150, 161, 188
Wheeler, William Marshall, 172
Wiener, Jack, 14
Williams, Colin, 10, 25, 51, 54, 55, 57, 63, 64–65, 69, 70, 73, 74, 107, 122, 124, 142, 150, 160, 162, 172, 182–83, 188, 197, 199, 204, 239n
Wilson, Marilyn, 198
Wolff, Charlotte, 142, 172
worry
    HFs and HTFs and, 209–10
    HMs and HTMs and, 200
Wortis, S. B., 51

Yolles, Stanley, 9